HORIMIYA 12

HERO X DAISUKE HAGIWARA

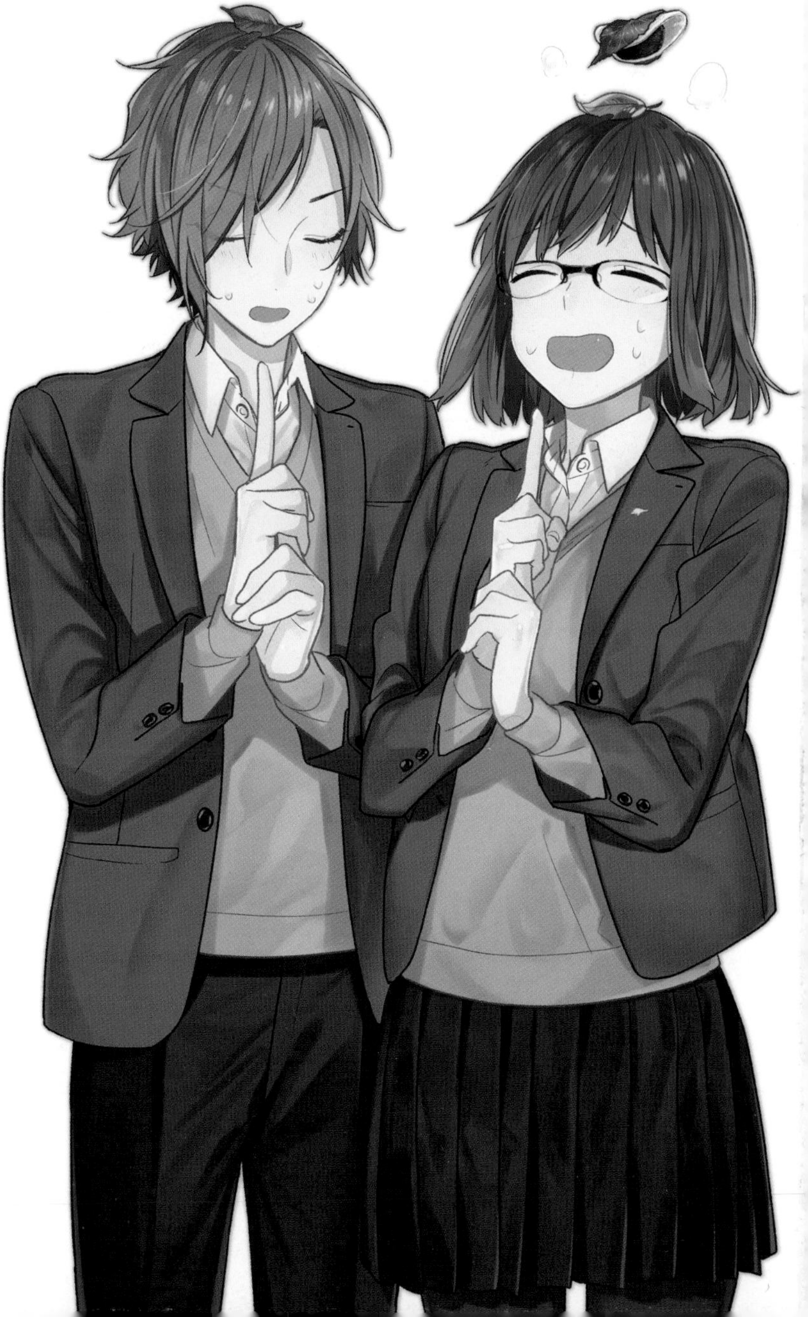

HORI-SAN AND
MIYAMURA-KUN

HORIMIYA

12

CONTENTS ✴

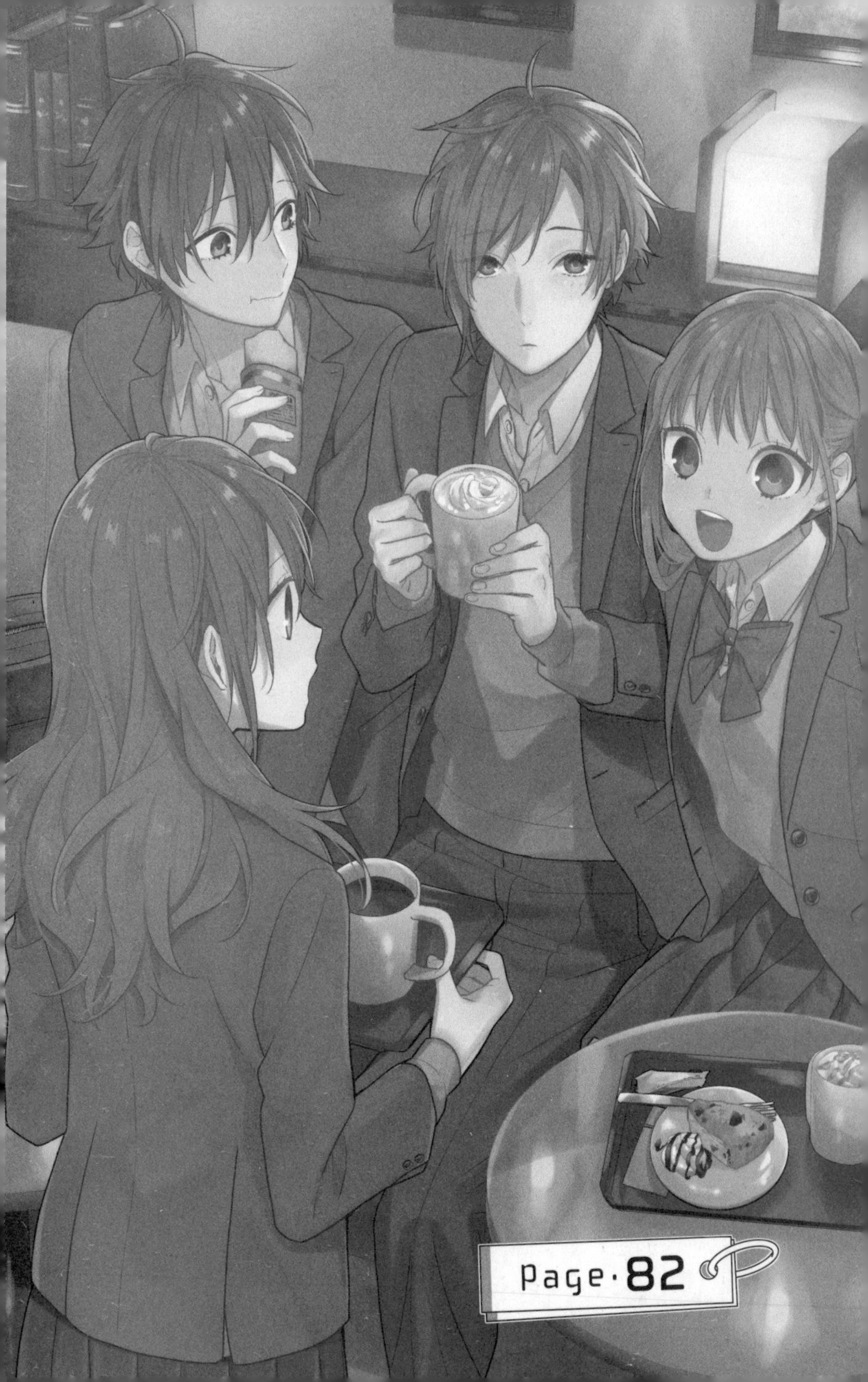
Page·82

HORIMIYA

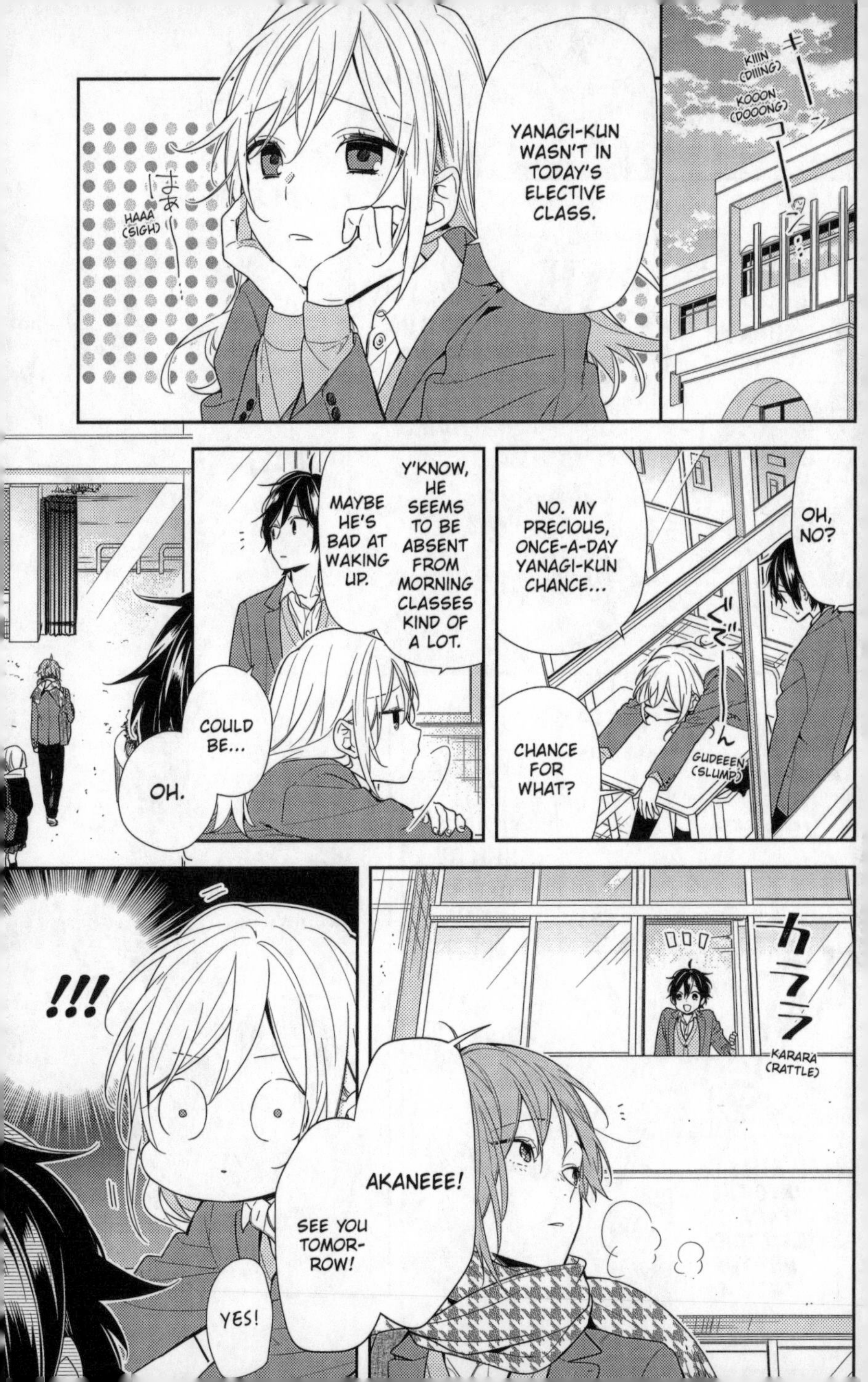
KIIN (DIIING)
KOOON (DOOONG)
YANAGI-KUN WASN'T IN TODAY'S ELECTIVE CLASS.
HAAA (SIGH)
OH, NO?
NO. MY PRECIOUS, ONCE-A-DAY YANAGI-KUN CHANCE...
GUDEEEN (SLUMP)
CHANCE FOR WHAT?
Y'KNOW, HE SEEMS TO BE ABSENT FROM MORNING CLASSES KIND OF A LOT.
MAYBE HE'S BAD AT WAKING UP.
COULD BE...
OH.
KARARA (RATTLE)
!!!
AKANEEE!
SEE YOU TOMOR-ROW!
YES!

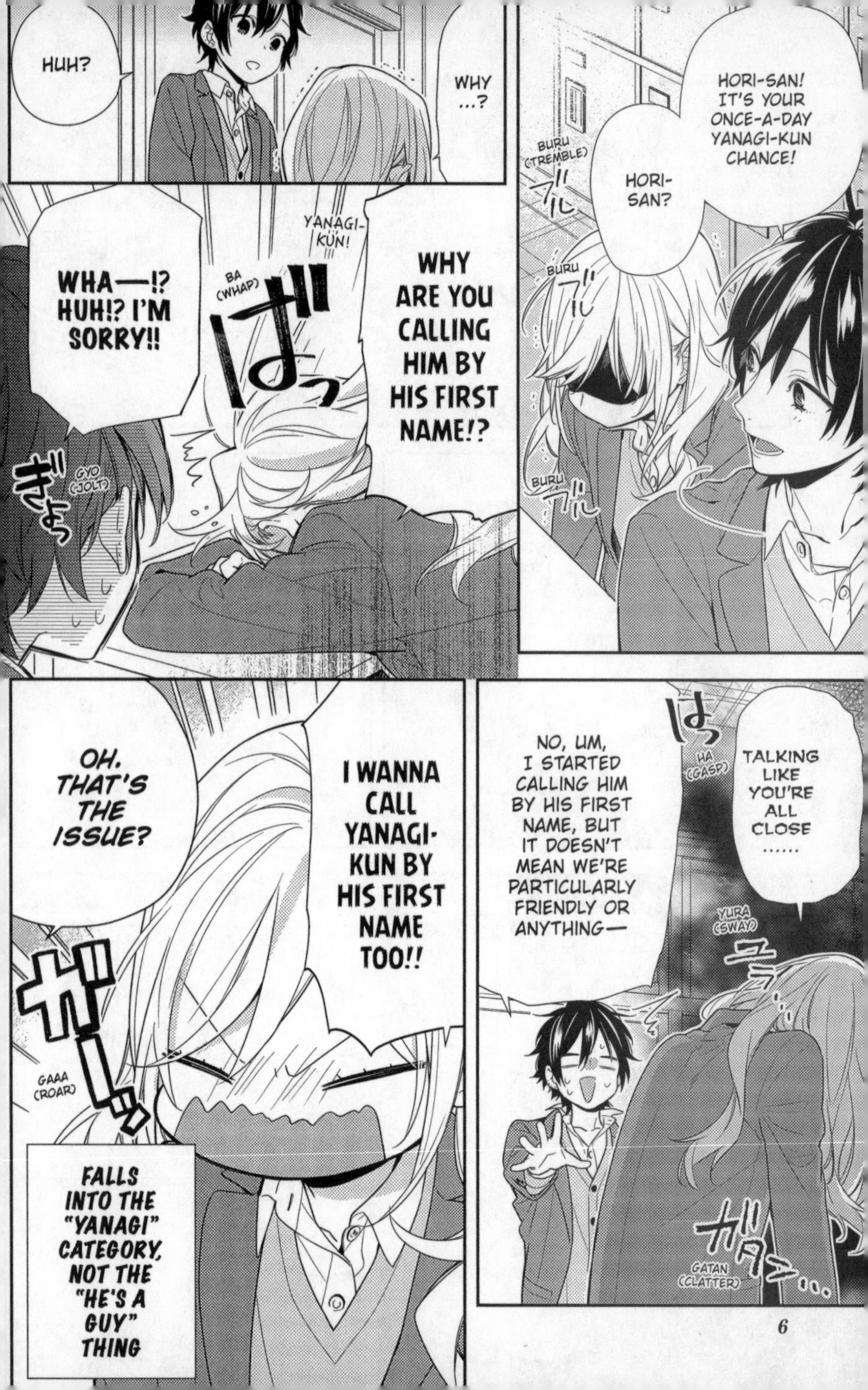
HORI-SAN! IT'S YOUR ONCE-A-DAY YANAGI-KUN CHANCE!
HORI-SAN?
BURU (TREMBLE)
BURU
BURU
WHY ...?
HUH?
WHY ARE YOU CALLING HIM BY HIS FIRST NAME!?
YANAGI-KUN!
BA (WHAP)
WHA—!? HUH!? I'M SORRY!!
GYO (JOLT)
TALKING LIKE YOU'RE ALL CLOSE ......
HA (GASP)
NO, UM, I STARTED CALLING HIM BY HIS FIRST NAME, BUT IT DOESN'T MEAN WE'RE PARTICULARLY FRIENDLY OR ANYTHING—
YURA (SWAY)
GATAN (CLATTER)
I WANNA CALL YANAGI-KUN BY HIS FIRST NAME TOO!!
OH. THAT'S THE ISSUE?
GAAA (ROAR)
FALLS INTO THE "YANAGI" CATEGORY, NOT THE "HE'S A GUY" THING

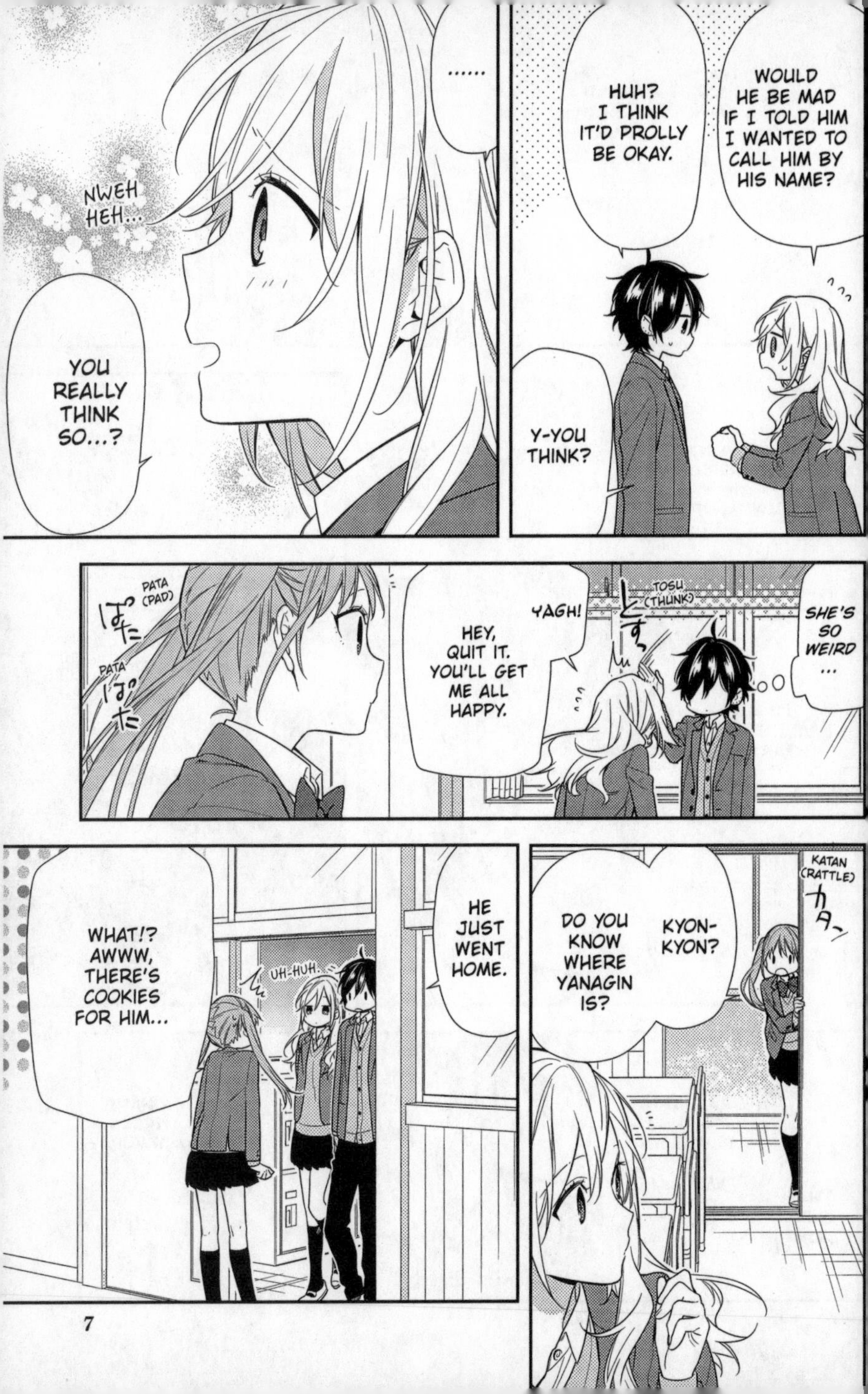
WOULD HE BE MAD IF I TOLD HIM I WANTED TO CALL HIM BY HIS NAME?
HUH? I THINK IT'D PROLLY BE OKAY.
Y-YOU THINK?
......
NWEH HEH...
YOU REALLY THINK SO...?
SHE'S SO WEIRD...
TOSU (THUNK)
YAGH!
HEY, QUIT IT. YOU'LL GET ME ALL HAPPY.
PATA (PAD)
PATA
KATAN (RATTLE)
KYON-KYON?
DO YOU KNOW WHERE YANAGIN IS?
HE JUST WENT HOME.
UH-HUH.
WHAT!? AWWW, THERE'S COOKIES FOR HIM...

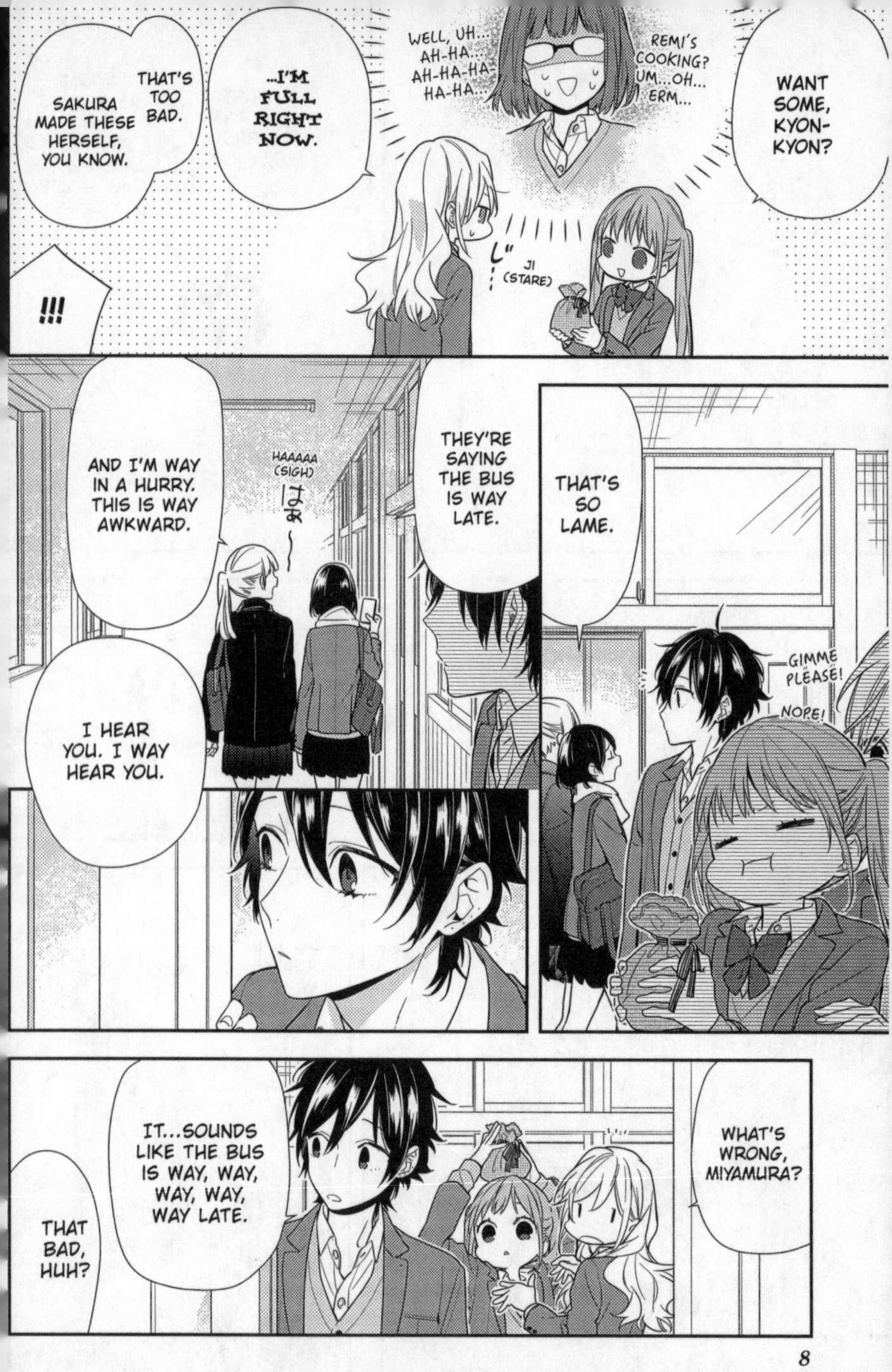
WANT SOME, KYON-KYON?
REMI'S COOKING? UM...OH... ERM...
WELL, UH... AH-HA... AH-HA-HA-HA-HA...
じ"
JI (STARE)
...I'M FULL RIGHT NOW.
THAT'S TOO BAD.
SAKURA MADE THESE HERSELF, YOU KNOW.
!!!
THAT'S SO LAME.
GIMME PLEASE!
NOPE!
THEY'RE SAYING THE BUS IS WAY LATE.
HAAAAA (SIGH)
はぁ~
AND I'M WAY IN A HURRY. THIS IS WAY AWKWARD.
I HEAR YOU. I WAY HEAR YOU.
WHAT'S WRONG, MIYAMURA?
IT...SOUNDS LIKE THE BUS IS WAY, WAY, WAY, WAY, WAY LATE.
THAT BAD, HUH?

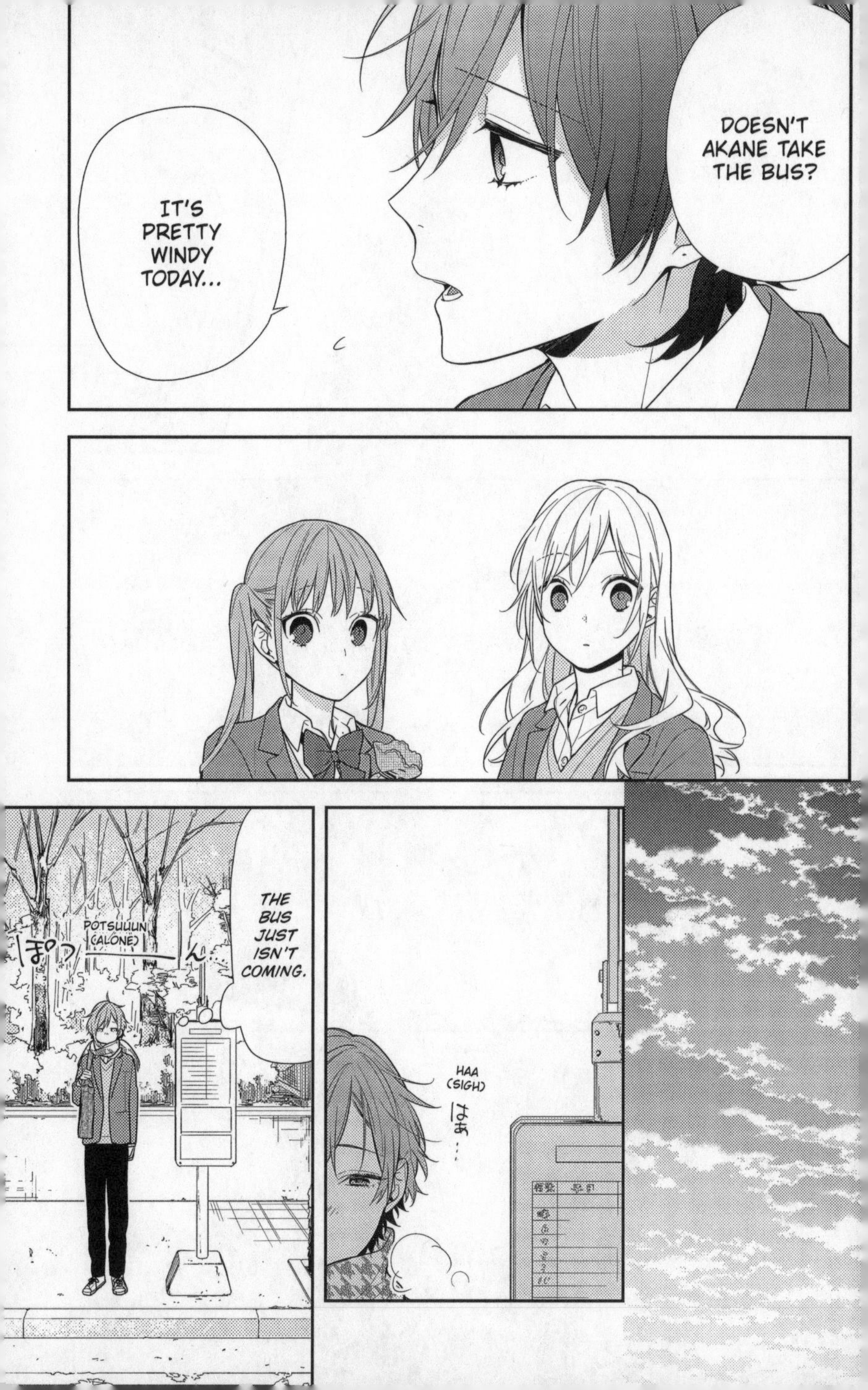
DOESN'T AKANE TAKE THE BUS?
IT'S PRETTY WINDY TODAY...
HAA (SIGH)
はぁ…
THE BUS JUST ISN'T COMING.
POTSUUUN (ALONE)
ぽつーーーん…

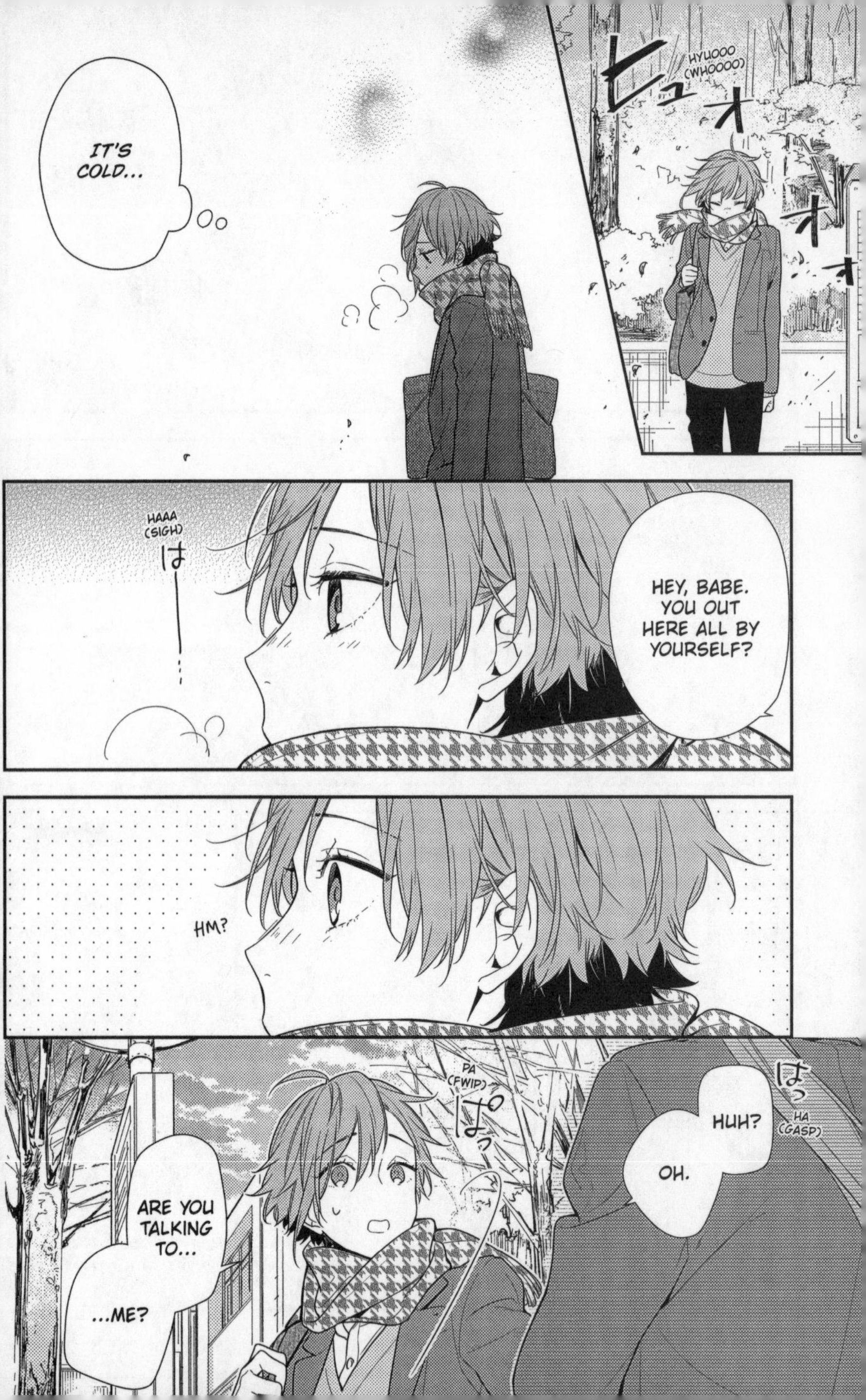
ヒュオオオ
HYUOOO (WHOOOO)
IT'S COLD...
HEY, BABE. YOU OUT HERE ALL BY YOURSELF?
は―…
HAAA (SIGH)
HM?
はっ
HA (GASP)
HUH?
OH.
ぱっ
PA (FWIP)
ARE YOU TALKING TO...
...ME?

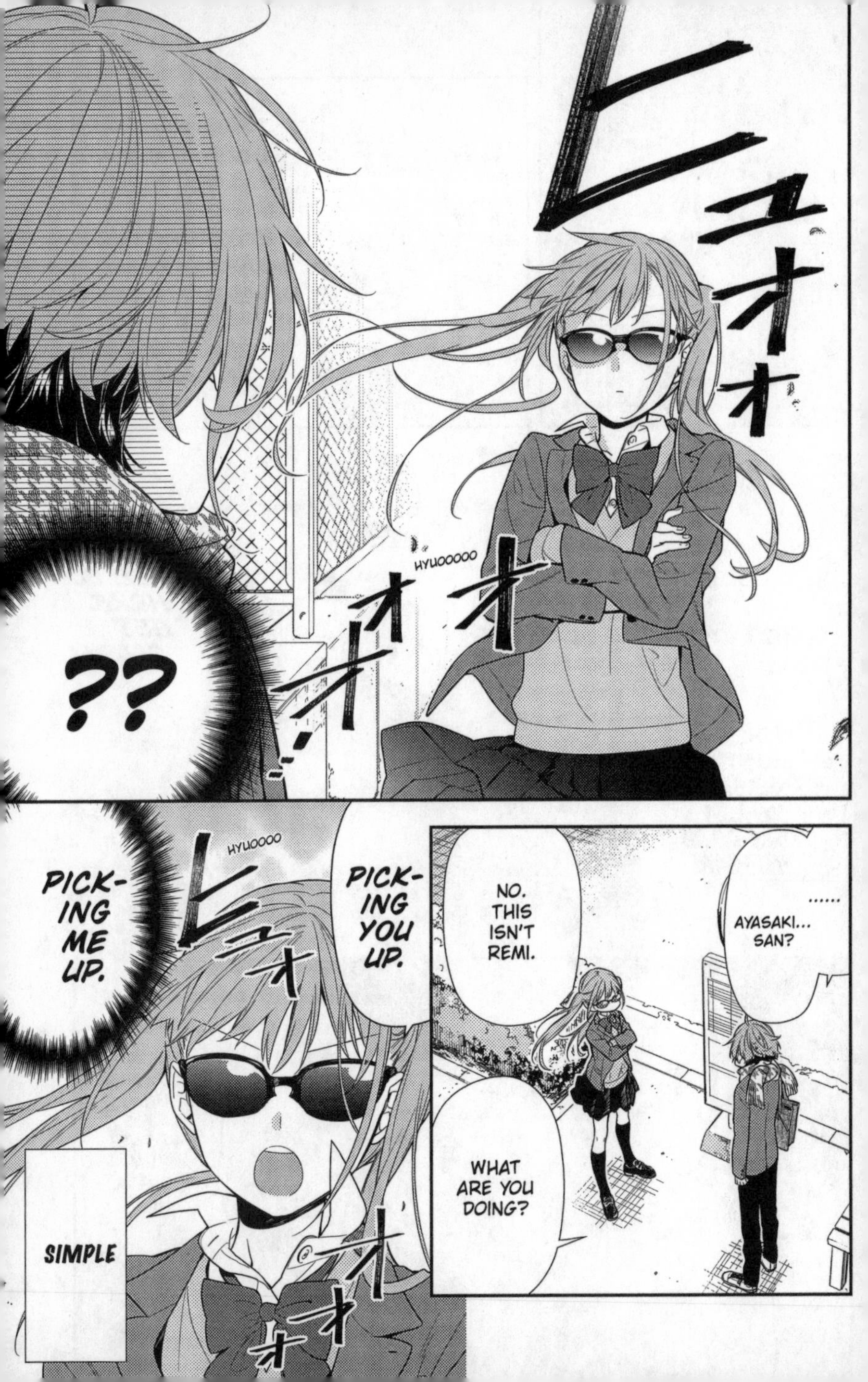
HYUOOOO
??
......
AYASAKI... SAN?
NO. THIS ISN'T REMI.
WHAT ARE YOU DOING?
HYUOOOO
PICK-ING YOU UP.
PICK-ING ME UP.
SIMPLE

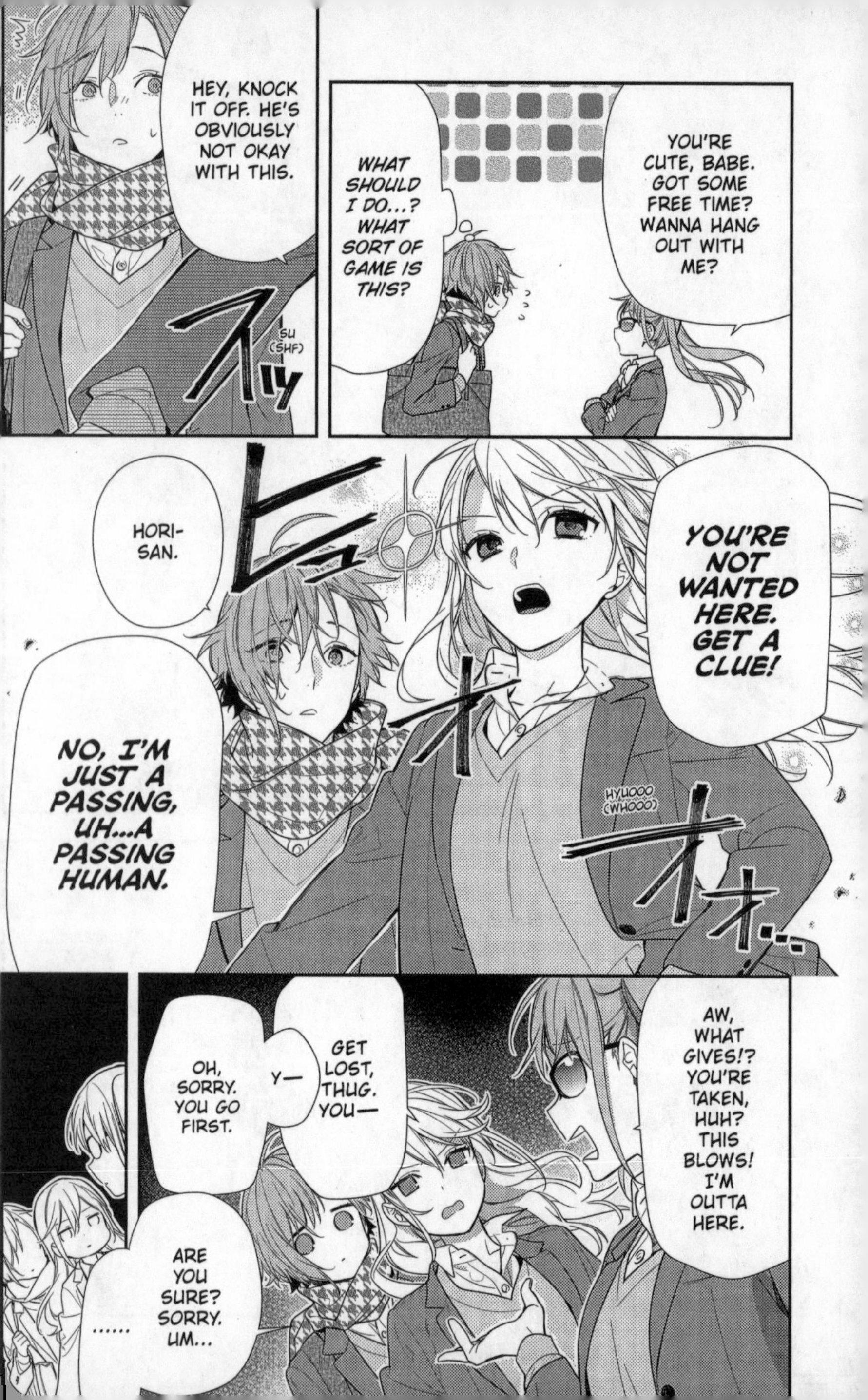
YOU'RE CUTE, BABE. GOT SOME FREE TIME? WANNA HANG OUT WITH ME?
WHAT SHOULD I DO...? WHAT SORT OF GAME IS THIS?
HEY, KNOCK IT OFF. HE'S OBVIOUSLY NOT OKAY WITH THIS.
SU (SHF)
YOU'RE NOT WANTED HERE. GET A CLUE!
HYUOOO (WHOOO)
HORI-SAN.
NO, I'M JUST A PASSING, UH...A PASSING HUMAN.
AW, WHAT GIVES!? YOU'RE TAKEN, HUH? THIS BLOWS! I'M OUTTA HERE.
GET LOST, THUG. YOU—
Y—
OH, SORRY. YOU GO FIRST.
ARE YOU SURE? SORRY. UM...
......

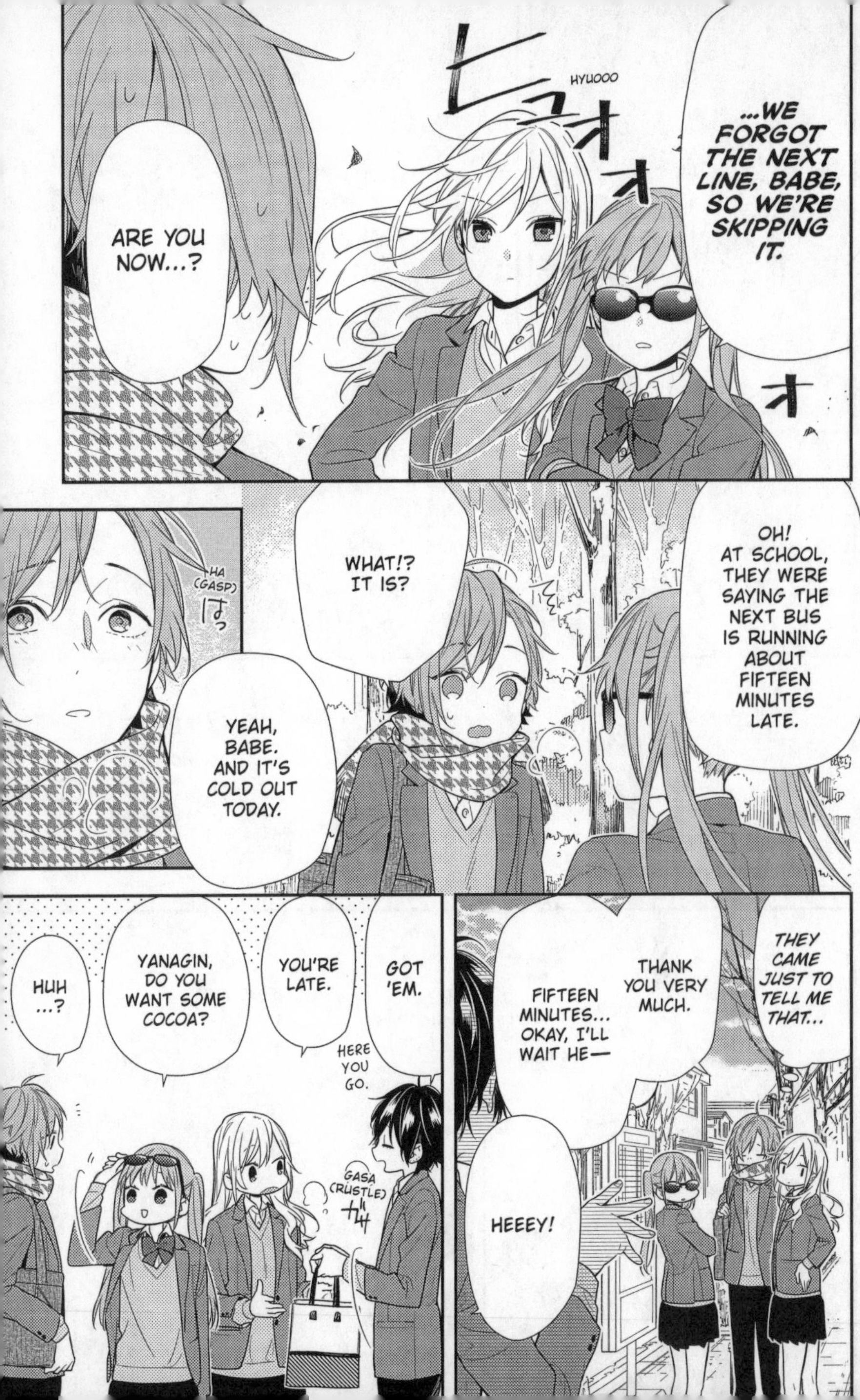
...WE FORGOT THE NEXT LINE, BABE, SO WE'RE SKIPPING IT.
HYUOOO
ARE YOU NOW...?
OH! AT SCHOOL, THEY WERE SAYING THE NEXT BUS IS RUNNING ABOUT FIFTEEN MINUTES LATE.
WHAT!? IT IS?
YEAH, BABE. AND IT'S COLD OUT TODAY.
HA (GASP)
THEY CAME JUST TO TELL ME THAT...
THANK YOU VERY MUCH.
FIFTEEN MINUTES... OKAY, I'LL WAIT HE—
HEEEY!
GOT 'EM.
YOU'RE LATE.
HERE YOU GO.
YANAGIN, DO YOU WANT SOME COCOA?
GASA (RUSTLE)
HUH ...?

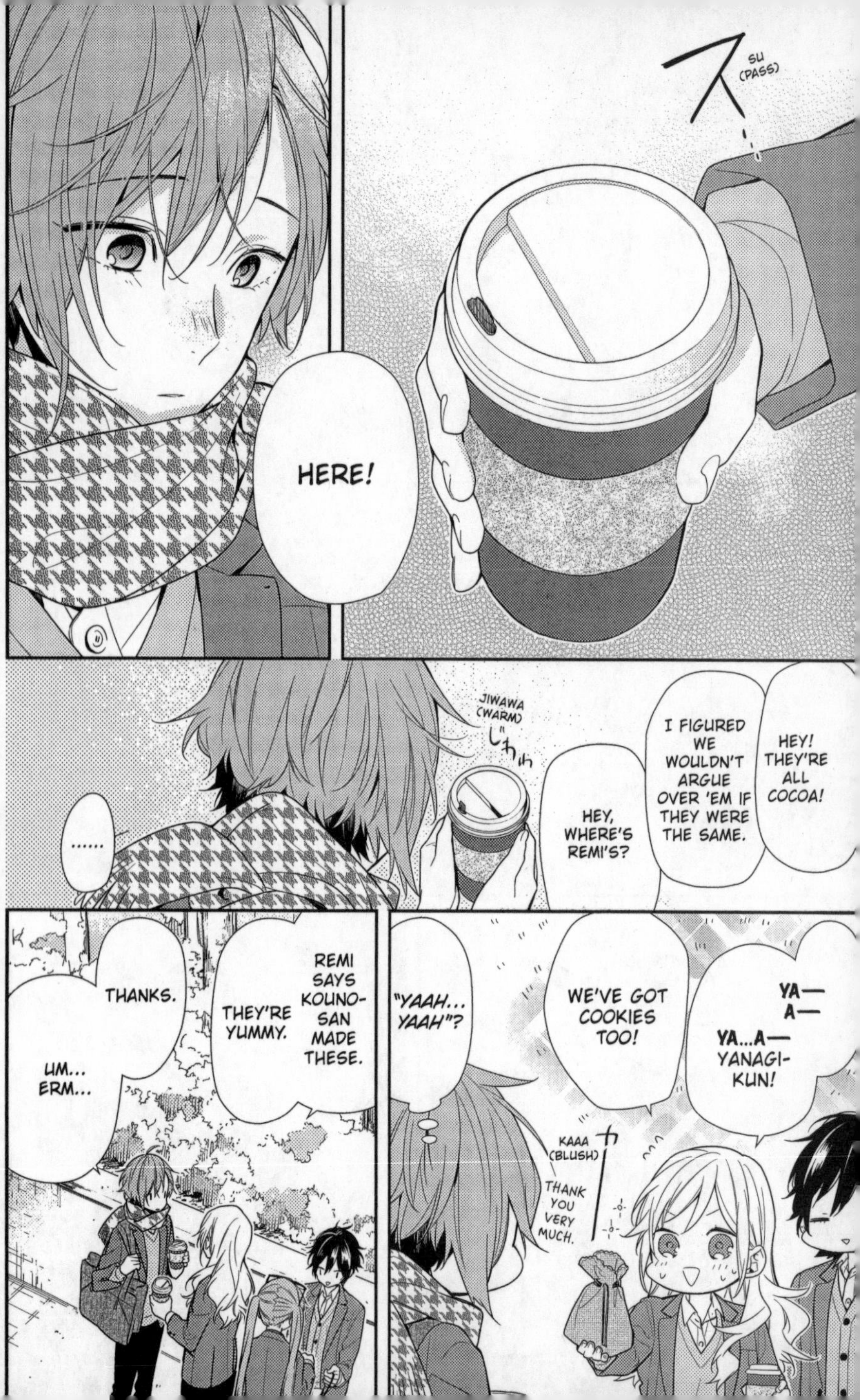
SU (PASS)
HERE!
HEY! THEY'RE ALL COCOA!
I FIGURED WE WOULDN'T ARGUE OVER 'EM IF THEY WERE THE SAME.
HEY, WHERE'S REMI'S?
JIWAWA (WARM)
......
YA— A— YA...A— YANAGI-KUN!
WE'VE GOT COOKIES TOO!
"YAAH... YAAH"?
KAAA (BLUSH)
THANK YOU VERY MUCH.
REMI SAYS KOUNO-SAN MADE THESE.
THEY'RE YUMMY.
THANKS.
UM... ERM...

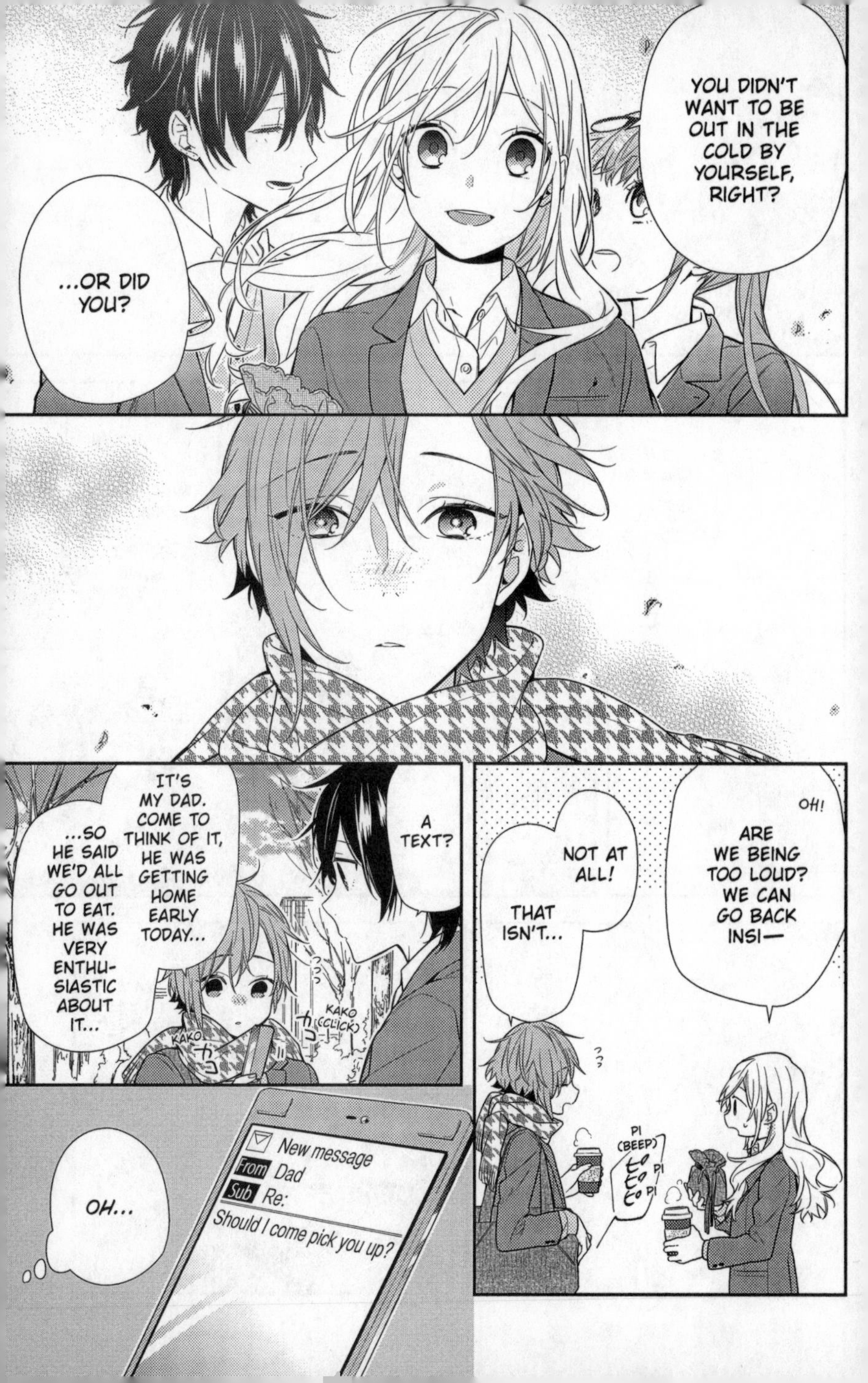
YOU DIDN'T WANT TO BE OUT IN THE COLD BY YOURSELF, RIGHT?
...OR DID YOU?
OH!
ARE WE BEING TOO LOUD? WE CAN GO BACK INSI—
NOT AT ALL!
THAT ISN'T...
PI (BEEP) PI PI
A TEXT?
IT'S MY DAD. COME TO THINK OF IT, HE WAS GETTING HOME EARLY TODAY...
...SO HE SAID WE'D ALL GO OUT TO EAT. HE WAS VERY ENTHUSIASTIC ABOUT IT...
KAKO (CLICK)
KAKO
New message
From Dad
Sub Re:
Should I come pick you up?
OH...

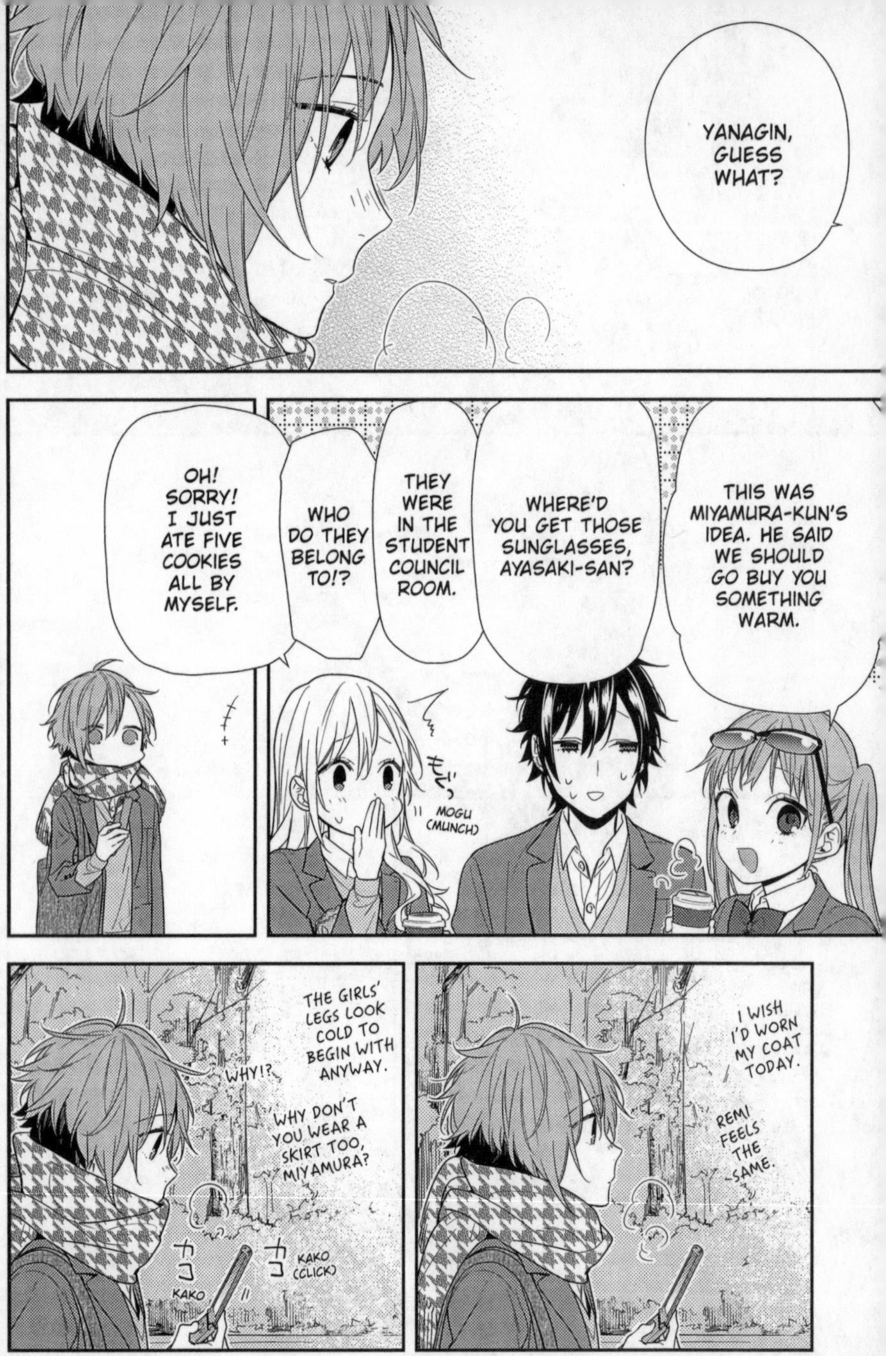
YANAGIN, GUESS WHAT?
THIS WAS MIYAMURA-KUN'S IDEA. HE SAID WE SHOULD GO BUY YOU SOMETHING WARM.
WHERE'D YOU GET THOSE SUNGLASSES, AYASAKI-SAN?
THEY WERE IN THE STUDENT COUNCIL ROOM.
WHO DO THEY BELONG TO!?
OH! SORRY! I JUST ATE FIVE COOKIES ALL BY MYSELF.
MOGU (MUNCH)
I WISH I'D WORN MY COAT TODAY.
REMI FEELS THE SAME.
THE GIRLS' LEGS LOOK COLD TO BEGIN WITH ANYWAY.
WHY!?
WHY DON'T YOU WEAR A SKIRT TOO, MIYAMURA?
KAKO (CLICK)
KAKO

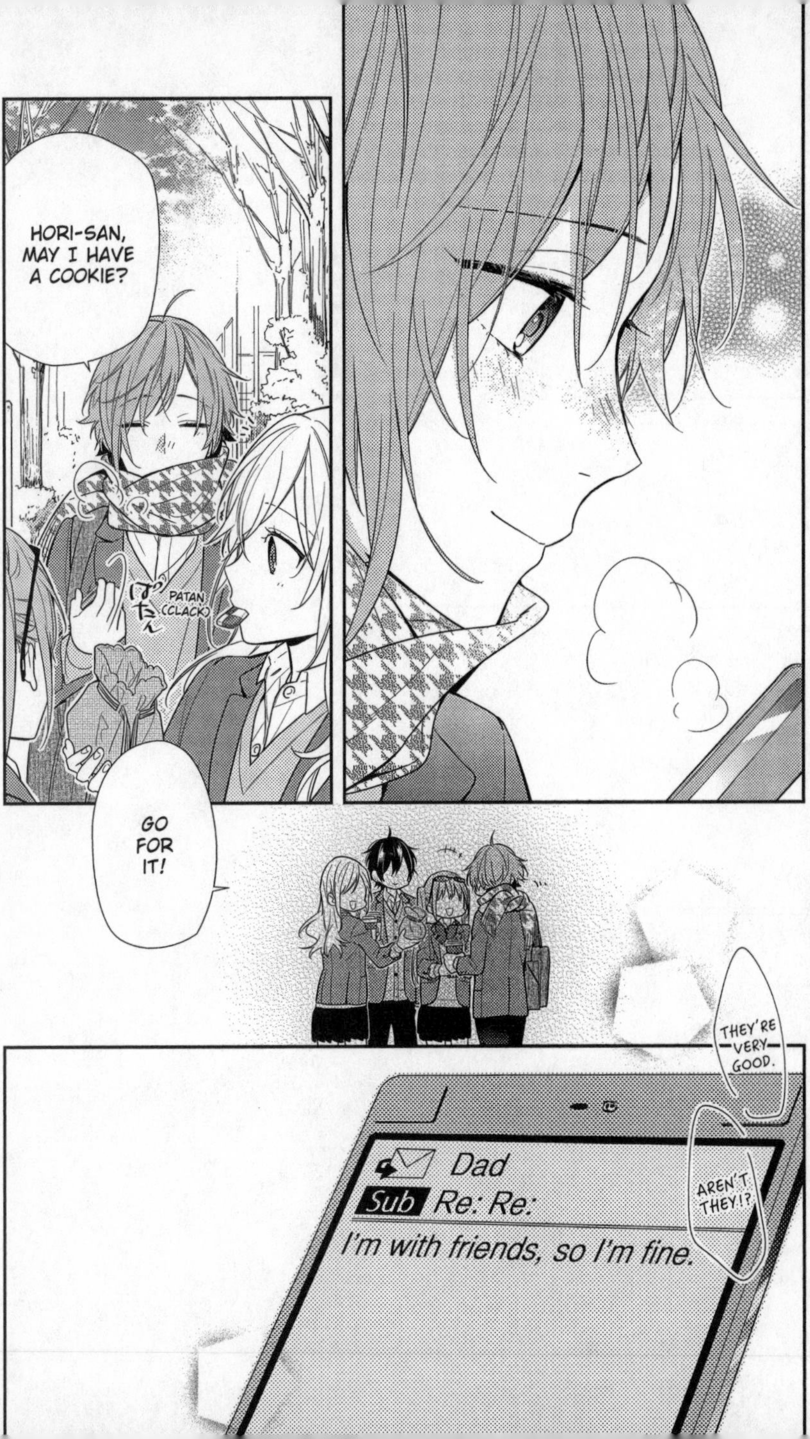
HORI-SAN, MAY I HAVE A COOKIE?
ぱたん
PATAN (CLACK)
GO FOR IT!
THEY'RE VERY GOOD.
AREN'T THEY!?
Dad
Sub Re: Re:
I'm with friends, so I'm fine.

HORIMIYA

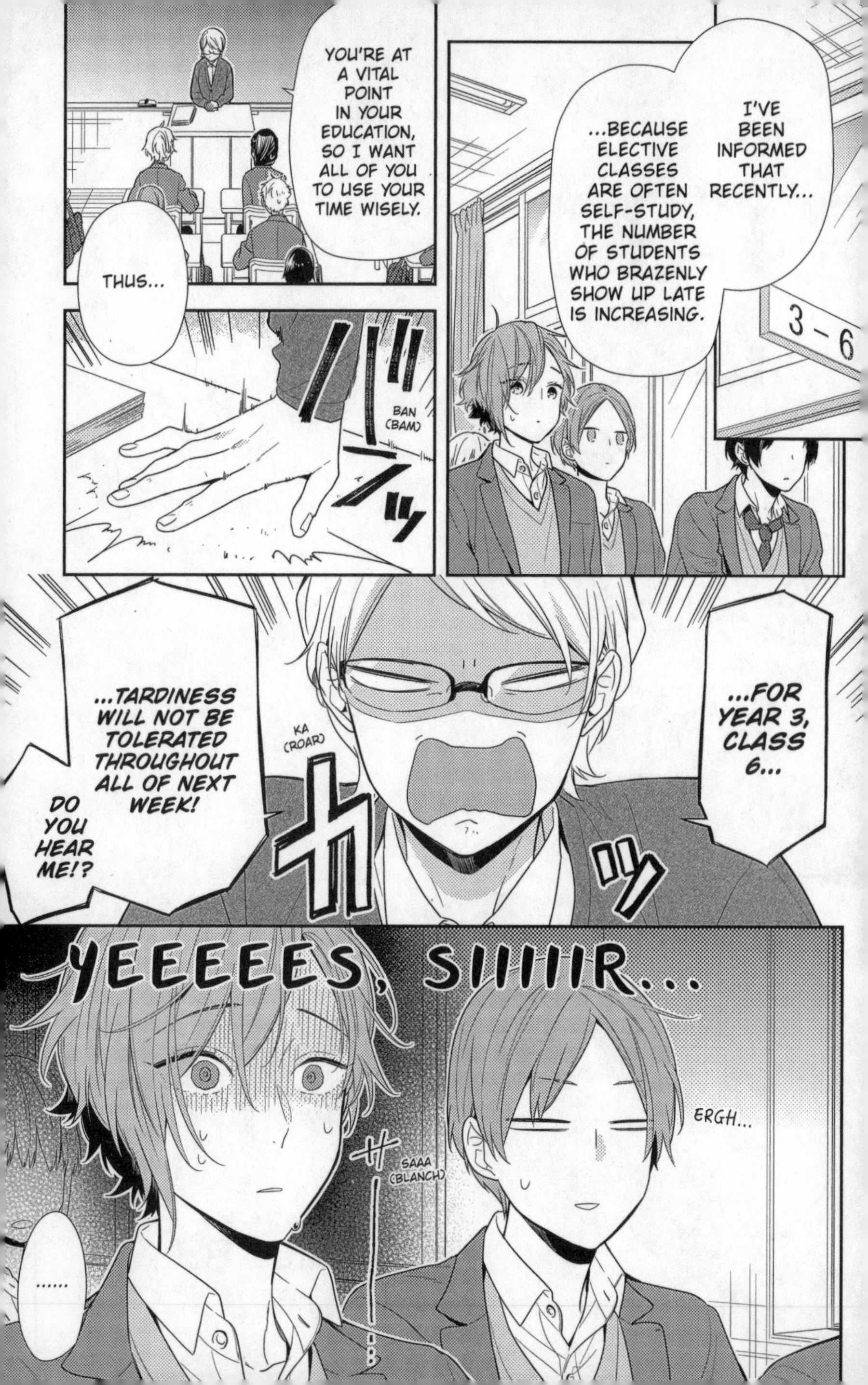
I'VE BEEN INFORMED THAT RECENTLY...
...BECAUSE ELECTIVE CLASSES ARE OFTEN SELF-STUDY, THE NUMBER OF STUDENTS WHO BRAZENLY SHOW UP LATE IS INCREASING.
3-6
YOU'RE AT A VITAL POINT IN YOUR EDUCATION, SO I WANT ALL OF YOU TO USE YOUR TIME WISELY.
THUS...
BAN (BAM)
...FOR YEAR 3, CLASS 6...
KA (ROAR)
...TARDINESS WILL NOT BE TOLERATED THROUGHOUT ALL OF NEXT WEEK!
DO YOU HEAR ME!?
YEEEEES, SIIIIR...
ERGH...
SAAA (BLANCH)
......

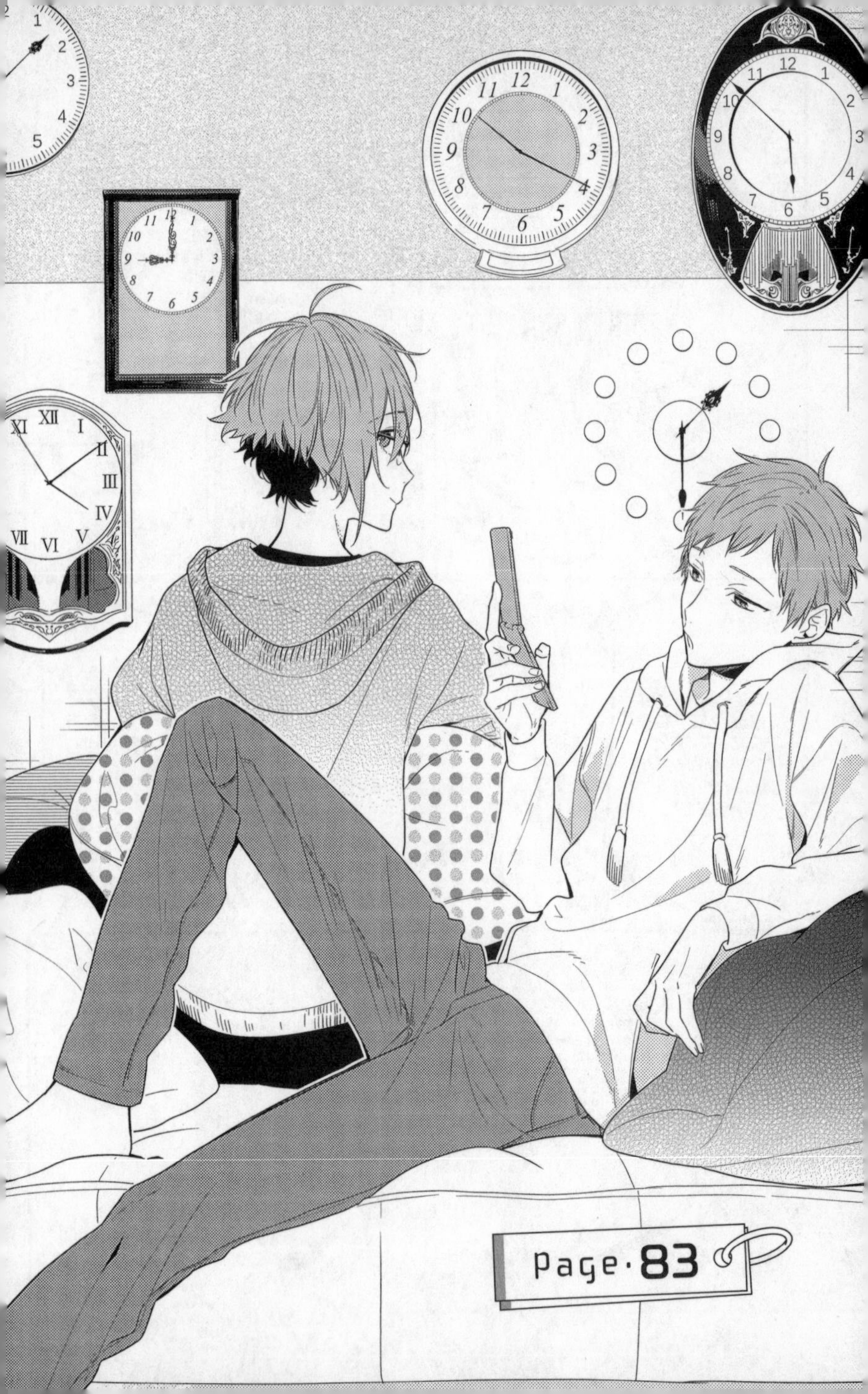
page·83

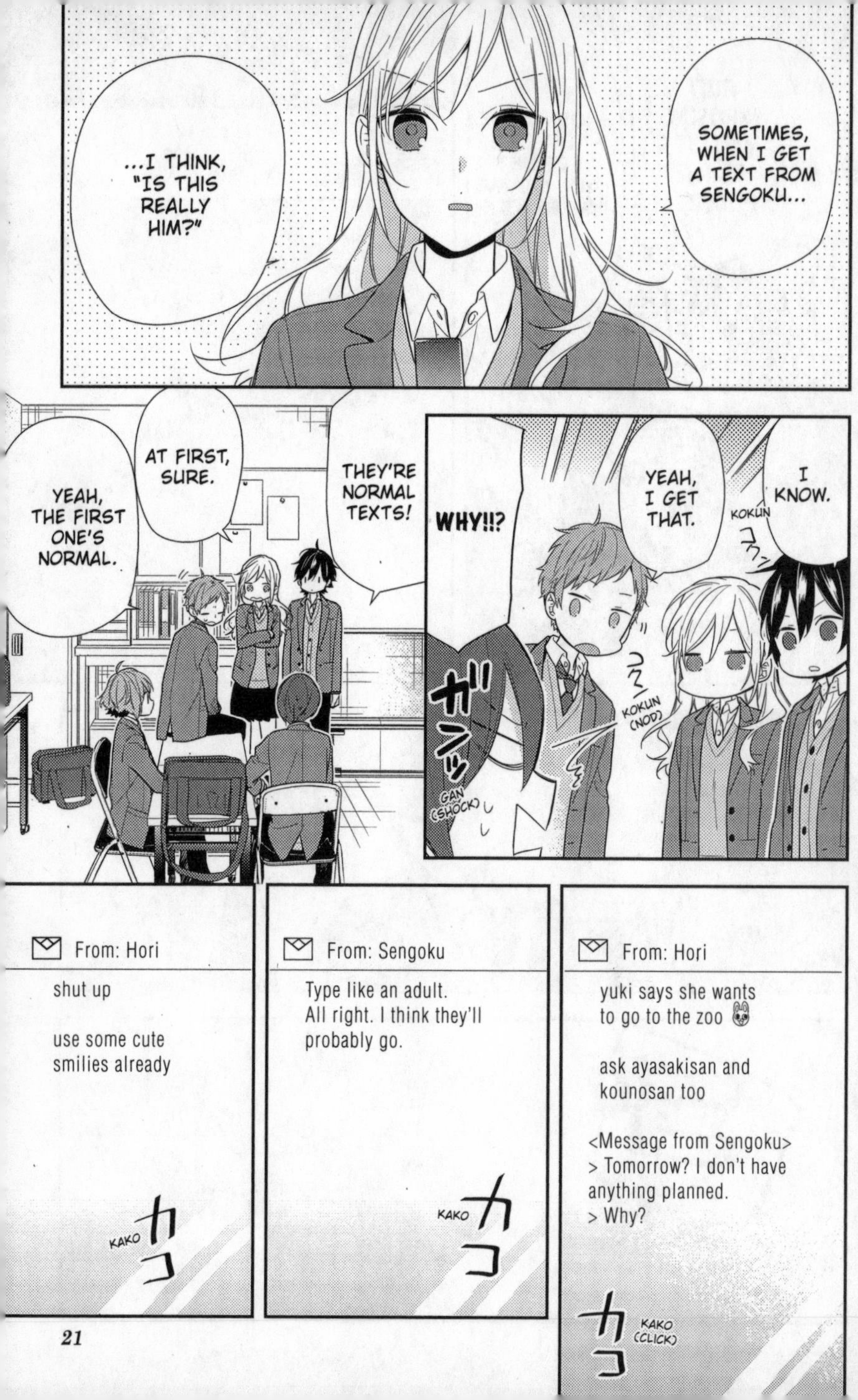
SOMETIMES, WHEN I GET A TEXT FROM SENGOKU...
...I THINK, "IS THIS REALLY HIM?"
I KNOW.
KOKUN
YEAH, I GET THAT.
KOKUN (NOD)
WHY!!?
GAN (SHOCK)
THEY'RE NORMAL TEXTS!
AT FIRST, SURE.
YEAH, THE FIRST ONE'S NORMAL.
From: Hori
yuki says she wants to go to the zoo
ask ayasakisan and kounosan too
<Message from Sengoku>
> Tomorrow? I don't have anything planned.
> Why?
KAKO (CLICK)
From: Sengoku
Type like an adult.
All right. I think they'll probably go.
KAKO
From: Hori
shut up
use some cute smilies already
KAKO

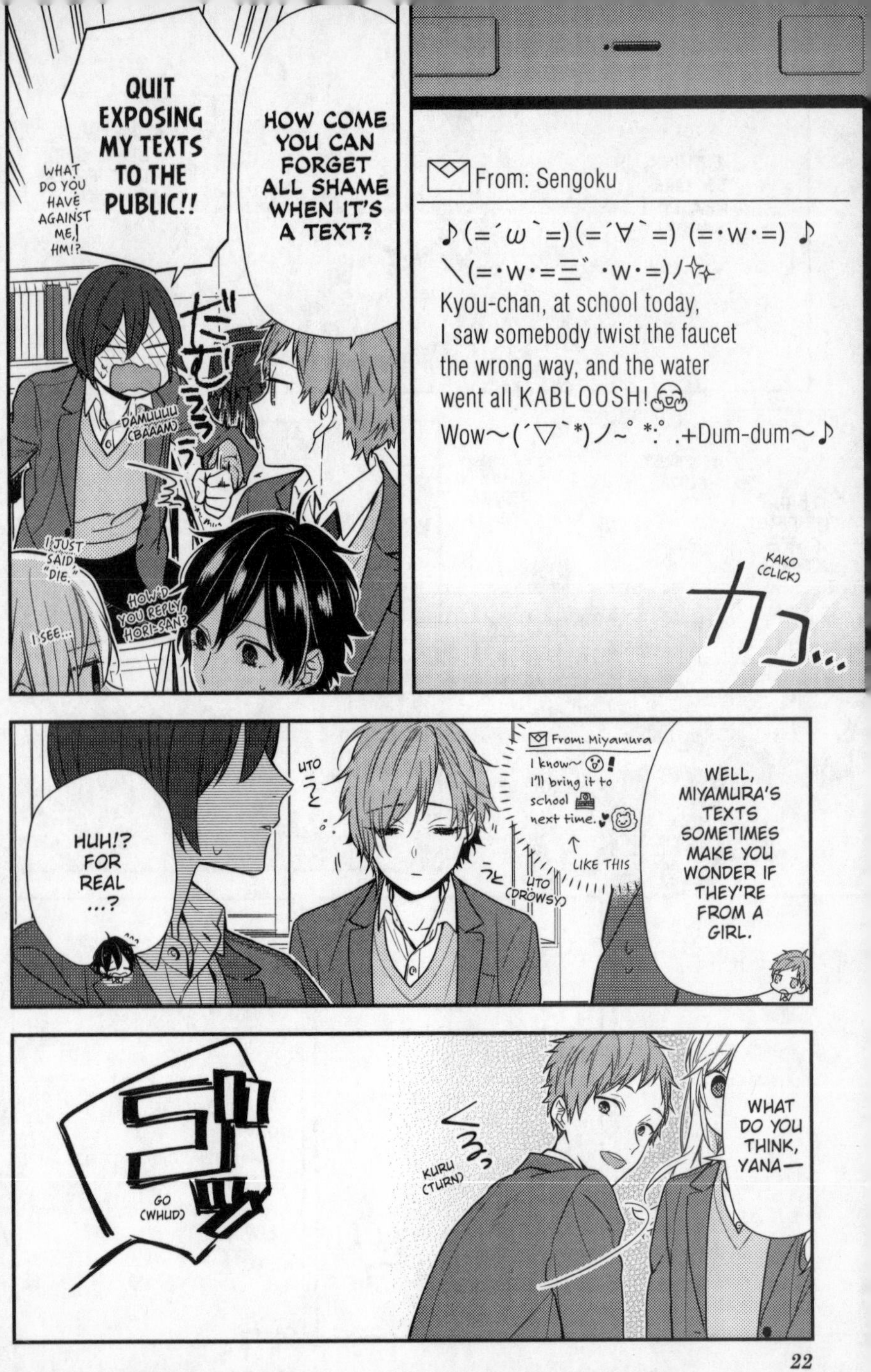
From: Sengoku
♪(=´ω`=)(=´∀`=) (=・w・=) ♪
╲(=・w・=三゛・w・=)ノ✧
Kyou-chan, at school today,
I saw somebody twist the faucet
the wrong way, and the water
went all KABLOOSH!
Wow～(´▽`*)ノ~゜*:゜.+Dum-dum～♪
KAKO (CLICK)
カコ…
HOW COME YOU CAN FORGET ALL SHAME WHEN IT'S A TEXT?
QUIT EXPOSING MY TEXTS TO THE PUBLIC!!
WHAT DO YOU HAVE AGAINST ME, HM!?
DAMUUUUU (BAAAM)
I JUST SAID "DIE."
HOW'D YOU REPLY, HORI-SAN?
I SEE...
WELL, MIYAMURA'S TEXTS SOMETIMES MAKE YOU WONDER IF THEY'RE FROM A GIRL.
From: Miyamura
I know~ !
I'll bring it to
school
next time.
LIKE THIS
UTO (DROWSY)
UTO
HUH!? FOR REAL ...?
WHAT DO YOU THINK, YANA—
KURU (TURN)
GO (WHUD)

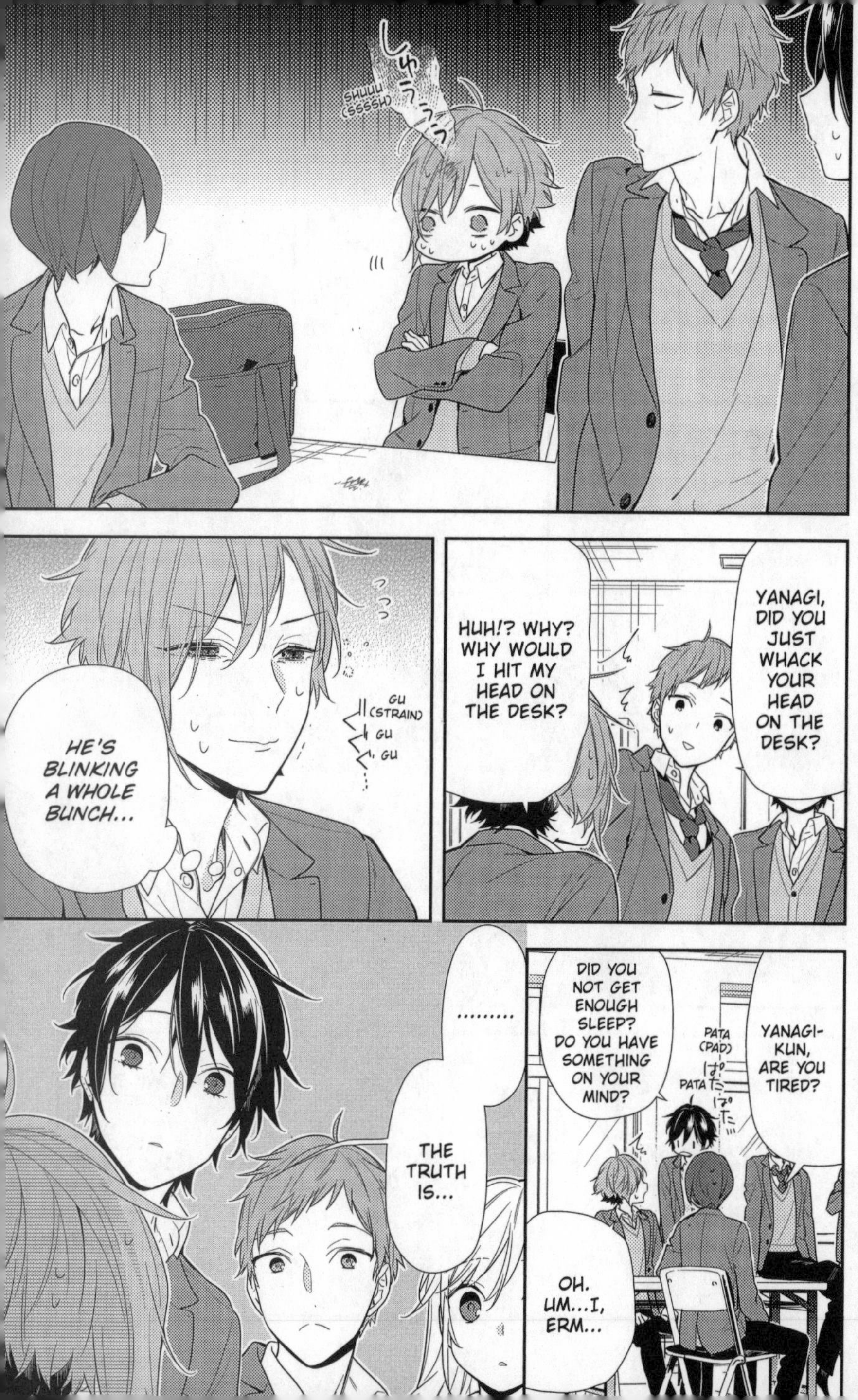
SHUUU (SSSSH)
YANAGI, DID YOU JUST WHACK YOUR HEAD ON THE DESK?
HUH!? WHY? WHY WOULD I HIT MY HEAD ON THE DESK?
GU (STRAIN) GU GU
HE'S BLINKING A WHOLE BUNCH...
YANAGI-KUN, ARE YOU TIRED?
PATA (PAD) PATA
DID YOU NOT GET ENOUGH SLEEP? DO YOU HAVE SOMETHING ON YOUR MIND?
OH. UM...I, ERM...
....
THE TRUTH IS...

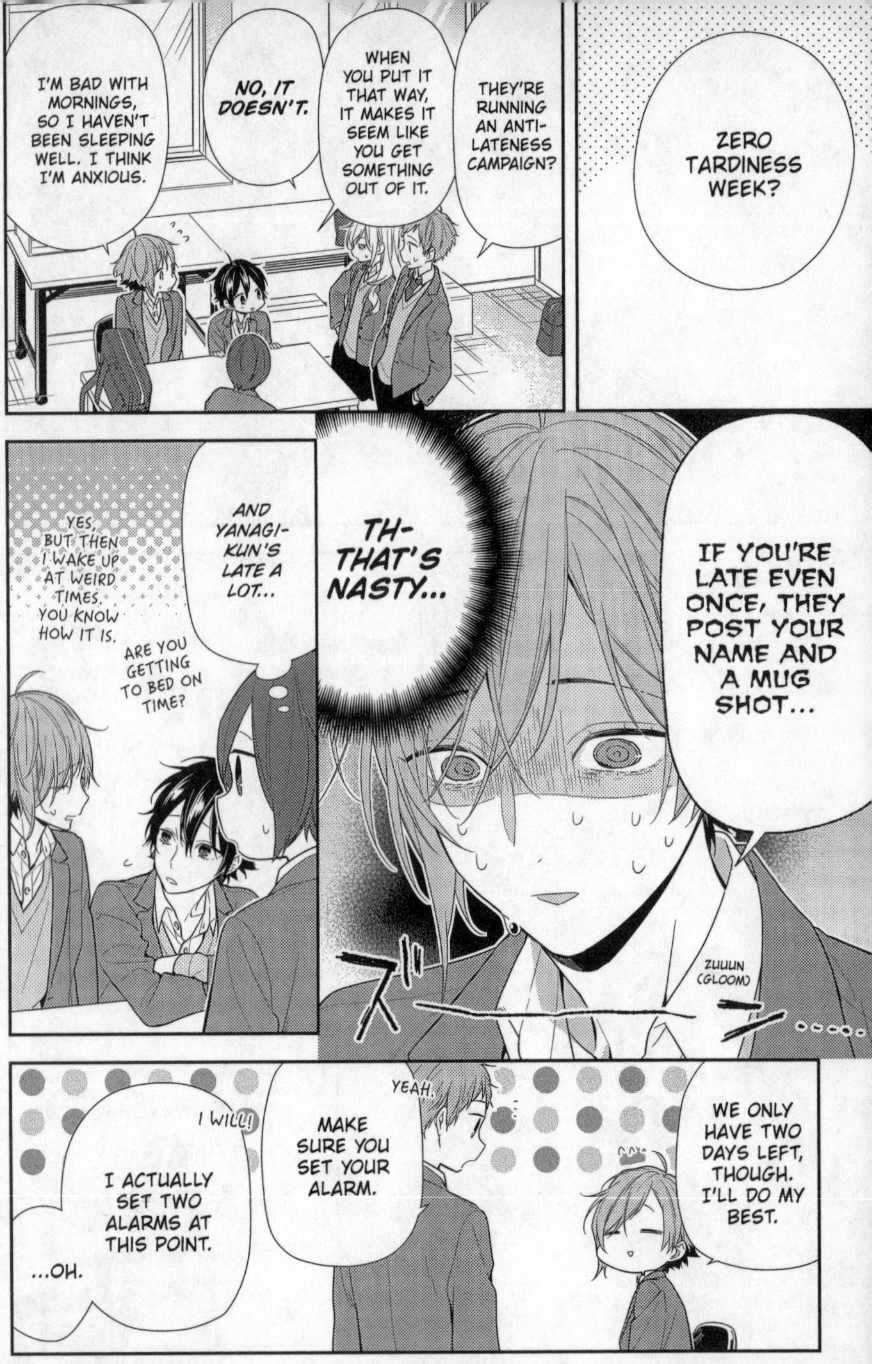
ZERO TARDINESS WEEK?
THEY'RE RUNNING AN ANTI-LATENESS CAMPAIGN?
WHEN YOU PUT IT THAT WAY, IT MAKES IT SEEM LIKE YOU GET SOMETHING OUT OF IT.
NO, IT DOESN'T.
I'M BAD WITH MORNINGS, SO I HAVEN'T BEEN SLEEPING WELL. I THINK I'M ANXIOUS.
IF YOU'RE LATE EVEN ONCE, THEY POST YOUR NAME AND A MUG SHOT...
TH-THAT'S NASTY...
ZUUUN (GLOOM)
AND YANAGI-KUN'S LATE A LOT...
ARE YOU GETTING TO BED ON TIME?
YES, BUT THEN I WAKE UP AT WEIRD TIMES. YOU KNOW HOW IT IS.
WE ONLY HAVE TWO DAYS LEFT, THOUGH. I'LL DO MY BEST.
YEAH.
MAKE SURE YOU SET YOUR ALARM.
I WILL!
I ACTUALLY SET TWO ALARMS AT THIS POINT.
...OH.

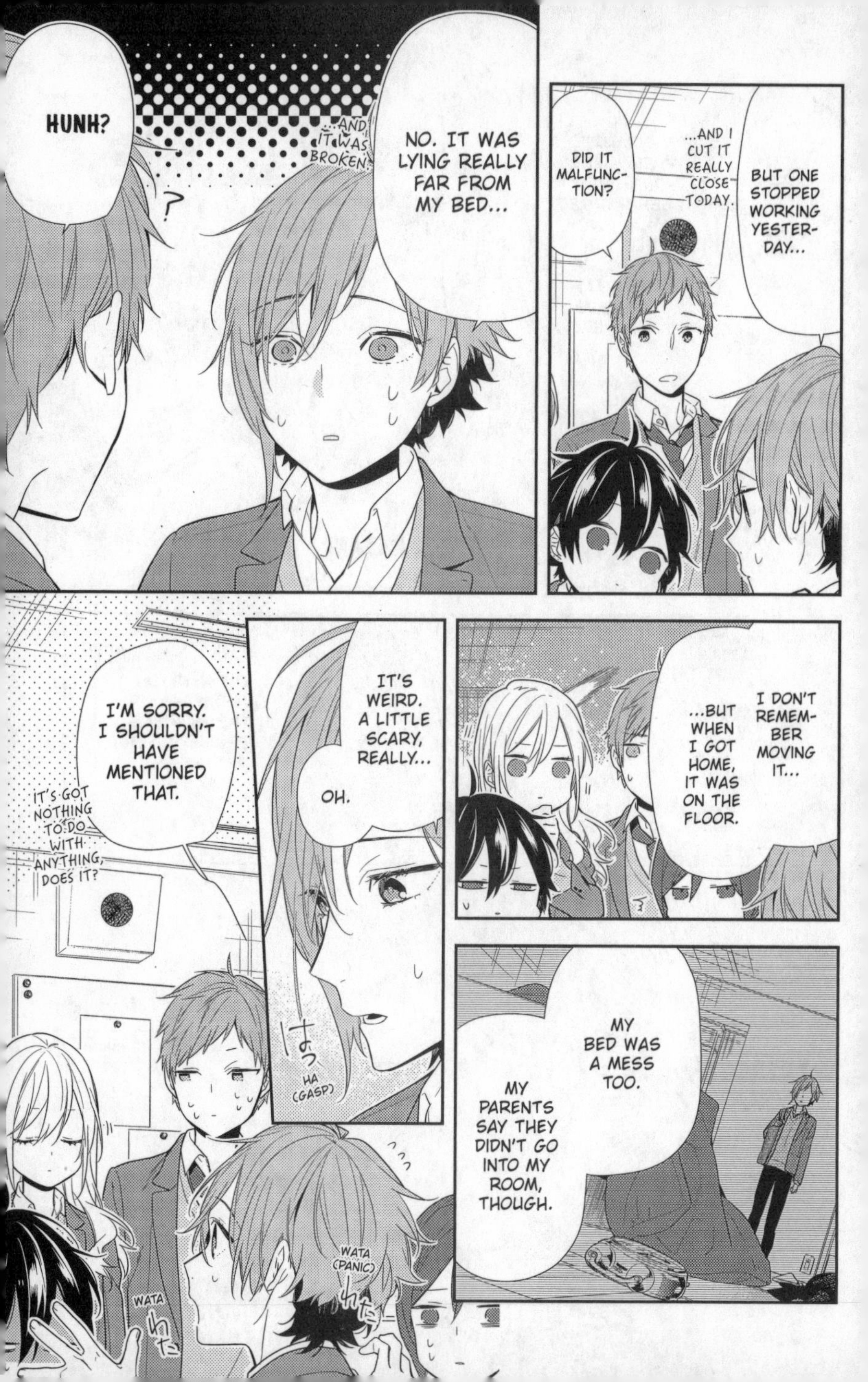
BUT ONE STOPPED WORKING YESTERDAY...
...AND I CUT IT REALLY CLOSE TODAY.
DID IT MALFUNCTION?
NO. IT WAS LYING REALLY FAR FROM MY BED...
...AND IT WAS BROKEN.
HUNH?
?
I DON'T REMEMBER MOVING IT...
...BUT WHEN I GOT HOME, IT WAS ON THE FLOOR.
MY BED WAS A MESS TOO.
MY PARENTS SAY THEY DIDN'T GO INTO MY ROOM, THOUGH.
IT'S WEIRD. A LITTLE SCARY, REALLY...
OH.
HA (GASP)
I'M SORRY. I SHOULDN'T HAVE MENTIONED THAT.
IT'S GOT NOTHING TO DO WITH ANYTHING, DOES IT?
WATA (PANIC)
WATA

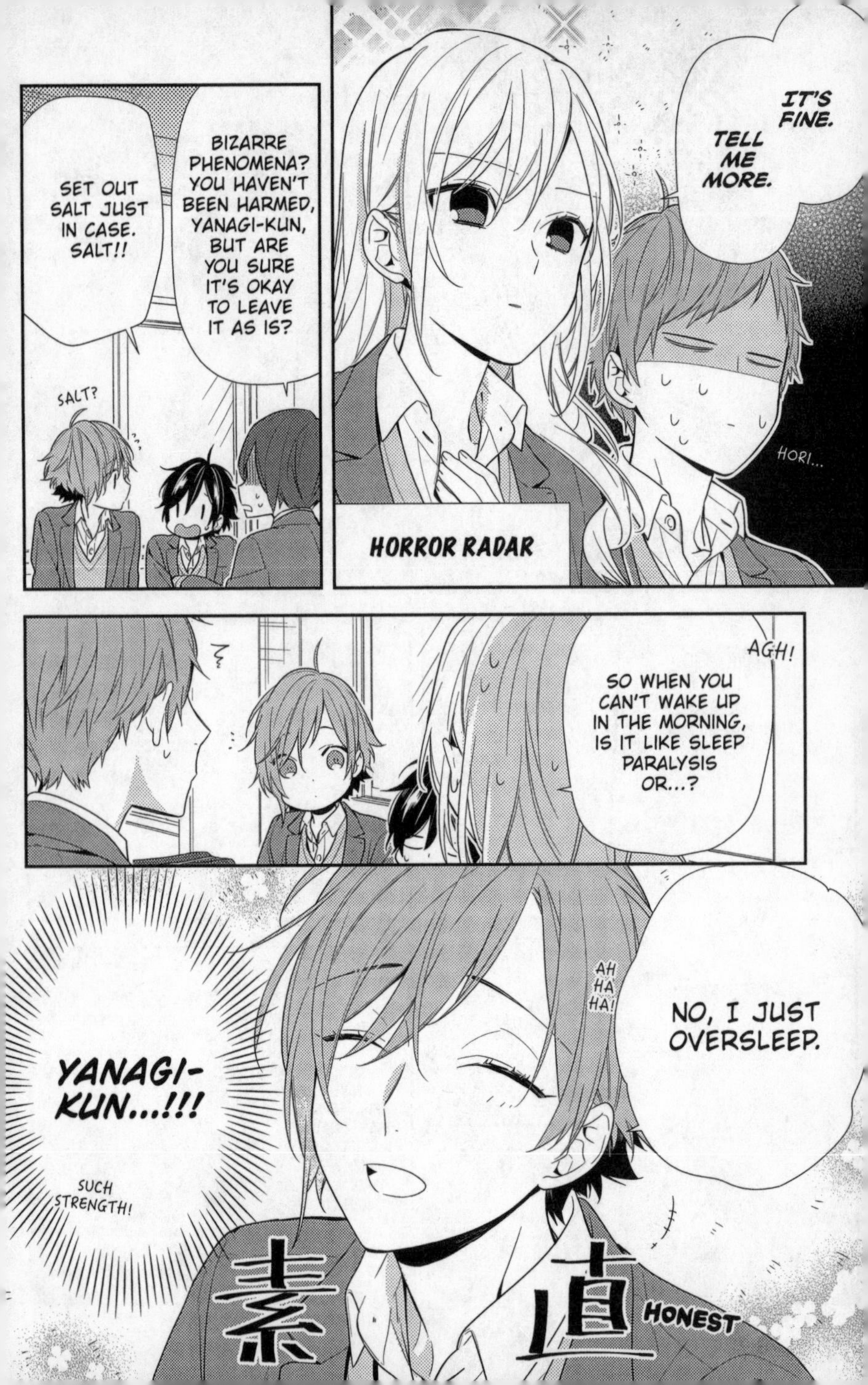
IT'S FINE.
TELL ME MORE.
HORI...
HORROR RADAR
BIZARRE PHENOMENA? YOU HAVEN'T BEEN HARMED, YANAGI-KUN, BUT ARE YOU SURE IT'S OKAY TO LEAVE IT AS IS?
SET OUT SALT JUST IN CASE. SALT!!
SALT?
AGH!
SO WHEN YOU CAN'T WAKE UP IN THE MORNING, IS IT LIKE SLEEP PARALYSIS OR...?
NO, I JUST OVERSLEEP.
AH HA HA!
YANAGI-KUN...!!!
SUCH STRENGTH!
素直
HONEST

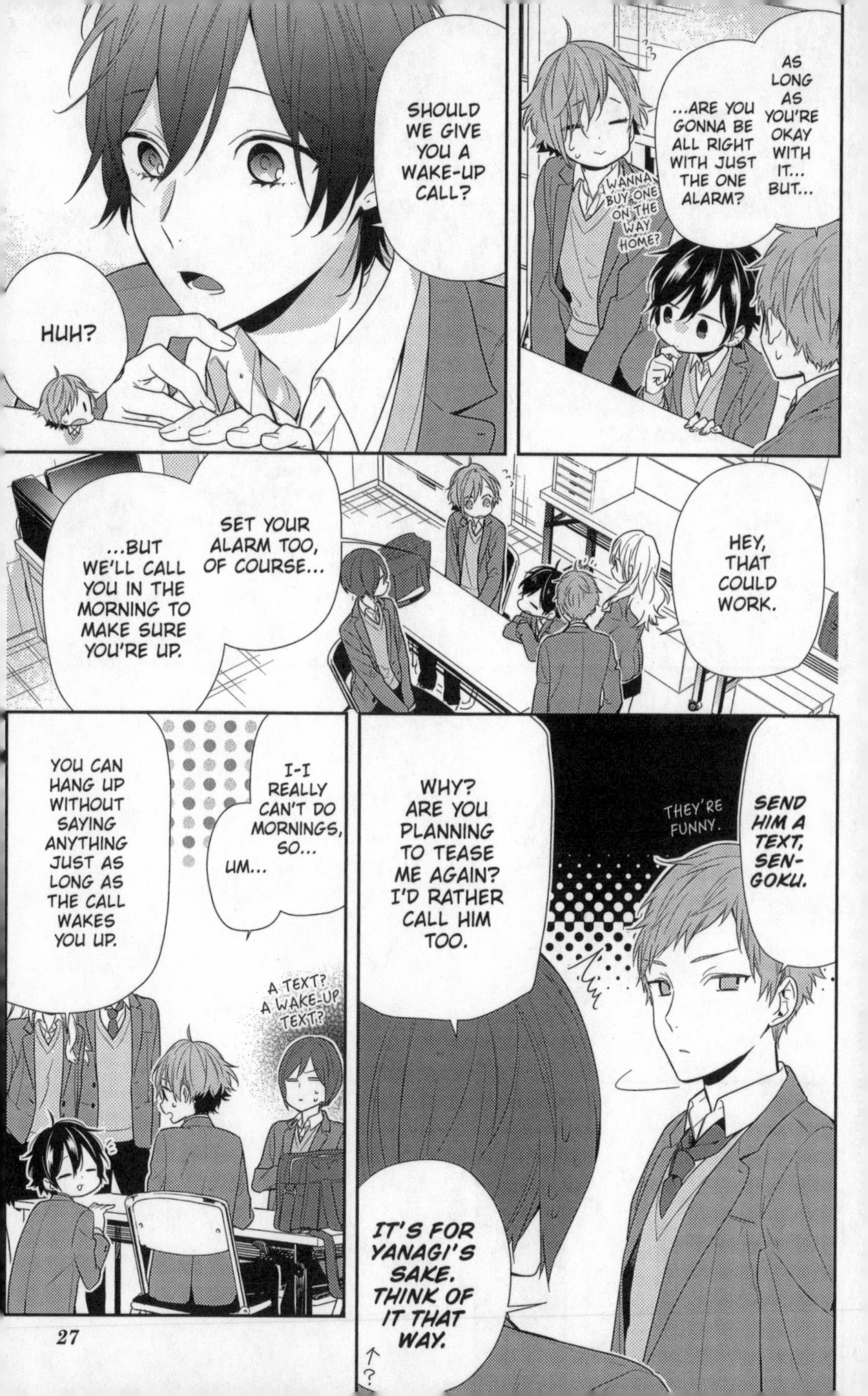
AS LONG AS YOU'RE OKAY WITH IT... BUT...
...ARE YOU GONNA BE ALL RIGHT WITH JUST THE ONE ALARM?
WANNA BUY ONE ON THE WAY HOME?
SHOULD WE GIVE YOU A WAKE-UP CALL?
HUH?
HEY, THAT COULD WORK.
SET YOUR ALARM TOO, OF COURSE...
...BUT WE'LL CALL YOU IN THE MORNING TO MAKE SURE YOU'RE UP.
SEND HIM A TEXT, SEN-GOKU.
THEY'RE FUNNY.
WHY? ARE YOU PLANNING TO TEASE ME AGAIN? I'D RATHER CALL HIM TOO.
IT'S FOR YANAGI'S SAKE. THINK OF IT THAT WAY.
?
I-I REALLY CAN'T DO MORNINGS, SO... UM...
YOU CAN HANG UP WITHOUT SAYING ANYTHING JUST AS LONG AS THE CALL WAKES YOU UP.
A TEXT? A WAKE-UP TEXT?

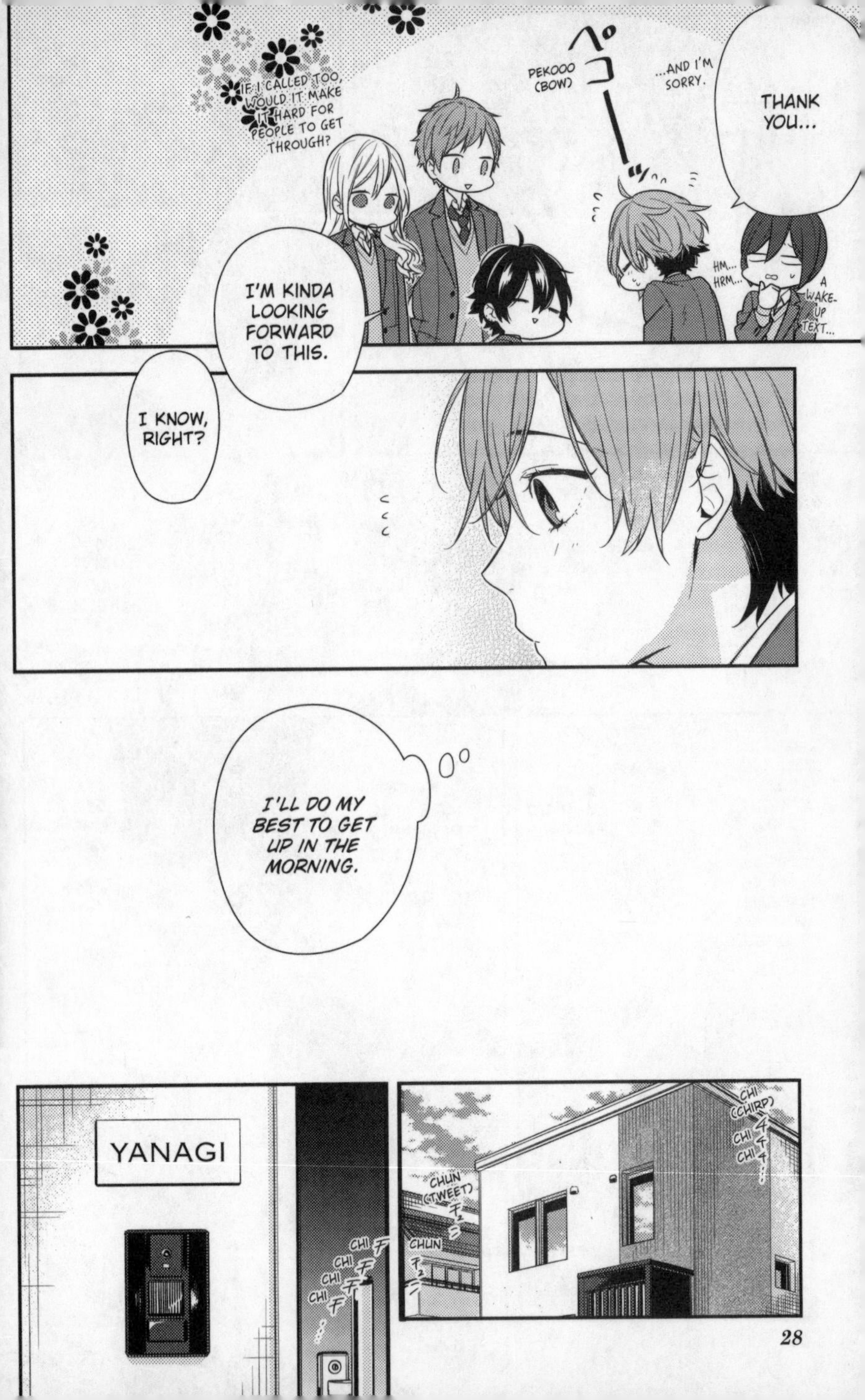
THANK YOU...
A WAKE-UP TEXT...
HM... HRM...
...AND I'M SORRY.
ペコー
PEKOOO (BOW)
IF I CALLED TOO, WOULD IT MAKE IT HARD FOR PEOPLE TO GET THROUGH?
I'M KINDA LOOKING FORWARD TO THIS.
I KNOW, RIGHT?
I'LL DO MY BEST TO GET UP IN THE MORNING.
CHI (CHIRP) CHI CHI
チチチ…
CHUN (TWEET)
チュ
CHUN
チュ
YANAGI
CHI CHI CHI CHI
チチチチ

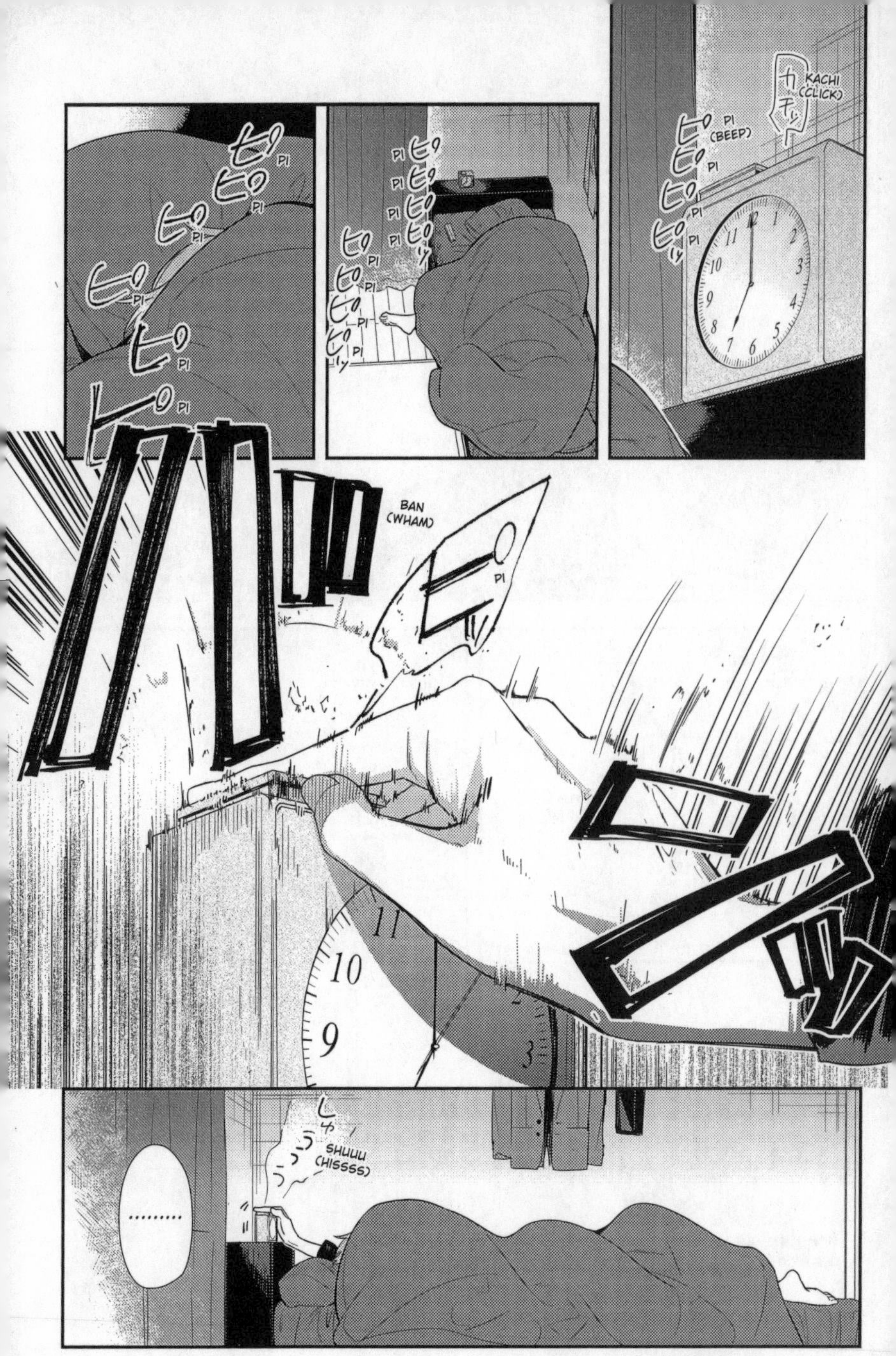

カチッ
KACHI (CLICK)
ピ PI (BEEP)
ピ PI
ピ PI
ピッ PI
ピ PI
ピ PI
ピ PI
ピッ PI
ピ PI
ピ PI
ピ PI
ピッ PI
ピ PI
ピ PI
ピ PI
ピ PI
ピ PI
ピ PI
ピ PI
バン
BAN (WHAM)
ピ PI
しゅううう
SHUUU (HISSSS)
....

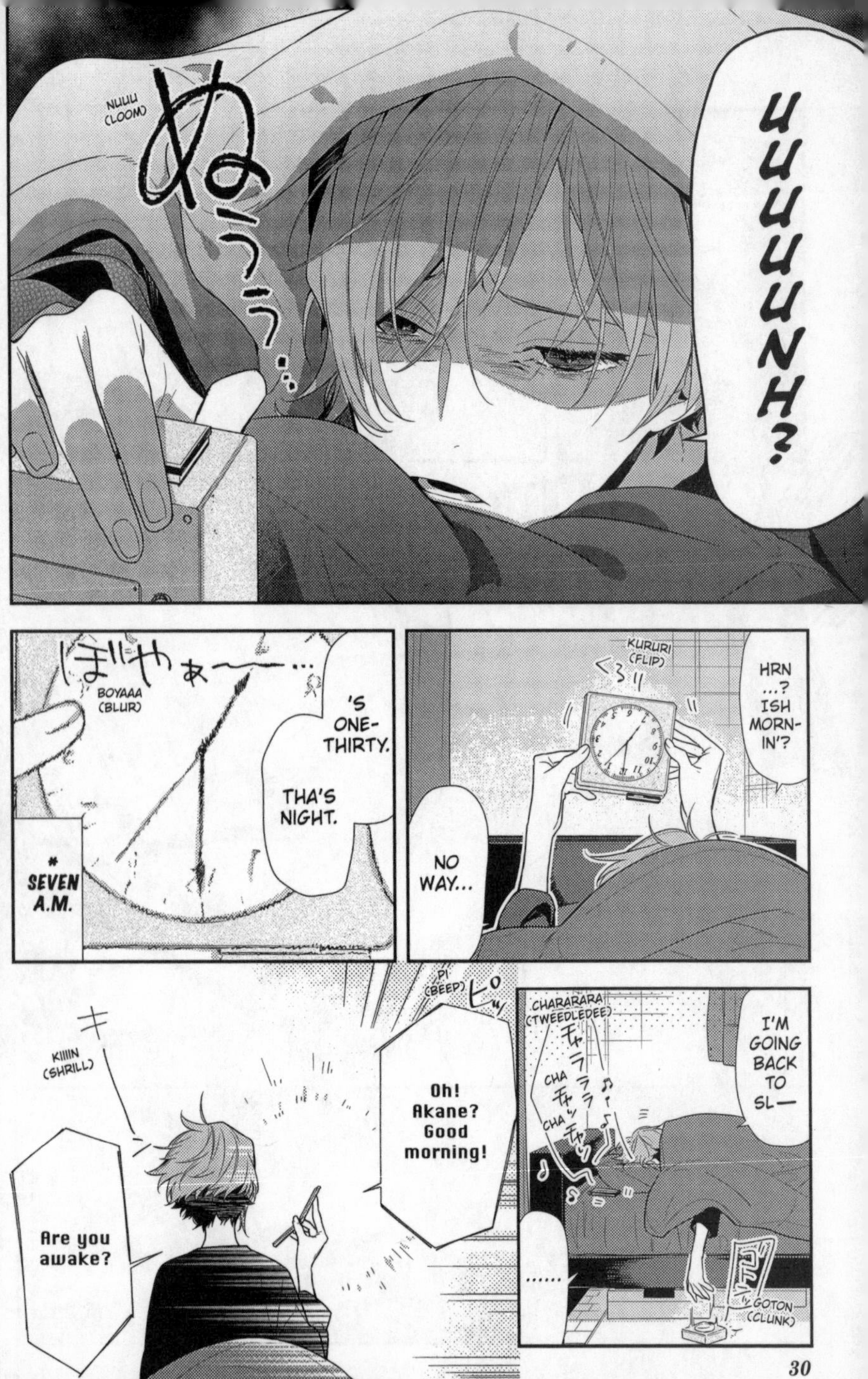
UUUUUNH?
NUUU (LOOM)
KURURI (FLIP)
HRN ...? ISH MORNIN'?
NO WAY...
BOYAAA (BLUR)
'S ONE-THIRTY.
THA'S NIGHT.
* SEVEN A.M.
CHARARARA (TWEEDLEDEE)
I'M GOING BACK TO SL—
CHA
CHA
GOTON (CLUNK)
......
PI (BEEP)
Oh! Akane? Good morning!
KIIIN (SHRILL)
Are you awake?

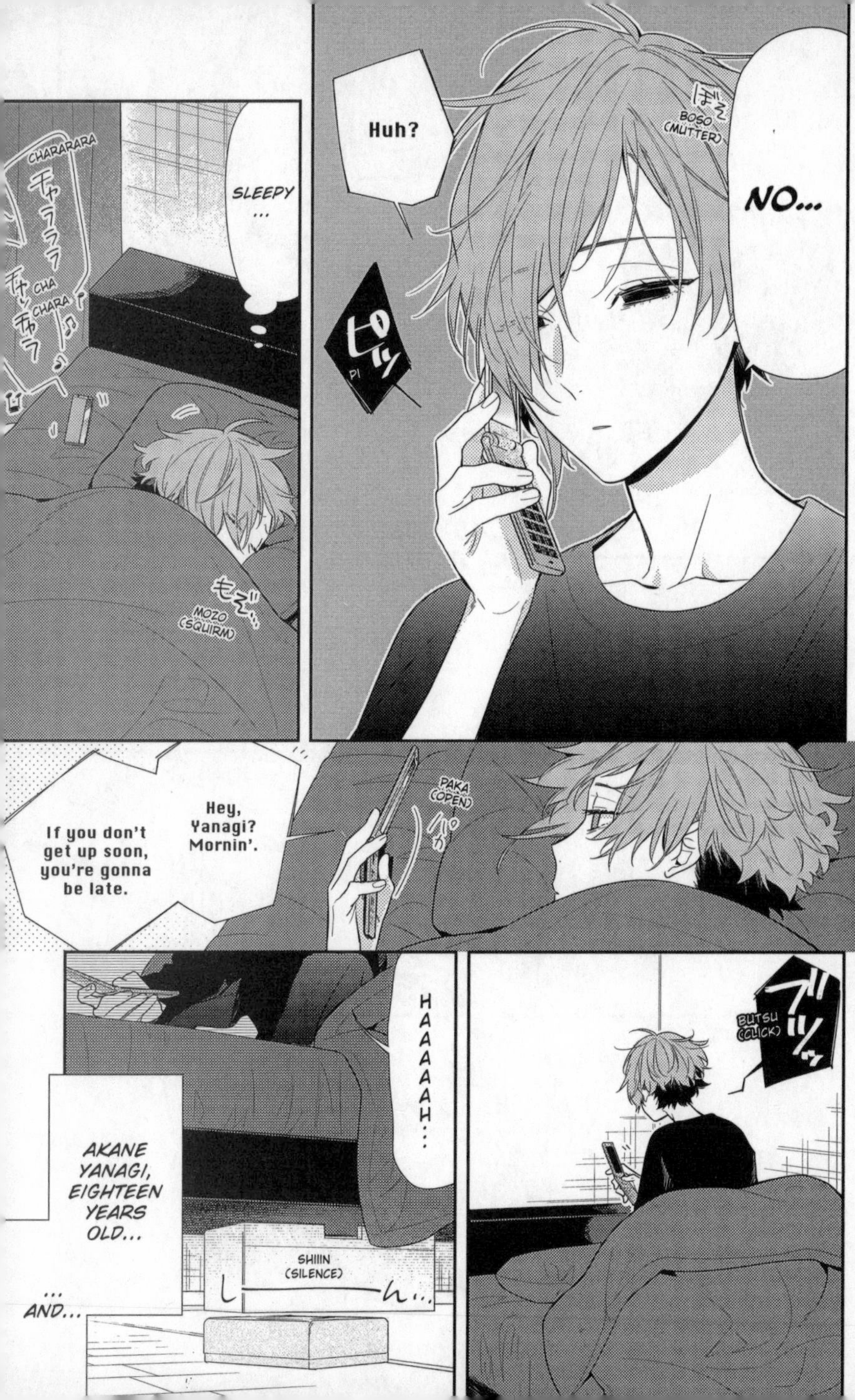
NO...
ぼそ
BOSO (MUTTER)
Huh?
ピッ
PI
SLEEPY ...
チャラララ
CHARARARA
チャチャラ
CHA CHARA
もぞ…
MOZO (SQUIRM)
パカ
PAKA (OPEN)
Hey, Yanagi? Mornin'.
If you don't get up soon, you're gonna be late.
ブツッ
BUTSU (CLICK)
HAAAAAAH...
AKANE YANAGI, EIGHTEEN YEARS OLD...
SHIIIN (SILENCE)
し——ん…
... AND...

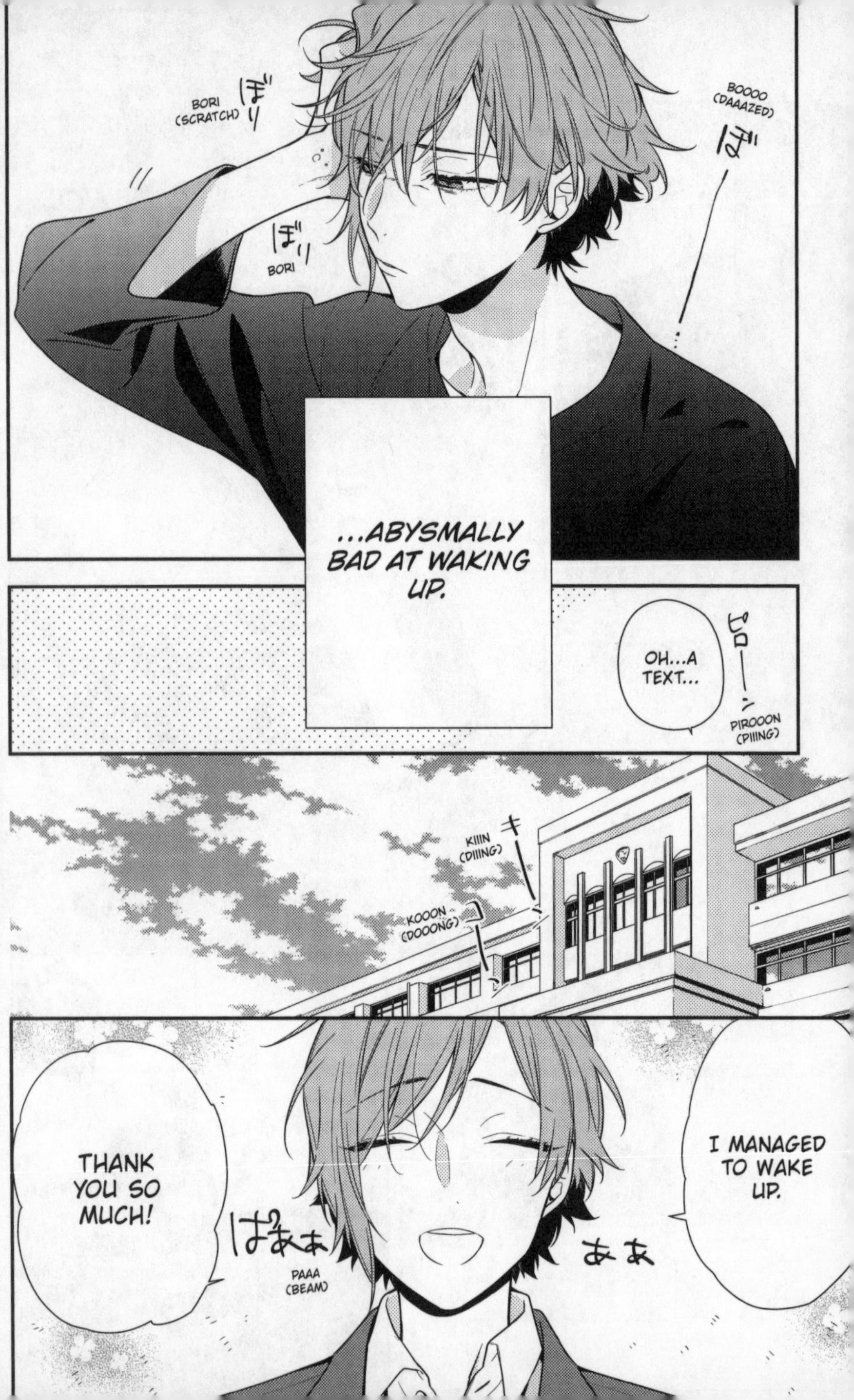
ぼー
BOOOO (DAAAZED)
ぼり
BORI (SCRATCH)
ぼり
BORI
...ABYSMALLY BAD AT WAKING UP.
ピロ—ン
PIROOON (PIIING)
OH...A TEXT...
キーン
KIIIN (DIIING)
コーン
KOOON (DOOONG)
I MANAGED TO WAKE UP.
ああ
ぱあぁ
PAAA (BEAM)
THANK YOU SO MUCH!

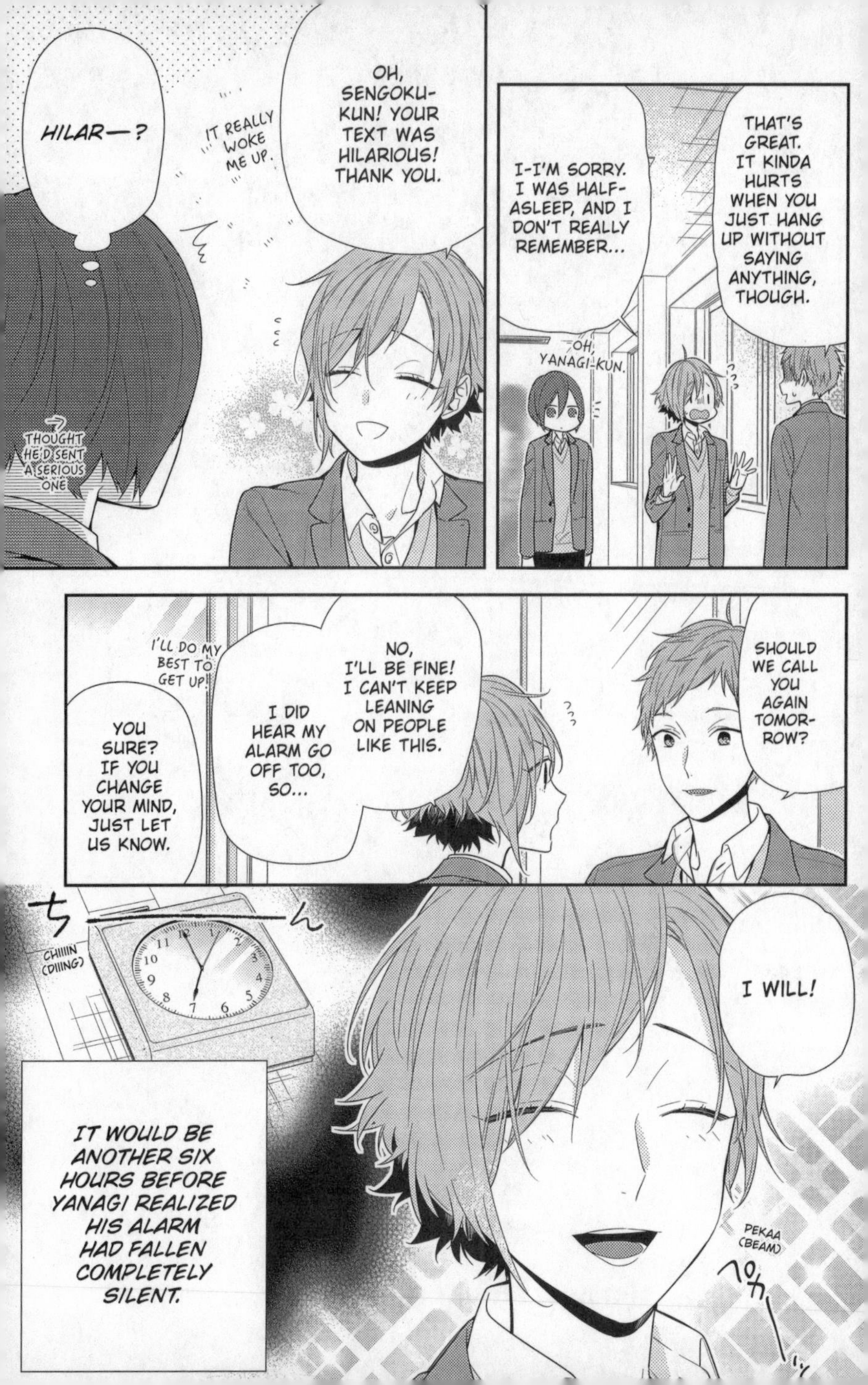
THAT'S GREAT. IT KINDA HURTS WHEN YOU JUST HANG UP WITHOUT SAYING ANYTHING, THOUGH.
I-I'M SORRY. I WAS HALF-ASLEEP, AND I DON'T REALLY REMEMBER...
OH, YANAGI-KUN.
OH, SENGOKU-KUN! YOUR TEXT WAS HILARIOUS! THANK YOU.
IT REALLY WOKE ME UP.
HILAR—?
THOUGHT HE'D SENT A SERIOUS ONE
SHOULD WE CALL YOU AGAIN TOMORROW?
NO, I'LL BE FINE! I CAN'T KEEP LEANING ON PEOPLE LIKE THIS.
I DID HEAR MY ALARM GO OFF TOO, SO...
I'LL DO MY BEST TO GET UP!
YOU SURE? IF YOU CHANGE YOUR MIND, JUST LET US KNOW.
I WILL!
PEKAA (BEAM)
CHIIIN (DIIING)
IT WOULD BE ANOTHER SIX HOURS BEFORE YANAGI REALIZED HIS ALARM HAD FALLEN COMPLETELY SILENT.

HORIMIYA

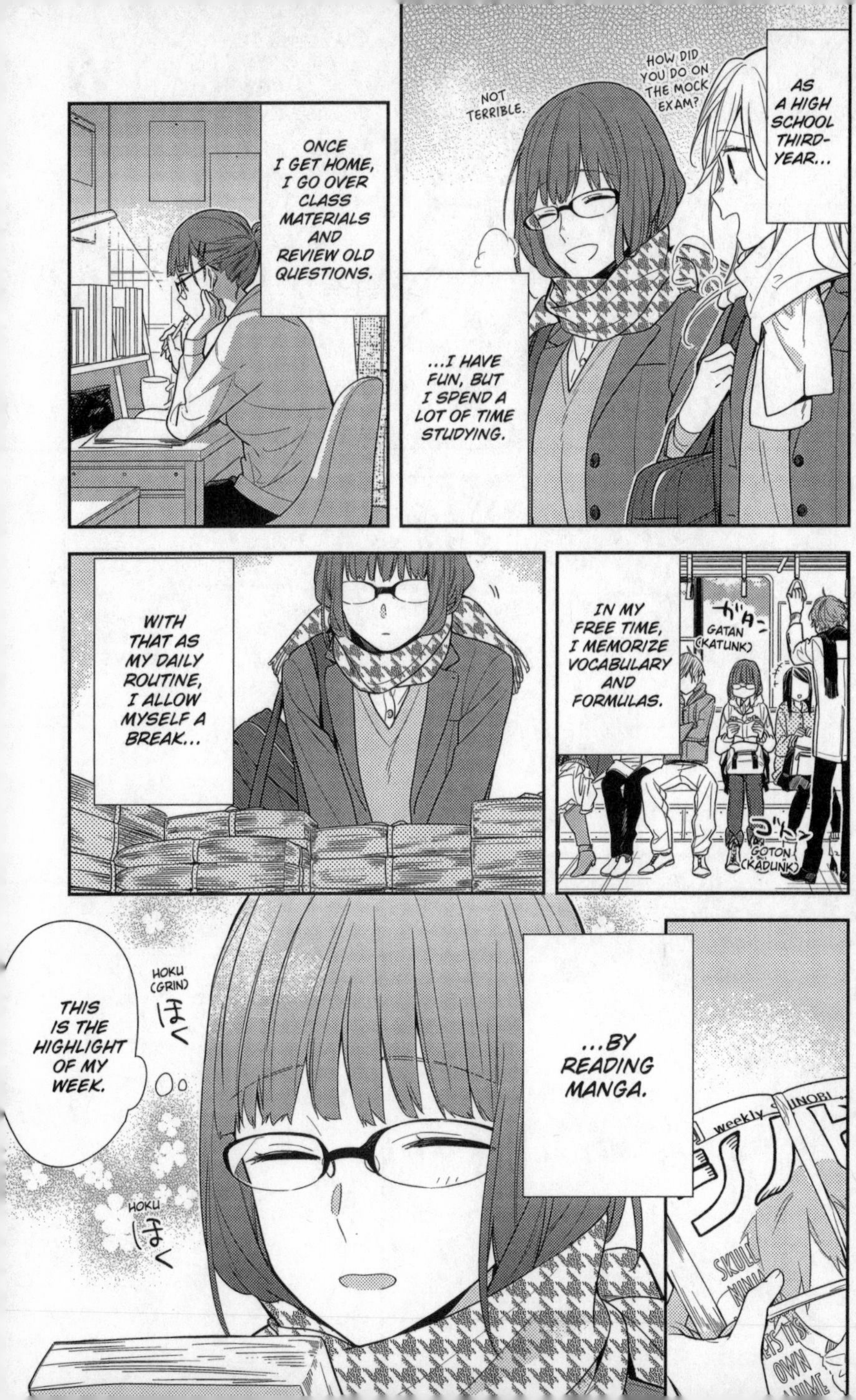
AS A HIGH SCHOOL THIRD-YEAR...
HOW DID YOU DO ON THE MOCK EXAM?
NOT TERRIBLE.
...I HAVE FUN, BUT I SPEND A LOT OF TIME STUDYING.
ONCE I GET HOME, I GO OVER CLASS MATERIALS AND REVIEW OLD QUESTIONS.
IN MY FREE TIME, I MEMORIZE VOCABULARY AND FORMULAS.
ガタン
GATAN (KATUNK)
ゴトン
GOTON (KADUNK)
WITH THAT AS MY DAILY ROUTINE, I ALLOW MYSELF A BREAK...
...BY READING MANGA.
weekly SHINOBI
HOKU (GRIND)
ほく
THIS IS THE HIGHLIGHT OF MY WEEK.
HOKU
ほく

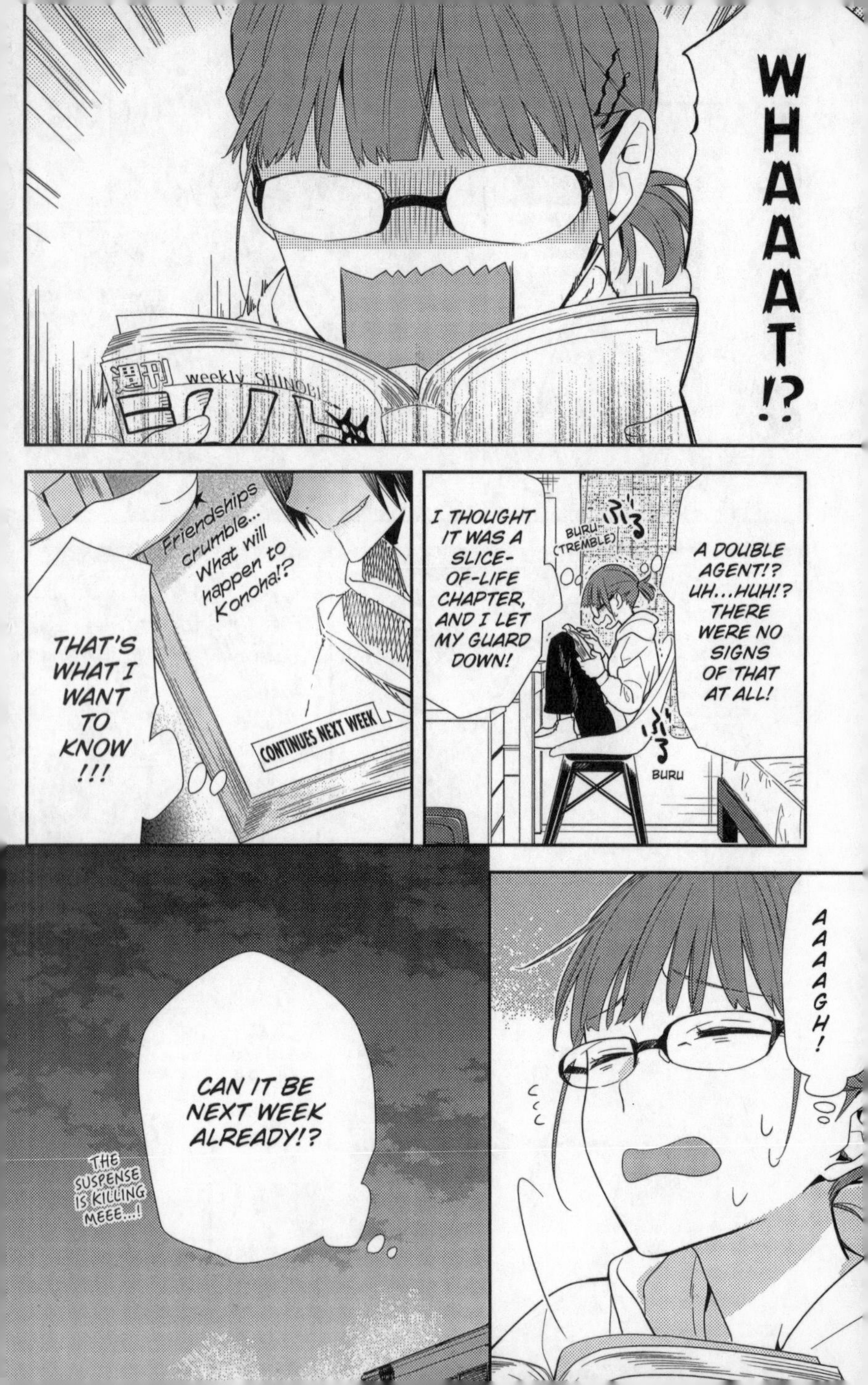
weekly SHINOBI
WHAAAT!?
A DOUBLE AGENT!? UH...HUH!? THERE WERE NO SIGNS OF THAT AT ALL!
BURU (TREMBLE)
I THOUGHT IT WAS A SLICE-OF-LIFE CHAPTER, AND I LET MY GUARD DOWN!
BURU
Friendships crumble... What will happen to Konoha!?
CONTINUES NEXT WEEK
THAT'S WHAT I WANT TO KNOW!!!
AAAAAGH!
CAN IT BE NEXT WEEK ALREADY!?
THE SUSPENSE IS KILLING MEEE...!

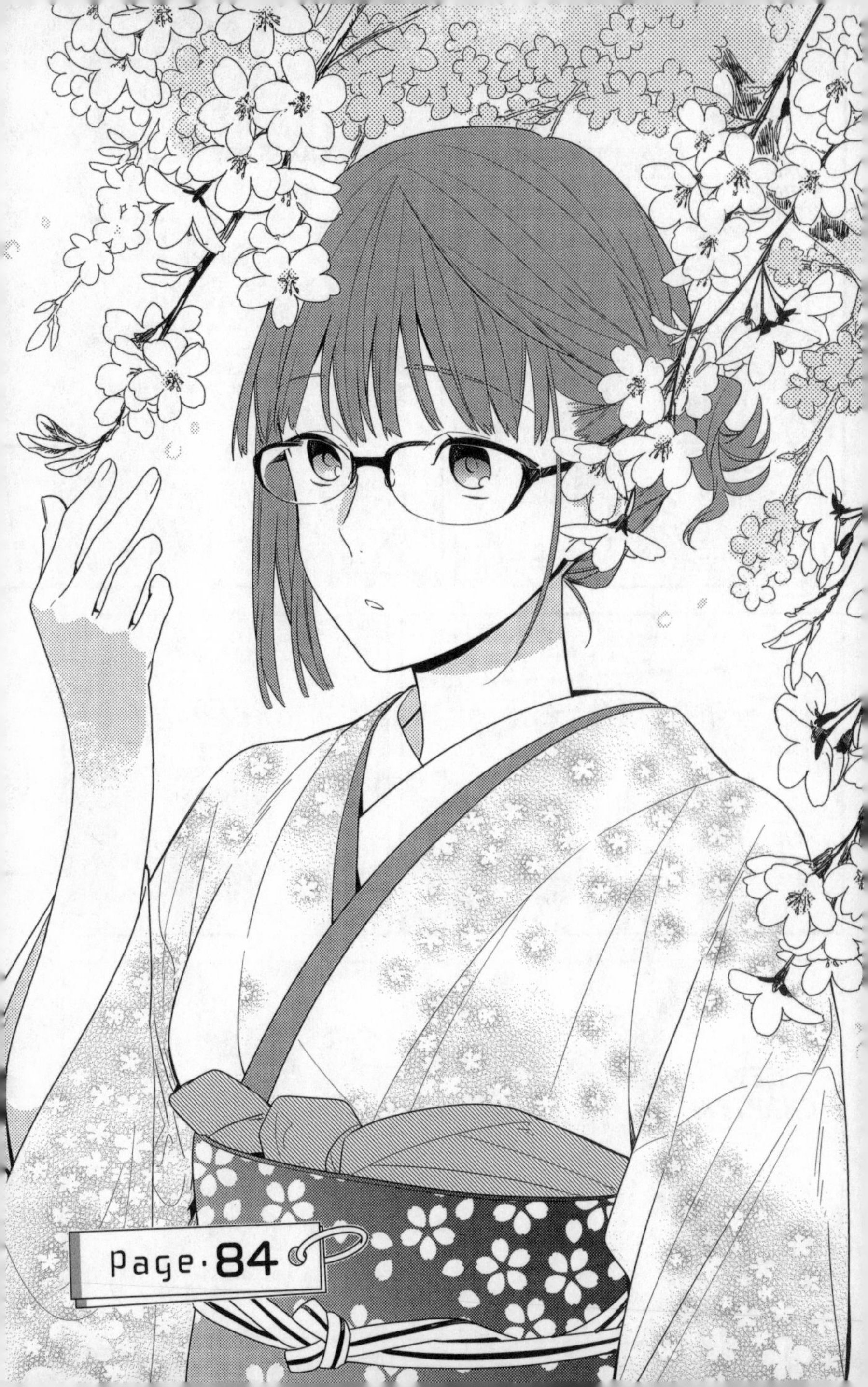
page·84

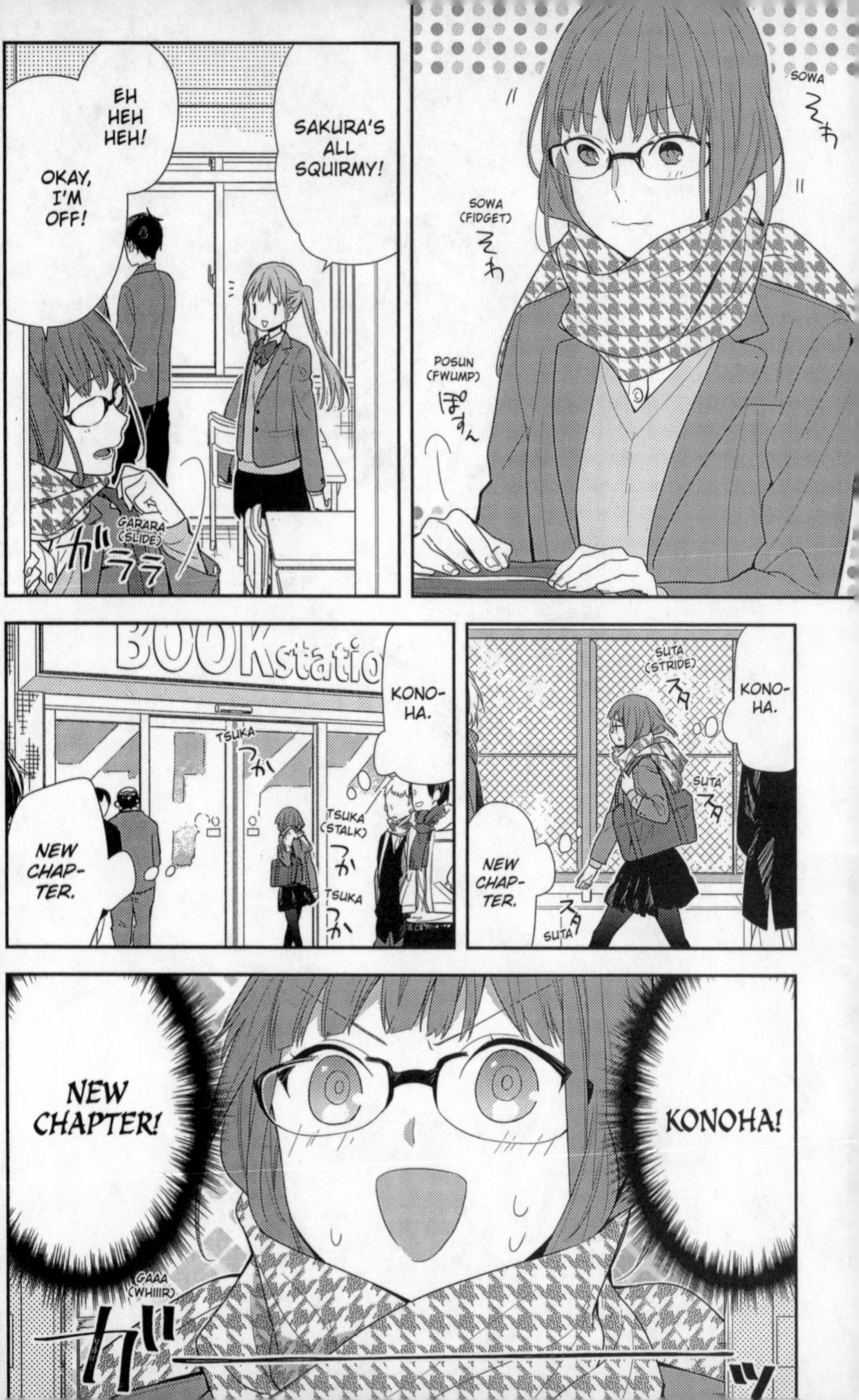

SOWA
そわ
SOWA (FIDGET)
そわ
POSUN (FWUMP)
ぽすん
SAKURA'S ALL SQUIRMY!
EH HEH HEH!
OKAY, I'M OFF!
GARARA (SLIDE)
ガララ
KONOHA.
SUTA (STRIDE)
スタ
SUTA
スタ
NEW CHAPTER.
SUTA
スタ
BOOKstatio
KONOHA.
TSUKA
つか
TSUKA (STALK)
つか
TSUKA
つか
NEW CHAPTER.
KONOHA!
NEW CHAPTER!
GAAA (WHIIIR)
ガーッ

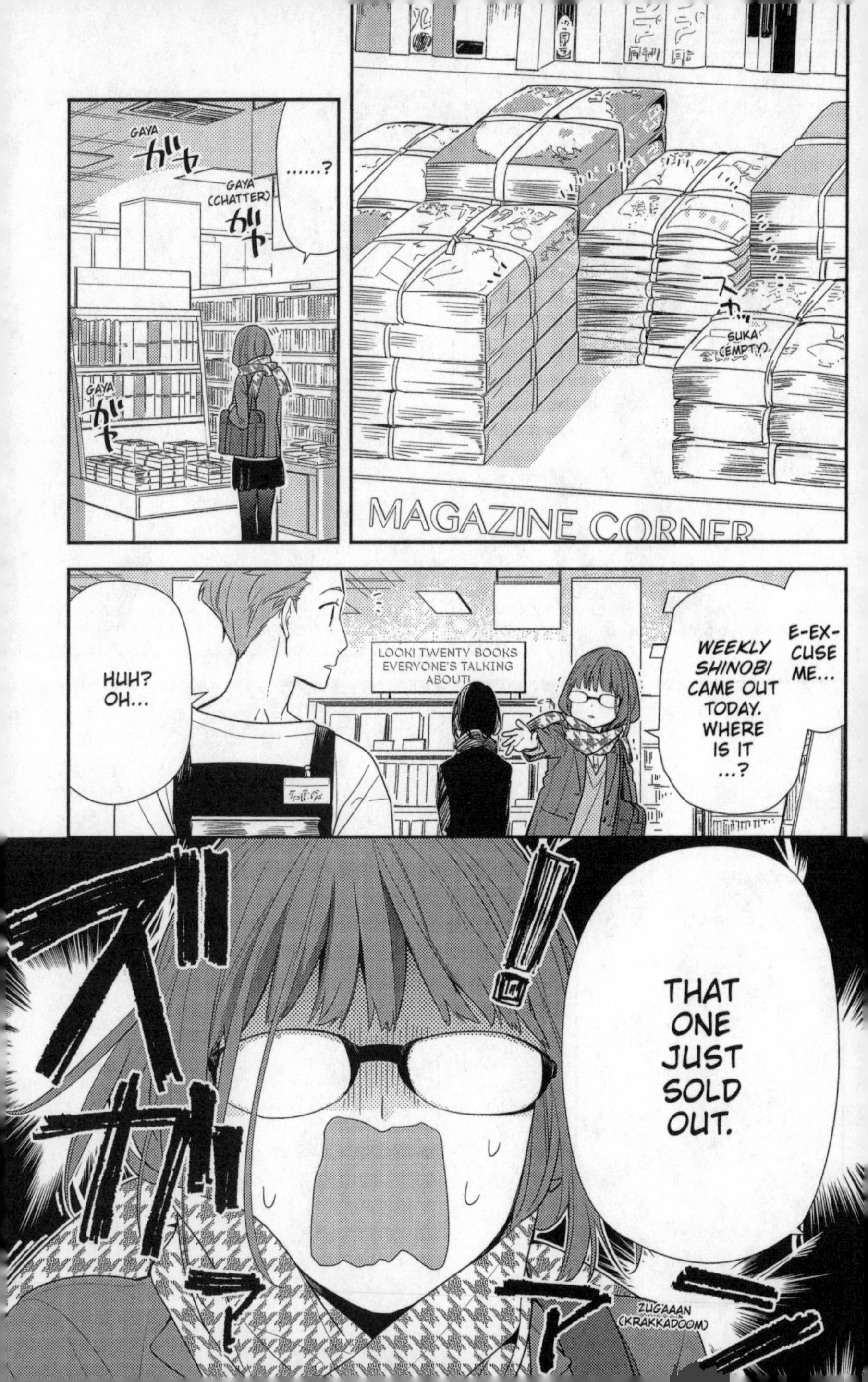
MAGAZINE CORNER
SUKA (EMPTY)
GAYA
GAYA (CHATTER)
GAYA
......?
E-EX-CUSE ME...
WEEKLY SHINOBI CAME OUT TODAY. WHERE IS IT ...?
LOOK! TWENTY BOOKS EVERYONE'S TALKING ABOUT!
HUH? OH...
THAT ONE JUST SOLD OUT.
ZUGAAAN (KRAKKADOOM)

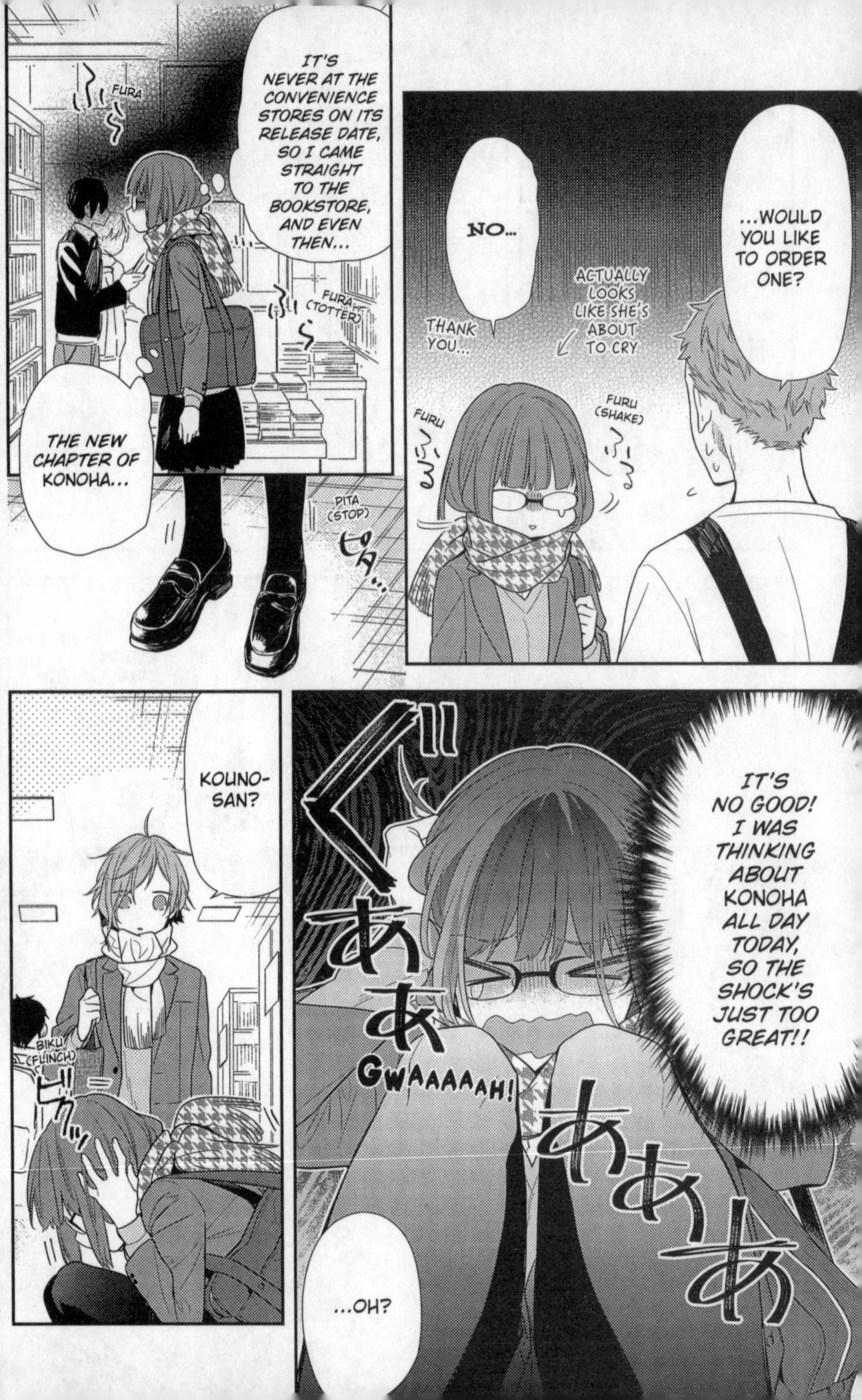

...WOULD YOU LIKE TO ORDER ONE?
NO...
ACTUALLY LOOKS LIKE SHE'S ABOUT TO CRY
THANK YOU...
FURU (SHAKE)
FURU
FURA
IT'S NEVER AT THE CONVENIENCE STORES ON ITS RELEASE DATE, SO I CAME STRAIGHT TO THE BOOKSTORE, AND EVEN THEN...
FURA (TOTTER)
THE NEW CHAPTER OF KONOHA...
PITA (STOP)
IT'S NO GOOD! I WAS THINKING ABOUT KONOHA ALL DAY TODAY, SO THE SHOCK'S JUST TOO GREAT!!
GWAAAAAH!
...OH?
KOUNO-SAN?
BIKU (FLINCH)

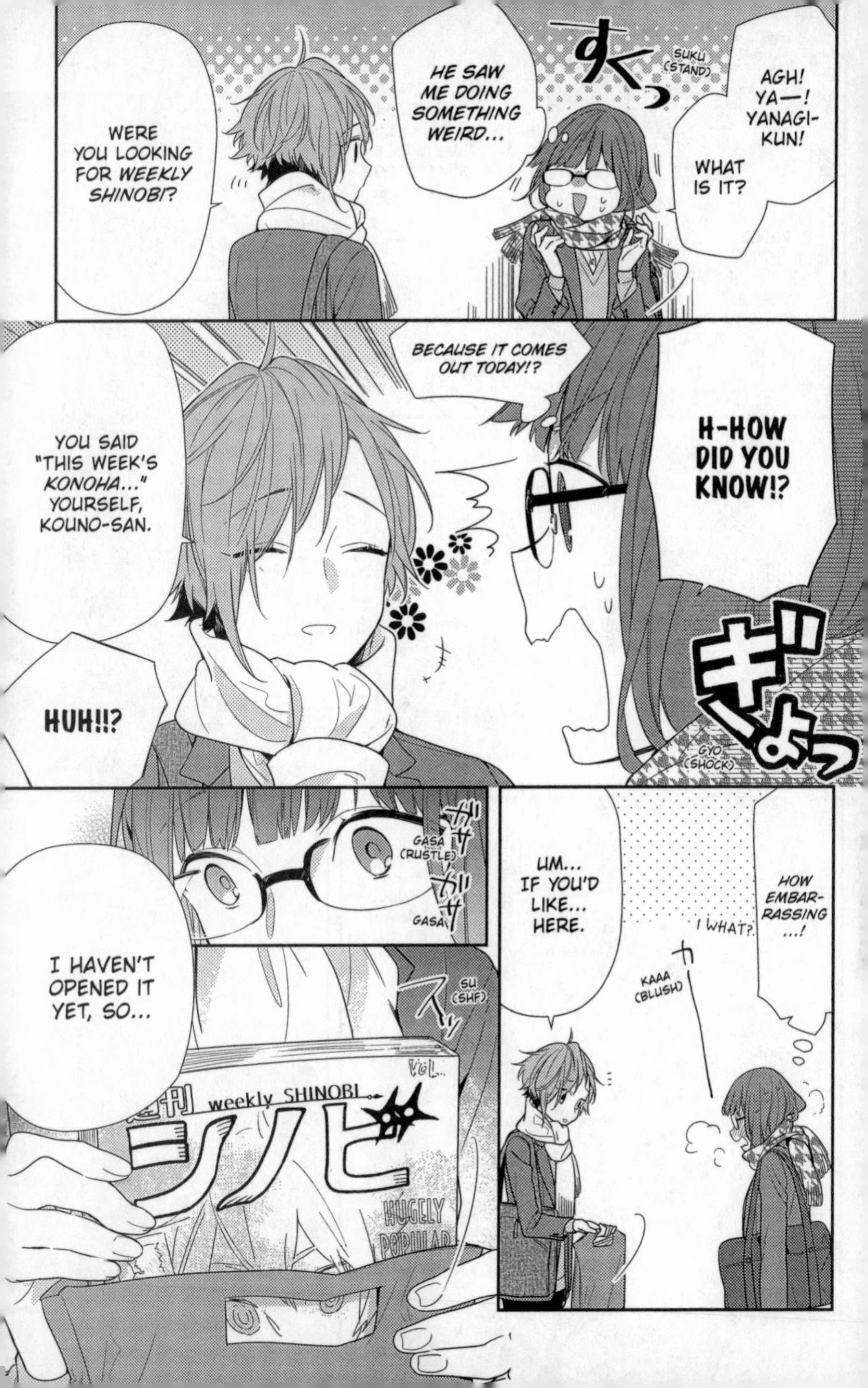
AGH! YA—! YANAGI-KUN! WHAT IS IT?
すくっ
SUKU (STAND)
HE SAW ME DOING SOMETHING WEIRD...
WERE YOU LOOKING FOR WEEKLY SHINOBI?
H-HOW DID YOU KNOW!?
BECAUSE IT COMES OUT TODAY!?
YOU SAID "THIS WEEK'S KONOHA..." YOURSELF, KOUNO-SAN.
ぎょっ
GYO (SHOCK)
HUH!!?
HOW EMBARRASSING...!
I WHAT?
UM... IF YOU'D LIKE... HERE.
KAAA (BLUSH)
GASA (RUSTLE)
GASA
SU (SHF)
I HAVEN'T OPENED IT YET, SO...
weekly SHINOBI
シノビ
HUGELY POPULAR

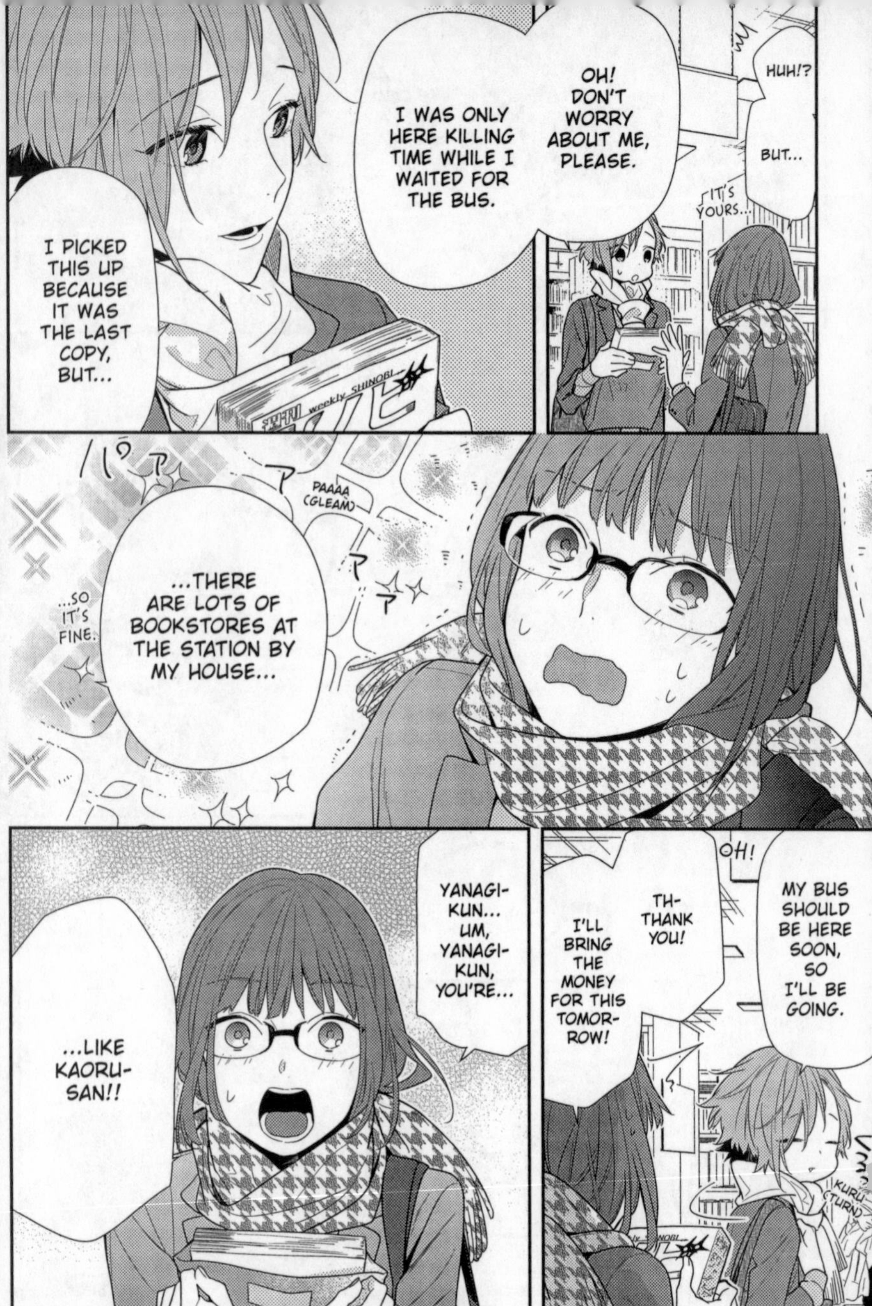
HUH!?
BUT...
IT'S YOURS...
OH! DON'T WORRY ABOUT ME, PLEASE.
I WAS ONLY HERE KILLING TIME WHILE I WAITED FOR THE BUS.
I PICKED THIS UP BECAUSE IT WAS THE LAST COPY, BUT...
PAAAA (GLEAM)
...THERE ARE LOTS OF BOOKSTORES AT THE STATION BY MY HOUSE...
...SO IT'S FINE.
MY BUS SHOULD BE HERE SOON, SO I'LL BE GOING.
OH!
TH-THANK YOU!
I'LL BRING THE MONEY FOR THIS TOMORROW!
KURU (TURN)
YANAGI-KUN... UM, YANAGI-KUN, YOU'RE...
...LIKE KAORU-SAN!!

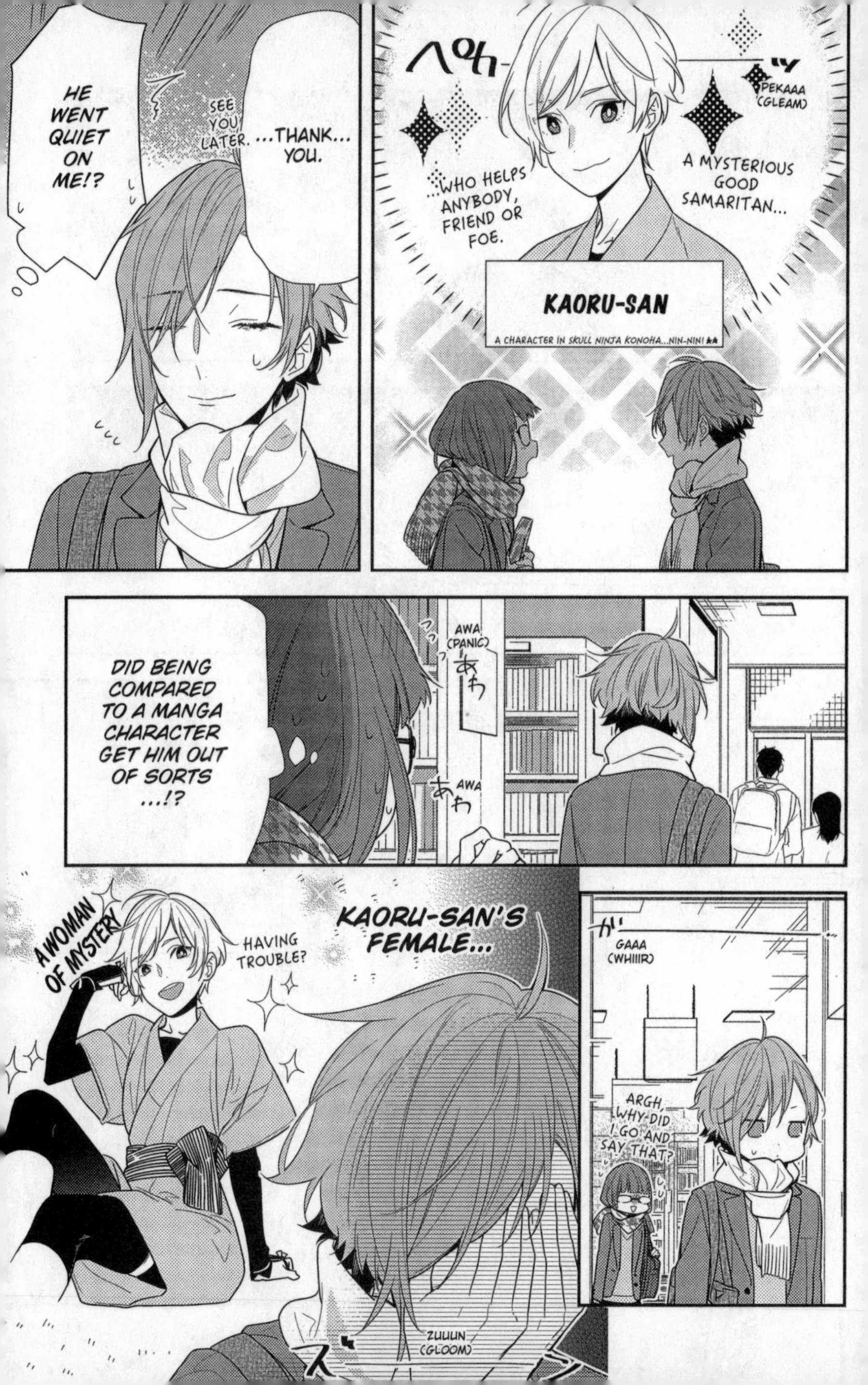
PEKAAA (GLEAM)
A MYSTERIOUS GOOD SAMARITAN...
...WHO HELPS ANYBODY, FRIEND OR FOE.
KAORU-SAN
A CHARACTER IN SKULL NINJA KONOHA...NIN-NIN!
...THANK... YOU.
SEE YOU LATER.
HE WENT QUIET ON ME!?
AWA (PANIC)
AWA
DID BEING COMPARED TO A MANGA CHARACTER GET HIM OUT OF SORTS ...!?
GAAA (WHIIIR)
ARGH, WHY DID I GO AND SAY THAT?
KAORU-SAN'S FEMALE...
A WOMAN OF MYSTERY
HAVING TROUBLE?
ZUUUN (GLOOM)

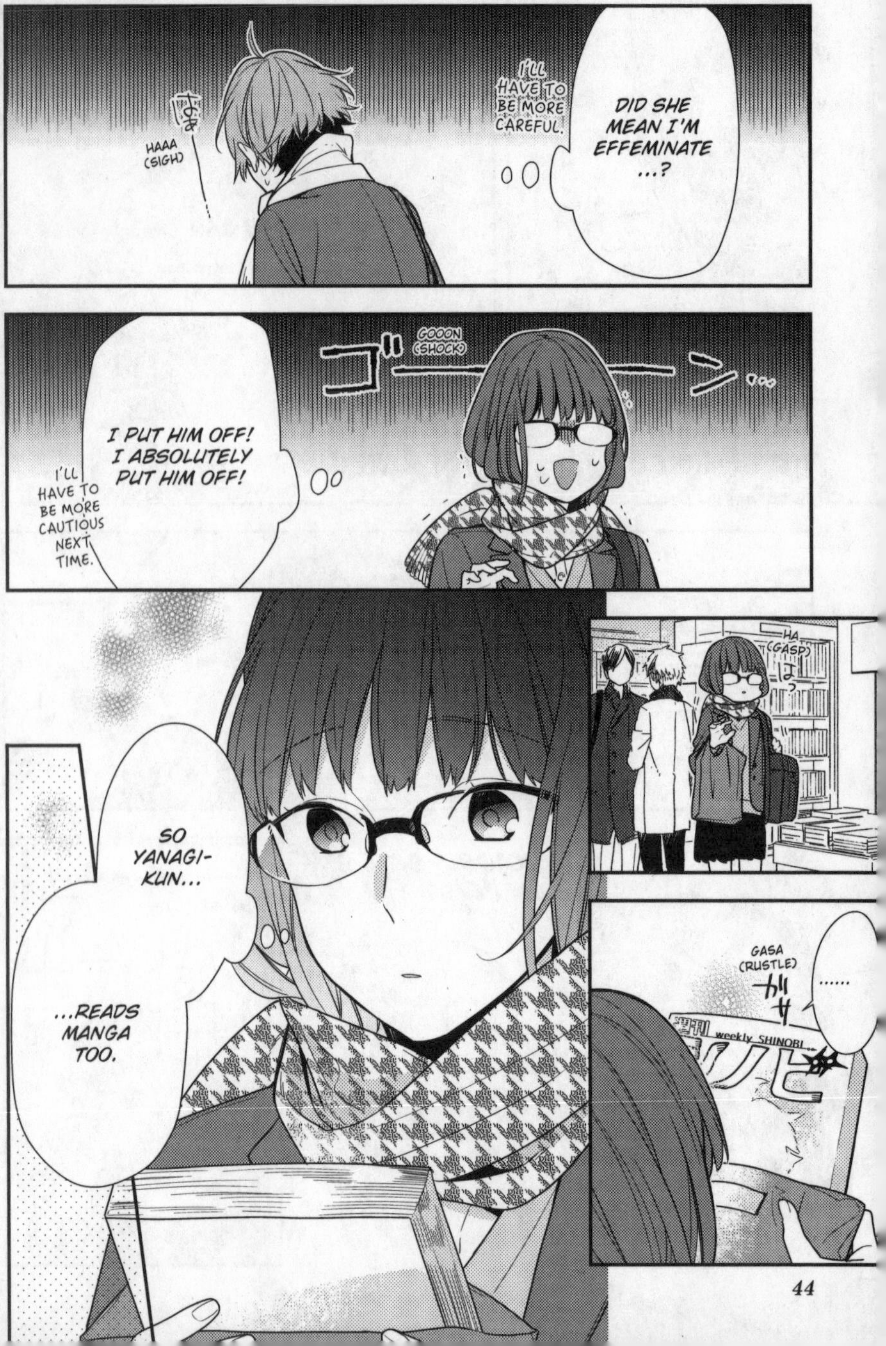
DID SHE MEAN I'M EFFEMINATE ...?
I'LL HAVE TO BE MORE CAREFUL.
HAAA (SIGH)
GOOON (SHOCK)
I PUT HIM OFF! I ABSOLUTELY PUT HIM OFF!
I'LL HAVE TO BE MORE CAUTIOUS NEXT TIME.
HA (GASP)
GASA (RUSTLE)
......
weekly SHINOBI
SO YANAGI-KUN...
...READS MANGA TOO.

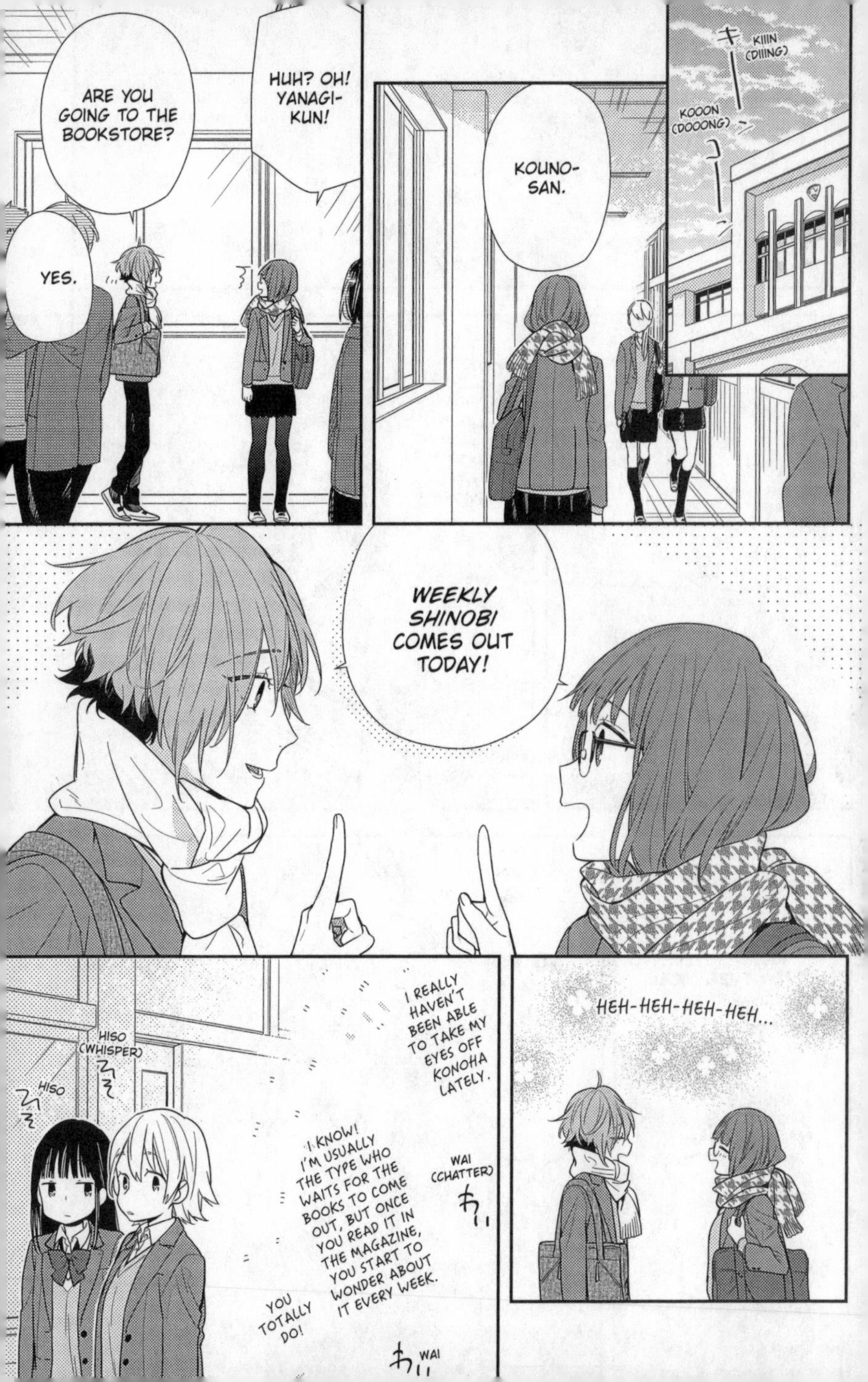
KIIN (DIIING)
KOOON (DOOONG)
KOUNO-SAN.
HUH? OH! YANAGI-KUN!
ARE YOU GOING TO THE BOOKSTORE?
YES.
WEEKLY SHINOBI COMES OUT TODAY!
HEH-HEH-HEH-HEH...
I REALLY HAVEN'T BEEN ABLE TO TAKE MY EYES OFF KONOHA LATELY.
WAI (CHATTER)
I KNOW! I'M USUALLY THE TYPE WHO WAITS FOR THE BOOKS TO COME OUT, BUT ONCE YOU READ IT IN THE MAGAZINE, YOU START TO WONDER ABOUT IT EVERY WEEK.
HISO (WHISPER)
HISO
YOU TOTALLY DO!
WAI

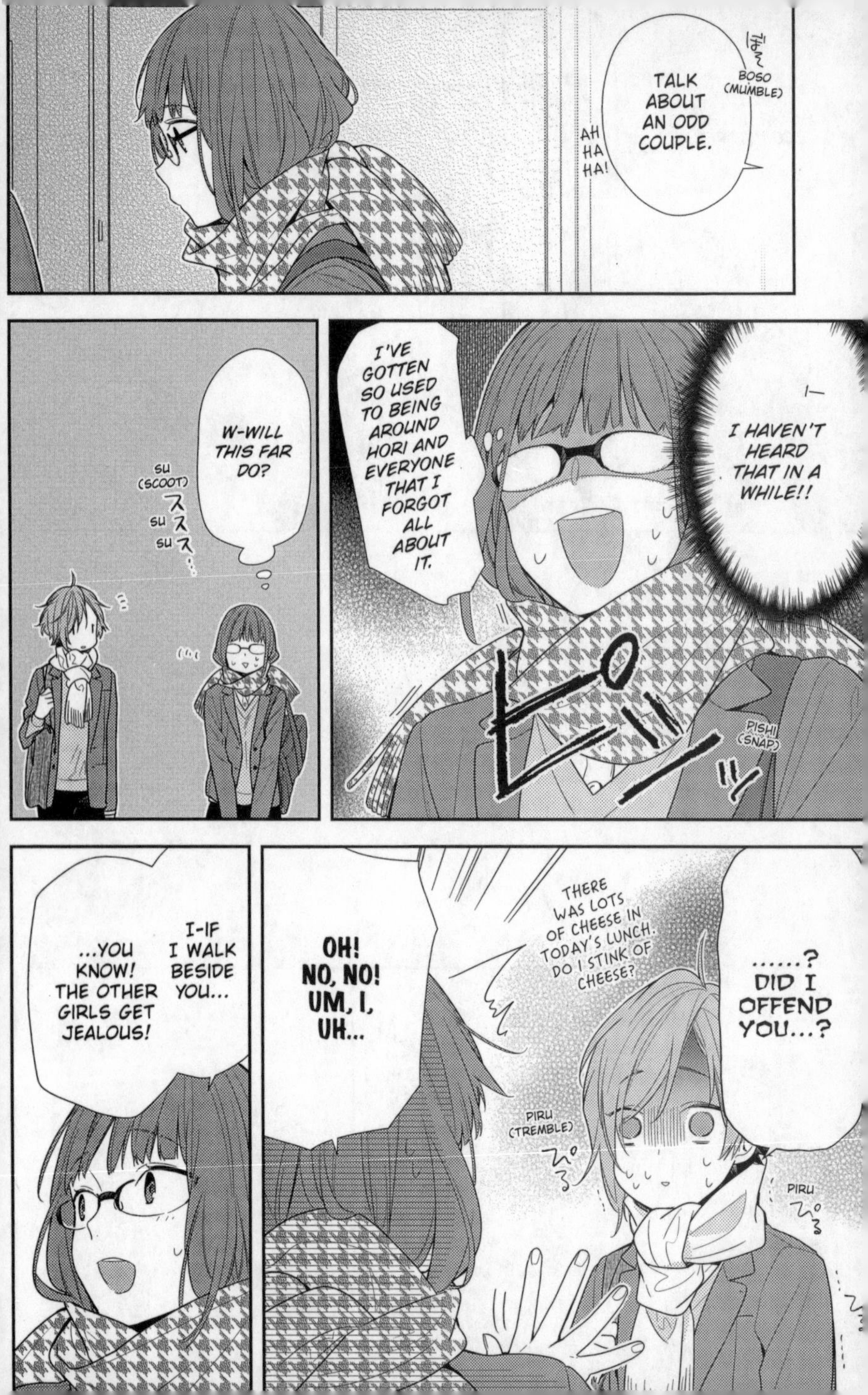
BOSO (MUMBLE)
TALK ABOUT AN ODD COUPLE.
AH HA HA!
I HAVEN'T HEARD THAT IN A WHILE!!
I'VE GOTTEN SO USED TO BEING AROUND HORI AND EVERYONE THAT I FORGOT ALL ABOUT IT.
PISHI (SNAP)
W-WILL THIS FAR DO?
SU (SCOOT)
SU
SU
......? DID I OFFEND YOU...?
PIRU
THERE WAS LOTS OF CHEESE IN TODAY'S LUNCH. DO I STINK OF CHEESE?
PIRU (TREMBLE)
OH! NO, NO! UM, I, UH...
I-IF I WALK BESIDE YOU...
...YOU KNOW! THE OTHER GIRLS GET JEALOUS!

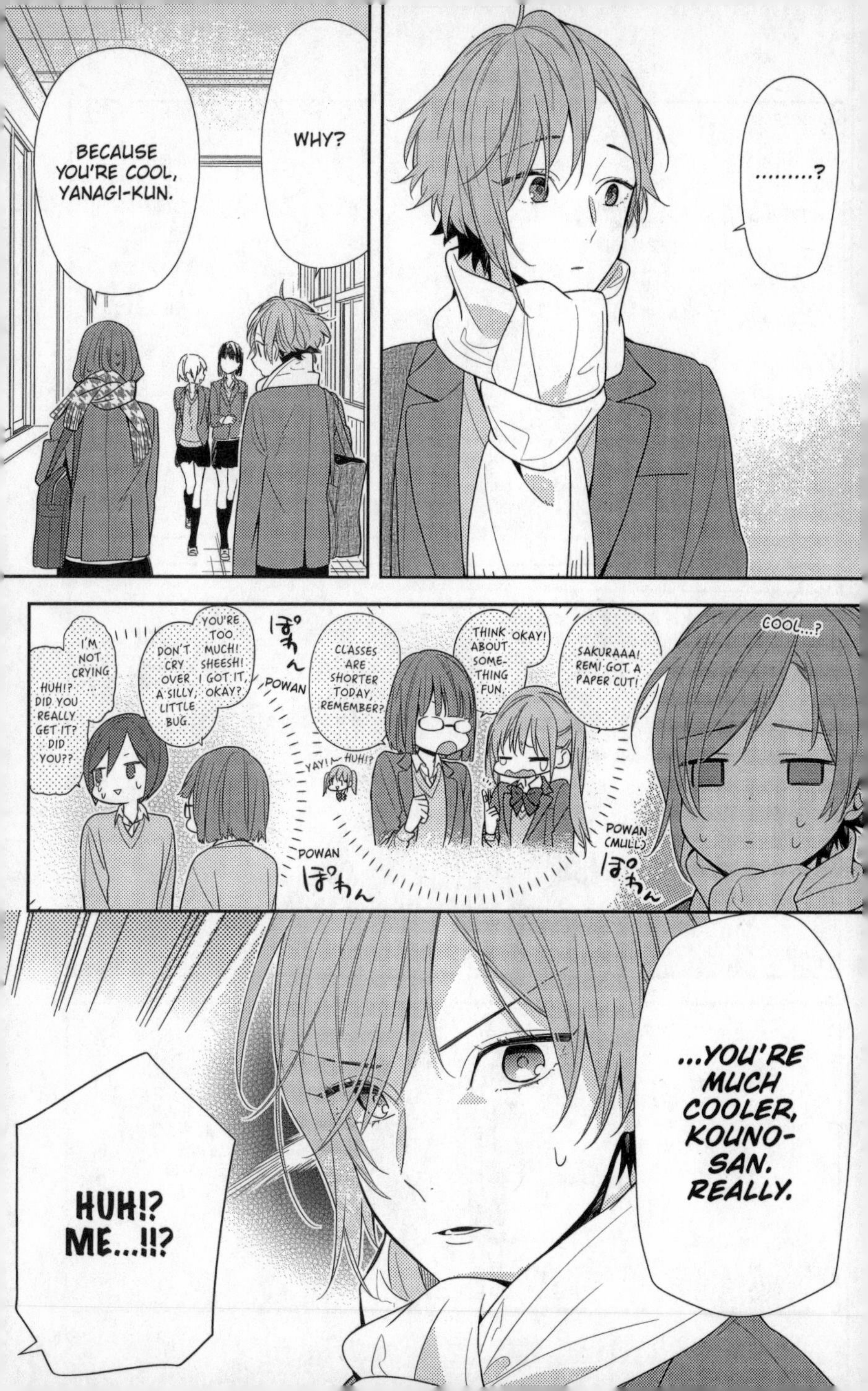
.........?
WHY?
BECAUSE YOU'RE COOL, YANAGI-KUN.
COOL...?
SAKURAAA! REMI GOT A PAPER CUT!
OKAY!
THINK ABOUT SOMETHING FUN.
ぽわん
POWAN
CLASSES ARE SHORTER TODAY, REMEMBER?
HUH!?
YAY!
YOU'RE TOO MUCH! SHEESH! I GOT IT, OKAY?
DON'T CRY OVER A SILLY, LITTLE BUG.
I'M NOT CRYING...
HUH!? DID YOU REALLY GET IT? DID YOU??
POWAN (MULL)
ぽわん
POWAN
ぽわん
...YOU'RE MUCH COOLER, KOUNO-SAN. REALLY.
HUH!? ME...!!?

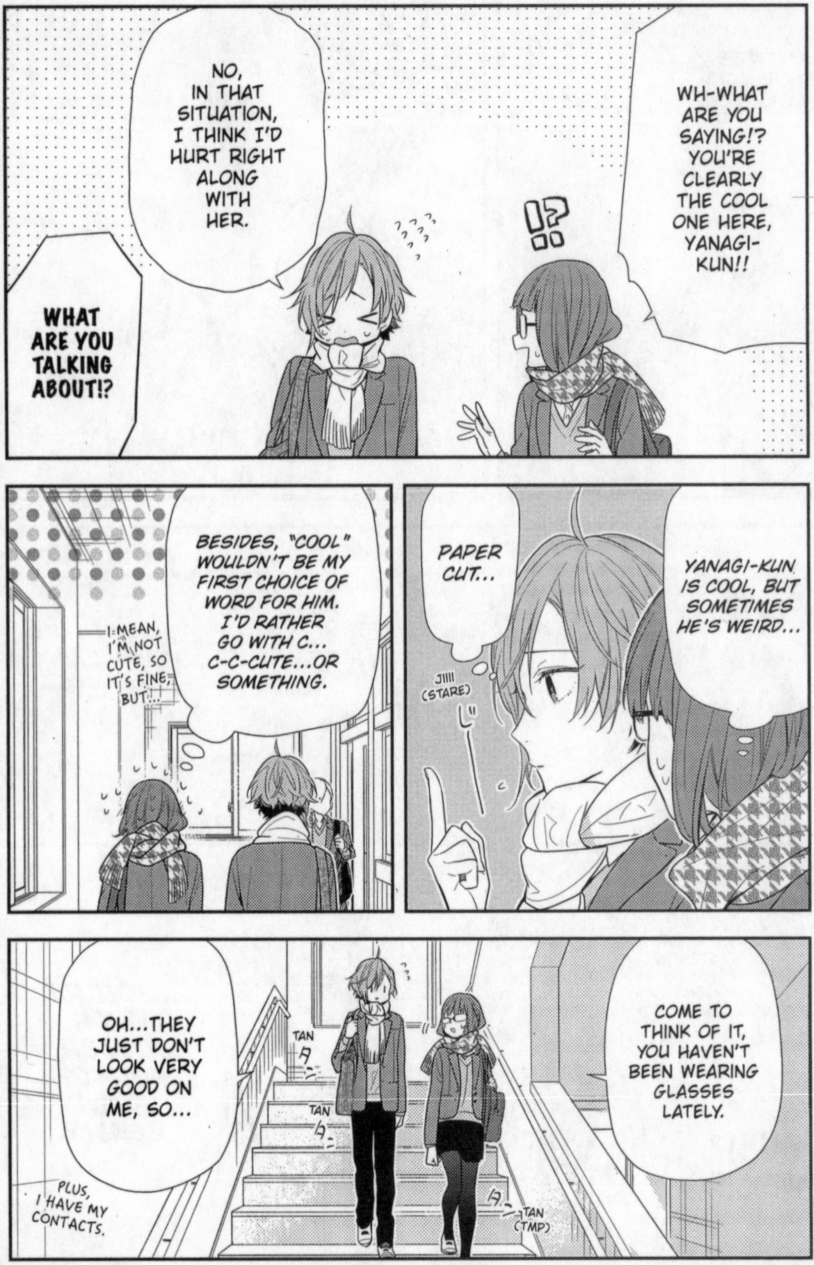
WH-WHAT ARE YOU SAYING!? YOU'RE CLEARLY THE COOL ONE HERE, YANAGI-KUN!!
!?
NO, IN THAT SITUATION, I THINK I'D HURT RIGHT ALONG WITH HER.
WHAT ARE YOU TALKING ABOUT!?
YANAGI-KUN IS COOL, BUT SOMETIMES HE'S WEIRD...
PAPER CUT...
JIIII (STARE)
BESIDES, "COOL" WOULDN'T BE MY FIRST CHOICE OF WORD FOR HIM. I'D RATHER GO WITH C... C-C-CUTE...OR SOMETHING.
I MEAN, I'M NOT CUTE, SO IT'S FINE, BUT...
COME TO THINK OF IT, YOU HAVEN'T BEEN WEARING GLASSES LATELY.
TAN (TMP)
TAN
TAN
OH...THEY JUST DON'T LOOK VERY GOOD ON ME, SO...
PLUS, I HAVE MY CONTACTS.

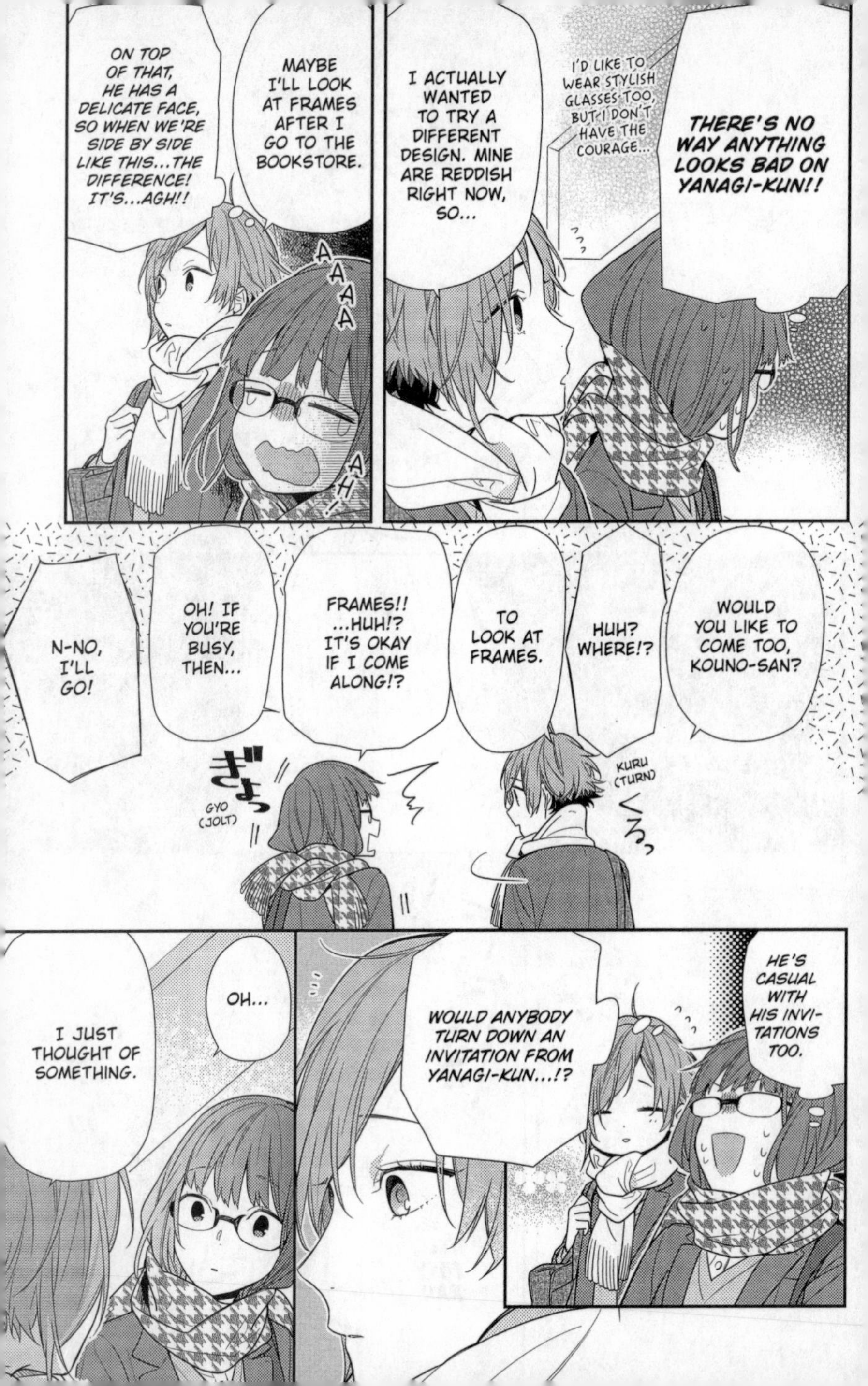
THERE'S NO WAY ANYTHING LOOKS BAD ON YANAGI-KUN!!
I'D LIKE TO WEAR STYLISH GLASSES TOO, BUT I DON'T HAVE THE COURAGE...
I ACTUALLY WANTED TO TRY A DIFFERENT DESIGN. MINE ARE REDDISH RIGHT NOW, SO...
MAYBE I'LL LOOK AT FRAMES AFTER I GO TO THE BOOKSTORE.
ON TOP OF THAT, HE HAS A DELICATE FACE, SO WHEN WE'RE SIDE BY SIDE LIKE THIS...THE DIFFERENCE! IT'S...AGH!!
AAAA
AH!
WOULD YOU LIKE TO COME TOO, KOUNO-SAN?
HUH? WHERE!?
TO LOOK AT FRAMES.
KURU (TURN)
FRAMES!! ...HUH!? IT'S OKAY IF I COME ALONG!?
GYO (JOLT)
OH! IF YOU'RE BUSY, THEN...
N-NO, I'LL GO!
HE'S CASUAL WITH HIS INVITATIONS TOO.
WOULD ANYBODY TURN DOWN AN INVITATION FROM YANAGI-KUN...!?
OH...
I JUST THOUGHT OF SOMETHING.

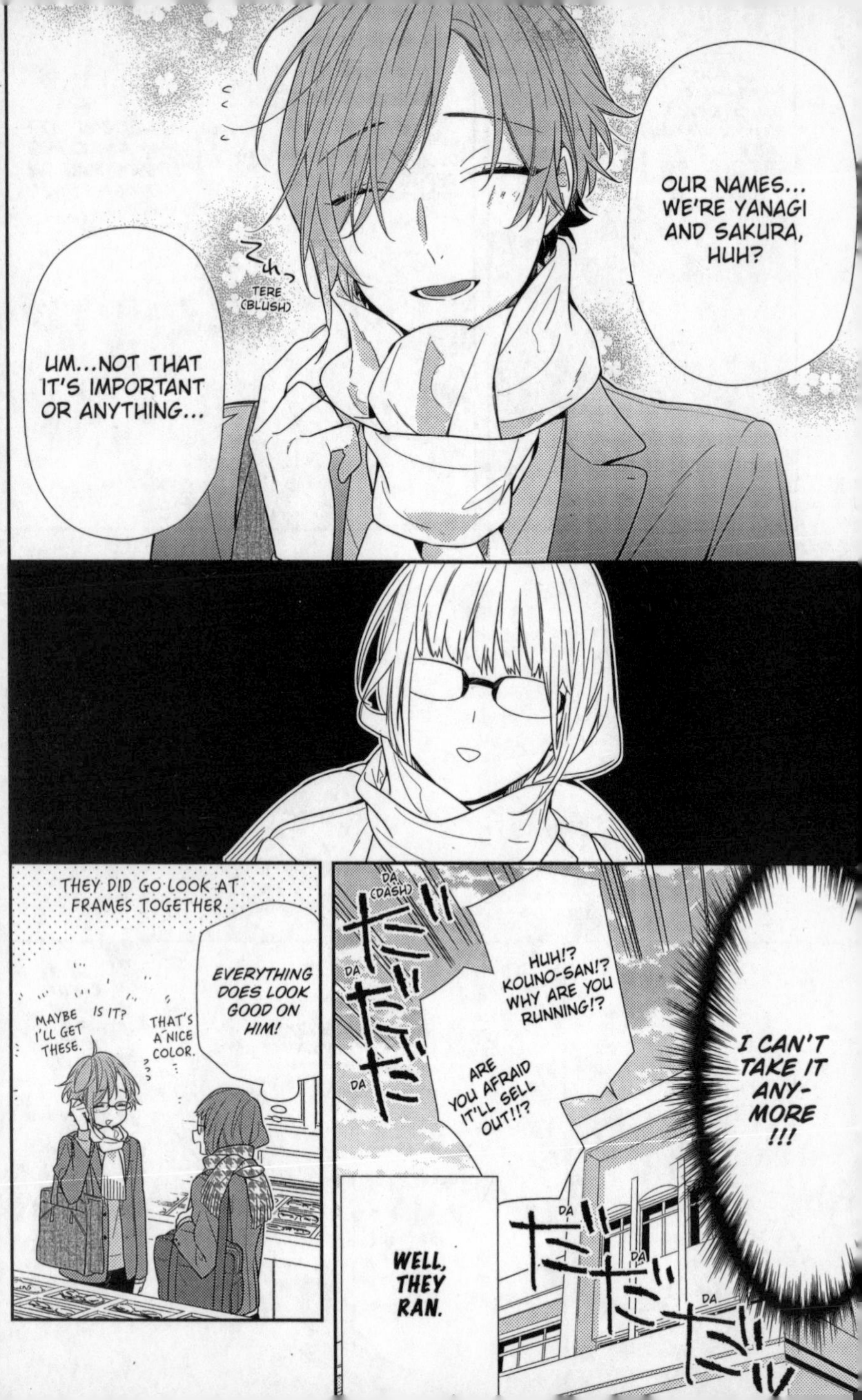

OUR NAMES... WE'RE YANAGI AND SAKURA, HUH?
TERE (BLUSH)
UM...NOT THAT IT'S IMPORTANT OR ANYTHING...
I CAN'T TAKE IT ANYMORE!!!
DA (DASH)
HUH!? KOUNO-SAN!? WHY ARE YOU RUNNING!?
DA
ARE YOU AFRAID IT'LL SELL OUT!!?
DA
DA
DA
DA
WELL, THEY RAN.
THEY DID GO LOOK AT FRAMES TOGETHER.
EVERYTHING DOES LOOK GOOD ON HIM!
THAT'S A NICE COLOR.
IS IT?
MAYBE I'LL GET THESE.

HORIMIYA

HORIMIYA

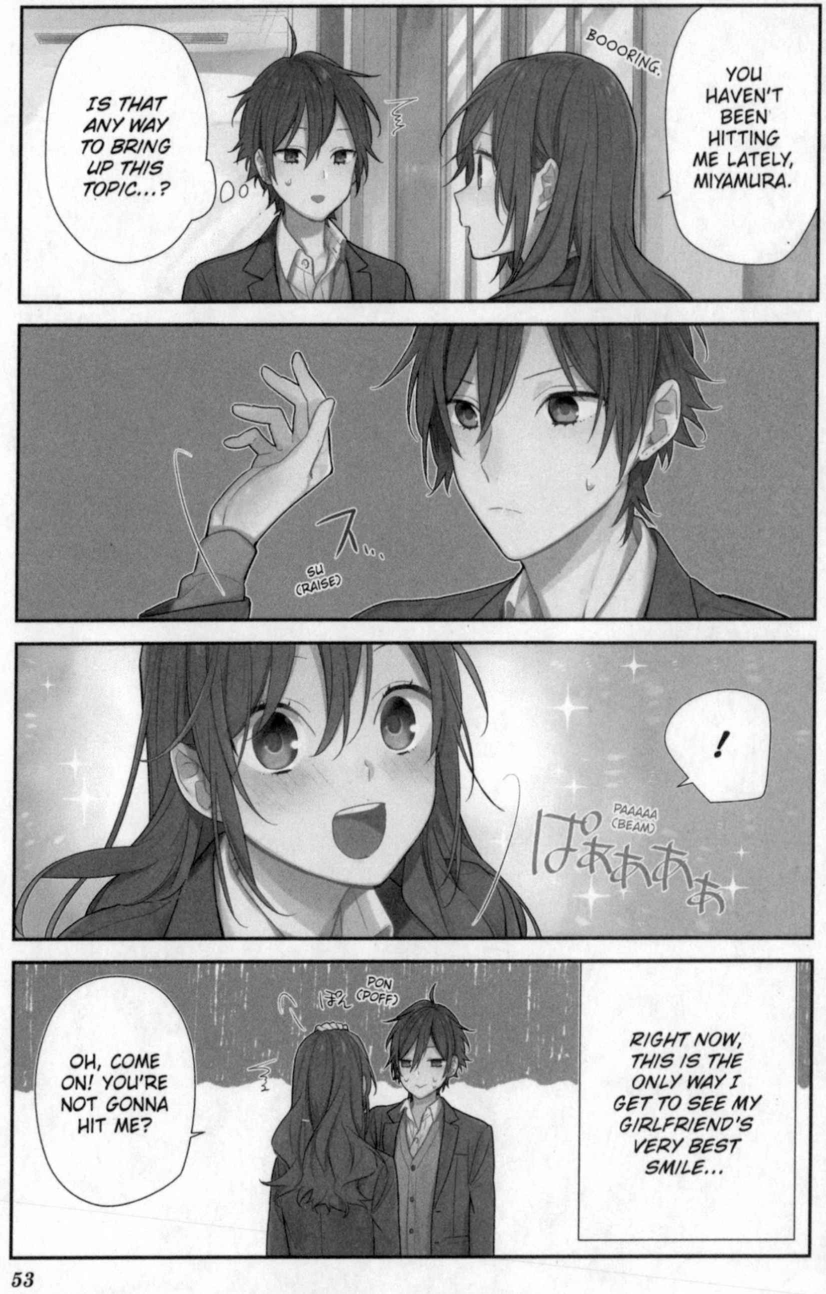
YOU HAVEN'T BEEN HITTING ME LATELY, MIYAMURA.
BOOORING.
IS THAT ANY WAY TO BRING UP THIS TOPIC...?
ス...
SU (RAISE)
!
ぱあああああ
PAAAAA (BEAM)
RIGHT NOW, THIS IS THE ONLY WAY I GET TO SEE MY GIRLFRIEND'S VERY BEST SMILE...
ぽん
PON (POFF)
OH, COME ON! YOU'RE NOT GONNA HIT ME?

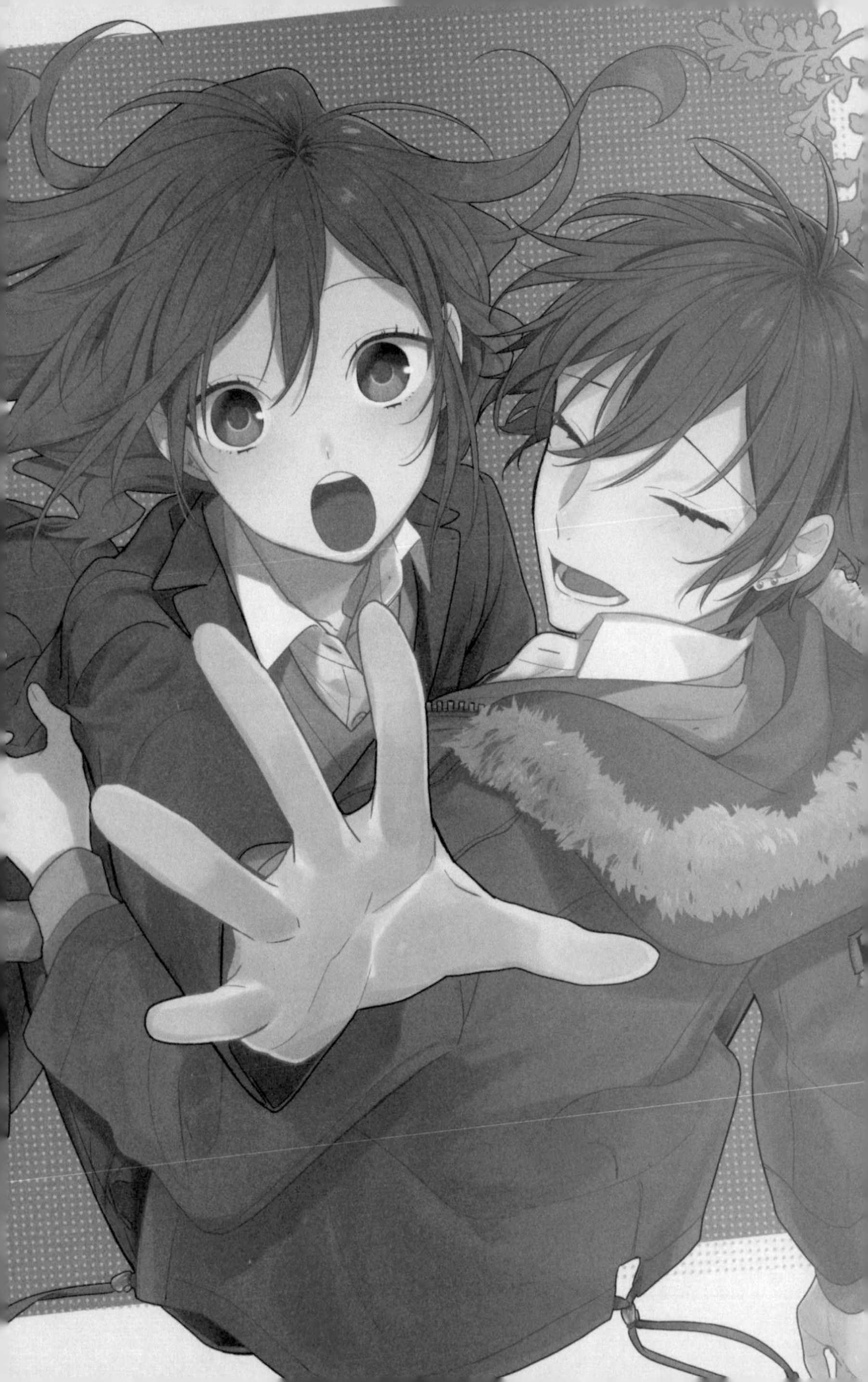

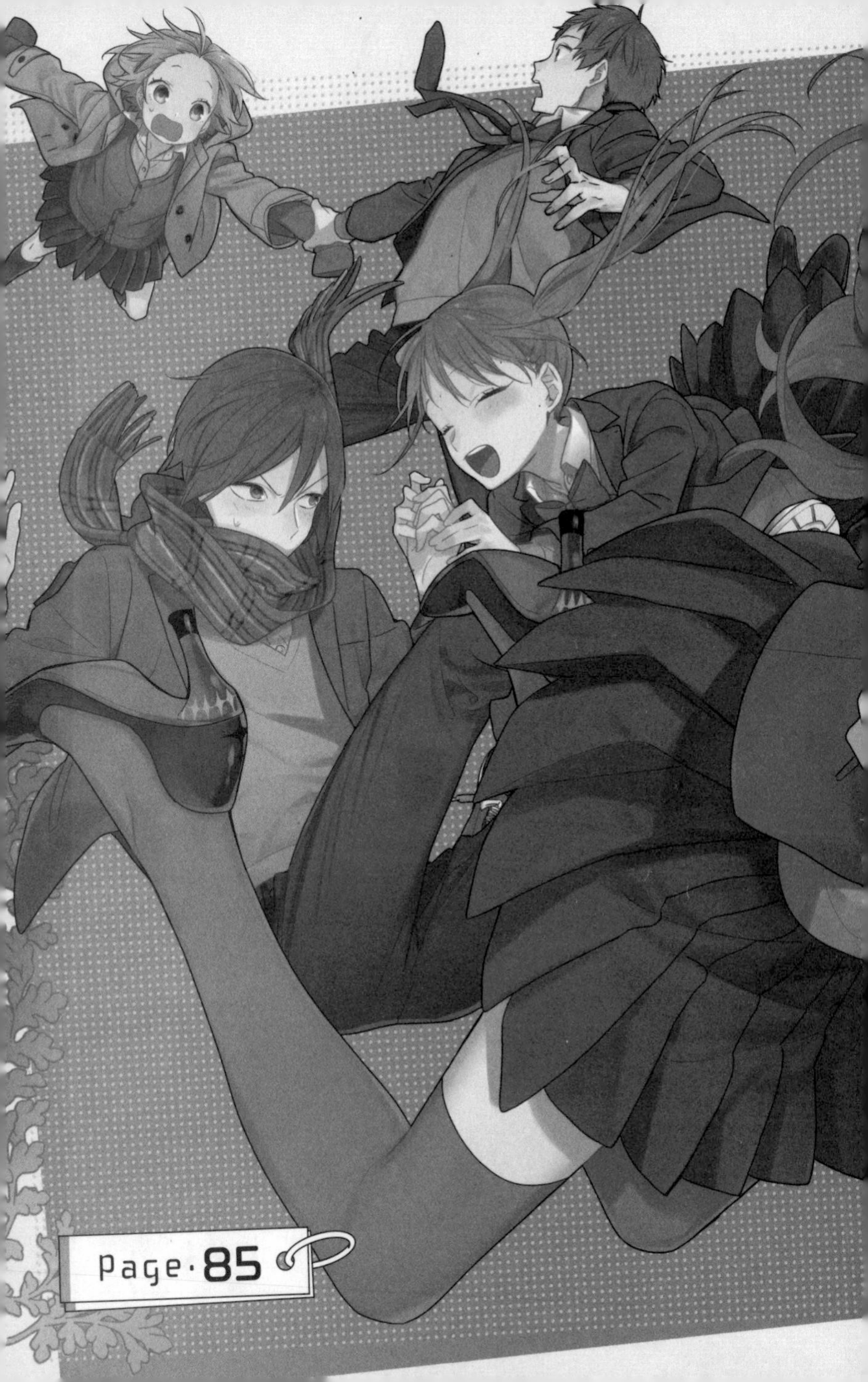
page·85

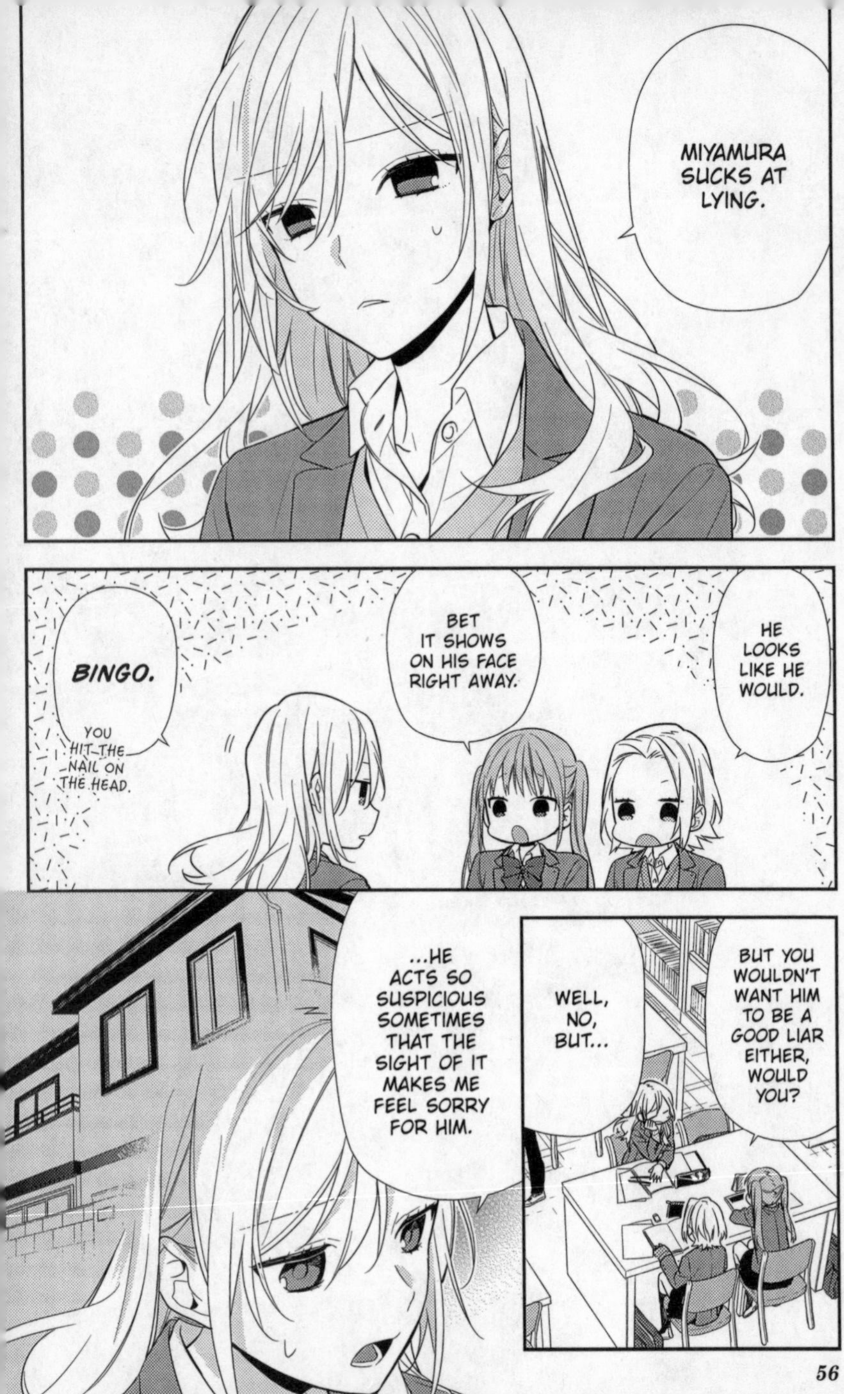
MIYAMURA SUCKS AT LYING.
HE LOOKS LIKE HE WOULD.
BET IT SHOWS ON HIS FACE RIGHT AWAY.
BINGO.
YOU HIT THE NAIL ON THE HEAD.
BUT YOU WOULDN'T WANT HIM TO BE A GOOD LIAR EITHER, WOULD YOU?
WELL, NO, BUT...
...HE ACTS SO SUSPICIOUS SOMETIMES THAT THE SIGHT OF IT MAKES ME FEEL SORRY FOR HIM.

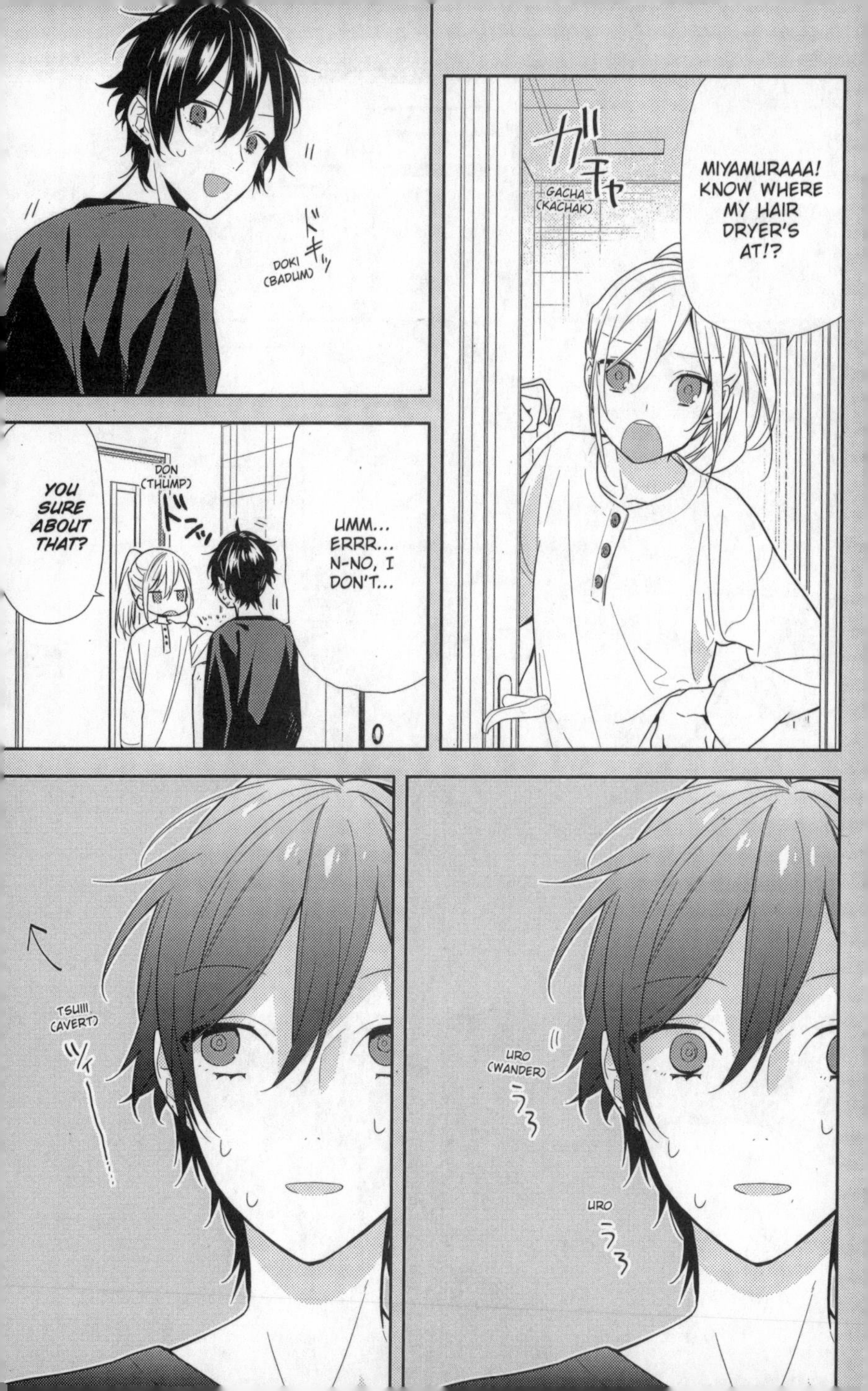
MIYAMURAAA! KNOW WHERE MY HAIR DRYER'S AT!?
GACHA (KACHAK)
DOKI (BADUM)
UMM... ERRR... N-NO, I DON'T...
DON (THUMP)
YOU SURE ABOUT THAT?
URO (WANDER)
URO
TSUIII (AVERT)

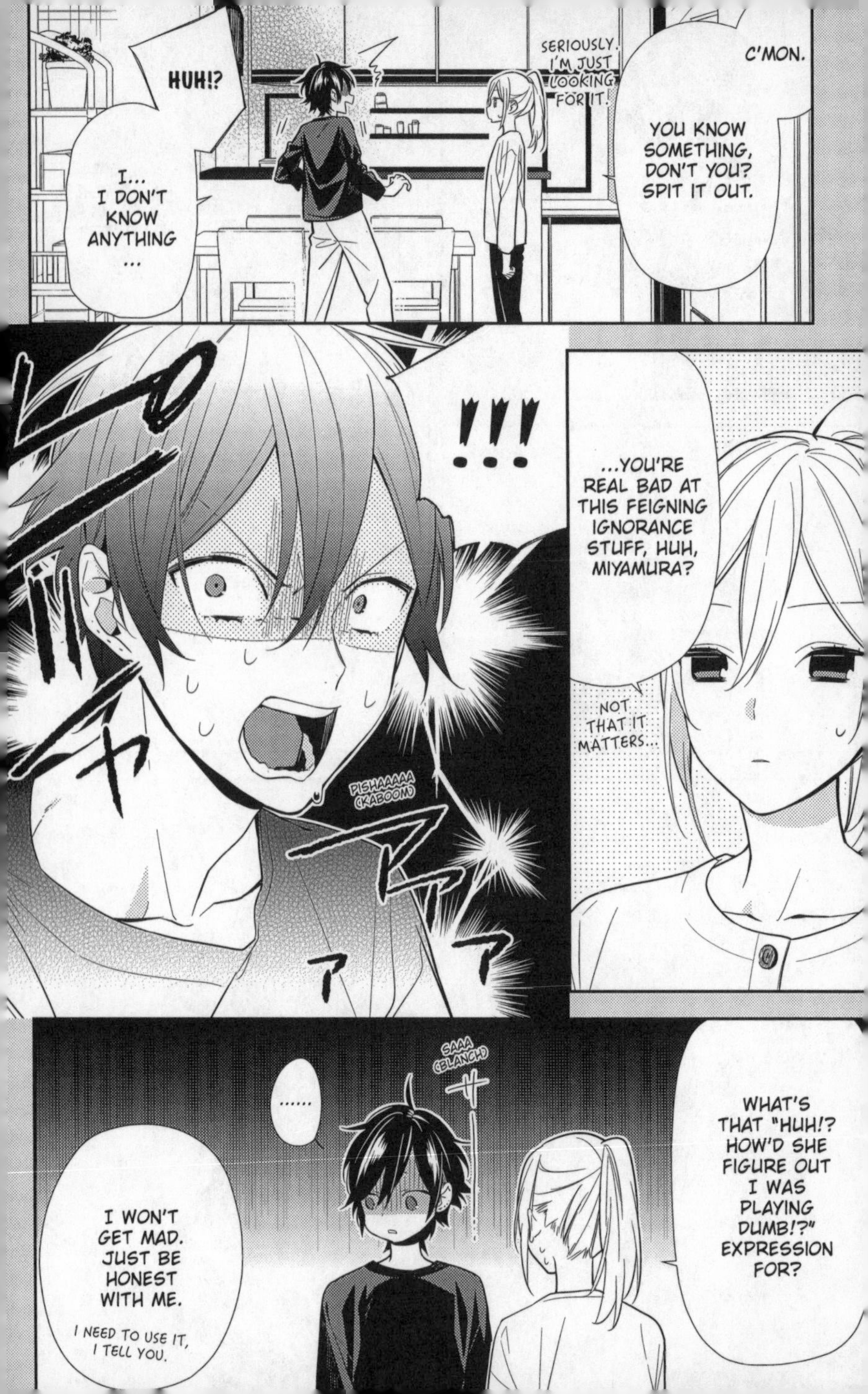
C'MON.
YOU KNOW SOMETHING, DON'T YOU? SPIT IT OUT.
SERIOUSLY. I'M JUST LOOKING FOR IT.
HUH!?
I... I DON'T KNOW ANYTHING...
...YOU'RE REAL BAD AT THIS FEIGNING IGNORANCE STUFF, HUH, MIYAMURA?
NOT THAT IT MATTERS...
!!!
PISHAAAAA (KABOOM)
WHAT'S THAT "HUH!? HOW'D SHE FIGURE OUT I WAS PLAYING DUMB!?" EXPRESSION FOR?
SAAA (BLANCH)
......
I WON'T GET MAD. JUST BE HONEST WITH ME.
I NEED TO USE IT, I TELL YOU.

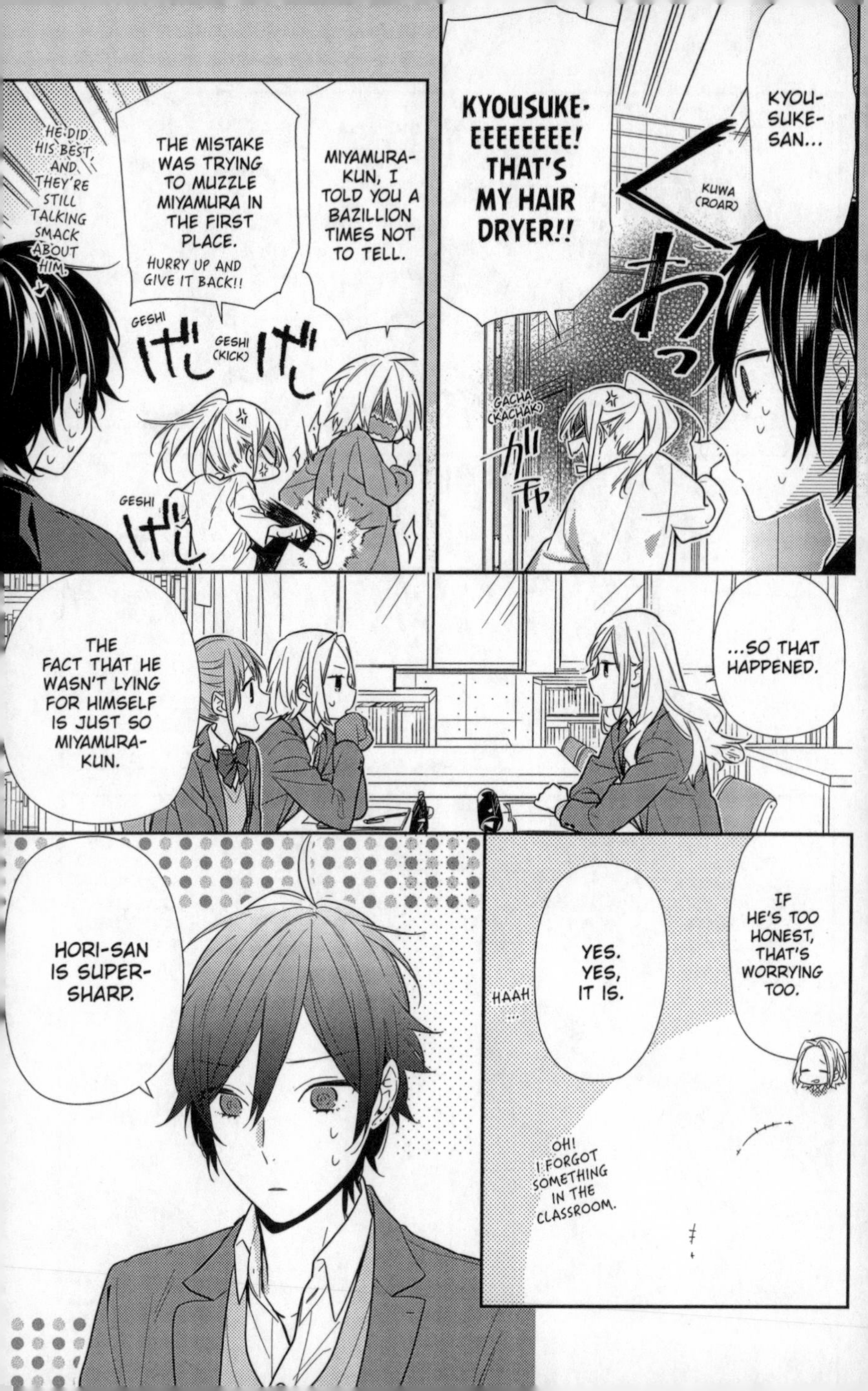
KYOU-SUKE-SAN...
KUWA (ROAR)
KYOUSUKE-EEEEEEEE! THAT'S MY HAIR DRYER!!
GACHA (KACHAK)
MIYAMURA-KUN, I TOLD YOU A BAZILLION TIMES NOT TO TELL.
THE MISTAKE WAS TRYING TO MUZZLE MIYAMURA IN THE FIRST PLACE.
HURRY UP AND GIVE IT BACK!!
HE DID HIS BEST, AND THEY'RE STILL TALKING SMACK ABOUT HIM.
GESHI
GESHI (KICK)
GESHI
...SO THAT HAPPENED.
THE FACT THAT HE WASN'T LYING FOR HIMSELF IS JUST SO MIYAMURA-KUN.
IF HE'S TOO HONEST, THAT'S WORRYING TOO.
YES. YES, IT IS.
HAAH...
OH! I FORGOT SOMETHING IN THE CLASSROOM.
HORI-SAN IS SUPER-SHARP.

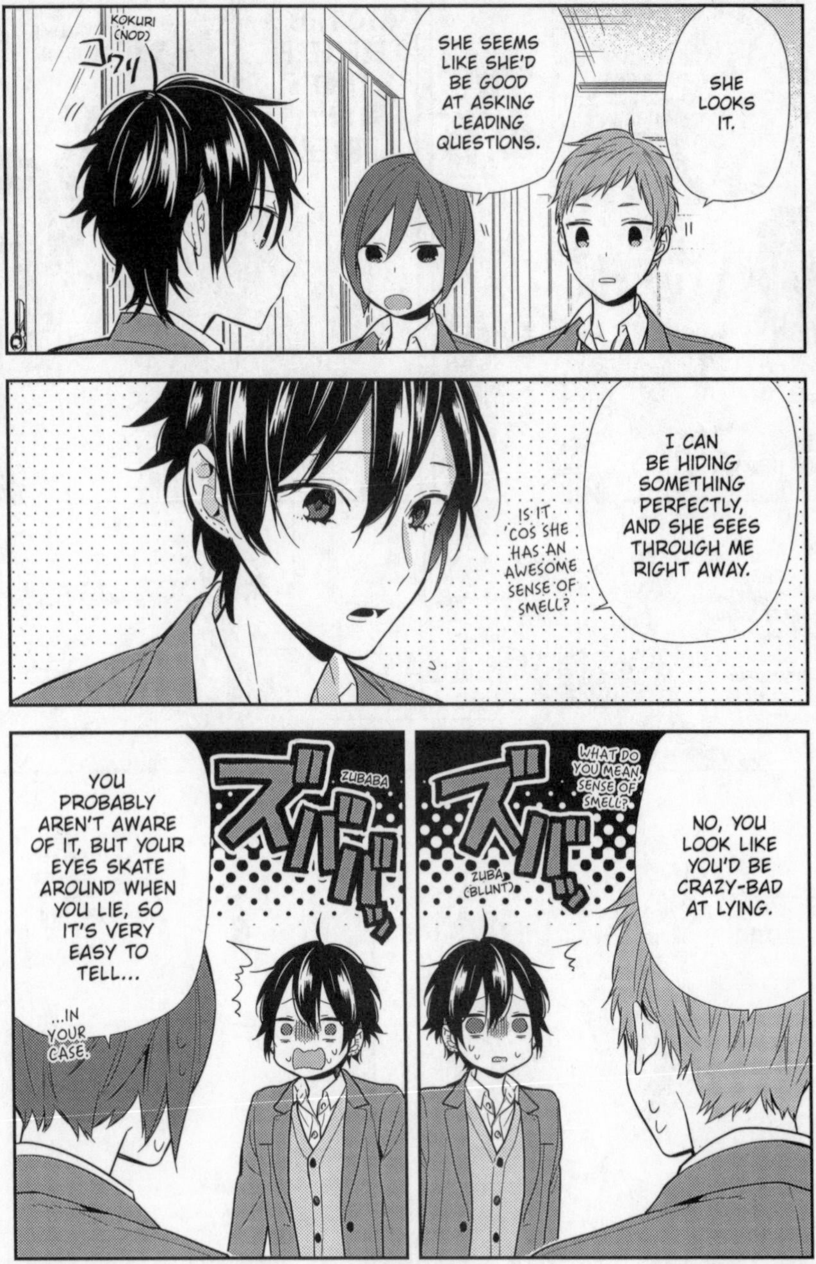
SHE LOOKS IT.
SHE SEEMS LIKE SHE'D BE GOOD AT ASKING LEADING QUESTIONS.
KOKURI (NOD)
I CAN BE HIDING SOMETHING PERFECTLY, AND SHE SEES THROUGH ME RIGHT AWAY.
IS IT COS SHE HAS AN AWESOME SENSE OF SMELL?
NO, YOU LOOK LIKE YOU'D BE CRAZY-BAD AT LYING.
WHAT DO YOU MEAN, SENSE OF SMELL?
ZUBA (BLUNT)
ZUBABA
YOU PROBABLY AREN'T AWARE OF IT, BUT YOUR EYES SKATE AROUND WHEN YOU LIE, SO IT'S VERY EASY TO TELL...
...IN YOUR CASE.

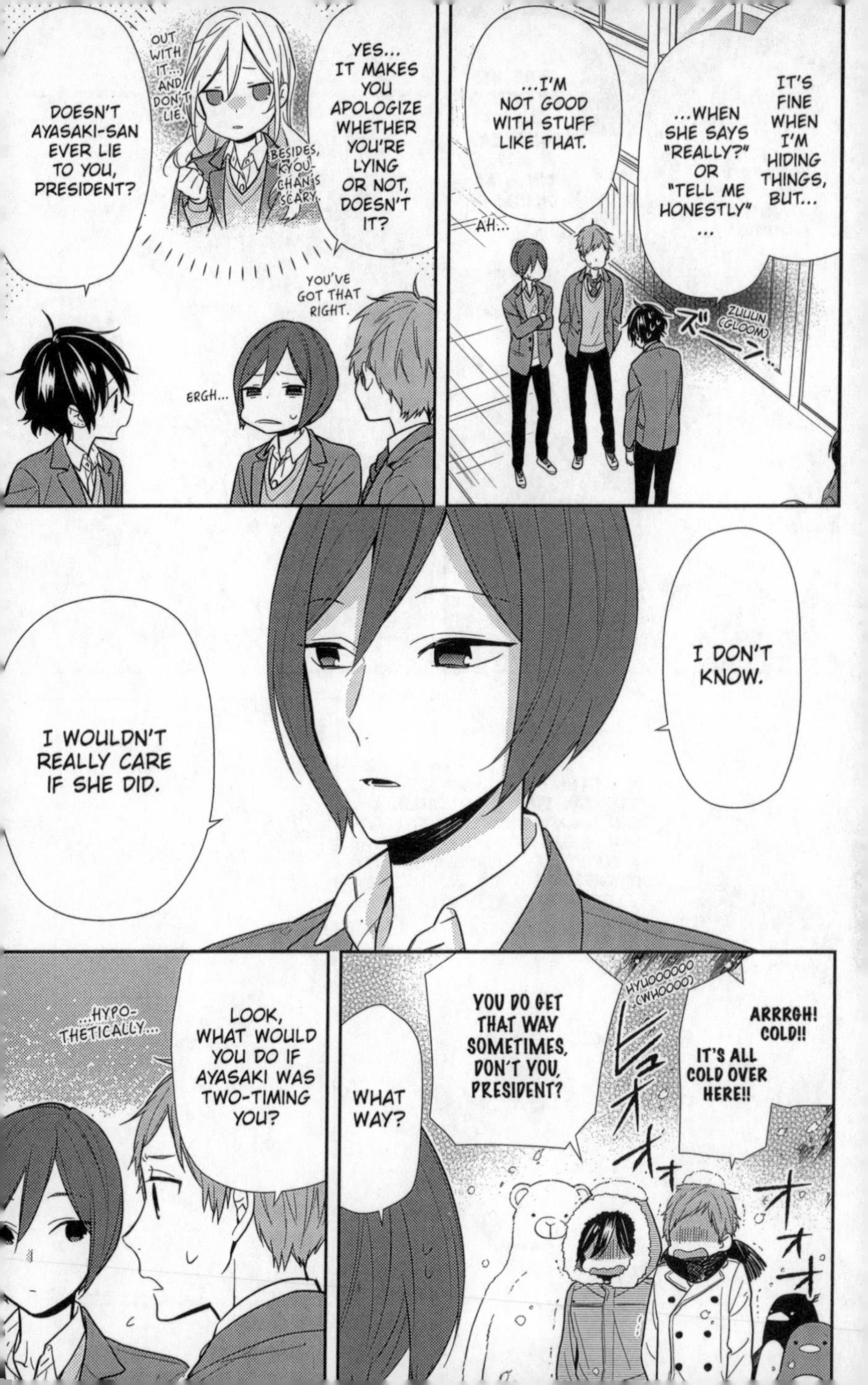
IT'S FINE WHEN I'M HIDING THINGS, BUT...
...WHEN SHE SAYS "REALLY?" OR "TELL ME HONESTLY"...
...I'M NOT GOOD WITH STUFF LIKE THAT.
AH...
ZUUUN (GLOOM)
YES... IT MAKES YOU APOLOGIZE WHETHER YOU'RE LYING OR NOT, DOESN'T IT?
OUT WITH IT... AND DON'T LIE.
BESIDES, KYOU-CHAN IS SCARY.
DOESN'T AYASAKI-SAN EVER LIE TO YOU, PRESIDENT?
YOU'VE GOT THAT RIGHT.
ERGH...
I DON'T KNOW.
I WOULDN'T REALLY CARE IF SHE DID.
ARRRGH! COLD!!
IT'S ALL COLD OVER HERE!!
HYUOOOOO (WHOOOO)
YOU DO GET THAT WAY SOMETIMES, DON'T YOU, PRESIDENT?
WHAT WAY?
LOOK, WHAT WOULD YOU DO IF AYASAKI WAS TWO-TIMING YOU?
...HYPO-THETICALLY...

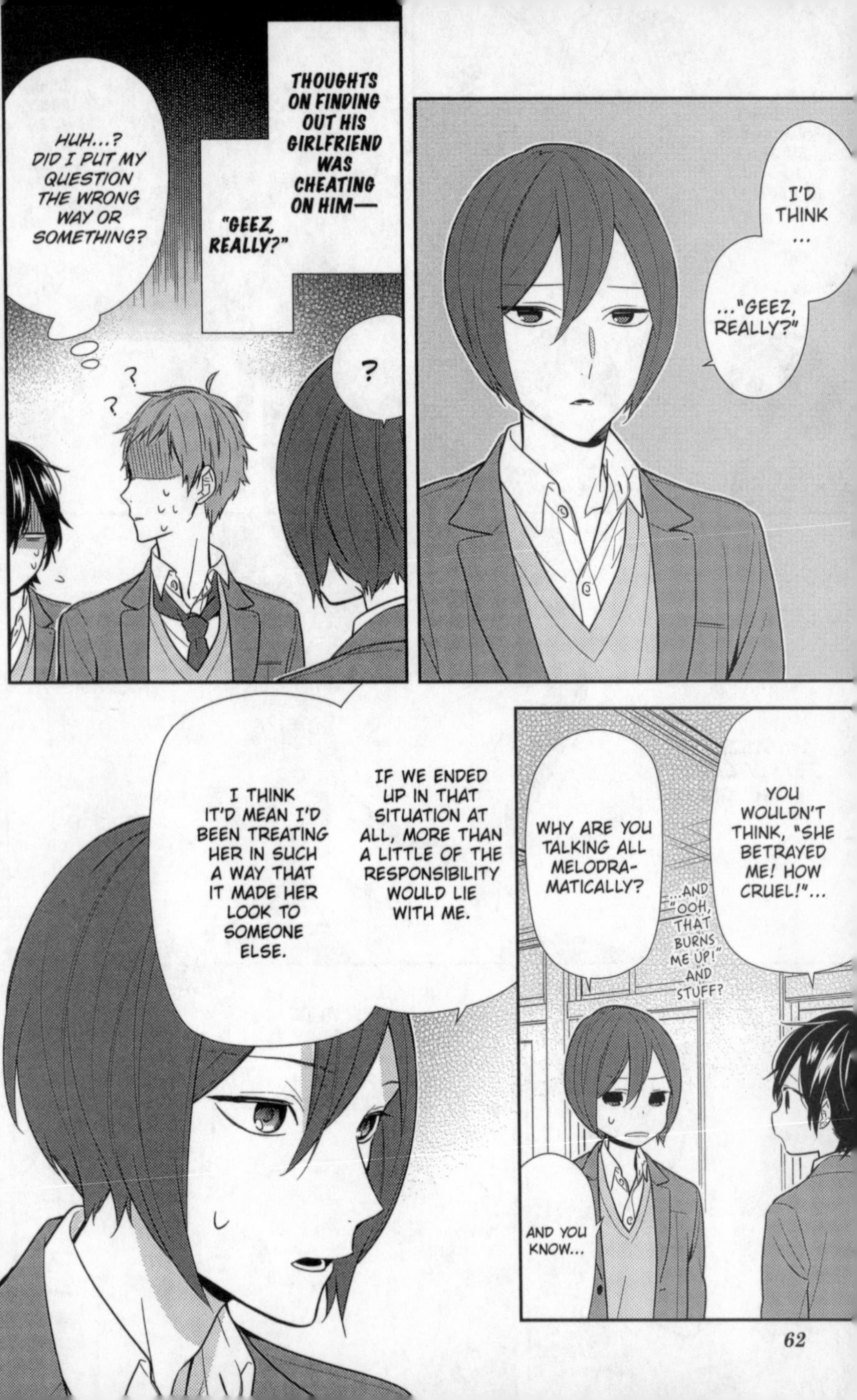
I'D THINK ...
..."GEEZ, REALLY?"
THOUGHTS ON FINDING OUT HIS GIRLFRIEND WAS CHEATING ON HIM—
"GEEZ, REALLY?"
HUH...? DID I PUT MY QUESTION THE WRONG WAY OR SOMETHING?
?
? ?
YOU WOULDN'T THINK, "SHE BETRAYED ME! HOW CRUEL!"...
...AND "OOH, THAT BURNS ME UP!" AND STUFF?
WHY ARE YOU TALKING ALL MELODRAMATICALLY?
AND YOU KNOW...
IF WE ENDED UP IN THAT SITUATION AT ALL, MORE THAN A LITTLE OF THE RESPONSIBILITY WOULD LIE WITH ME.
I THINK IT'D MEAN I'D BEEN TREATING HER IN SUCH A WAY THAT IT MADE HER LOOK TO SOMEONE ELSE.

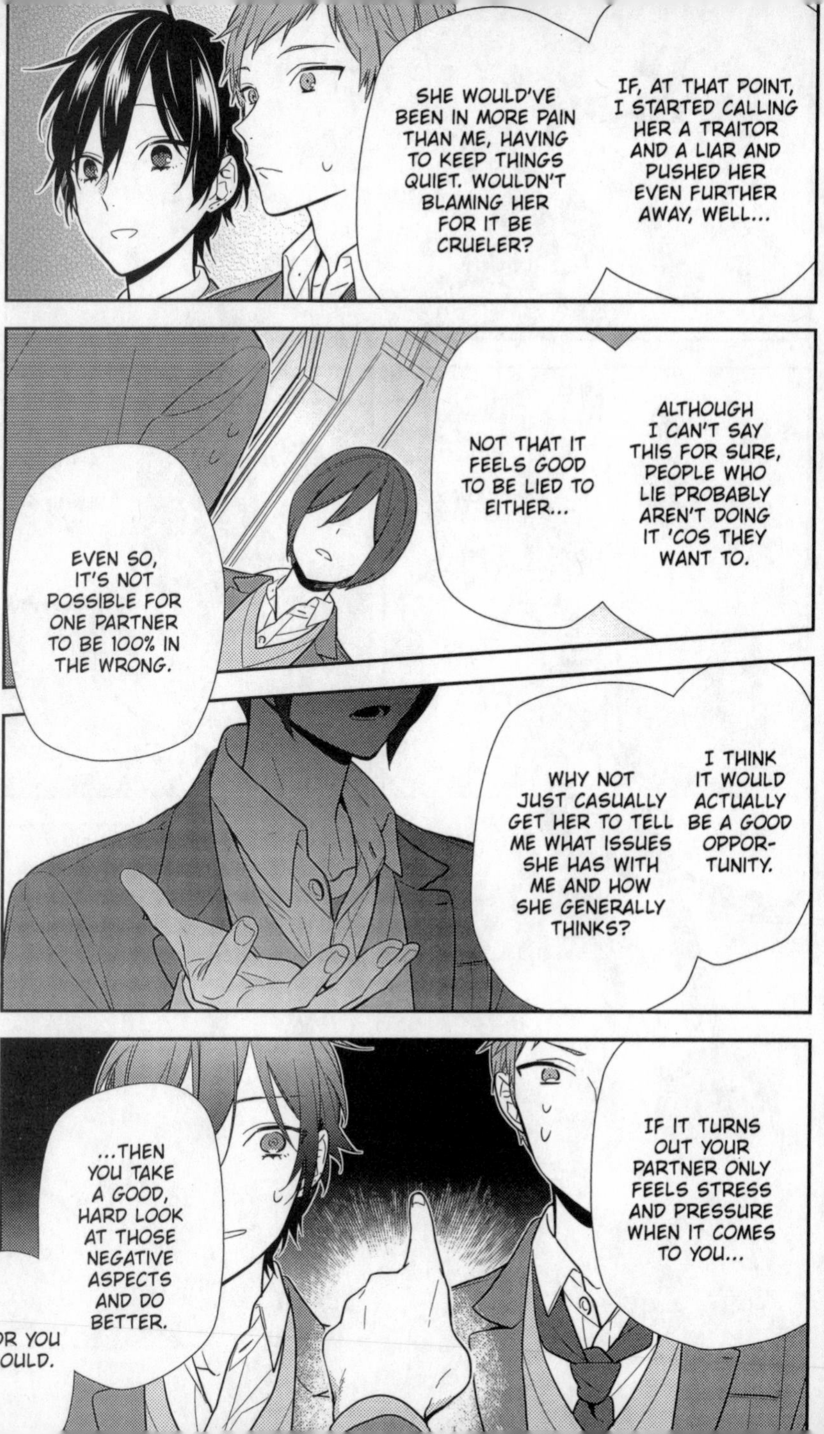
IF, AT THAT POINT, I STARTED CALLING HER A TRAITOR AND A LIAR AND PUSHED HER EVEN FURTHER AWAY, WELL...
SHE WOULD'VE BEEN IN MORE PAIN THAN ME, HAVING TO KEEP THINGS QUIET. WOULDN'T BLAMING HER FOR IT BE CRUELER?
ALTHOUGH I CAN'T SAY THIS FOR SURE, PEOPLE WHO LIE PROBABLY AREN'T DOING IT 'COS THEY WANT TO.
NOT THAT IT FEELS GOOD TO BE LIED TO EITHER...
EVEN SO, IT'S NOT POSSIBLE FOR ONE PARTNER TO BE 100% IN THE WRONG.
I THINK IT WOULD ACTUALLY BE A GOOD OPPOR-TUNITY.
WHY NOT JUST CASUALLY GET HER TO TELL ME WHAT ISSUES SHE HAS WITH ME AND HOW SHE GENERALLY THINKS?
IF IT TURNS OUT YOUR PARTNER ONLY FEELS STRESS AND PRESSURE WHEN IT COMES TO YOU...
...THEN YOU TAKE A GOOD, HARD LOOK AT THOSE NEGATIVE ASPECTS AND DO BETTER.
...OR YOU SHOULD.

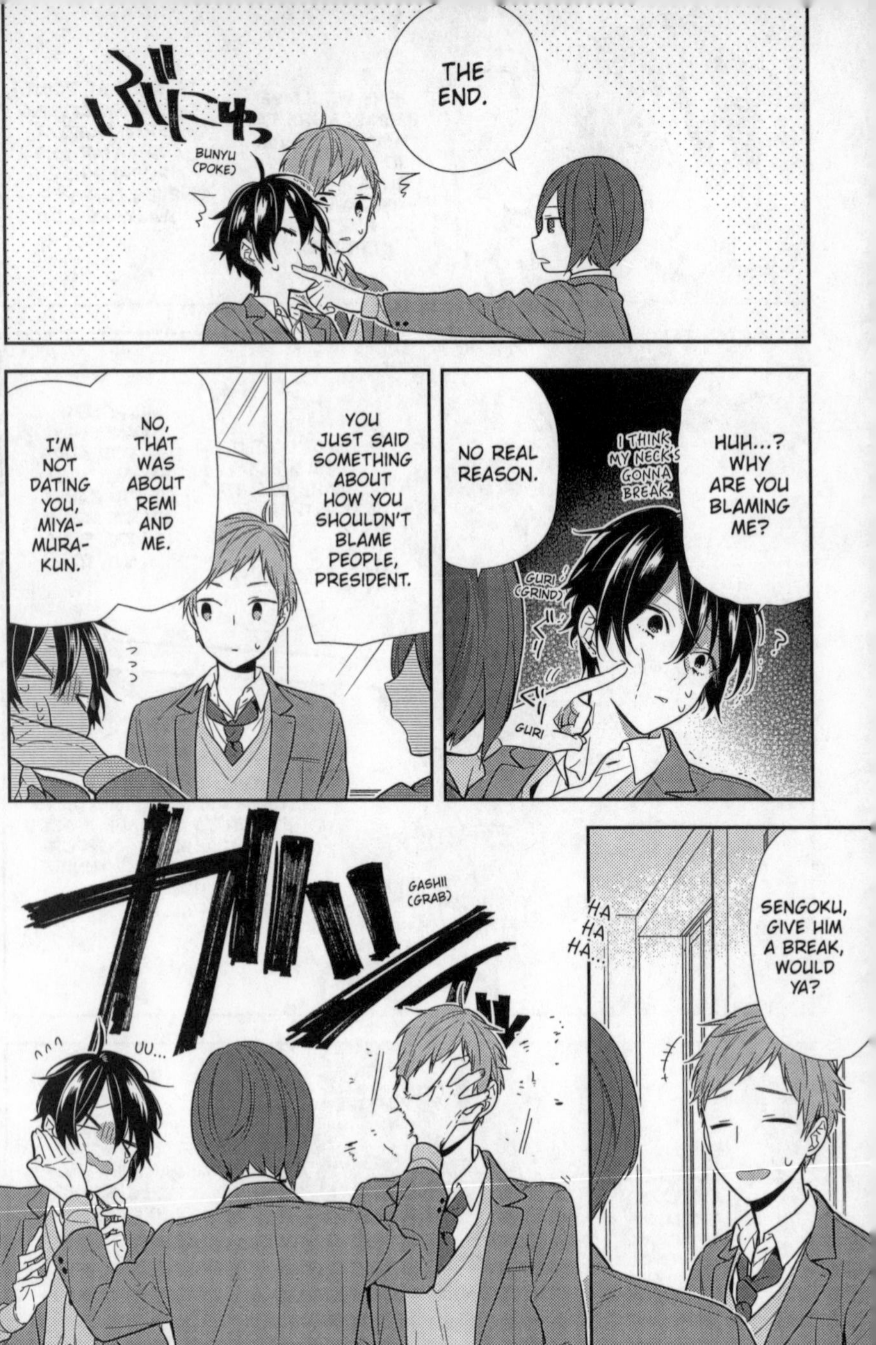
ぶにゅっ
BUNYU (POKE)
THE END.
HUH...? WHY ARE YOU BLAMING ME?
I THINK MY NECK'S GONNA BREAK.
NO REAL REASON.
GURI (GRIND)
GURI
YOU JUST SAID SOMETHING ABOUT HOW YOU SHOULDN'T BLAME PEOPLE, PRESIDENT.
NO, THAT WAS ABOUT REMI AND ME.
I'M NOT DATING YOU, MIYAMURA-KUN.
SENGOKU, GIVE HIM A BREAK, WOULD YA?
HA HA HA...
ガシッ
GASHII (GRAB)
UU...

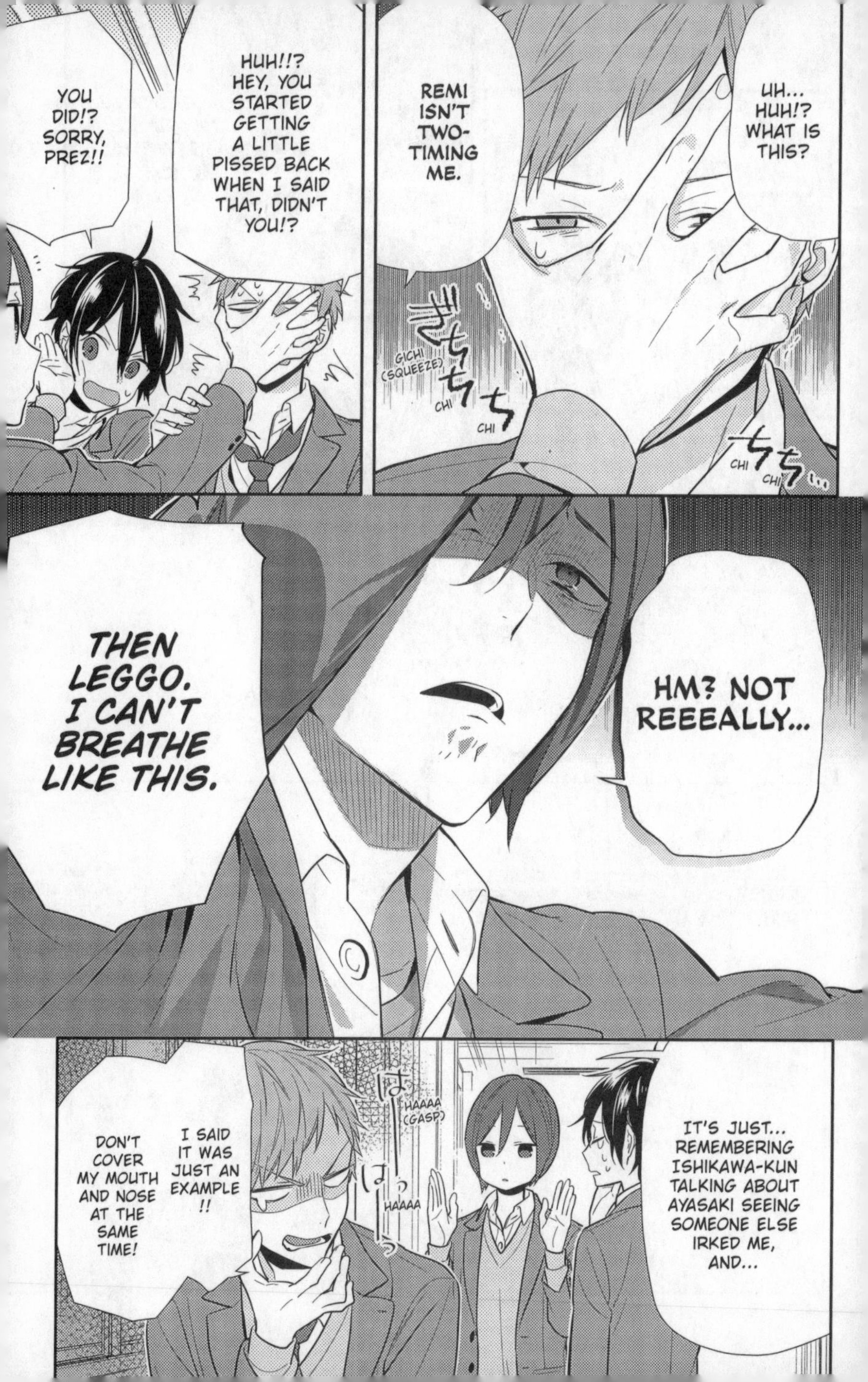
UH... HUH!? WHAT IS THIS?
REMI ISN'T TWO-TIMING ME.
GICHI (SQUEEZE)
CHI
CHI
CHI
CHI...
HUH!!? HEY, YOU STARTED GETTING A LITTLE PISSED BACK WHEN I SAID THAT, DIDN'T YOU!?
YOU DID!? SORRY, PREZ!!
HM? NOT REEEALLY...
THEN LEGGO. I CAN'T BREATHE LIKE THIS.
IT'S JUST... REMEMBERING ISHIKAWA-KUN TALKING ABOUT AYASAKI SEEING SOMEONE ELSE IRKED ME, AND...
HAAAA (GASP)
HAAAA
I SAID IT WAS JUST AN EXAMPLE!!
DON'T COVER MY MOUTH AND NOSE AT THE SAME TIME!

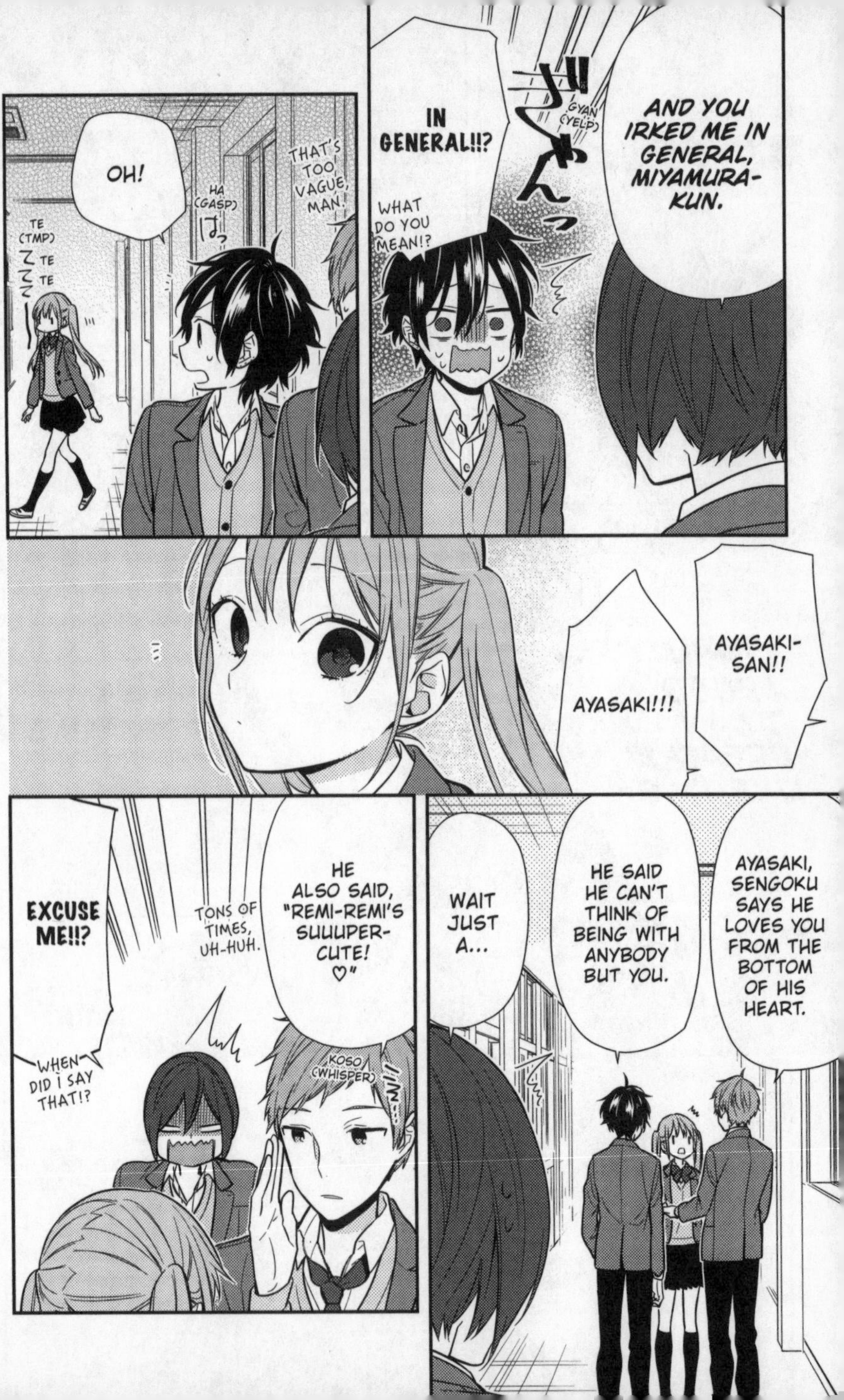
AND YOU IRKED ME IN GENERAL, MIYAMURA-KUN.
GYAN (YELP)
IN GENERAL!!?
WHAT DO YOU MEAN!?
THAT'S TOO VAGUE, MAN!
OH!
HA (GASP)
TE (TMP) TE TE
AYASAKI-SAN!!
AYASAKI!!!
AYASAKI, SENGOKU SAYS HE LOVES YOU FROM THE BOTTOM OF HIS HEART.
HE SAID HE CAN'T THINK OF BEING WITH ANYBODY BUT YOU.
WAIT JUST A...
HE ALSO SAID, "REMI-REMI'S SUUUPER-CUTE! ♡"
TONS OF TIMES, UH-HUH.
EXCUSE ME!!?
KOSO (WHISPER)
WHEN DID I SAY THAT!?

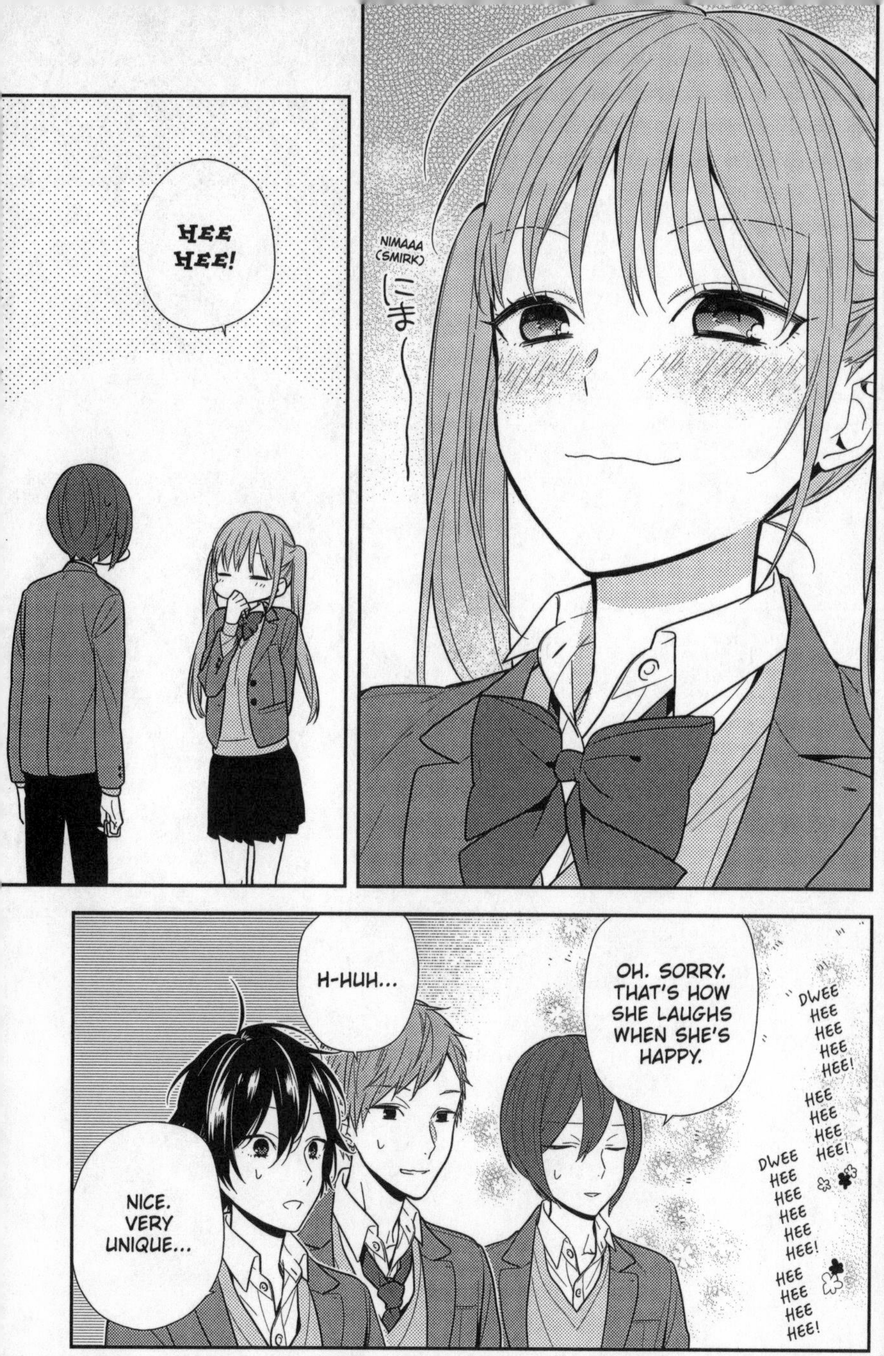
NIMAAA (SMIRK)
にまー
HEE HEE!
DWEE HEE HEE HEE HEE! HEE HEE HEE HEE! DWEE HEE HEE HEE HEE HEE! HEE HEE HEE HEE!
OH. SORRY. THAT'S HOW SHE LAUGHS WHEN SHE'S HAPPY.
H-HUH...
NICE. VERY UNIQUE...

HORIMIYA

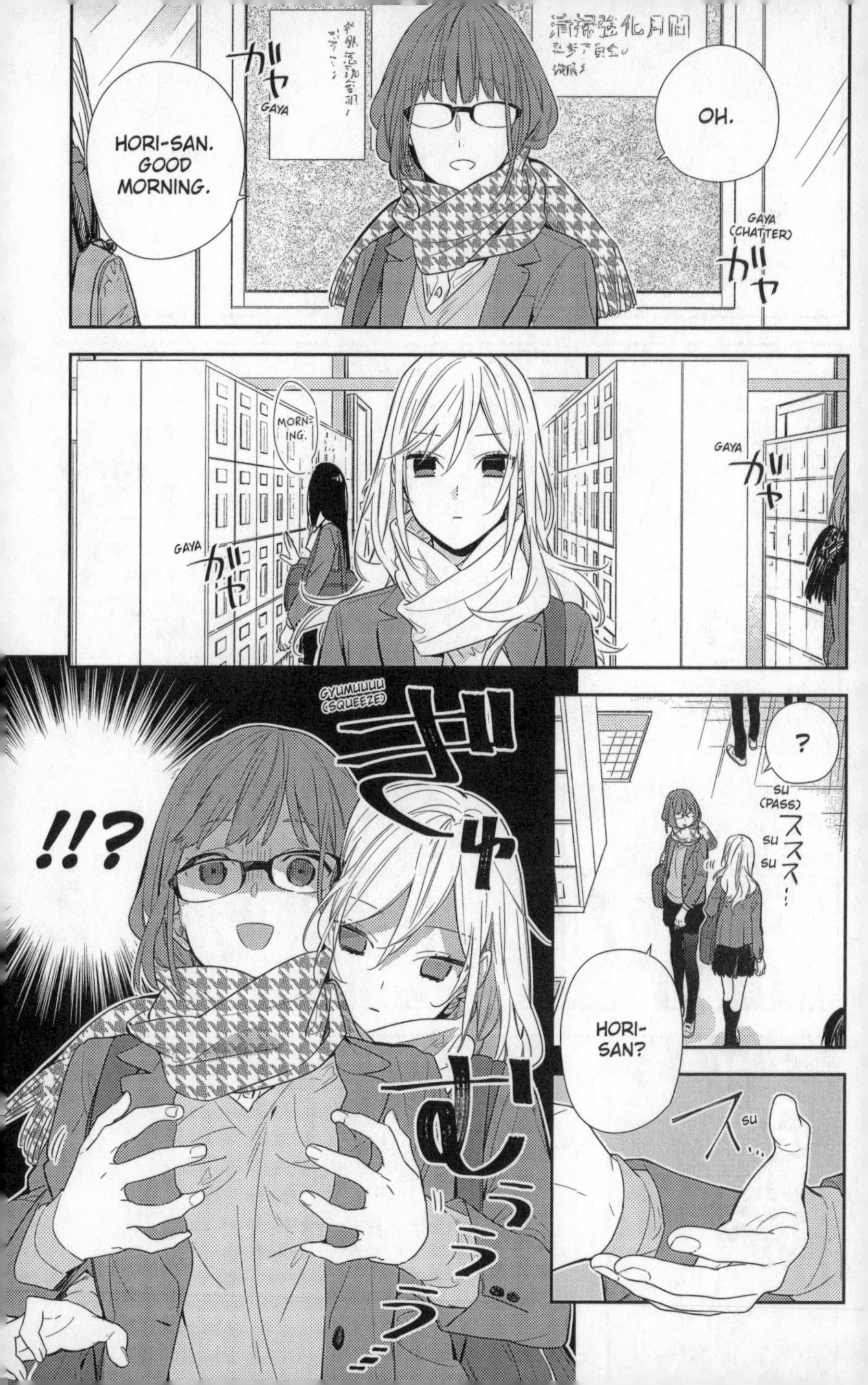
OH.
GAYA (CHATTER)
ガヤ
HORI-SAN. GOOD MORNING.
ガヤ
GAYA
GAYA
ガヤ
MORNING.
GAYA
ガヤ
?
SU (PASS)
SU
SU
ススス…
HORI-SAN?
ス…
SU
GYUMUUUU (SQUEEZE)
ぎゅむぅぅぅ…
!!?

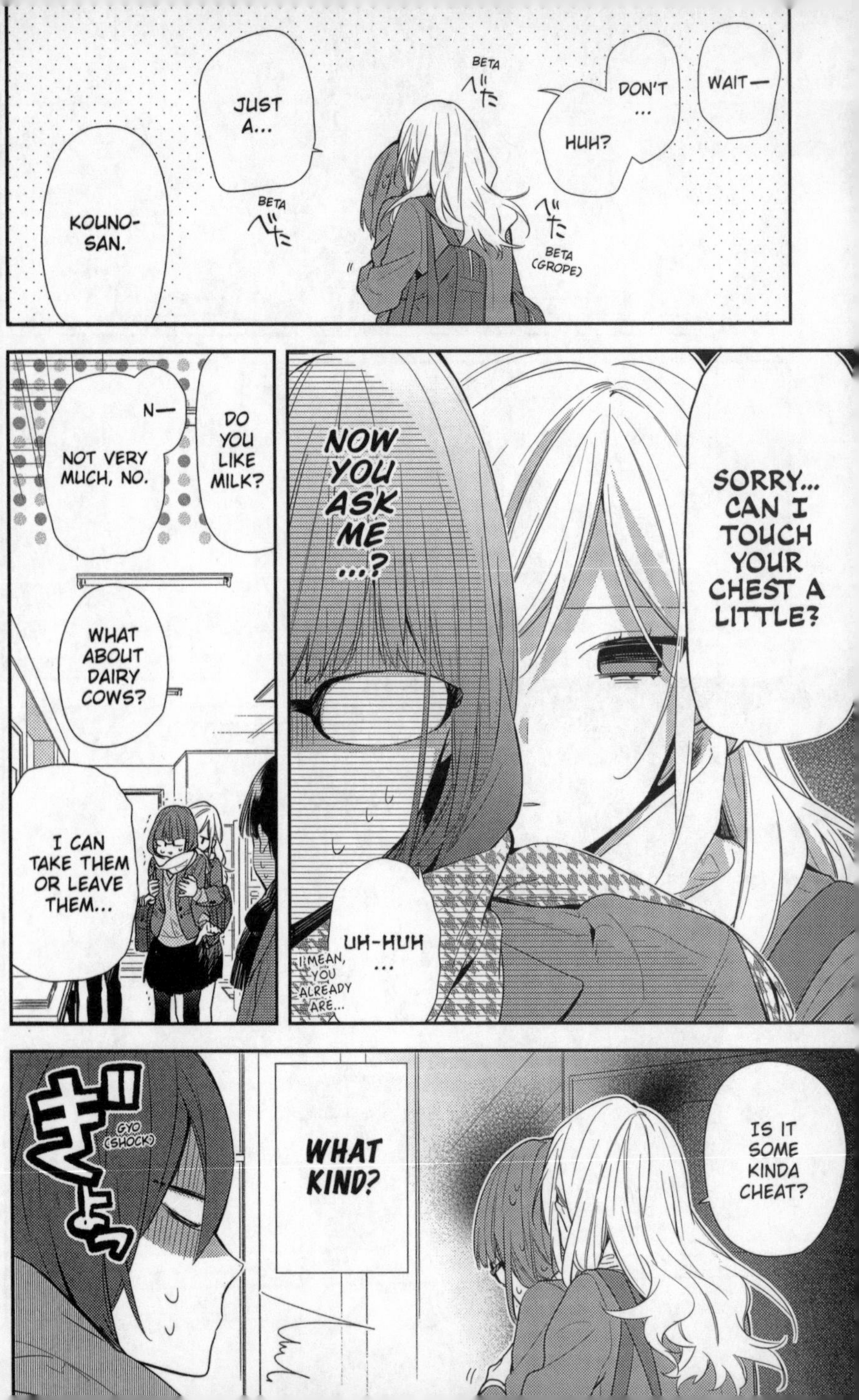
WAIT—
DON'T ...
HUH?
べた
BETA (GROPE)
べた
BETA
JUST A...
べた
BETA
KOUNO-SAN.
SORRY... CAN I TOUCH YOUR CHEST A LITTLE?
NOW YOU ASK ME ...?
UH-HUH ...
I MEAN, YOU ALREADY ARE...
DO YOU LIKE MILK?
N— NOT VERY MUCH, NO.
WHAT ABOUT DAIRY COWS?
I CAN TAKE THEM OR LEAVE THEM...
IS IT SOME KINDA CHEAT?
WHAT KIND?
GYO (SHOCK)

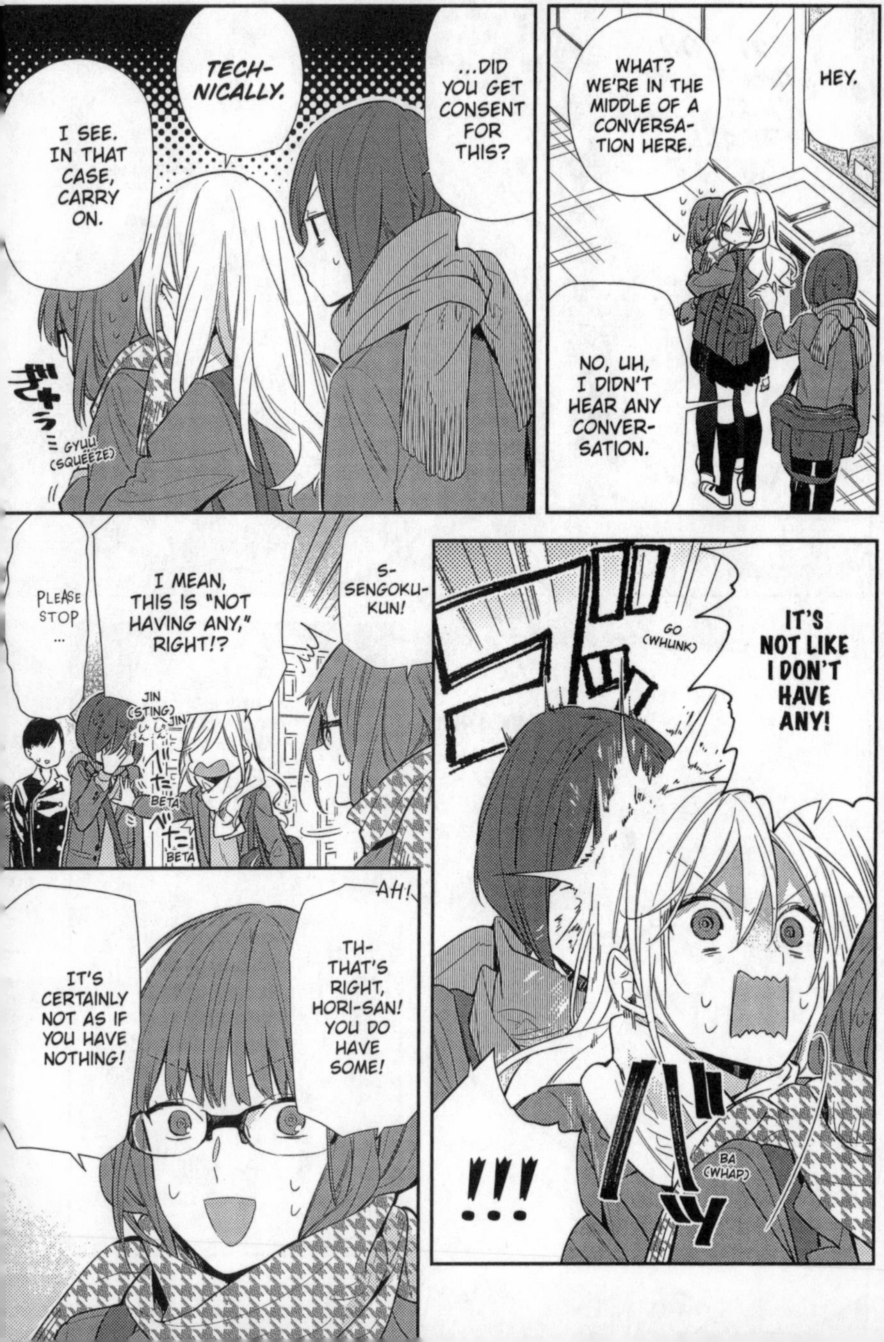
HEY.
WHAT? WE'RE IN THE MIDDLE OF A CONVERSATION HERE.
NO, UH, I DIDN'T HEAR ANY CONVERSATION.
...DID YOU GET CONSENT FOR THIS?
TECH-NICALLY.
I SEE. IN THAT CASE, CARRY ON.
GYUU (SQUEEZE)
IT'S NOT LIKE I DON'T HAVE ANY!
GO (WHUNK)
BA (WHAP)
!!!
S-SENGOKU-KUN!
I MEAN, THIS IS "NOT HAVING ANY," RIGHT!?
PLEASE STOP ...
JIN (STING) JIN
BETA
BETA
AH!
TH-THAT'S RIGHT, HORI-SAN! YOU DO HAVE SOME!
IT'S CERTAINLY NOT AS IF YOU HAVE NOTHING!

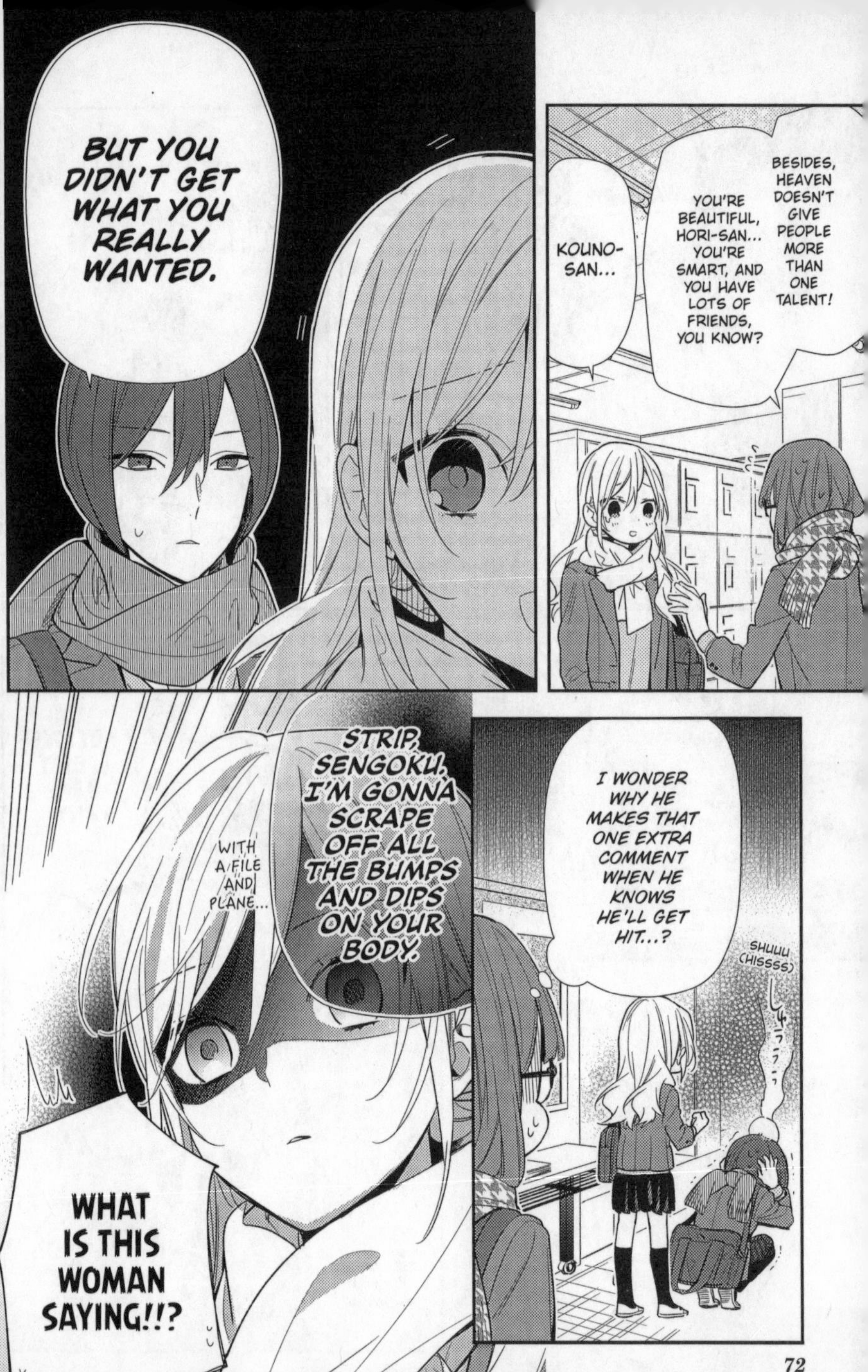
YOU'RE BEAUTIFUL, HORI-SAN... YOU'RE SMART, AND YOU HAVE LOTS OF FRIENDS, YOU KNOW?
BESIDES, HEAVEN DOESN'T GIVE PEOPLE MORE THAN ONE TALENT!
KOUNO-SAN...
BUT YOU DIDN'T GET WHAT YOU REALLY WANTED.
I WONDER WHY HE MAKES THAT ONE EXTRA COMMENT WHEN HE KNOWS HE'LL GET HIT...?
SHUUU (HISSSS)
STRIP, SENGOKU. I'M GONNA SCRAPE OFF ALL THE BUMPS AND DIPS ON YOUR BODY.
WITH A FILE AND PLANE...
WHAT IS THIS WOMAN SAYING!!?

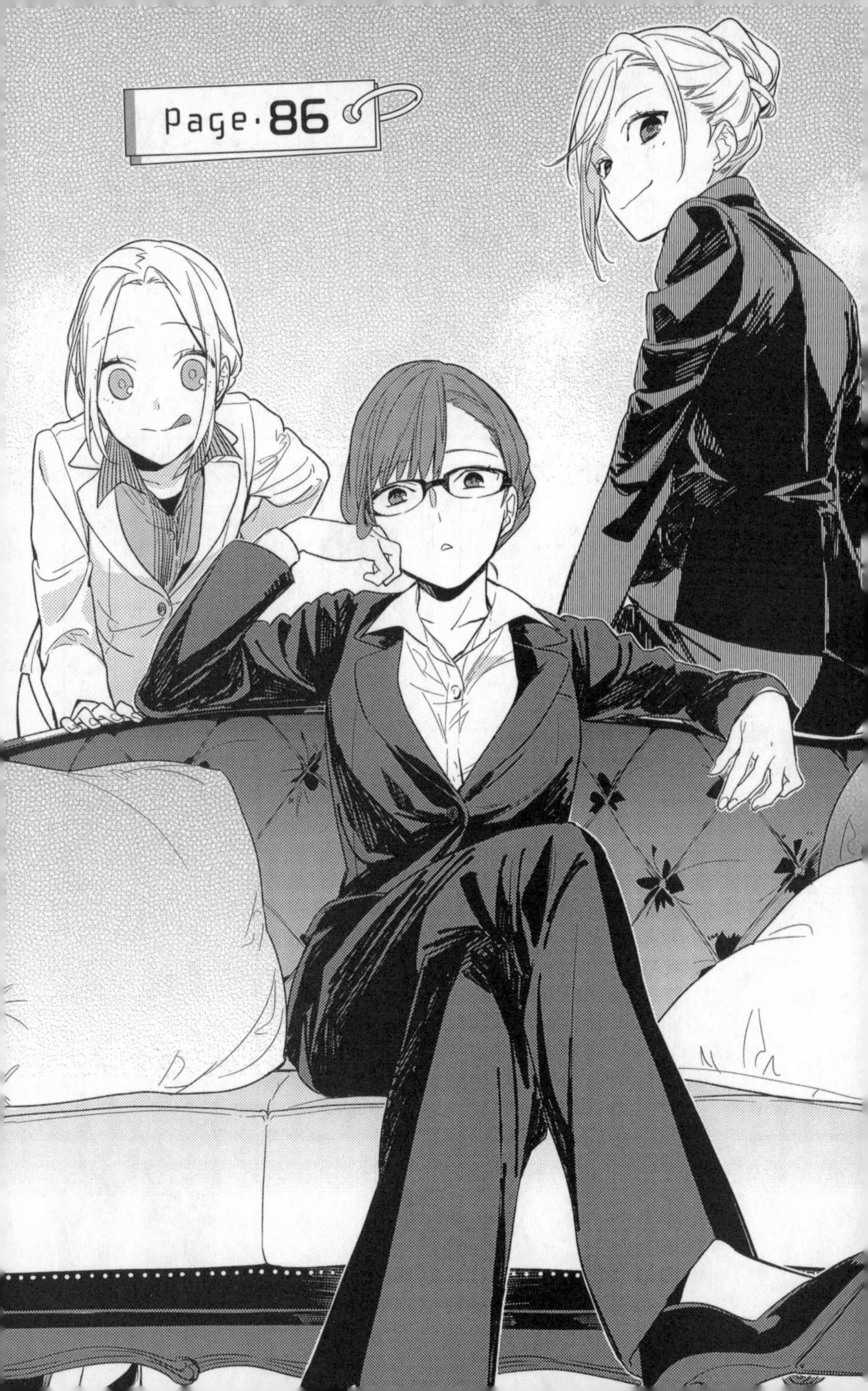
Page·86

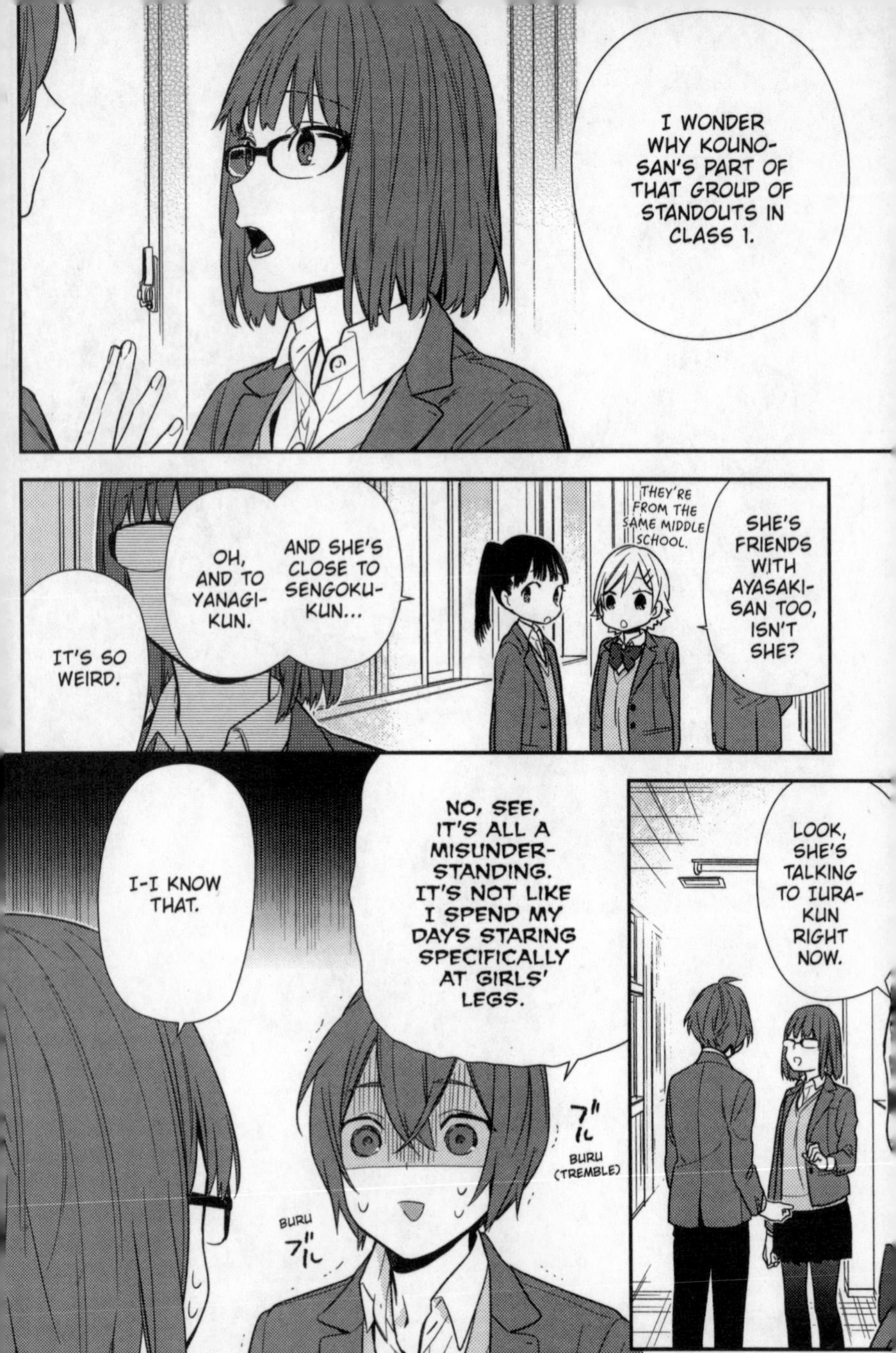
I WONDER WHY KOUNO-SAN'S PART OF THAT GROUP OF STANDOUTS IN CLASS 1.
SHE'S FRIENDS WITH AYASAKI-SAN TOO, ISN'T SHE?
THEY'RE FROM THE SAME MIDDLE SCHOOL.
AND SHE'S CLOSE TO SENGOKU-KUN...
OH, AND TO YANAGI-KUN.
IT'S SO WEIRD.
LOOK, SHE'S TALKING TO IURA-KUN RIGHT NOW.
NO, SEE, IT'S ALL A MISUNDERSTANDING. IT'S NOT LIKE I SPEND MY DAYS STARING SPECIFICALLY AT GIRLS' LEGS.
ブル
BURU (TREMBLE)
I-I KNOW THAT.
BURU
ブル

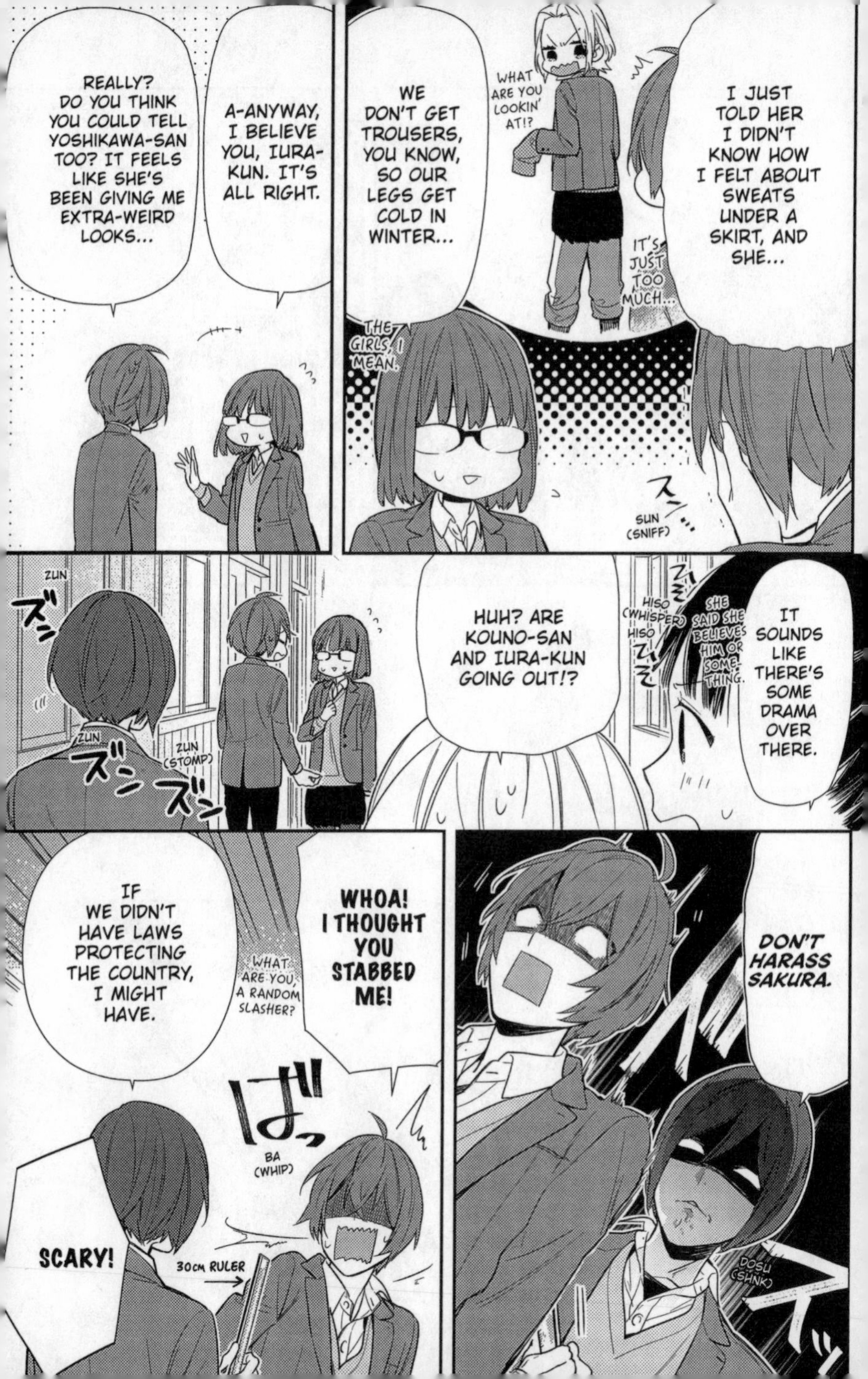
I JUST TOLD HER I DIDN'T KNOW HOW I FELT ABOUT SWEATS UNDER A SKIRT, AND SHE...
WHAT ARE YOU LOOKIN' AT!?
IT'S JUST TOO MUCH...
WE DON'T GET TROUSERS, YOU KNOW, SO OUR LEGS GET COLD IN WINTER...
THE GIRLS, I MEAN.
SUN (SNIFF)
A-ANYWAY, I BELIEVE YOU, IURA-KUN. IT'S ALL RIGHT.
REALLY? DO YOU THINK YOU COULD TELL YOSHIKAWA-SAN TOO? IT FEELS LIKE SHE'S BEEN GIVING ME EXTRA-WEIRD LOOKS...
IT SOUNDS LIKE THERE'S SOME DRAMA OVER THERE.
SHE SAID SHE BELIEVES HIM OR SOMETHING.
HISO (WHISPER) HISO
HUH? ARE KOUNO-SAN AND IURA-KUN GOING OUT!?
ZUN
ZUN
ZUN (STOMP)
DON'T HARASS SAKURA.
DOSU (SHNK)
WHOA! I THOUGHT YOU STABBED ME!
WHAT ARE YOU, A RANDOM SLASHER?
IF WE DIDN'T HAVE LAWS PROTECTING THE COUNTRY, I MIGHT HAVE.
BA (WHIP)
SCARY!
30CM RULER

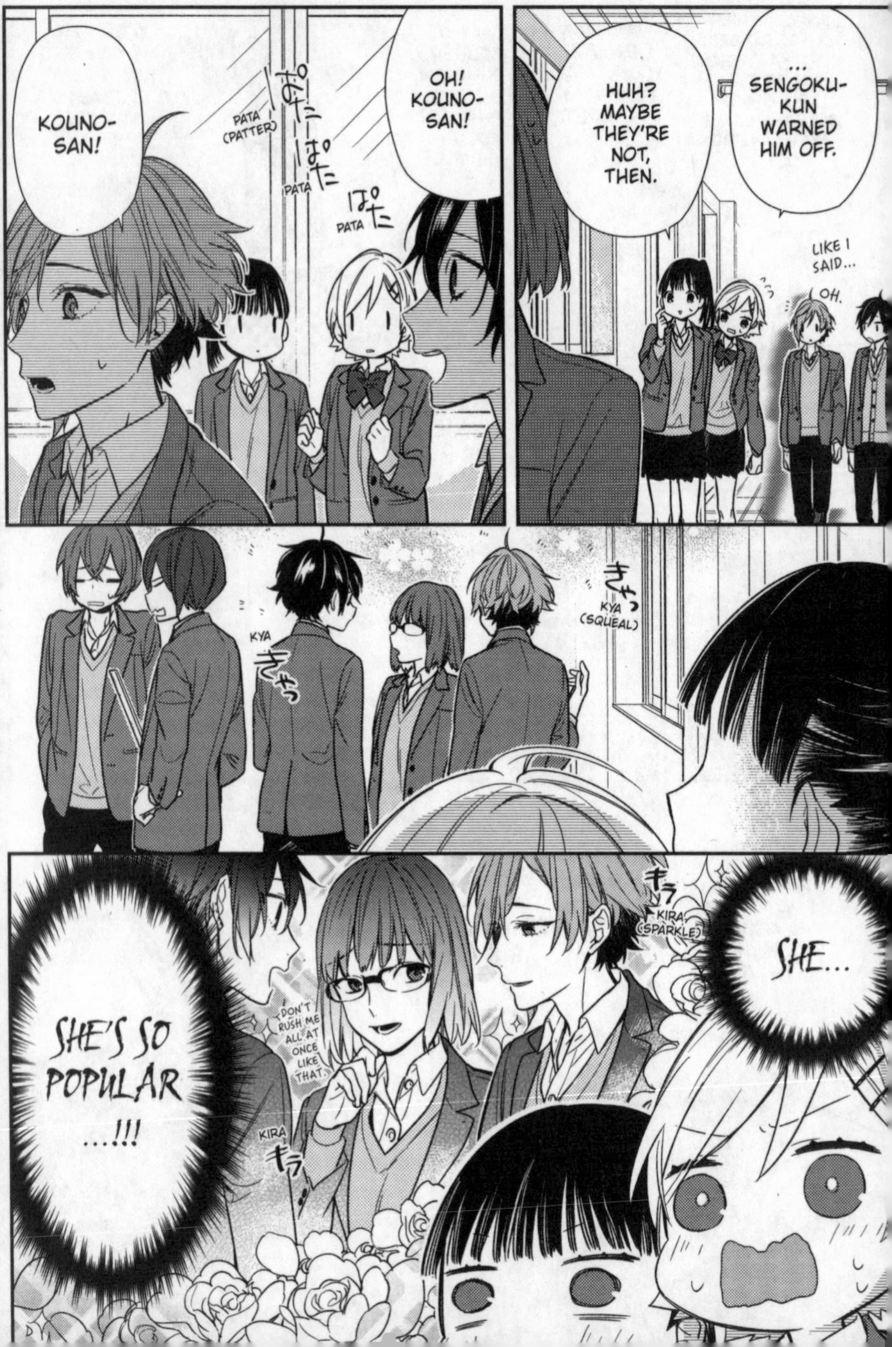
...SENGOKU-KUN WARNED HIM OFF.
HUH? MAYBE THEY'RE NOT, THEN.
LIKE I SAID...
OH.
OH! KOUNO-SAN!
ぱた PATA
ぱた PATA
ぱたぱた PATA (PATTER)
KOUNO-SAN!
きゃっ KYA (SQUEAL)
KYA きゃっ
SHE...
キラ KIRA (SPARKLE)
DON'T RUSH ME ALL AT ONCE LIKE THAT.
KIRA キラ
SHE'S SO POPULAR ...!!!

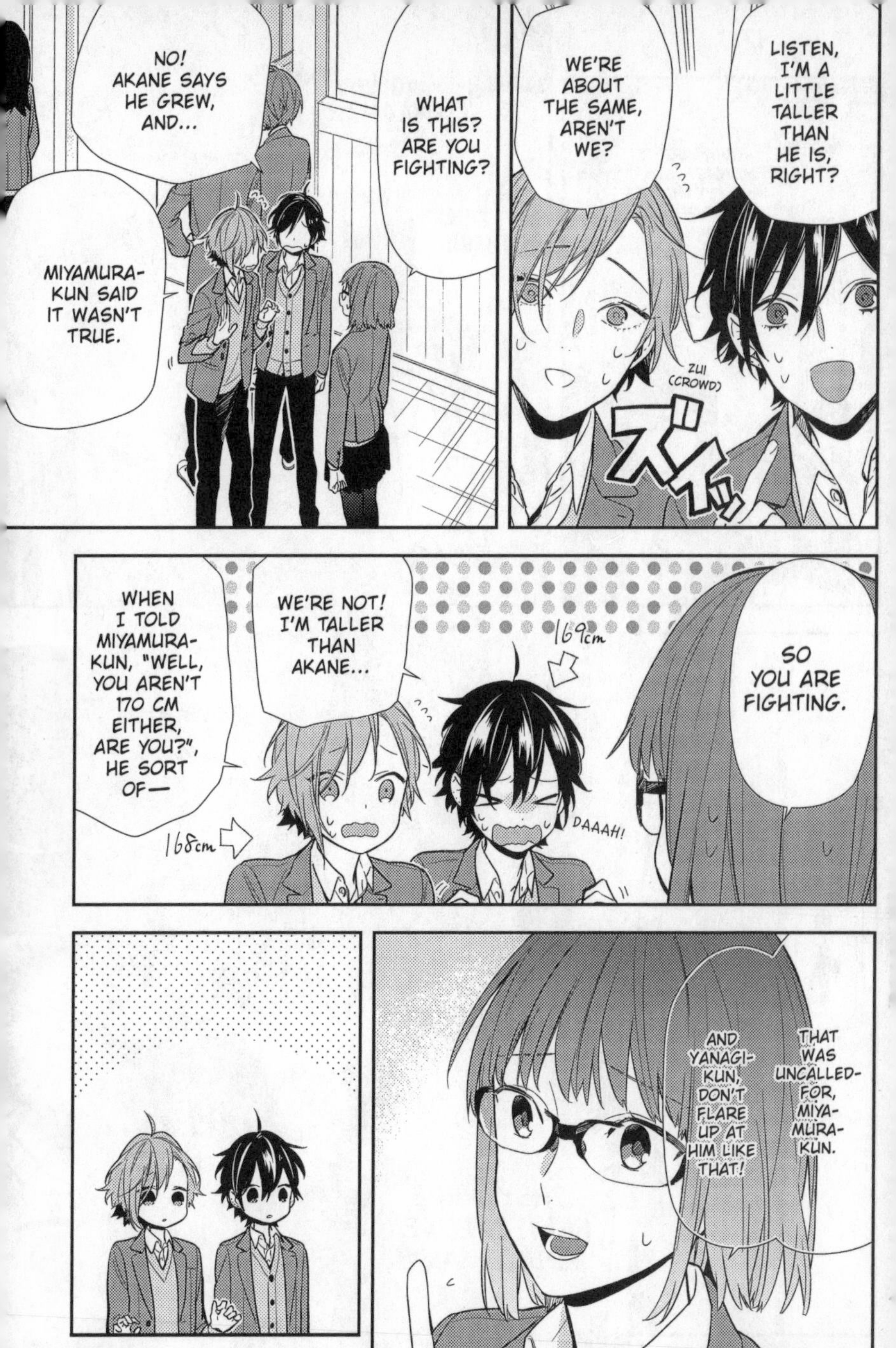
LISTEN, I'M A LITTLE TALLER THAN HE IS, RIGHT?
WE'RE ABOUT THE SAME, AREN'T WE?
ZUI (CROWD)
WHAT IS THIS? ARE YOU FIGHTING?
NO! AKANE SAYS HE GREW, AND...
MIYAMURA-KUN SAID IT WASN'T TRUE.
SO YOU ARE FIGHTING.
169cm
WE'RE NOT! I'M TALLER THAN AKANE...
DAAAH!
WHEN I TOLD MIYAMURA-KUN, "WELL, YOU AREN'T 170 CM EITHER, ARE YOU?", HE SORT OF—
168cm
THAT WAS UNCALLED-FOR, MIYAMURA-KUN.
AND YANAGI-KUN, DON'T FLARE UP AT HIM LIKE THAT!

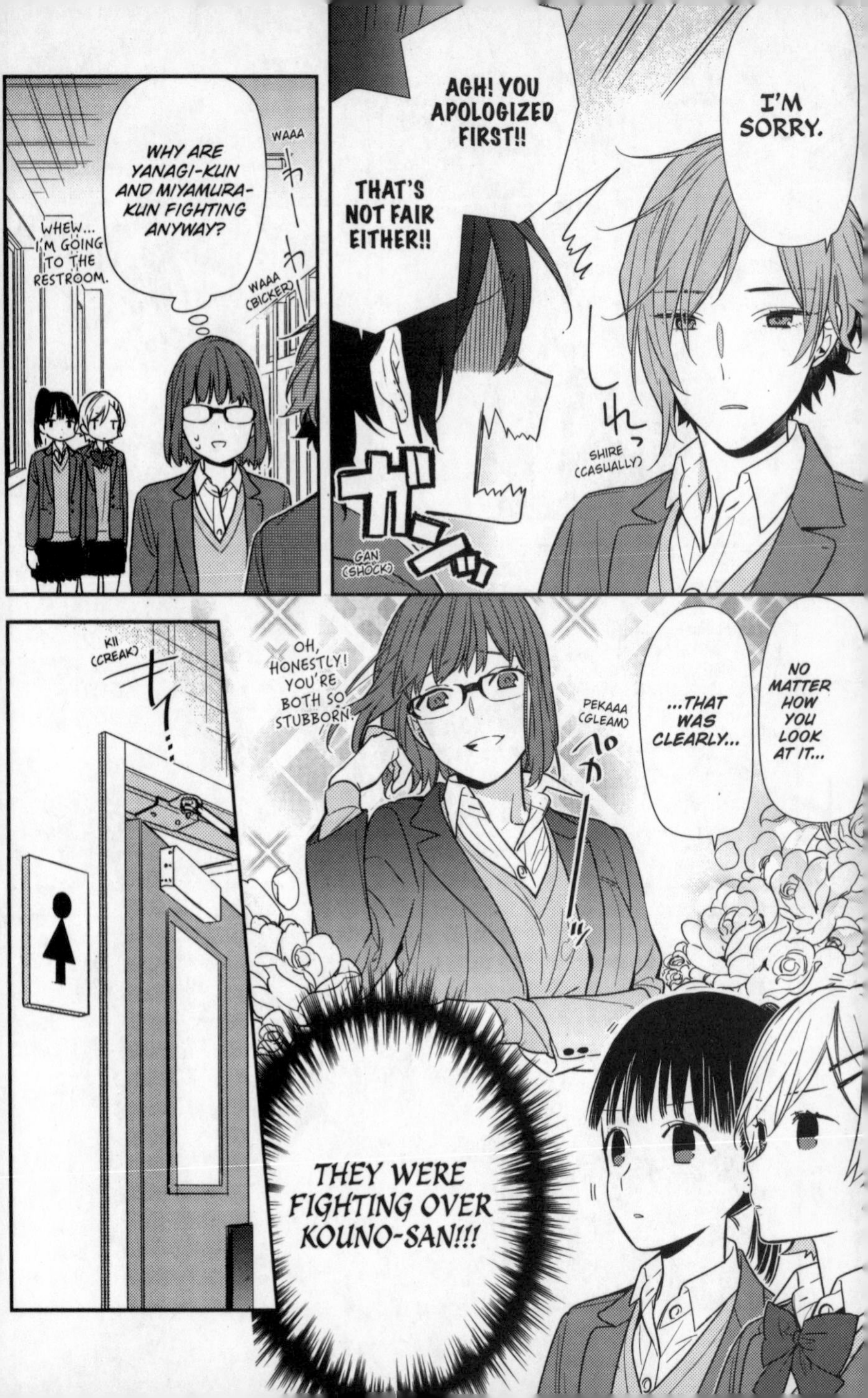
I'M SORRY.
AGH! YOU APOLOGIZED FIRST!!
THAT'S NOT FAIR EITHER!!
SHIRE (CASUALLY)
GAN (SHOCK)
WHY ARE YANAGI-KUN AND MIYAMURA-KUN FIGHTING ANYWAY?
WAAA
WAAA (BICKER)
WHEW... I'M GOING TO THE RESTROOM.
NO MATTER HOW YOU LOOK AT IT...
...THAT WAS CLEARLY...
PEKAAA (GLEAM)
OH, HONESTLY! YOU'RE BOTH SO STUBBORN.
THEY WERE FIGHTING OVER KOUNO-SAN!!!
KII (CREAK)

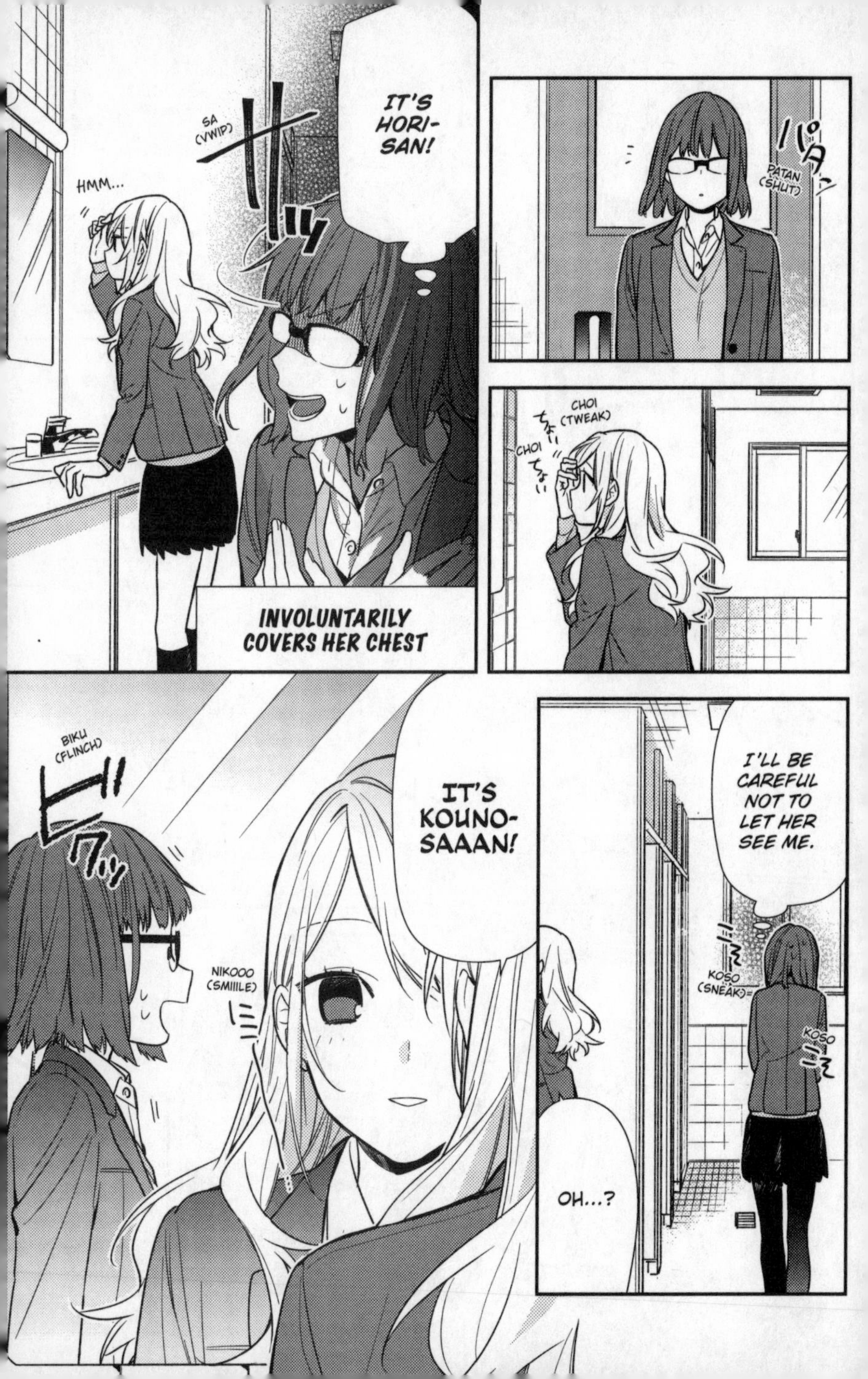
パタン
PATAN (SHUT)
ちょい ちょい
CHOI (TWEAK)
CHOI
IT'S HORI-SAN!
SA (VWIP)
HMM...
INVOLUNTARILY COVERS HER CHEST
I'LL BE CAREFUL NOT TO LET HER SEE ME.
KOSO (SNEAK)
KOSO
OH...?
IT'S KOUNO-SAAAN!
BIKU (FLINCH)
NIKOOO (SMIIILE)

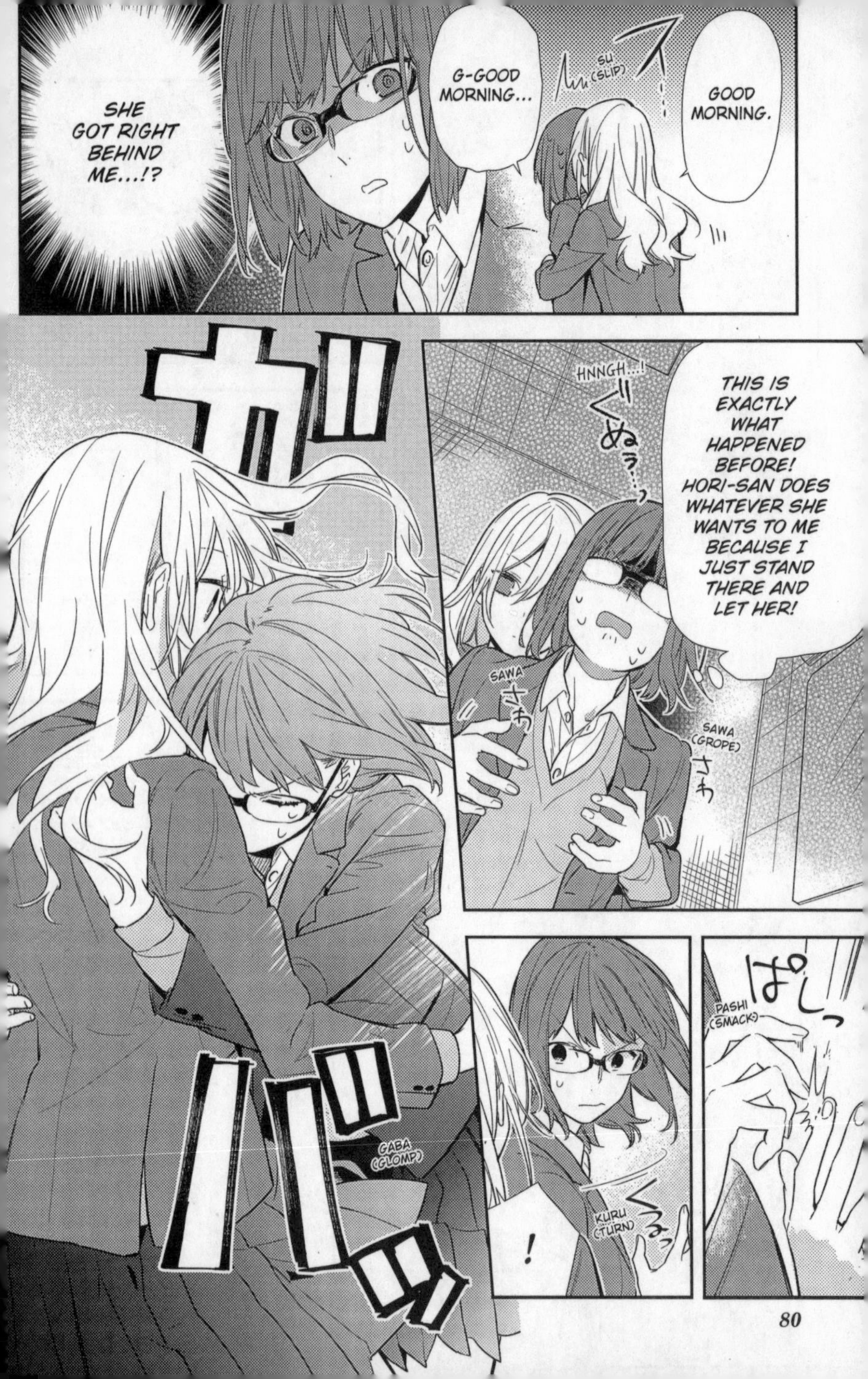
GOOD MORNING.
SU (SLIP)
G-GOOD MORNING...
SHE GOT RIGHT BEHIND ME...!?
HNNGH...!
THIS IS EXACTLY WHAT HAPPENED BEFORE! HORI-SAN DOES WHATEVER SHE WANTS TO ME BECAUSE I JUST STAND THERE AND LET HER!
SAWA
SAWA (GROPE)
PASHI (SMACK)
KURU (TURN)
!
GABA (GLOMP)

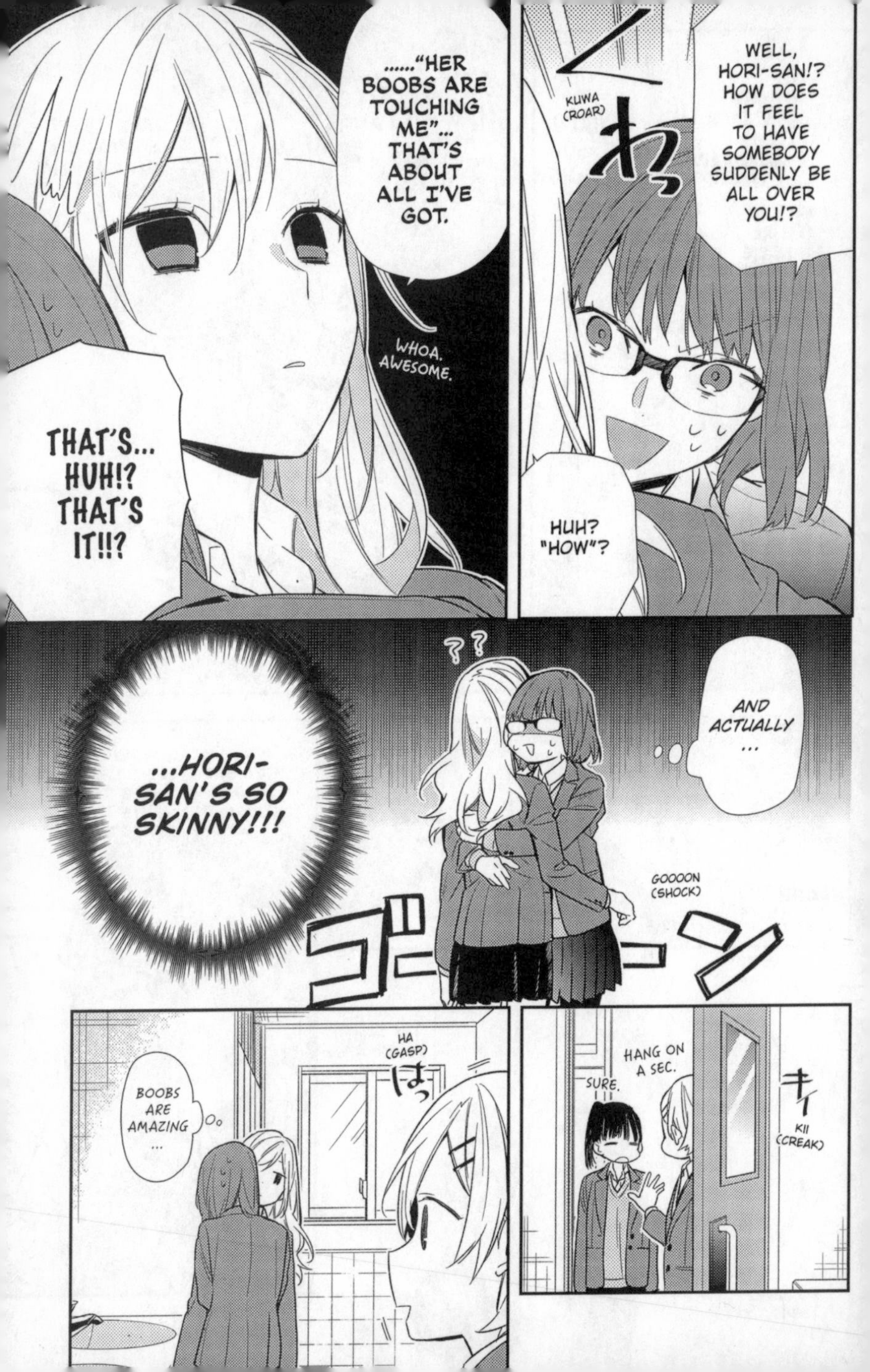
WELL, HORI-SAN!? HOW DOES IT FEEL TO HAVE SOMEBODY SUDDENLY BE ALL OVER YOU!?
KUWA (ROAR)
HUH? "HOW"?
......"HER BOOBS ARE TOUCHING ME"... THAT'S ABOUT ALL I'VE GOT.
WHOA. AWESOME.
THAT'S... HUH!? THAT'S IT!!?
AND ACTUALLY ...
??
GOOOON (SHOCK)
...HORI-SAN'S SO SKINNY!!!
HANG ON A SEC.
SURE.
KII (CREAK)
HA (GASP)
BOOBS ARE AMAZING ...

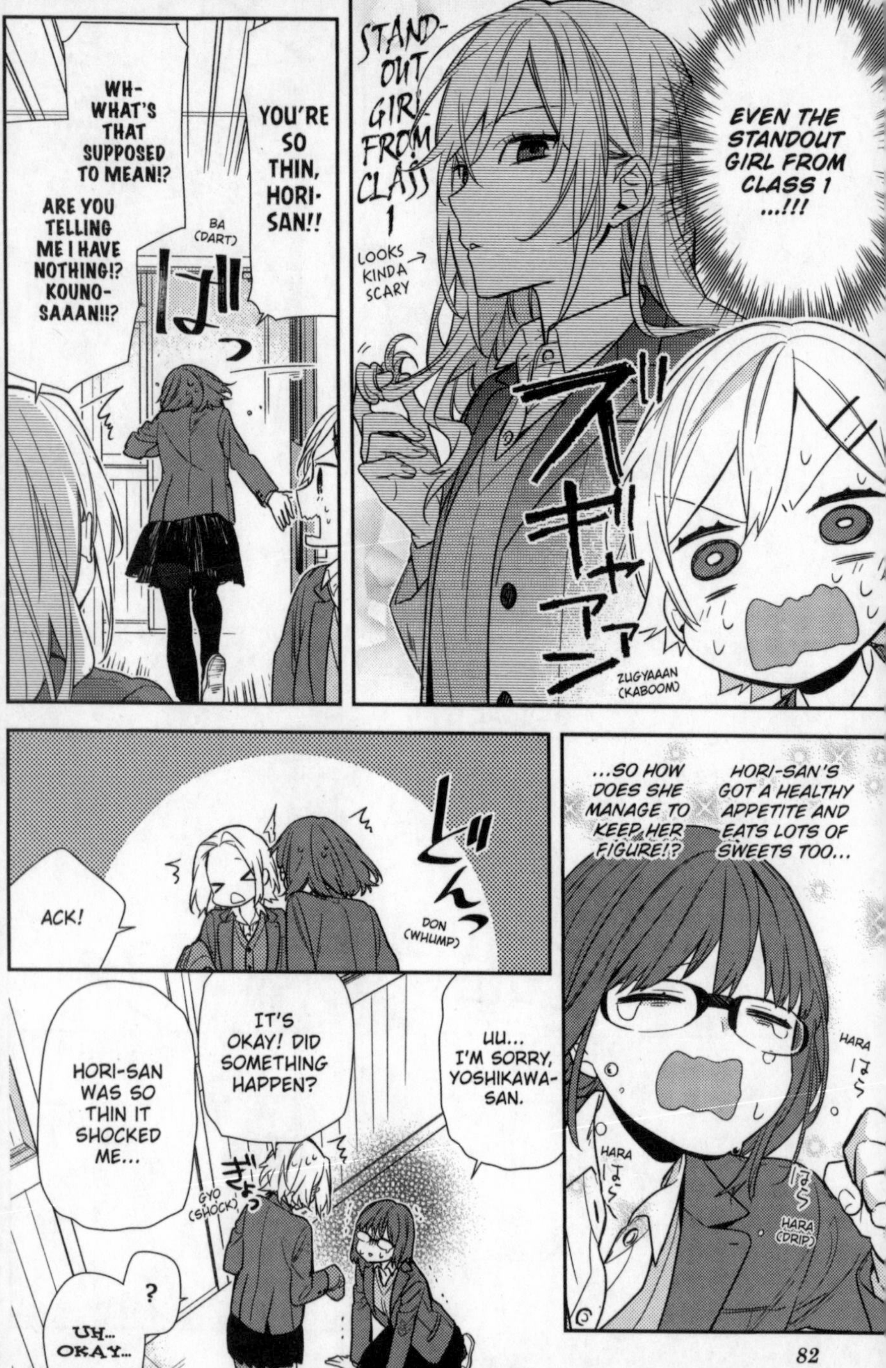
EVEN THE STANDOUT GIRL FROM CLASS 1 ...!!!
STAND-OUT GIRL FROM CLASS 1
LOOKS KINDA SCARY
ズギャアーン
ZUGYAAAN (KABOOM)
YOU'RE SO THIN, HORI-SAN!!
ばっ
BA (DART)
WH-WHAT'S THAT SUPPOSED TO MEAN!?
ARE YOU TELLING ME I HAVE NOTHING!? KOUNO-SAAAN!!?
HORI-SAN'S GOT A HEALTHY APPETITE AND EATS LOTS OF SWEETS TOO...
...SO HOW DOES SHE MANAGE TO KEEP HER FIGURE!?
はら
HARA
はら
HARA
はら
HARA (DRIP)
どんっ
DON (WHUMP)
ACK!
UU... I'M SORRY, YOSHIKAWA-SAN.
IT'S OKAY! DID SOMETHING HAPPEN?
HORI-SAN WAS SO THIN IT SHOCKED ME...
ぎょっ
GYO (SHOCK)
?
UH... OKAY...

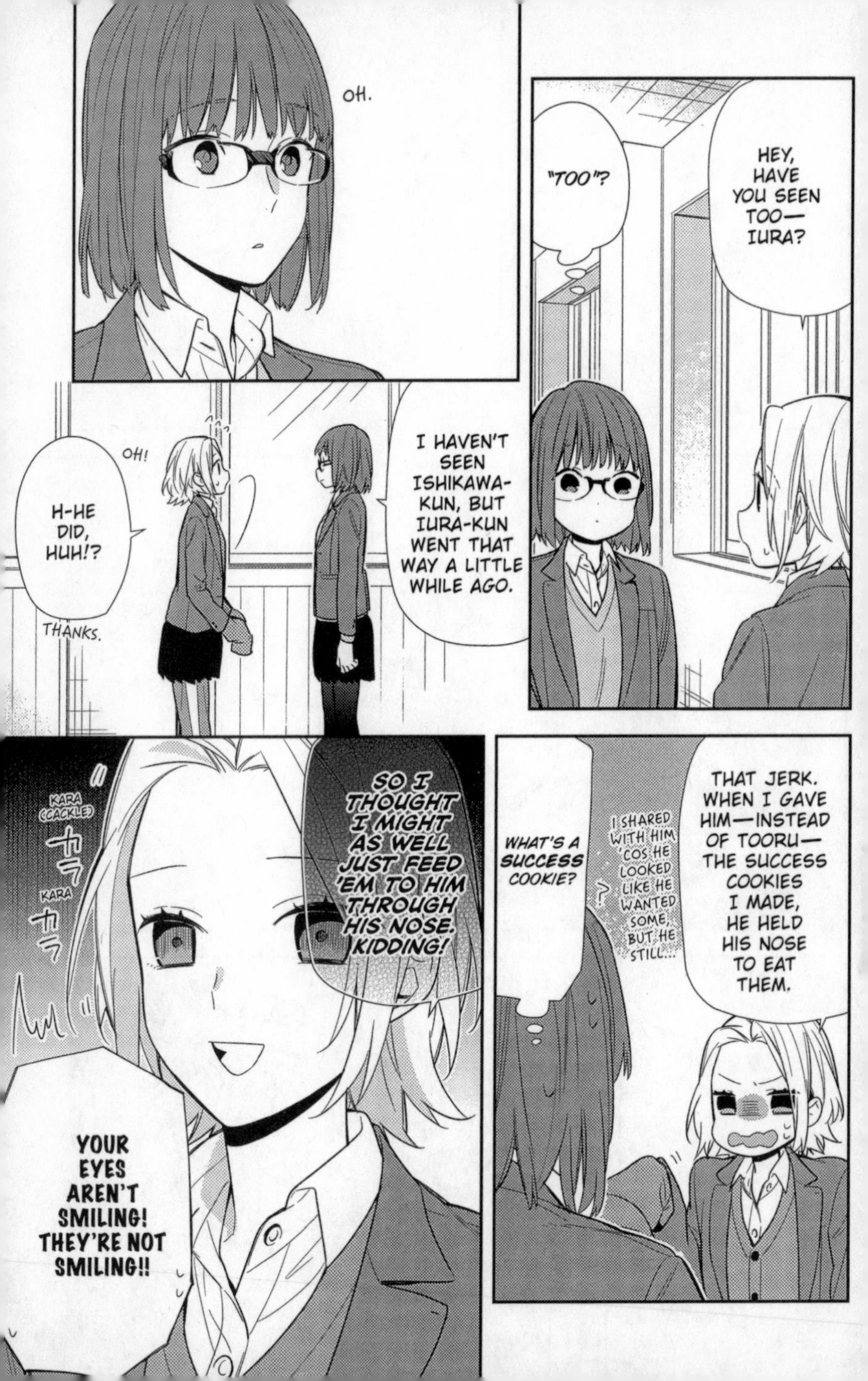
HEY, HAVE YOU SEEN TOO— IURA?
"TOO"?
OH.
I HAVEN'T SEEN ISHIKAWA-KUN, BUT IURA-KUN WENT THAT WAY A LITTLE WHILE AGO.
OH!
H-HE DID, HUH!?
THANKS.
THAT JERK. WHEN I GAVE HIM—INSTEAD OF TOORU—THE SUCCESS COOKIES I MADE, HE HELD HIS NOSE TO EAT THEM.
I SHARED WITH HIM 'COS HE LOOKED LIKE HE WANTED SOME, BUT HE STILL...
WHAT'S A SUCCESS COOKIE?
?
SO I THOUGHT I MIGHT AS WELL JUST FEED 'EM TO HIM THROUGH HIS NOSE. KIDDING!
KARA (CACKLE)
カラ
KARA
カラ
YOUR EYES AREN'T SMILING! THEY'RE NOT SMILING!!

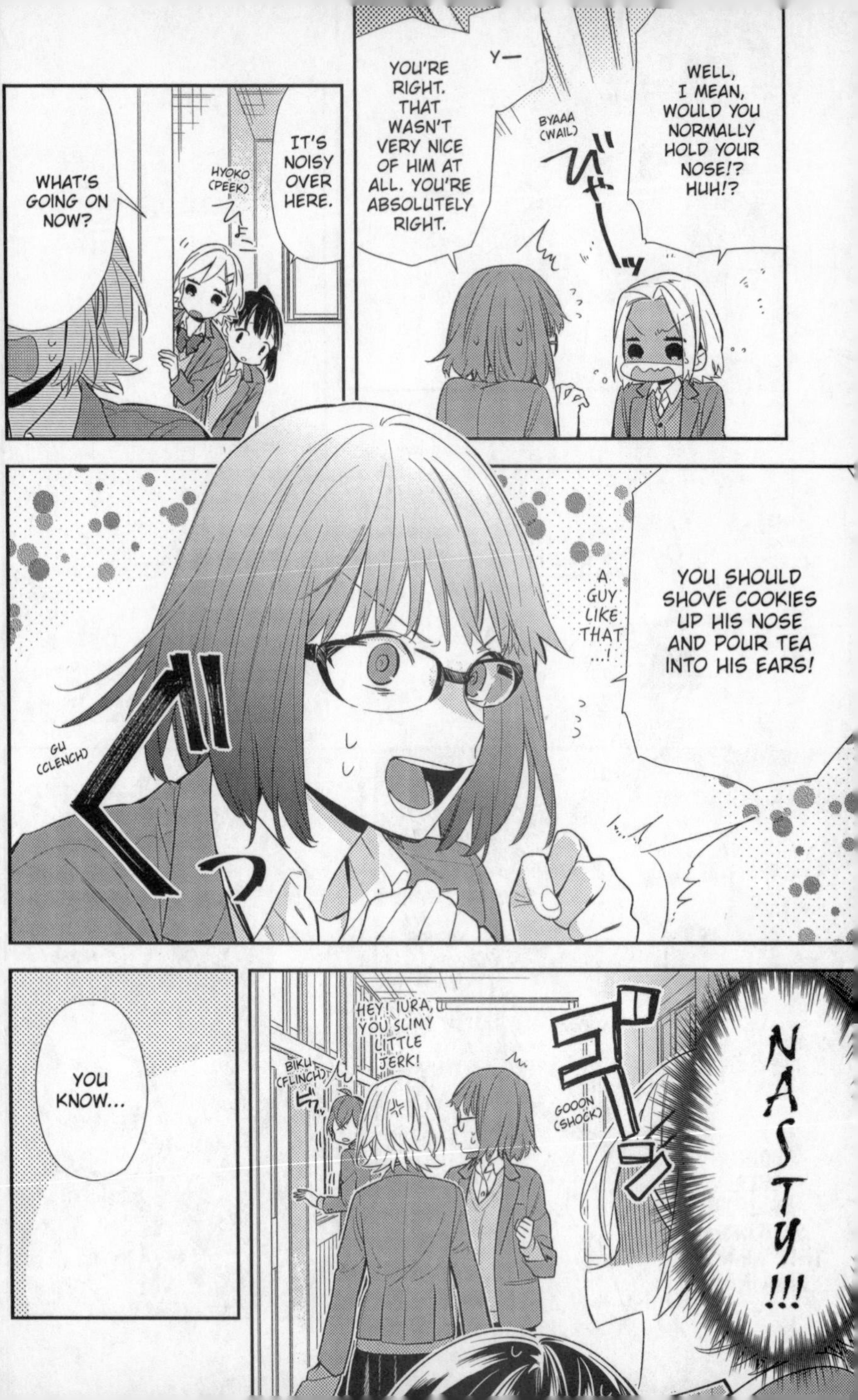
WELL, I MEAN, WOULD YOU NORMALLY HOLD YOUR NOSE!? HUH!?
Y—
BYAAA (WAIL)
YOU'RE RIGHT. THAT WASN'T VERY NICE OF HIM AT ALL. YOU'RE ABSOLUTELY RIGHT.
IT'S NOISY OVER HERE.
HYOKO (PEEK)
WHAT'S GOING ON NOW?
YOU SHOULD SHOVE COOKIES UP HIS NOSE AND POUR TEA INTO HIS EARS!
A GUY LIKE THAT ...!
GU (CLENCH)
NASTY!!!
GOOON (SHOCK)
HEY! IURA, YOU SLIMY LITTLE JERK!
BIKU (FLINCH)
YOU KNOW...

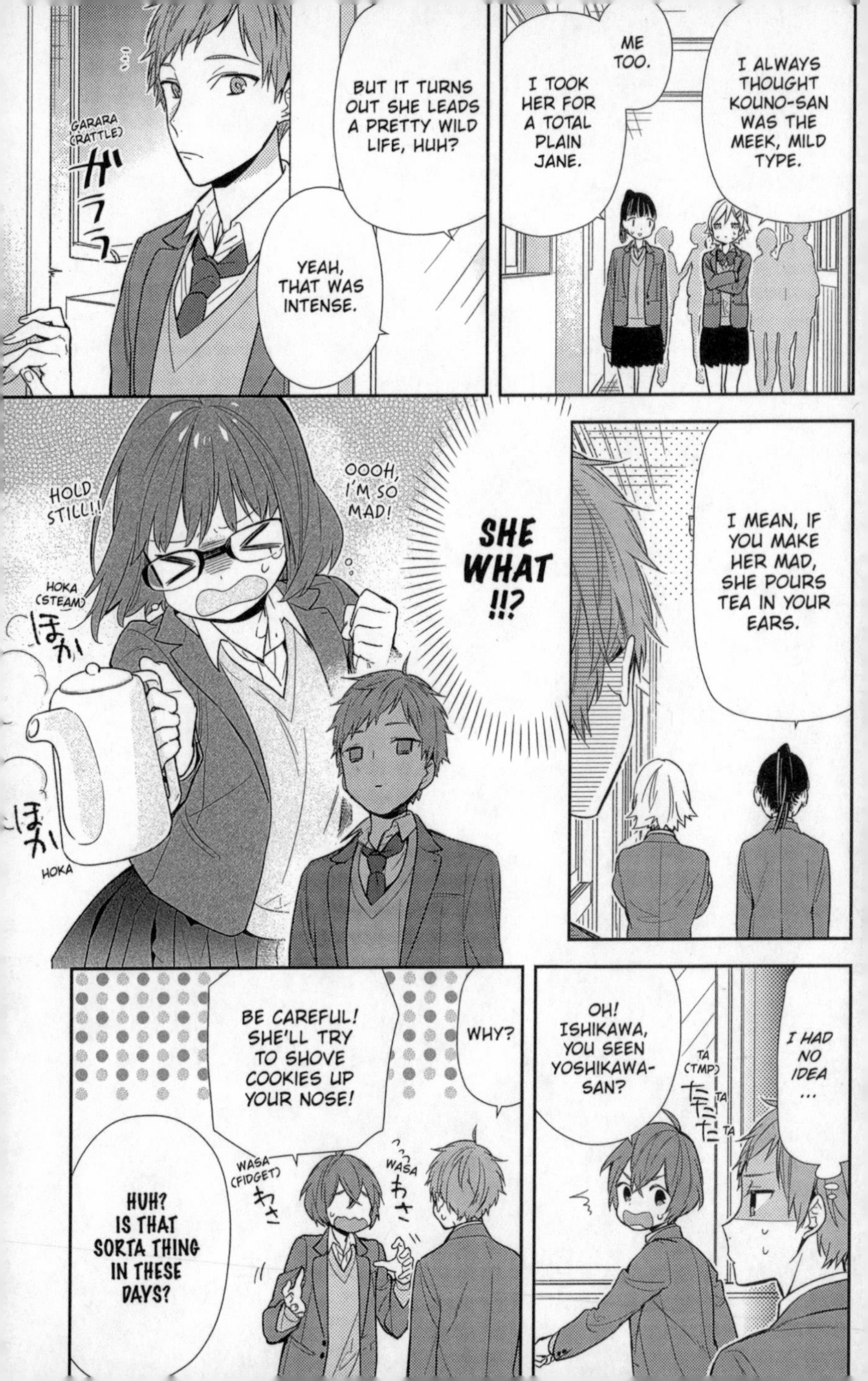
I ALWAYS THOUGHT KOUNO-SAN WAS THE MEEK, MILD TYPE.
ME TOO.
I TOOK HER FOR A TOTAL PLAIN JANE.
BUT IT TURNS OUT SHE LEADS A PRETTY WILD LIFE, HUH?
GARARA (RATTLE)
ガララ
YEAH, THAT WAS INTENSE.
I MEAN, IF YOU MAKE HER MAD, SHE POURS TEA IN YOUR EARS.
SHE WHAT!!?
OOOH, I'M SO MAD!
HOLD STILL!!
HOKA (STEAM)
ほか
ほか
HOKA
I HAD NO IDEA...
OH! ISHIKAWA, YOU SEEN YOSHIKAWA-SAN?
TA (TMP) TA TA
たたた
WHY?
BE CAREFUL! SHE'LL TRY TO SHOVE COOKIES UP YOUR NOSE!
WASA (FIDGET)
わさ
WASA
わさ
HUH? IS THAT SORTA THING IN THESE DAYS?

HORIMIYA

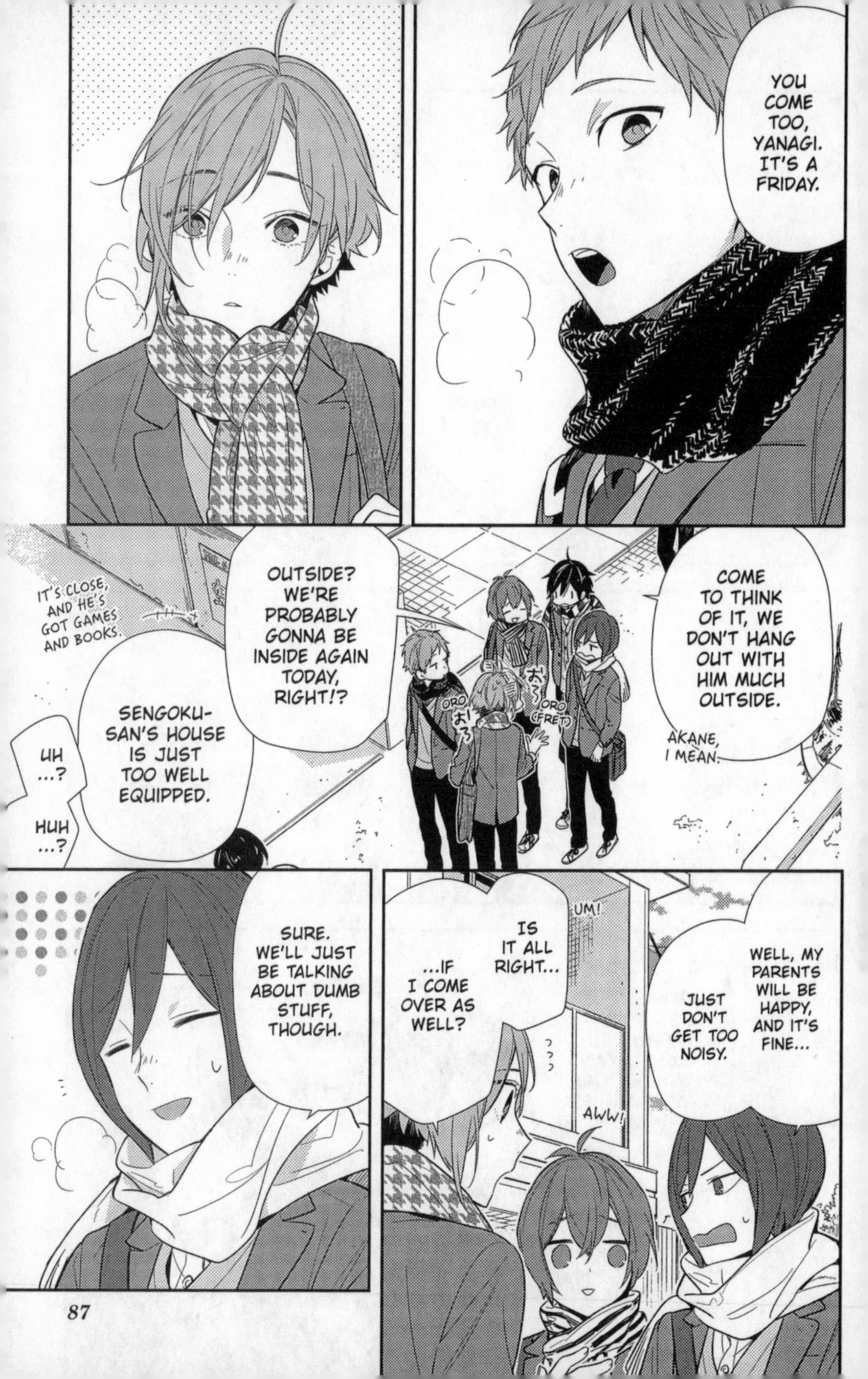
YOU COME TOO, YANAGI. IT'S A FRIDAY.
COME TO THINK OF IT, WE DON'T HANG OUT WITH HIM MUCH OUTSIDE.
AKANE, I MEAN.
OUTSIDE? WE'RE PROBABLY GONNA BE INSIDE AGAIN TODAY, RIGHT!?
ORO (FRET)
ORO
IT'S CLOSE, AND HE'S GOT GAMES AND BOOKS.
SENGOKU-SAN'S HOUSE IS JUST TOO WELL EQUIPPED.
UH ...?
HUH ...?
WELL, MY PARENTS WILL BE HAPPY, AND IT'S FINE...
JUST DON'T GET TOO NOISY.
UM!
IS IT ALL RIGHT...
...IF I COME OVER AS WELL?
AWW!
SURE. WE'LL JUST BE TALKING ABOUT DUMB STUFF, THOUGH.

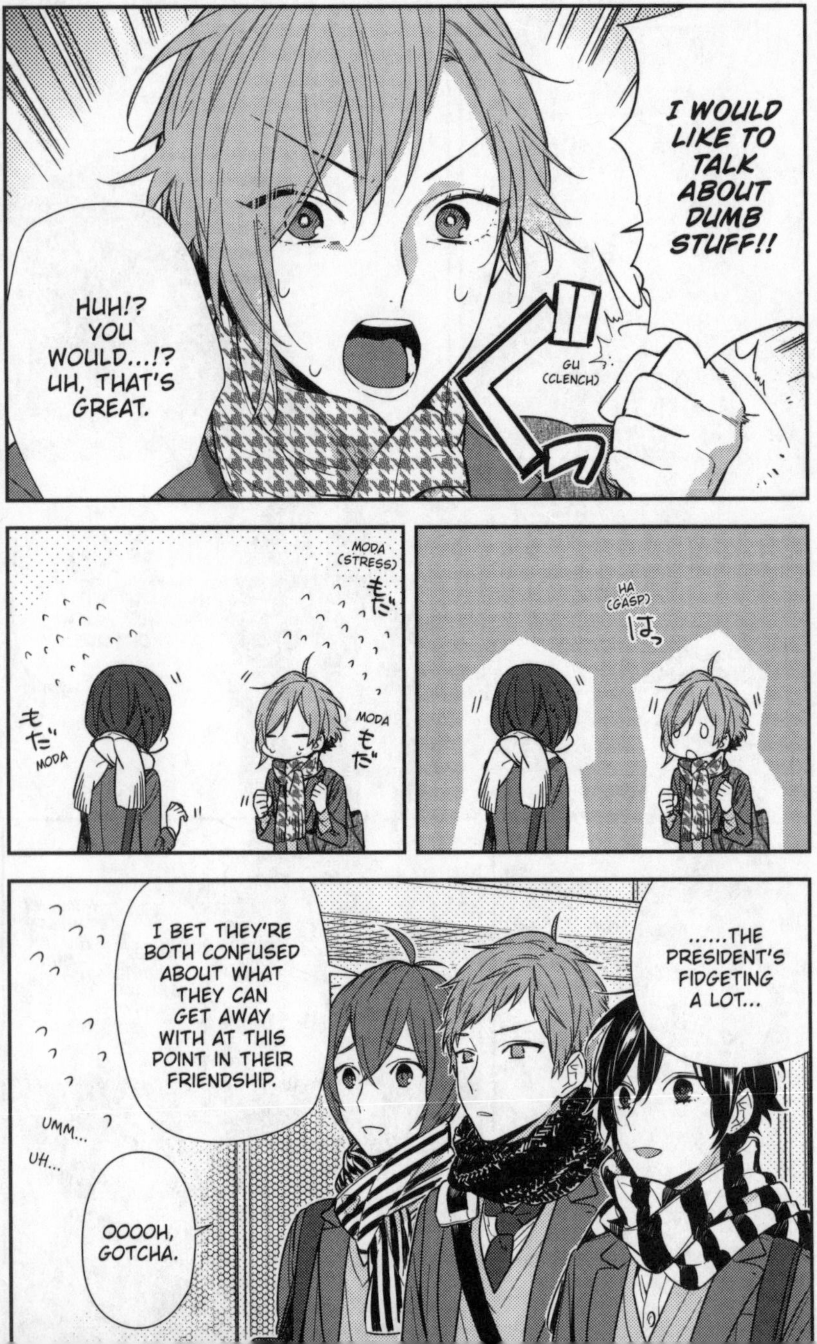
I WOULD LIKE TO TALK ABOUT DUMB STUFF!!
GU (CLENCH)
HUH!? YOU WOULD...!? UH, THAT'S GREAT.
HA (GASP)
はっ
MODA (STRESS)
もだ
MODA
もだ
もだ
MODA
......THE PRESIDENT'S FIDGETING A LOT...
I BET THEY'RE BOTH CONFUSED ABOUT WHAT THEY CAN GET AWAY WITH AT THIS POINT IN THEIR FRIENDSHIP.
UMM...
UH...
OOOOH, GOTCHA.

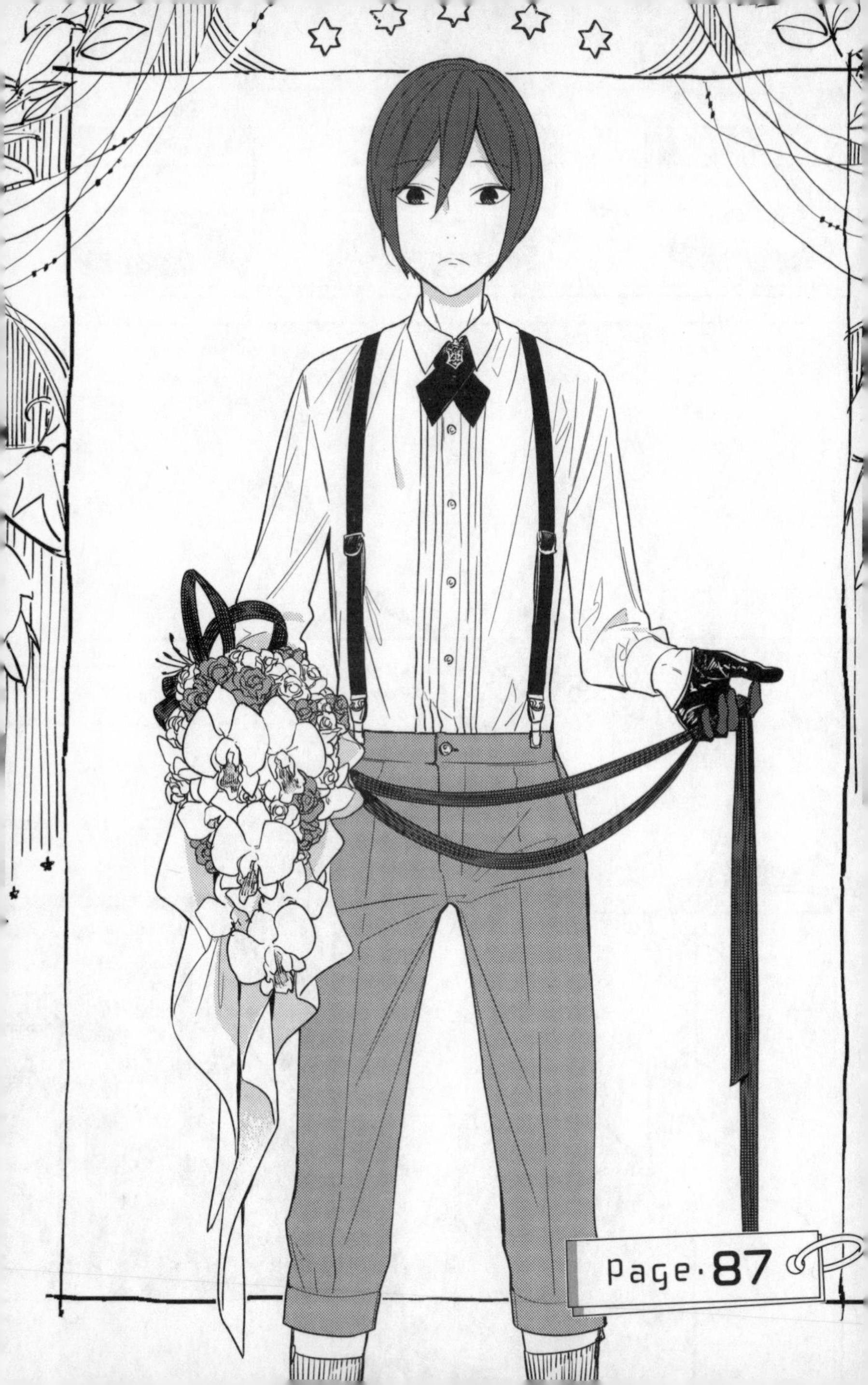
Page·87

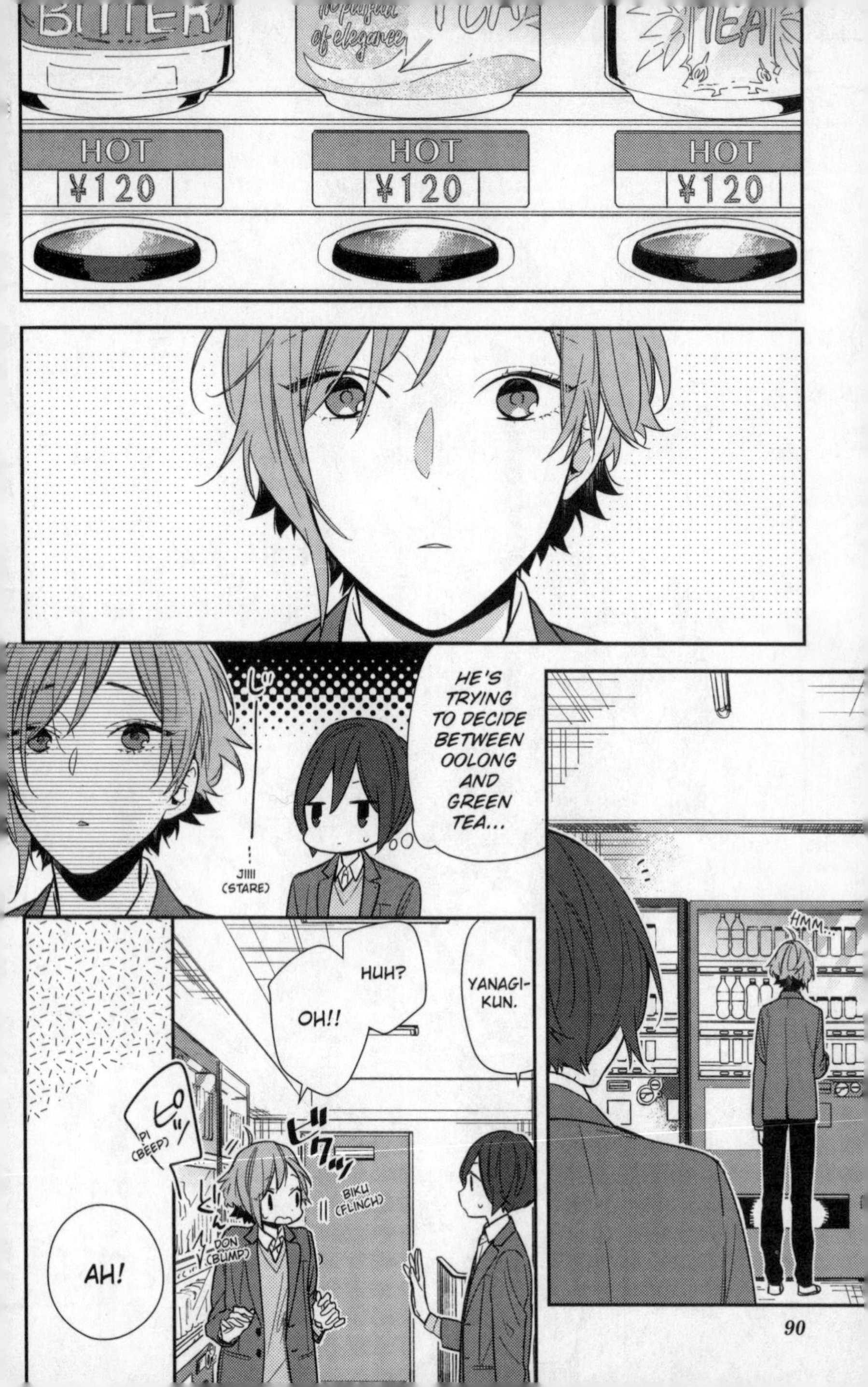
of elegance
TEA
HOT
¥120
HOT
¥120
HOT
¥120
HMM...
HE'S TRYING TO DECIDE BETWEEN OOLONG AND GREEN TEA...
JIIII (STARE)
YANAGI-KUN.
HUH?
OH!!
BIKU (FLINCH)
PI (BEEP)
DON (BUMP)
AH!

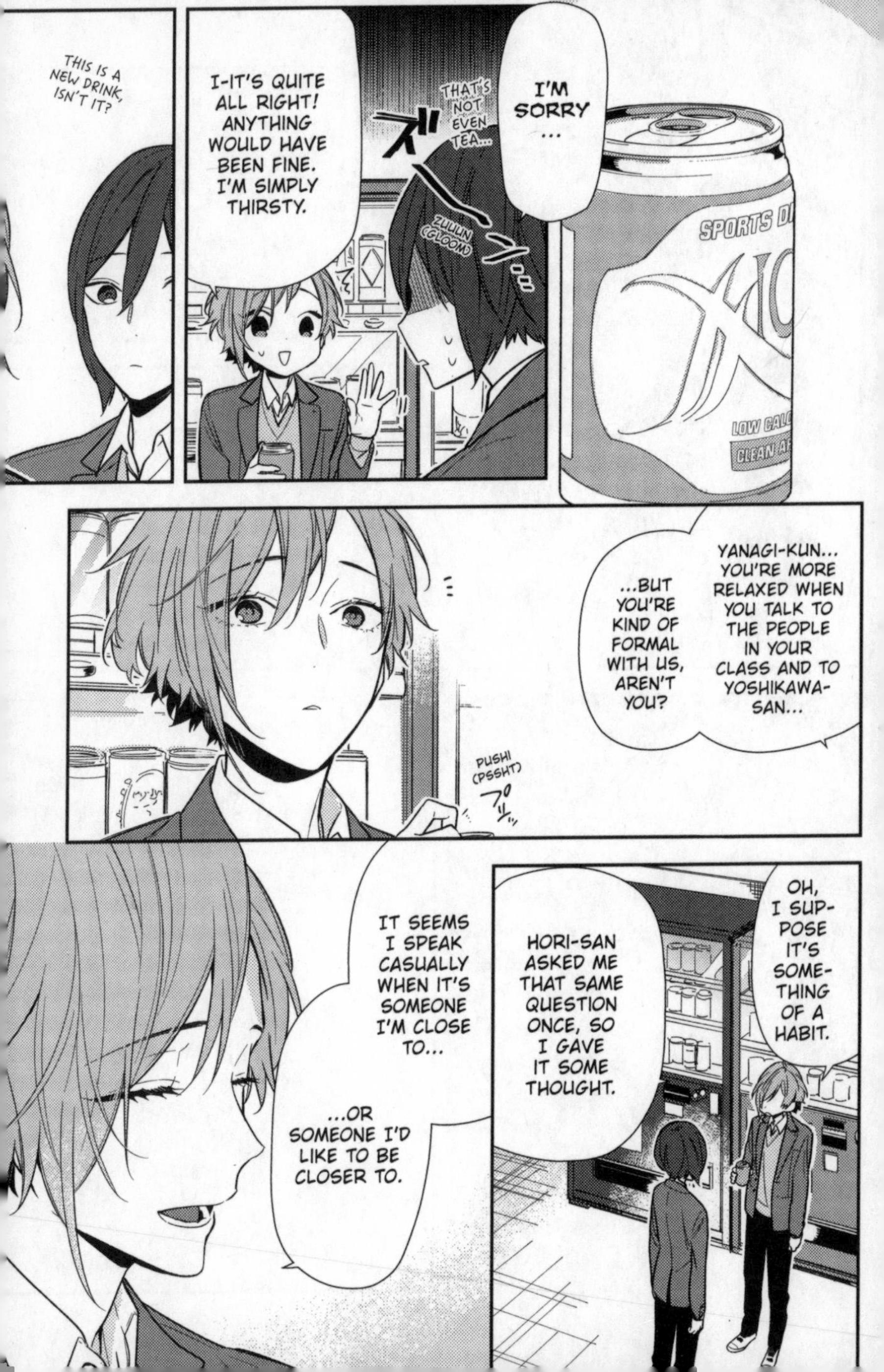
I'M SORRY ...
THAT'S NOT EVEN TEA...
ZUUUN (GLOOM)
I-IT'S QUITE ALL RIGHT! ANYTHING WOULD HAVE BEEN FINE. I'M SIMPLY THIRSTY.
THIS IS A NEW DRINK, ISN'T IT?
YANAGI-KUN... YOU'RE MORE RELAXED WHEN YOU TALK TO THE PEOPLE IN YOUR CLASS AND TO YOSHIKAWA-SAN...
...BUT YOU'RE KIND OF FORMAL WITH US, AREN'T YOU?
PUSHI (PSSHT)
OH, I SUP-POSE IT'S SOME-THING OF A HABIT.
HORI-SAN ASKED ME THAT SAME QUESTION ONCE, SO I GAVE IT SOME THOUGHT.
IT SEEMS I SPEAK CASUALLY WHEN IT'S SOMEONE I'M CLOSE TO...
...OR SOMEONE I'D LIKE TO BE CLOSER TO.

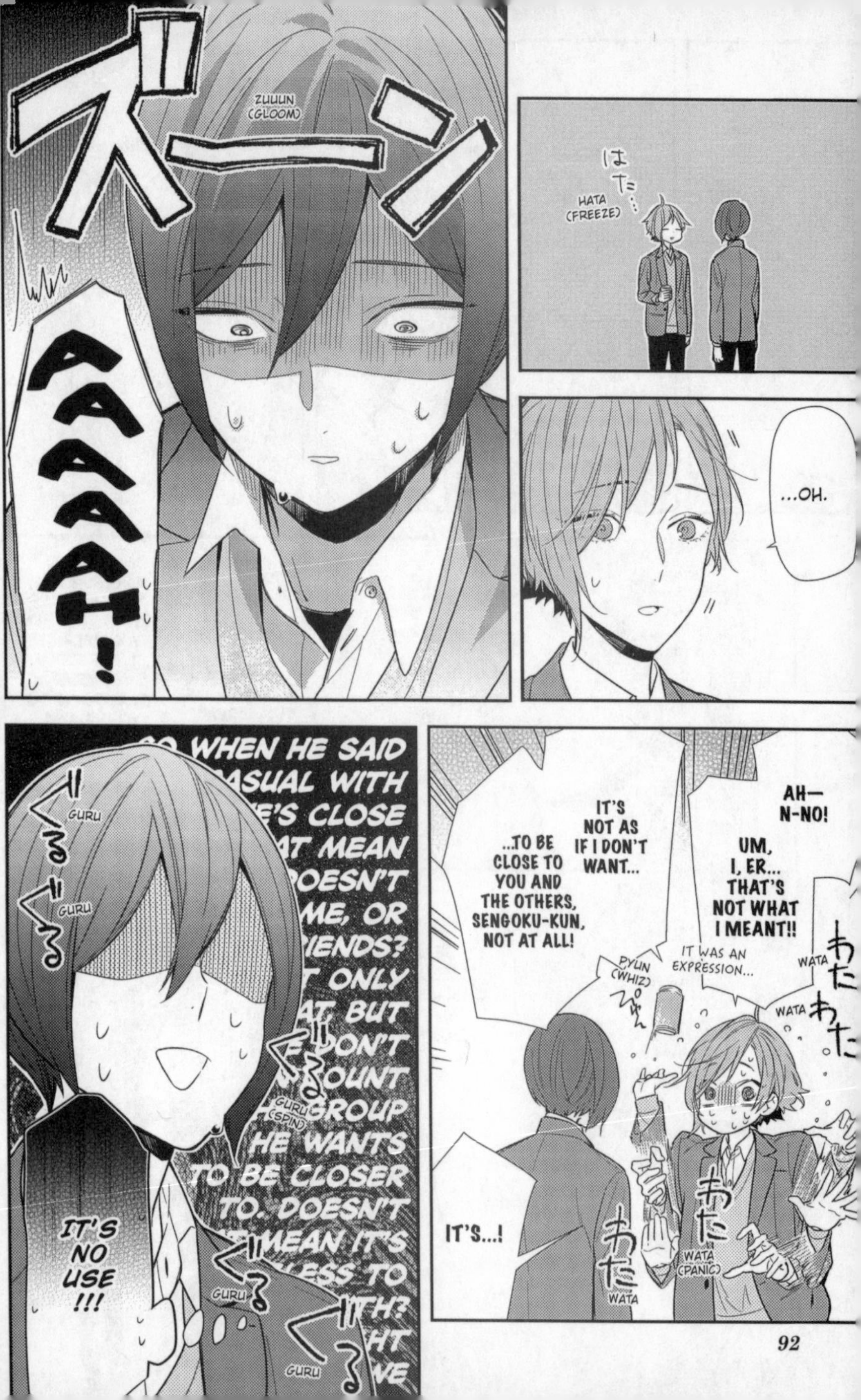
はた…
HATA (FREEZE)
...OH.
ズーン
ZUUUN (GLOOM)
AAAAAH!
AH— N-NO!
UM, I, ER... THAT'S NOT WHAT I MEANT!!
IT WAS AN EXPRESSION...
IT'S NOT AS IF I DON'T WANT...
...TO BE CLOSE TO YOU AND THE OTHERS, SENGOKU-KUN, NOT AT ALL!
PYUN (WHIZ)
ぴゅん
わたわた
WATA
WATA
わたわた
WATA (PANIC)
WATA
IT'S...!
WHEN HE SAID
WITH
CLOSE
MEAN
OR
ONLY
BUT
GROUP HE WANTS TO BE CLOSER TO. DOESN'T
MEAN IT'S
TO
ぐるぐる
GURU
GURU
ぐる
GURU (SPIN)
ぐるぐる
GURU
GURU
IT'S NO USE!!!

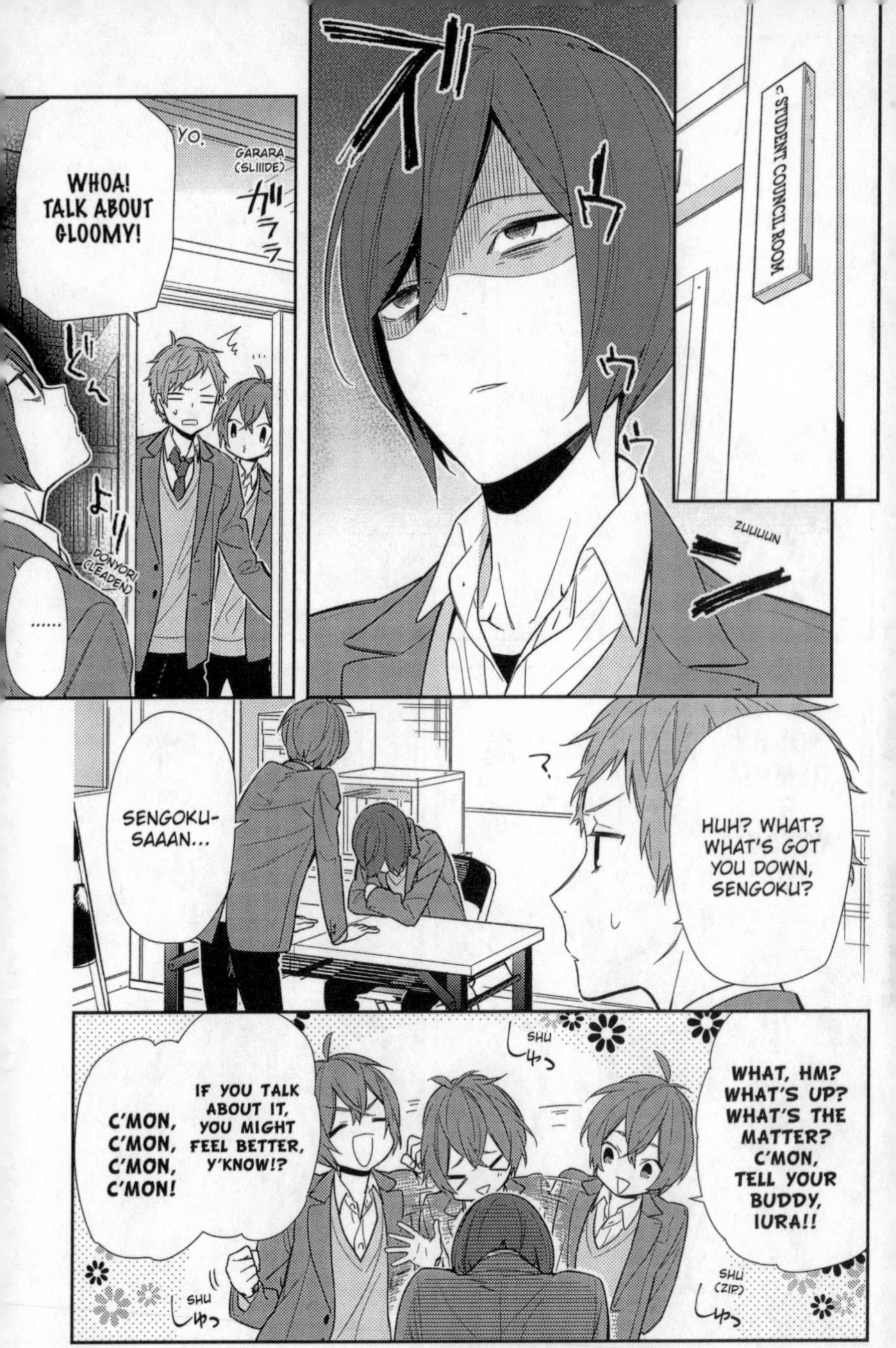
STUDENT COUNCIL ROOM
ZUUUUN
YO.
GARARA (SLIIIDE)
WHOA! TALK ABOUT GLOOMY!
DONYORI (LEADEN)
......
HUH? WHAT? WHAT'S GOT YOU DOWN, SENGOKU?
SENGOKU-SAAAN...
WHAT, HM? WHAT'S UP? WHAT'S THE MATTER? C'MON, TELL YOUR BUDDY, IURA!!
SHU (ZIP)
SHU
IF YOU TALK ABOUT IT, YOU MIGHT FEEL BETTER, Y'KNOW!?
C'MON, C'MON, C'MON, C'MON!
SHU

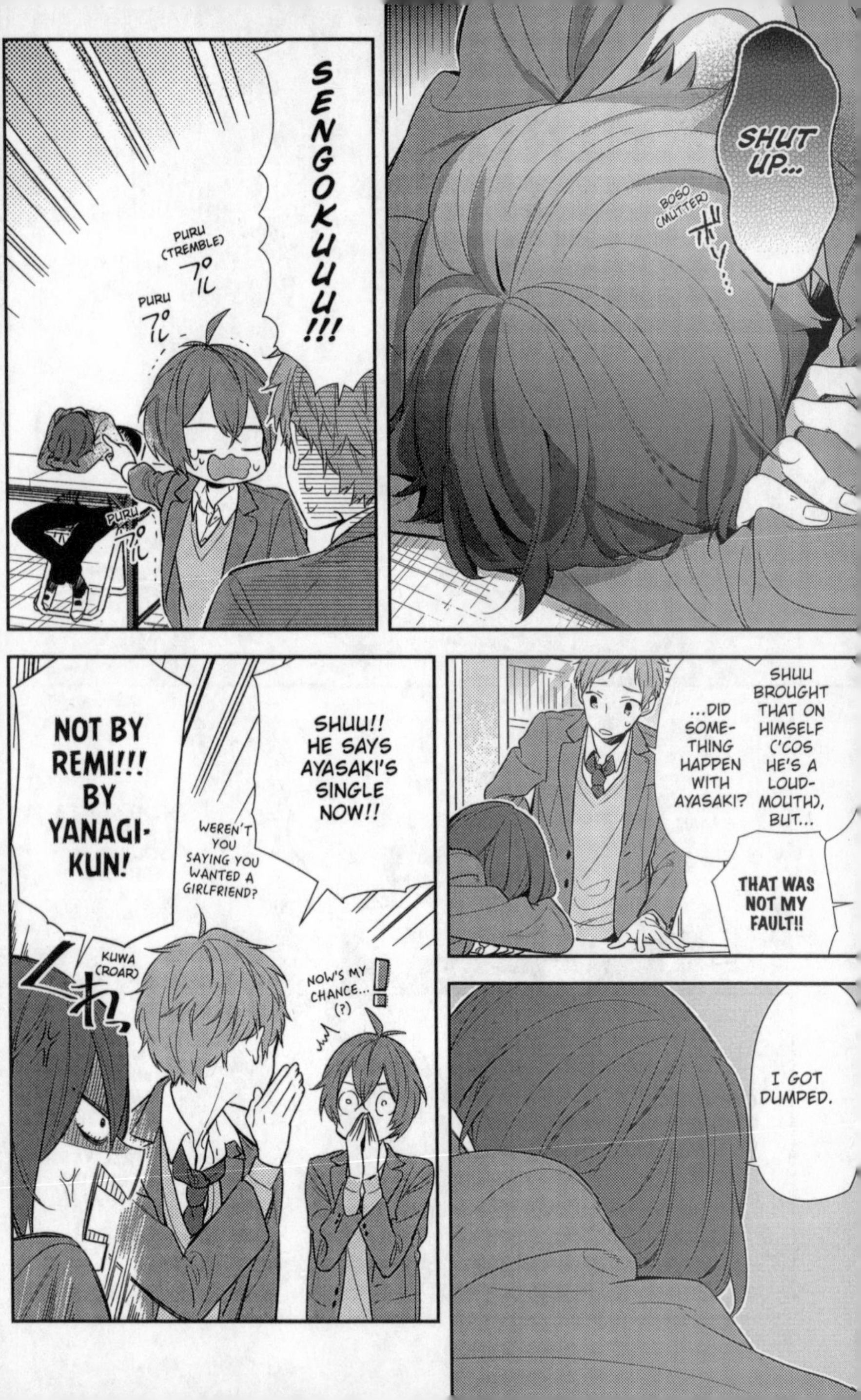
SHUT UP...
BOSO (MUTTER)
SENGOKUUUU!!!
PURU (TREMBLE)
プル
PURU
プル
PURU
プル
SHUU BROUGHT THAT ON HIMSELF ('COS HE'S A LOUD-MOUTH), BUT...
...DID SOMETHING HAPPEN WITH AYASAKI?
THAT WAS NOT MY FAULT!!
I GOT DUMPED.
SHUU!! HE SAYS AYASAKI'S SINGLE NOW!!
WEREN'T YOU SAYING YOU WANTED A GIRLFRIEND?
NOT BY REMI!!! BY YANAGI-KUN!
KUWA (ROAR)
NOW'S MY CHANCE... (?)

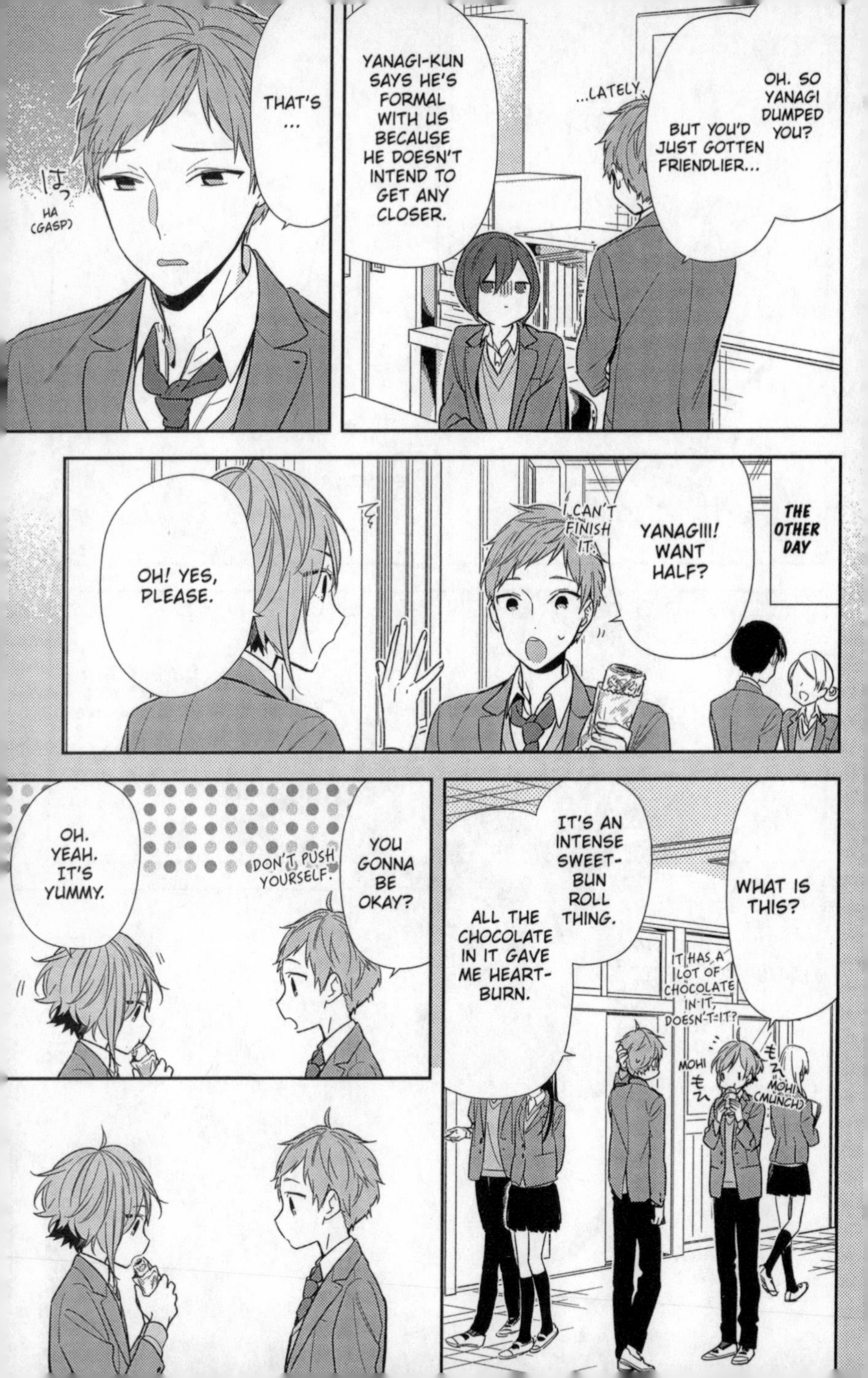
OH. SO YANAGI DUMPED YOU?
BUT YOU'D JUST GOTTEN FRIENDLIER...
...LATELY.
YANAGI-KUN SAYS HE'S FORMAL WITH US BECAUSE HE DOESN'T INTEND TO GET ANY CLOSER.
THAT'S ...
はっ
HA (GASP)
THE OTHER DAY
YANAGIII! WANT HALF?
I CAN'T FINISH IT.
OH! YES, PLEASE.
WHAT IS THIS?
IT HAS A LOT OF CHOCOLATE IN IT, DOESN'T IT?
IT'S AN INTENSE SWEET-BUN ROLL THING.
ALL THE CHOCOLATE IN IT GAVE ME HEART-BURN.
MOHI
MOHI (MUNCH)
YOU GONNA BE OKAY?
DON'T PUSH YOURSELF.
OH. YEAH. IT'S YUMMY.

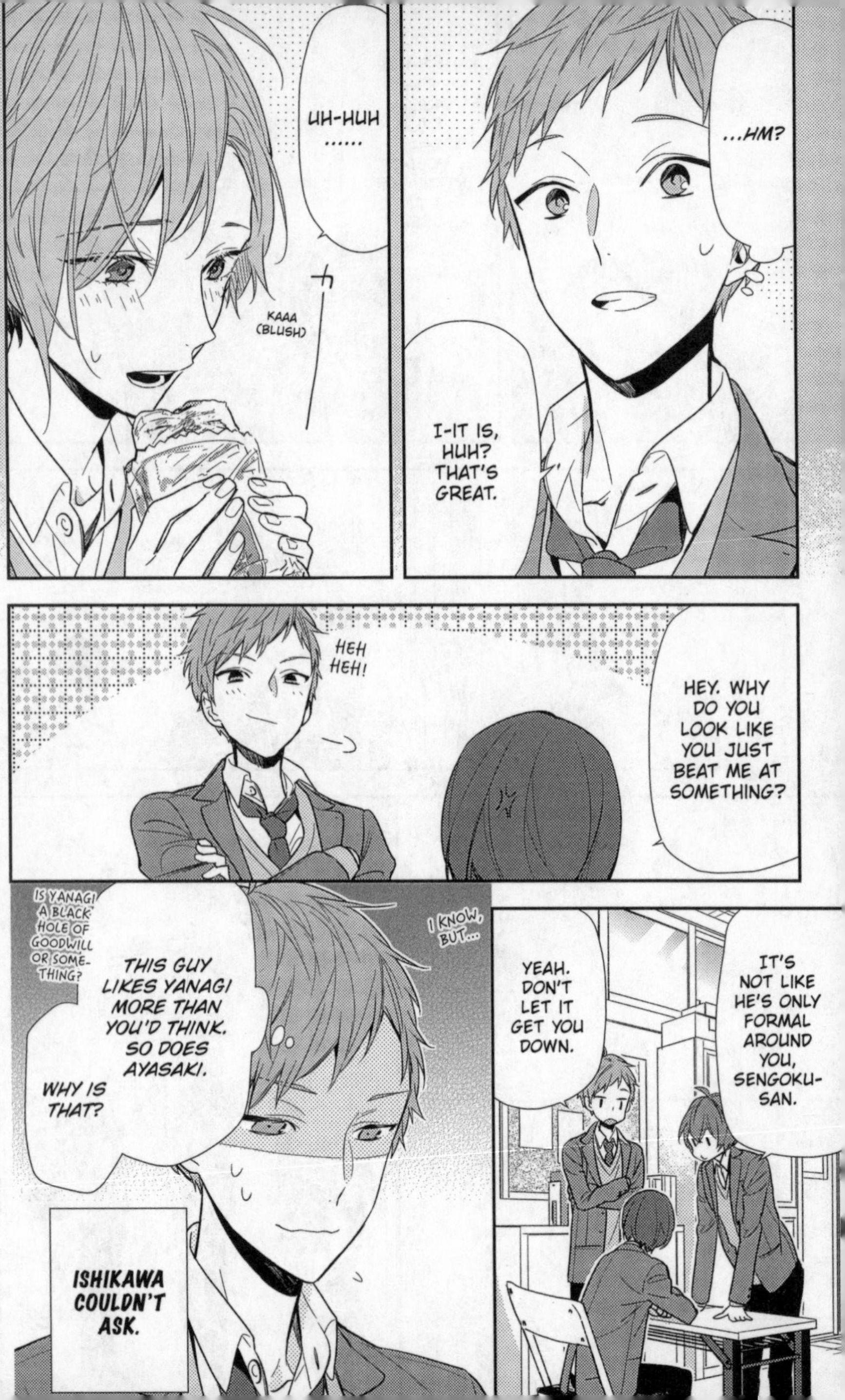
...HM?
I-IT IS, HUH? THAT'S GREAT.
UH-HUH ......
KAAA (BLUSH)
HEY. WHY DO YOU LOOK LIKE YOU JUST BEAT ME AT SOMETHING?
HEH HEH!
IT'S NOT LIKE HE'S ONLY FORMAL AROUND YOU, SENGOKU-SAN.
YEAH. DON'T LET IT GET YOU DOWN.
I KNOW, BUT...
IS YANAGI A BLACK HOLE OF GOODWILL OR SOME-THING?
THIS GUY LIKES YANAGI MORE THAN YOU'D THINK. SO DOES AYASAKI.
WHY IS THAT?
ISHIKAWA COULDN'T ASK.

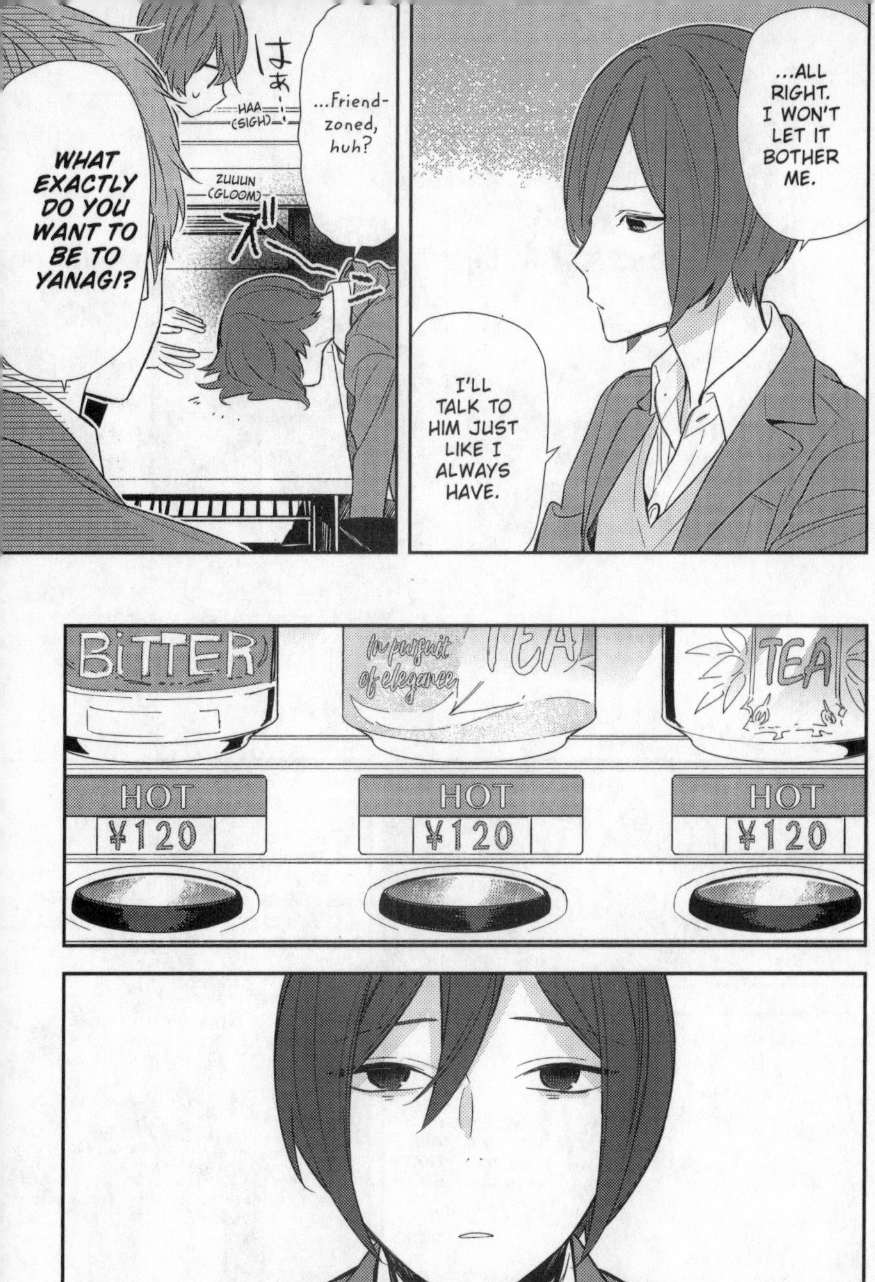
...ALL RIGHT. I WON'T LET IT BOTHER ME.
I'LL TALK TO HIM JUST LIKE I ALWAYS HAVE.
...Friend-zoned, huh?
はぁ…
HAA (SIGH)
ズーン
ZUUUN (GLOOM)
WHAT EXACTLY DO YOU WANT TO BE TO YANAGI?
BiTTER
In pursuit of elegance
TEA
TEA
HOT
¥120
HOT
¥120
HOT
¥120

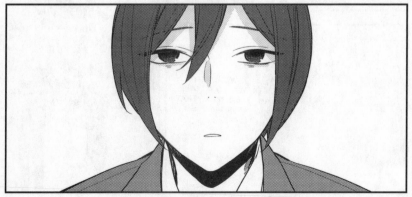

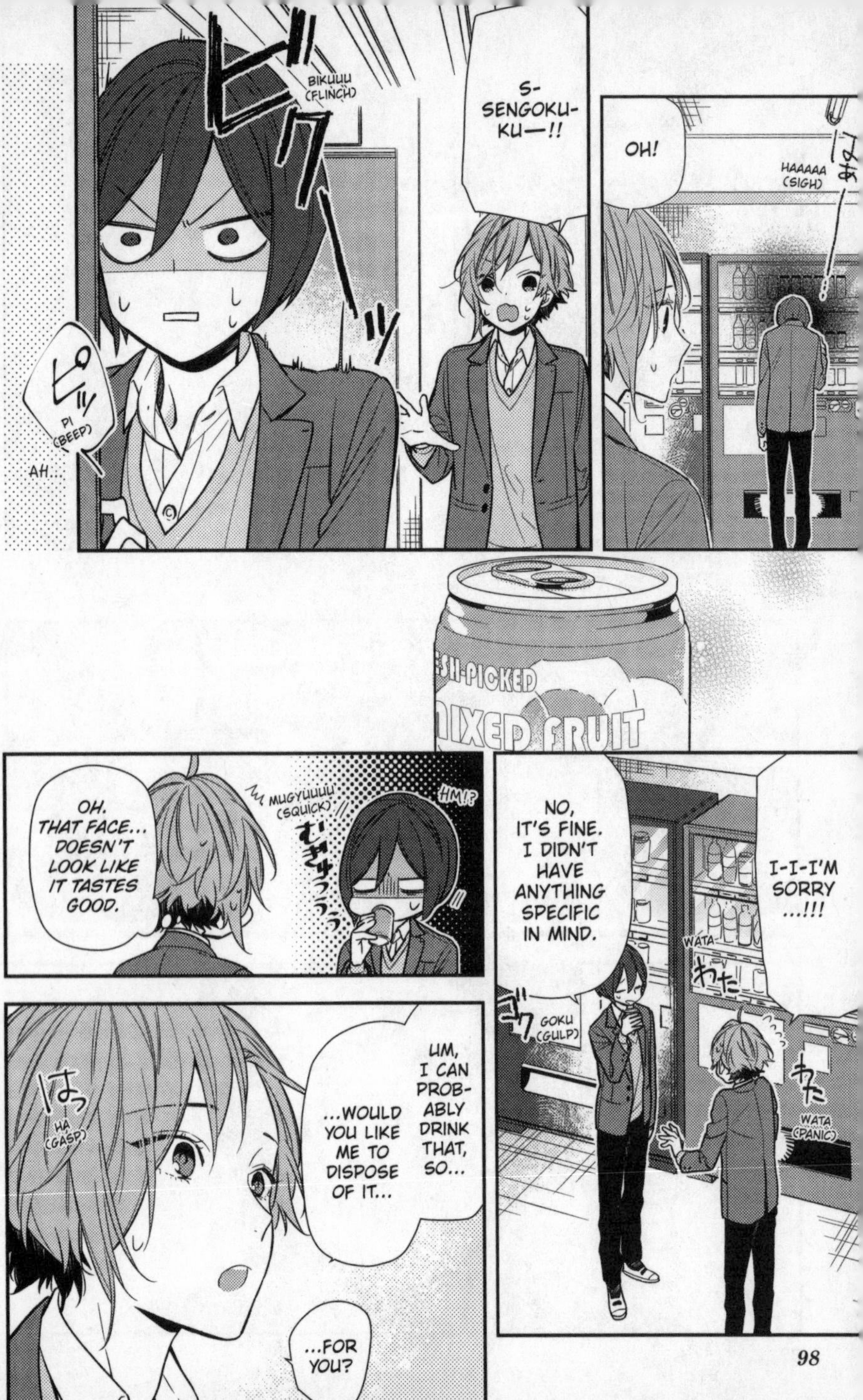
OH!
HAAAAA (SIGH)
はぁー
S-SENGOKUKU—!!
BIKUUU (FLINCH)
ビクーッ
ピッ
PI (BEEP)
AH...
ESH-PICKED
IXED FRUIT
I-I-I'M SORRY ...!!!
NO, IT'S FINE. I DIDN'T HAVE ANYTHING SPECIFIC IN MIND.
WATA
わた
わた
WATA (PANIC)
GOKU (GULP)
HM!?
MUGYUUUU (SQUICK)
OH. THAT FACE... DOESN'T LOOK LIKE IT TASTES GOOD.
UM, I CAN PROBABLY DRINK THAT, SO...
...WOULD YOU LIKE ME TO DISPOSE OF IT...
はっ
HA (GASP)
...FOR YOU?

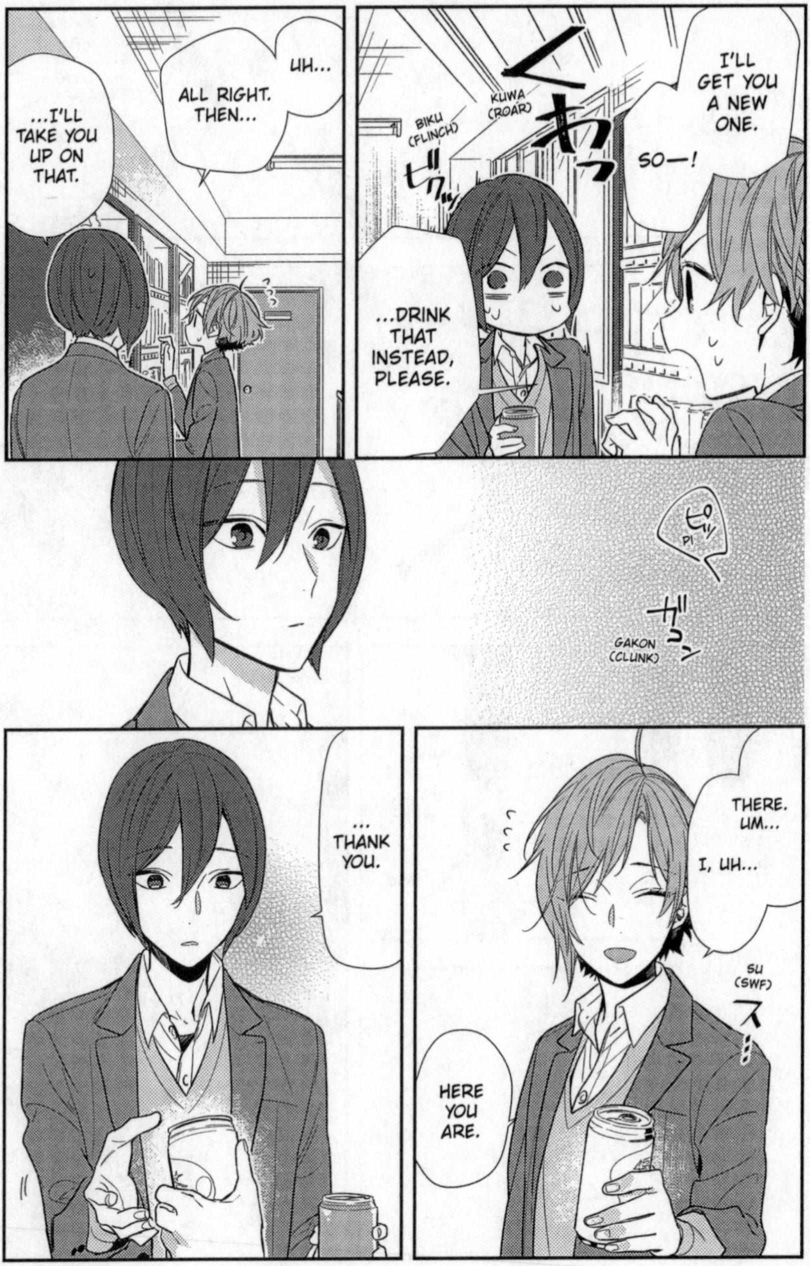
I'LL GET YOU A NEW ONE.
SO—!
KUWA (ROAR)
BIKU (FLINCH)
...DRINK THAT INSTEAD, PLEASE.
UH...
ALL RIGHT. THEN...
...I'LL TAKE YOU UP ON THAT.
PI
GAKON (CLUNK)
THERE. UM... I, UH...
SU (SWF)
HERE YOU ARE.
... THANK YOU.

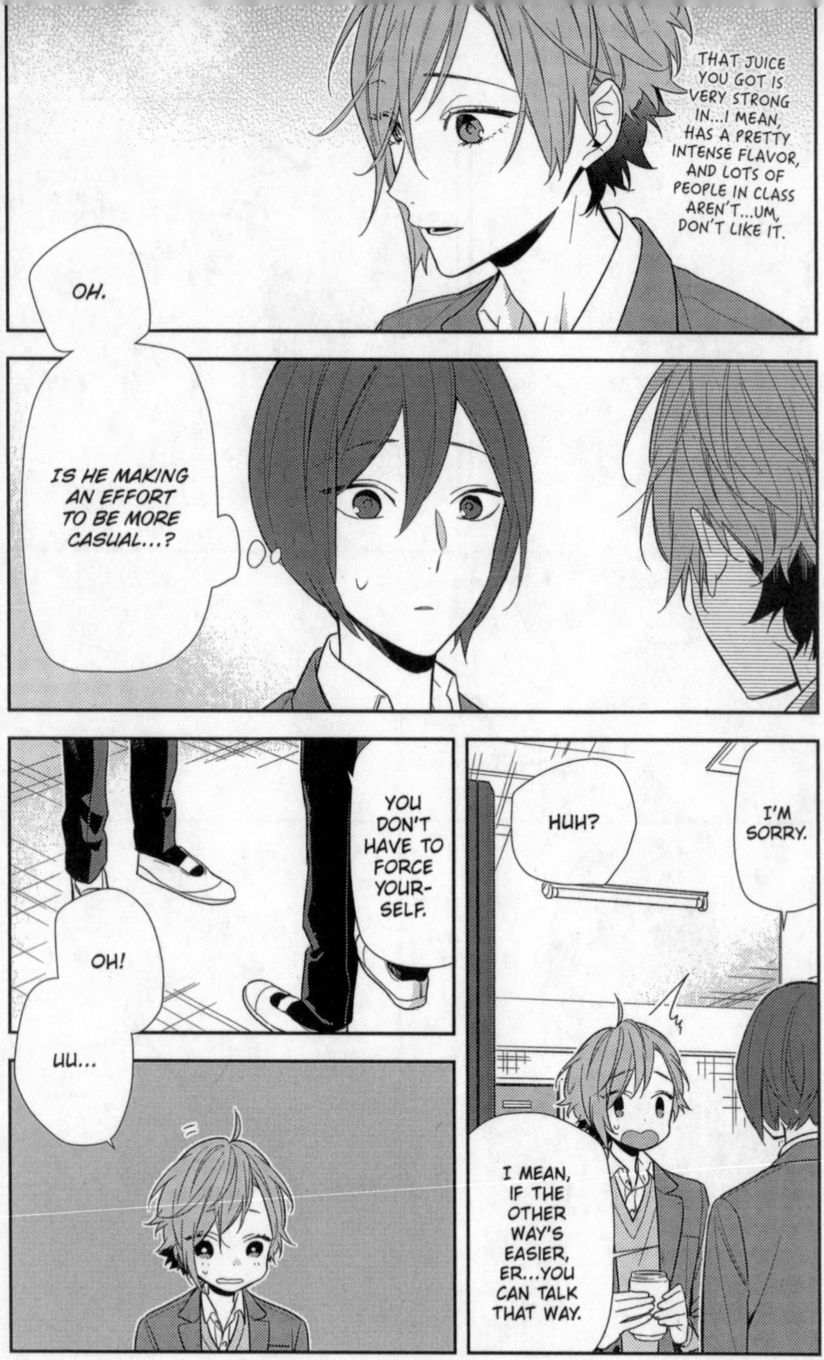
THAT JUICE YOU GOT IS VERY STRONG IN...I MEAN, HAS A PRETTY INTENSE FLAVOR, AND LOTS OF PEOPLE IN CLASS AREN'T...UM, DON'T LIKE IT.
OH.
IS HE MAKING AN EFFORT TO BE MORE CASUAL...?
I'M SORRY.
HUH?
I MEAN, IF THE OTHER WAY'S EASIER, ER...YOU CAN TALK THAT WAY.
YOU DON'T HAVE TO FORCE YOUR-SELF.
OH!
UU...

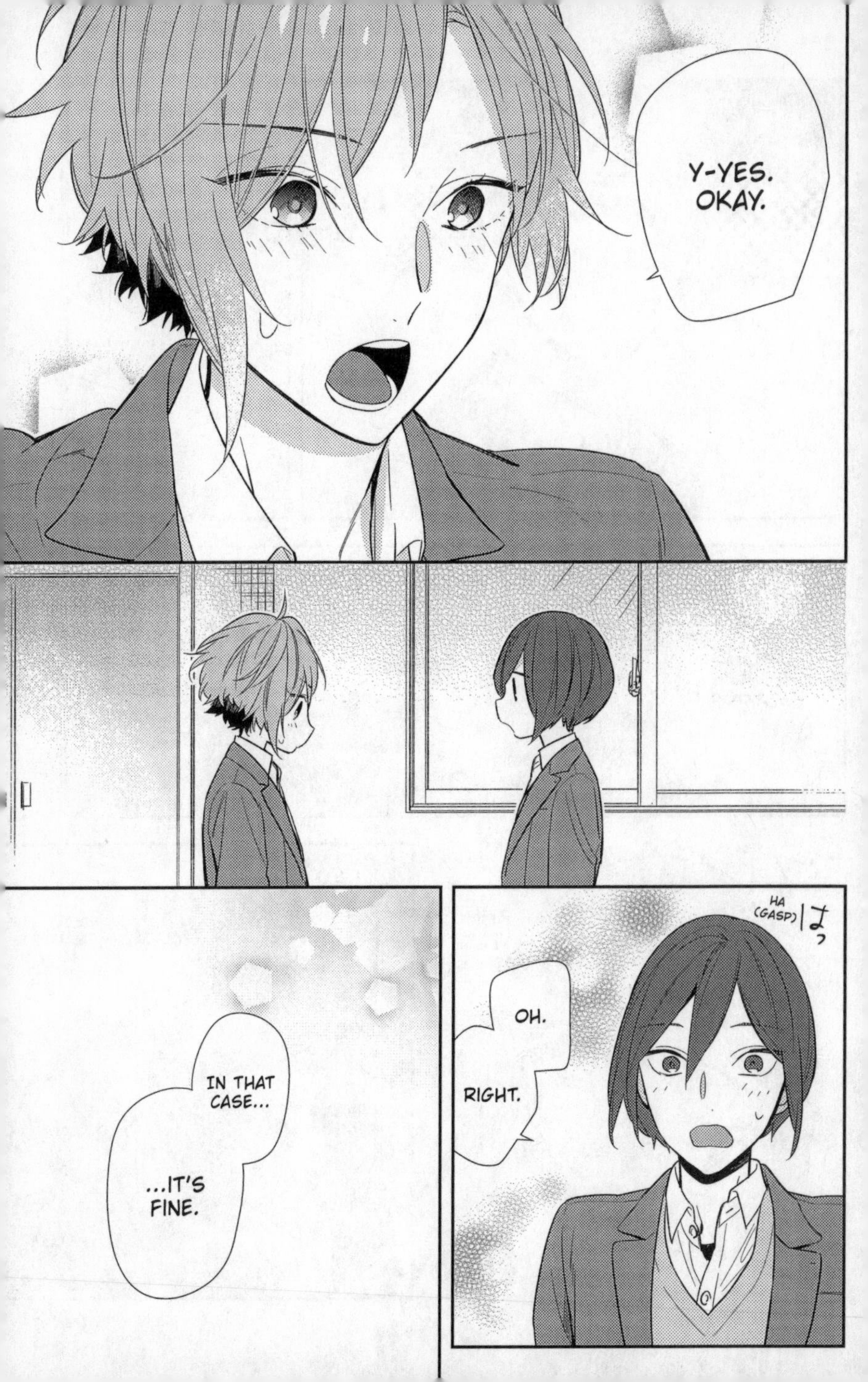
Y-YES. OKAY.
HA (GASP) はっ
OH.
RIGHT.
IN THAT CASE...
...IT'S FINE.

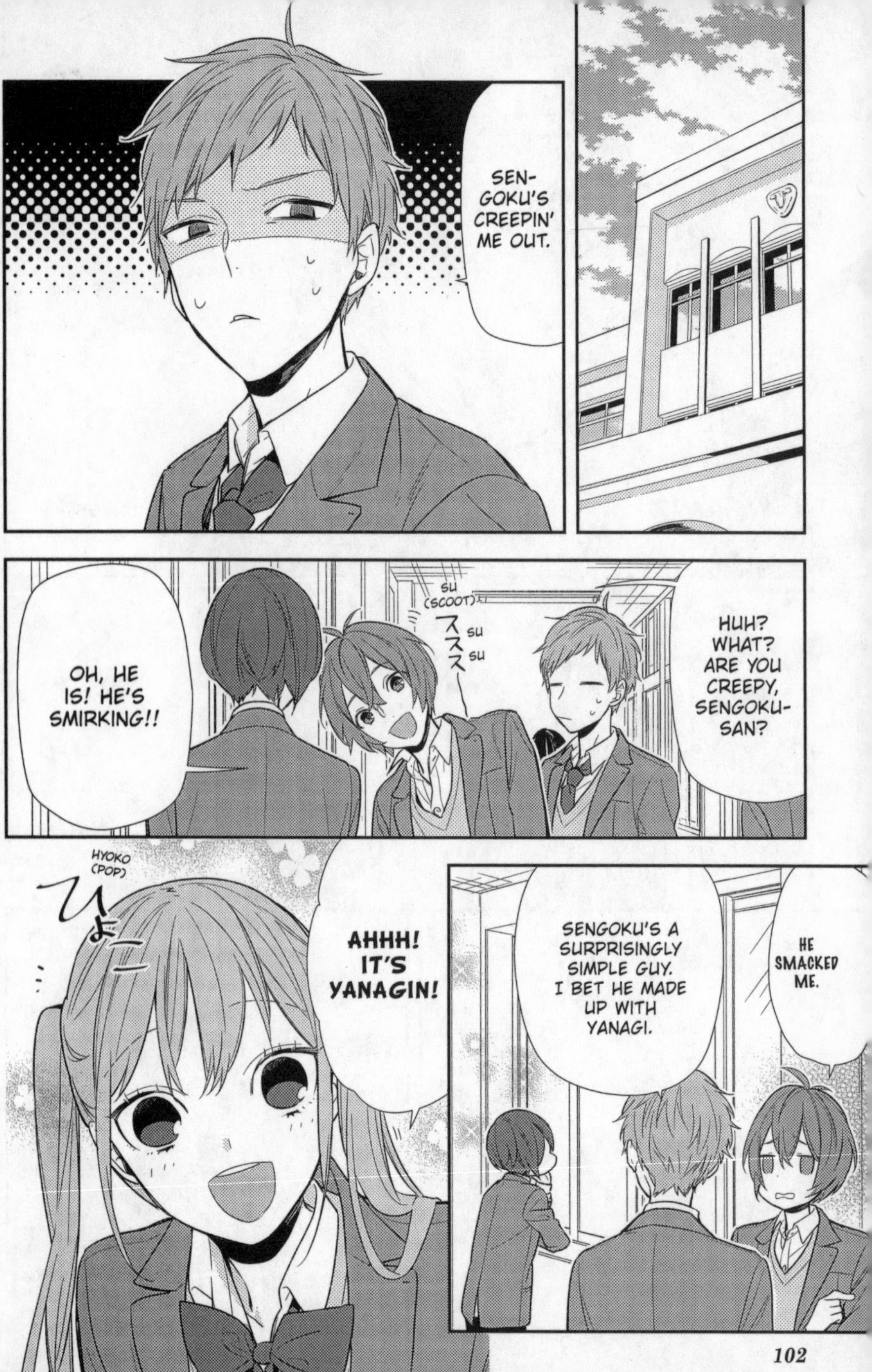
SEN-GOKU'S CREEPIN' ME OUT.
HUH? WHAT? ARE YOU CREEPY, SENGOKU-SAN?
SU (SCOOT)
ススス
SU SU
OH, HE IS! HE'S SMIRKING!!
HE SMACKED ME.
SENGOKU'S A SURPRISINGLY SIMPLE GUY. I BET HE MADE UP WITH YANAGI.
AHHH! IT'S YANAGIN!
HYOKO (POP)
ひょこ

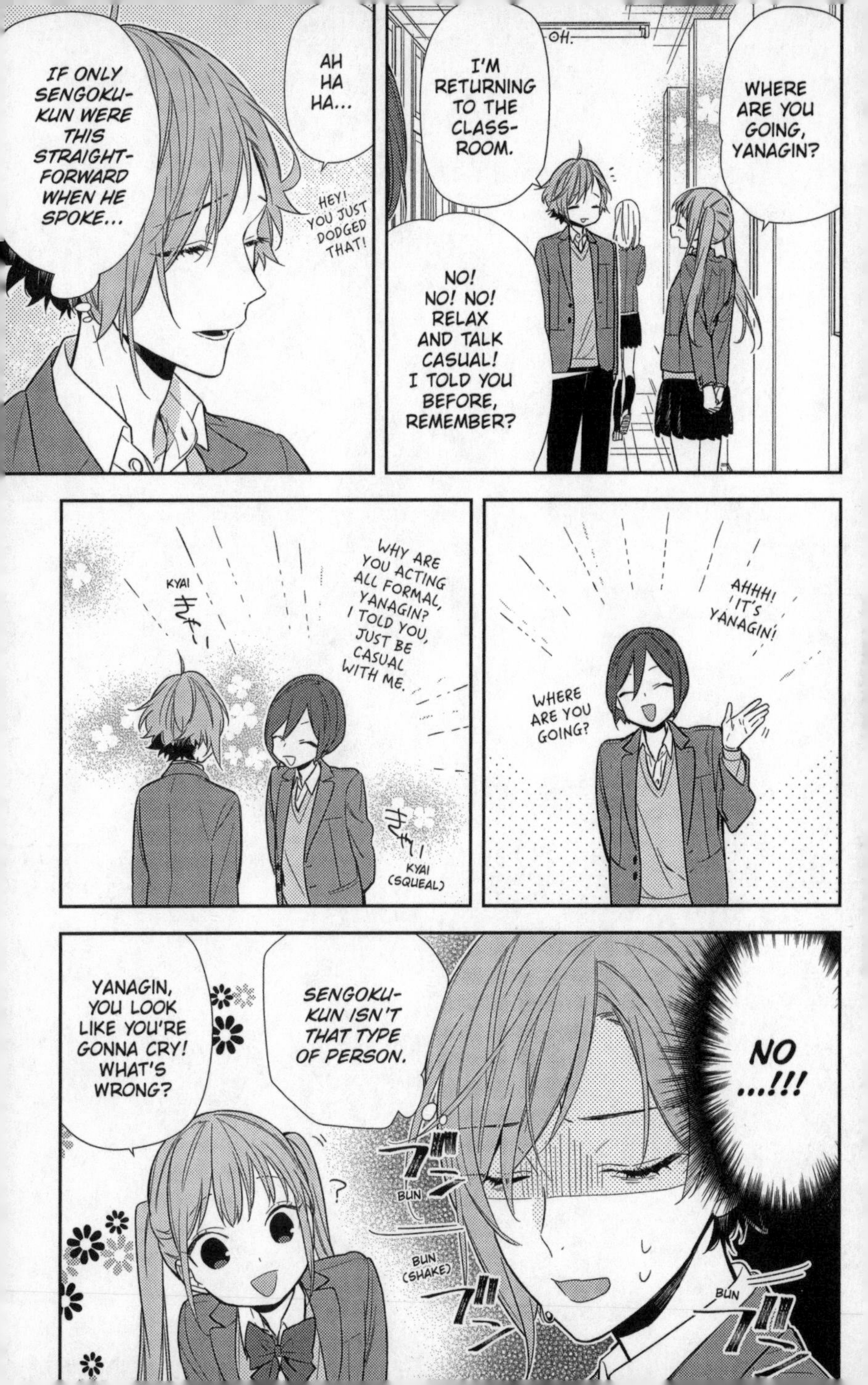

WHERE ARE YOU GOING, YANAGIN?
OH.
I'M RETURNING TO THE CLASS-ROOM.
NO! NO! NO! RELAX AND TALK CASUAL! I TOLD YOU BEFORE, REMEMBER?
AH HA HA...
HEY! YOU JUST DODGED THAT!
IF ONLY SENGOKU-KUN WERE THIS STRAIGHT-FORWARD WHEN HE SPOKE...
AHHH! IT'S YANAGIN!
WHERE ARE YOU GOING?
WHY ARE YOU ACTING ALL FORMAL, YANAGIN? I TOLD YOU, JUST BE CASUAL WITH ME.
KYAI
KYAI (SQUEAL)
NO ...!!!
BUN
SENGOKU-KUN ISN'T THAT TYPE OF PERSON.
YANAGIN, YOU LOOK LIKE YOU'RE GONNA CRY! WHAT'S WRONG?
BUN
BUN (SHAKE)

HORIMIYA

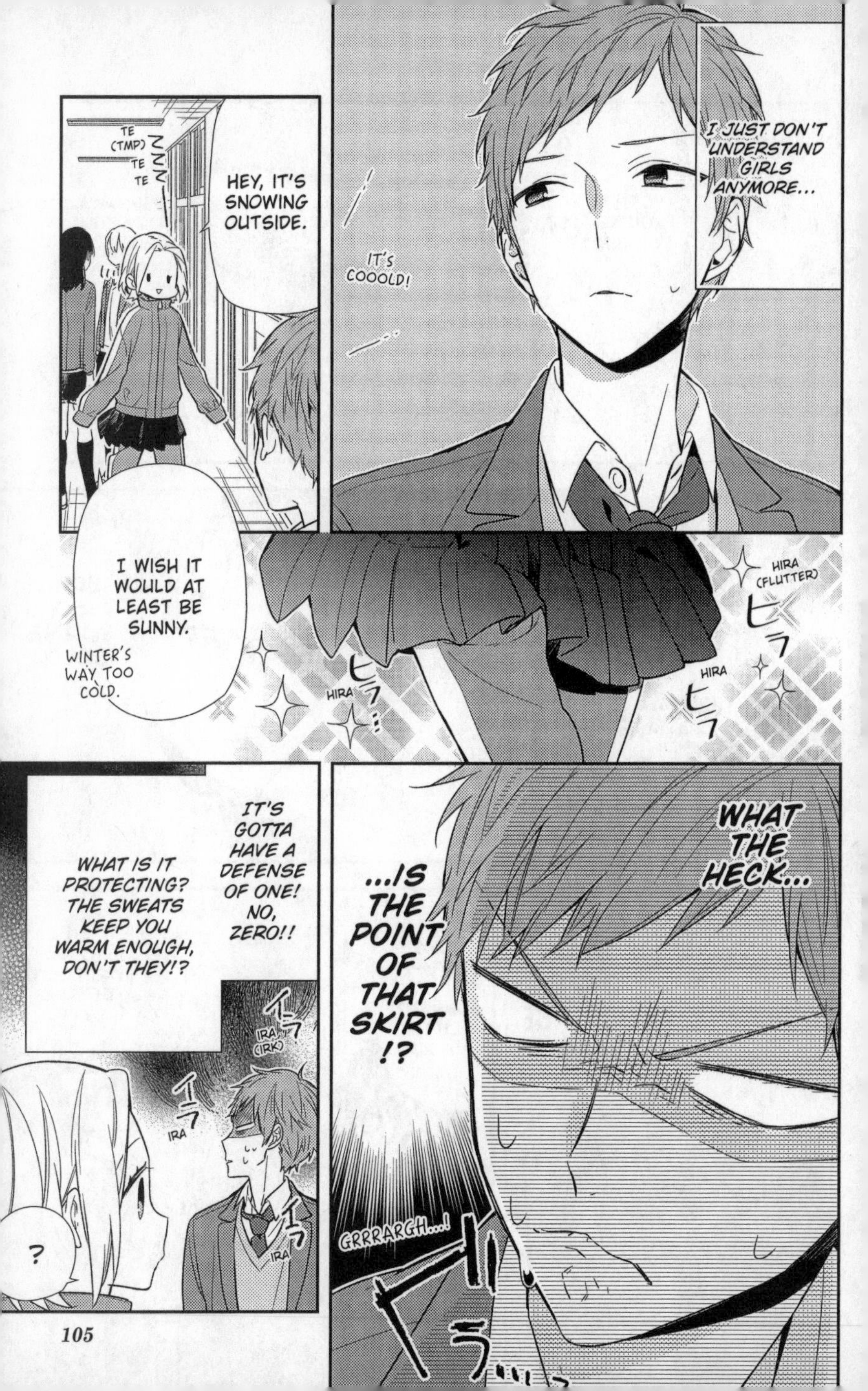
I JUST DON'T UNDERSTAND GIRLS ANYMORE...
IT'S COOOLD!
HEY, IT'S SNOWING OUTSIDE.
TE (TMP) TE TE
HIRA (FLUTTER)
HIRA
HIRA
I WISH IT WOULD AT LEAST BE SUNNY.
WINTER'S WAY TOO COLD.
WHAT THE HECK...
...IS THE POINT OF THAT SKIRT!?
GRRRARGH...!
IT'S GOTTA HAVE A DEFENSE OF ONE! NO, ZERO!!
WHAT IS IT PROTECTING? THE SWEATS KEEP YOU WARM ENOUGH, DON'T THEY!?
IRA (IRK)
IRA
IRA
?

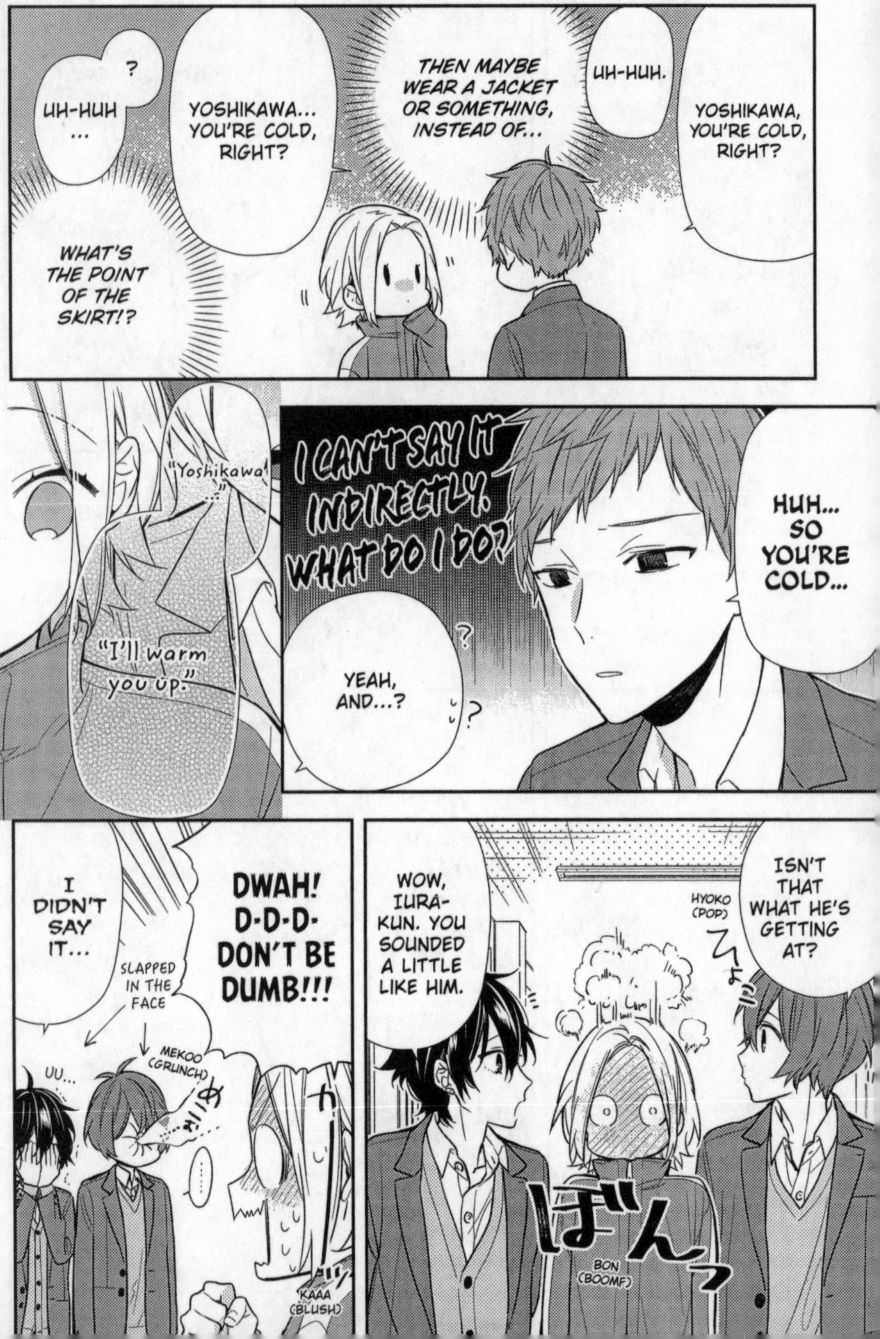
YOSHIKAWA, YOU'RE COLD, RIGHT?
UH-HUH.
THEN MAYBE WEAR A JACKET OR SOMETHING, INSTEAD OF...
YOSHIKAWA... YOU'RE COLD, RIGHT?
?
UH-HUH ...
WHAT'S THE POINT OF THE SKIRT!?
HUH... SO YOU'RE COLD...
I CAN'T SAY IT INDIRECTLY. WHAT DO I DO?
YEAH, AND...?
"Yoshikawa"
"I'll warm you up."
ISN'T THAT WHAT HE'S GETTING AT?
HYOKO (POP)
WOW, IURA-KUN. YOU SOUNDED A LITTLE LIKE HIM.
ばんっ
BON (BOOMF)
DWAH! D-D-D-DON'T BE DUMB!!!
I DIDN'T SAY IT...
SLAPPED IN THE FACE
MEKOO (GRUNCH)
UU...
KAAA (BLUSH)

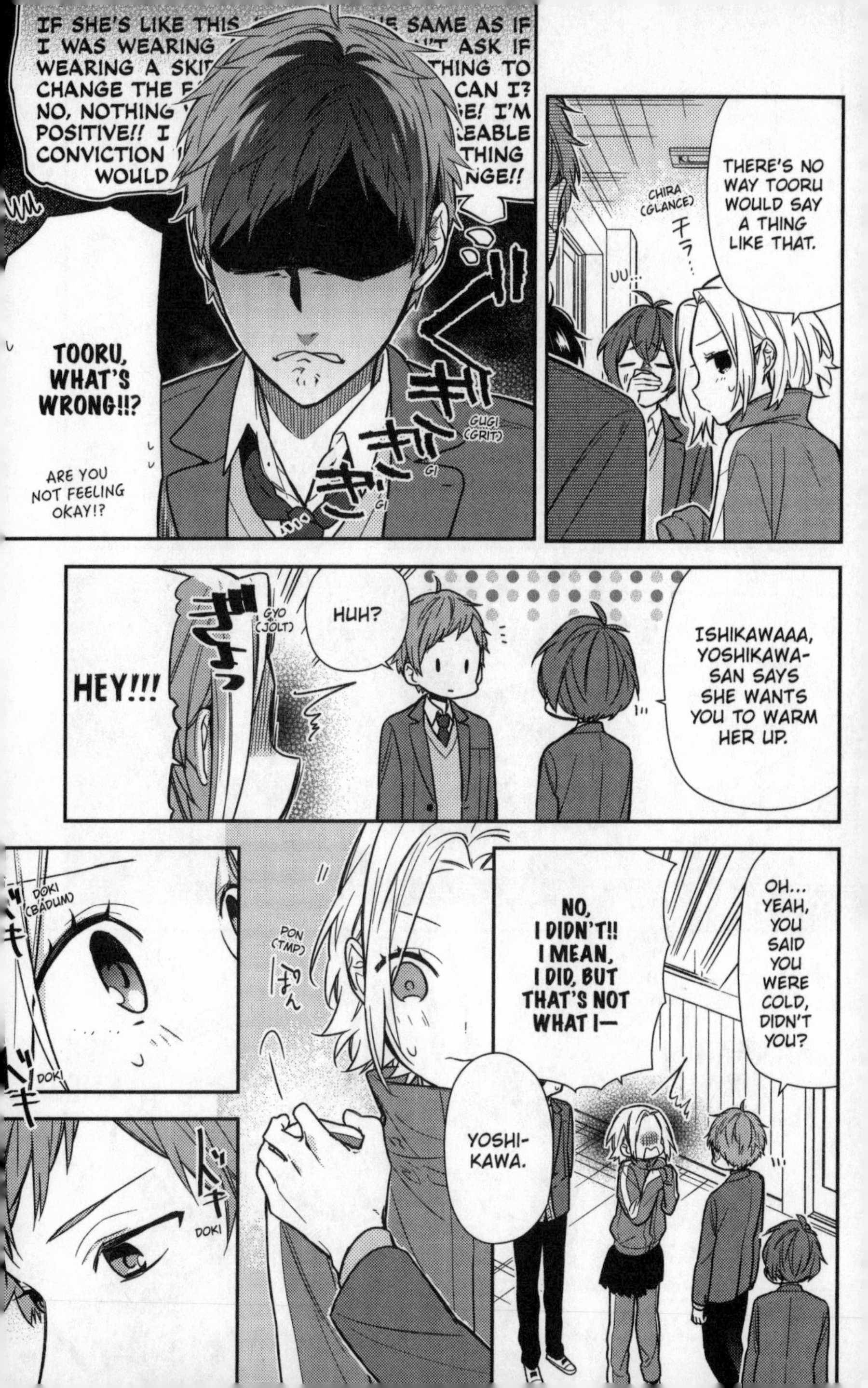
THERE'S NO WAY TOORU WOULD SAY A THING LIKE THAT.
CHIRA (GLANCE)
UU...
IF SHE'S LIKE THIS ... SAME AS IF I WAS WEARING ... 'T ASK IF WEARING A SKI ... THING TO CHANGE THE ... CAN I? NO, NOTHING ... GE! I'M POSITIVE!! I ... EABLE CONVICTION ... THING WOULD ... NGE!!
TOORU, WHAT'S WRONG!!?
ARE YOU NOT FEELING OKAY!?
GUGI (GRIT)
GI
GI
ISHIKAWAAA, YOSHIKAWA-SAN SAYS SHE WANTS YOU TO WARM HER UP.
HUH?
GYO (JOLT)
HEY!!!
OH... YEAH, YOU SAID YOU WERE COLD, DIDN'T YOU?
NO, I DIDN'T!! I MEAN, I DID, BUT THAT'S NOT WHAT I—
PON (TMP)
YOSHI-KAWA.
DOKI (BADUM)
DOKI
DOKI

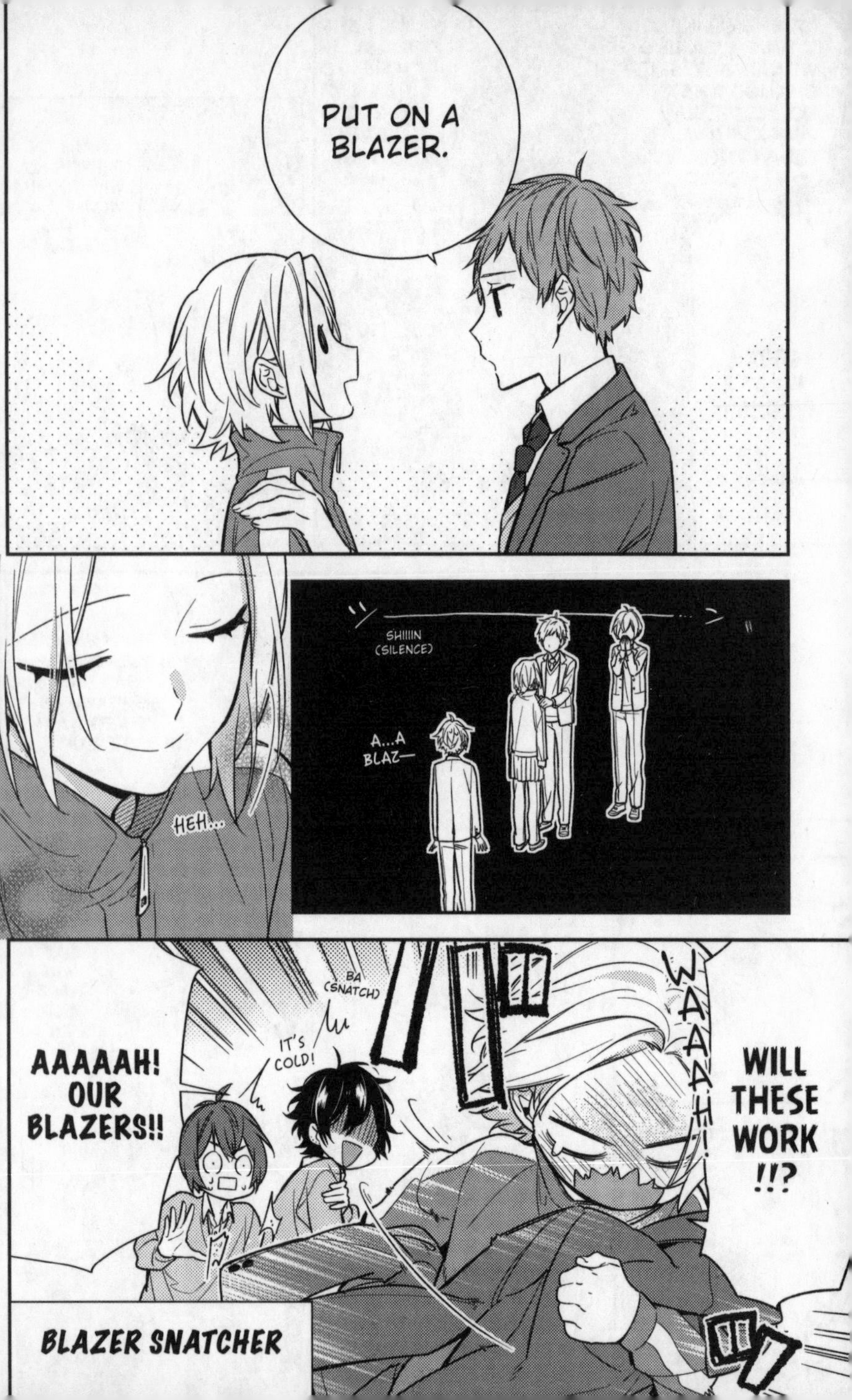
PUT ON A BLAZER.
SHIIIN (SILENCE)
A...A BLAZ—
HEH...
WAAAH!
WILL THESE WORK!!?
BA (SNATCH)
IT'S COLD!
AAAAAH! OUR BLAZERS!!
BLAZER SNATCHER

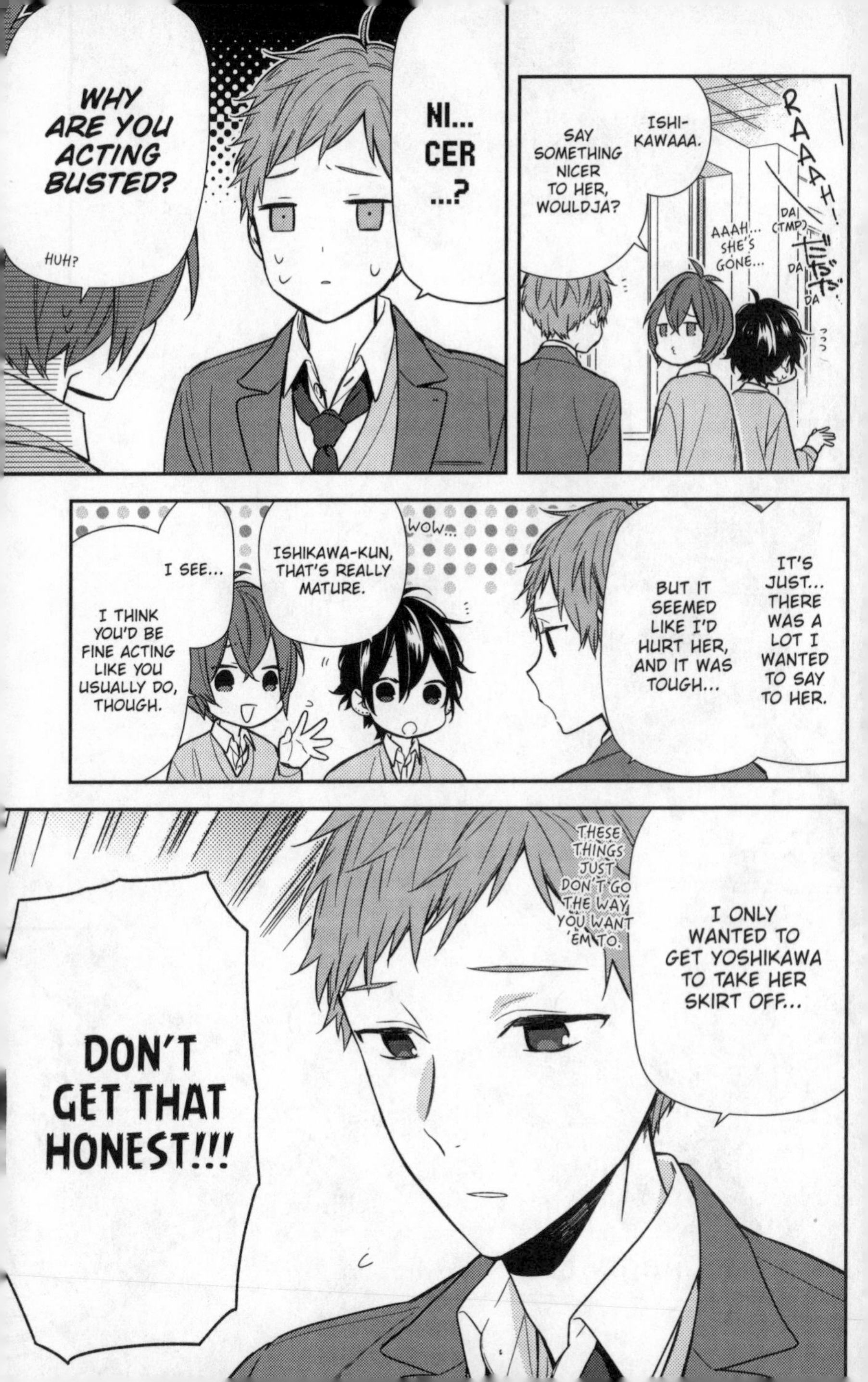
RAAAAH!
ISHI-KAWAAA.
SAY SOMETHING NICER TO HER, WOULDJA?
AAAH... SHE'S GONE...
DA (TMP)
DA
DA
NI... CER ...?
WHY ARE YOU ACTING BUSTED?
HUH?
IT'S JUST... THERE WAS A LOT I WANTED TO SAY TO HER.
BUT IT SEEMED LIKE I'D HURT HER, AND IT WAS TOUGH...
WOW...
ISHIKAWA-KUN, THAT'S REALLY MATURE.
I SEE...
I THINK YOU'D BE FINE ACTING LIKE YOU USUALLY DO, THOUGH.
I ONLY WANTED TO GET YOSHIKAWA TO TAKE HER SKIRT OFF...
THESE THINGS JUST DON'T GO THE WAY YOU WANT 'EM TO.
DON'T GET THAT HONEST!!!

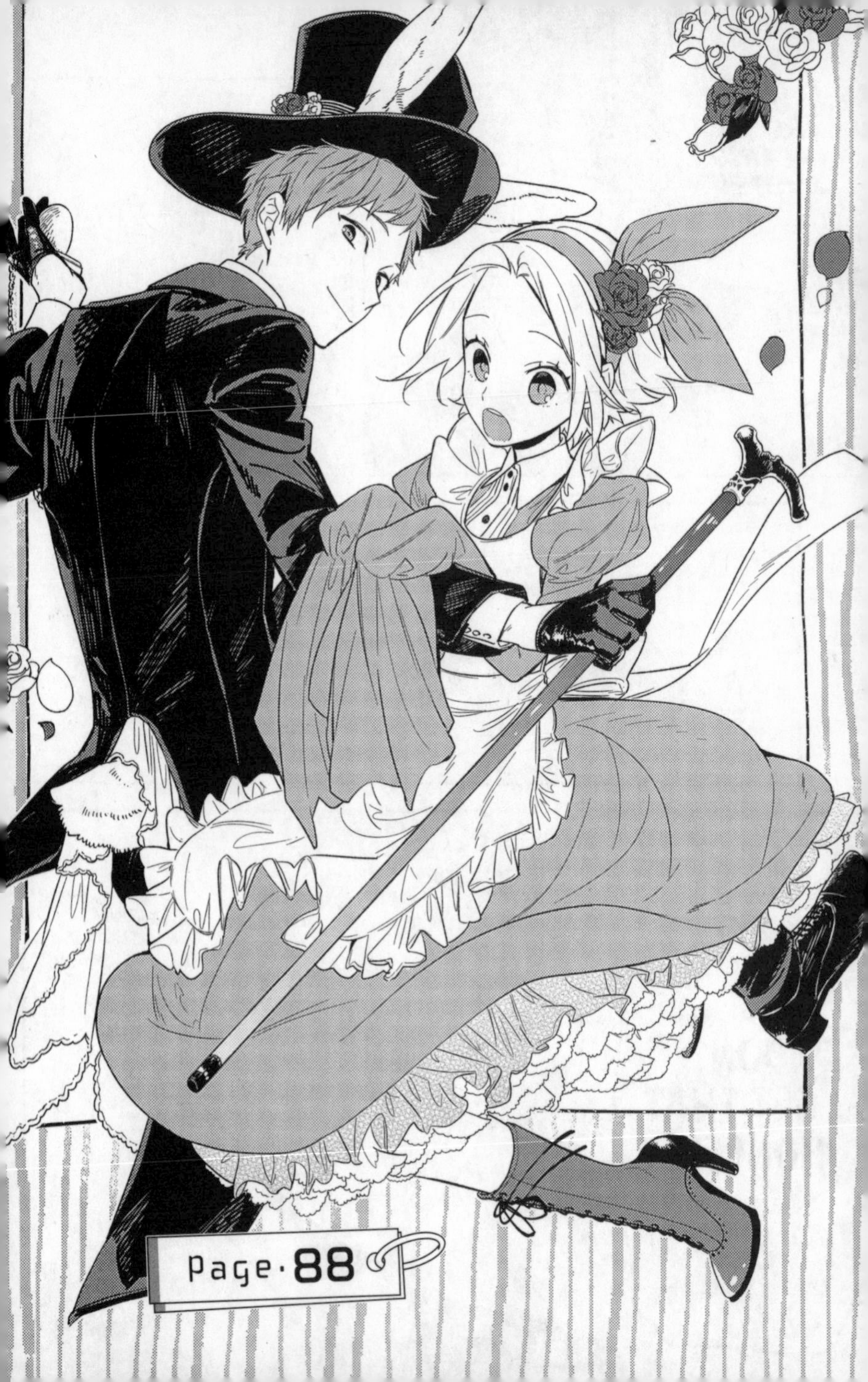
page・88

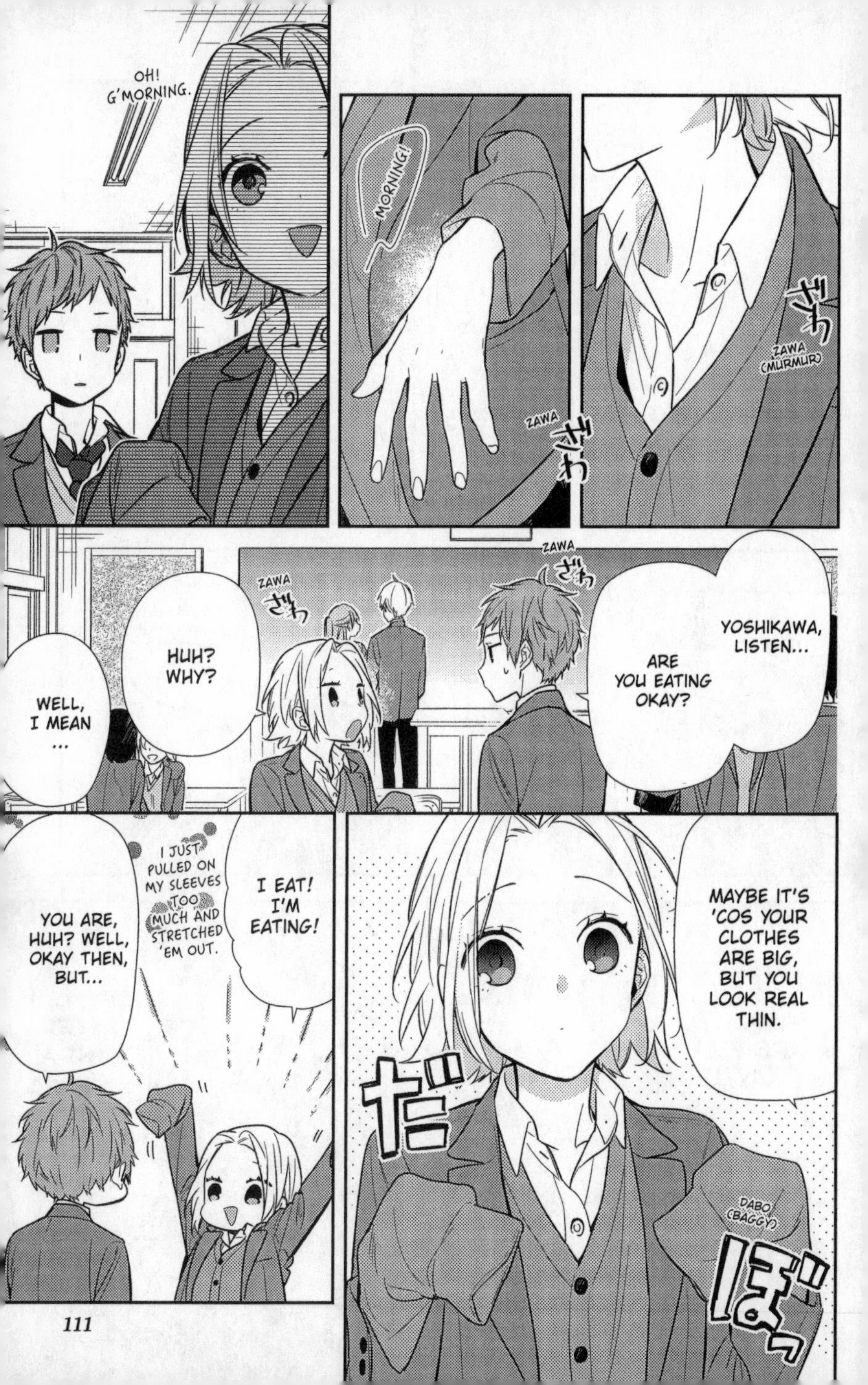
ZAWA (MURMUR)
MORNING!
ZAWA
OH! G'MORNING.
YOSHIKAWA, LISTEN...
ARE YOU EATING OKAY?
ZAWA
ZAWA
HUH? WHY?
WELL, I MEAN ...
MAYBE IT'S 'COS YOUR CLOTHES ARE BIG, BUT YOU LOOK REAL THIN.
DABO (BAGGY)
I EAT! I'M EATING!
I JUST PULLED ON MY SLEEVES TOO MUCH AND STRETCHED 'EM OUT.
YOU ARE, HUH? WELL, OKAY THEN, BUT...

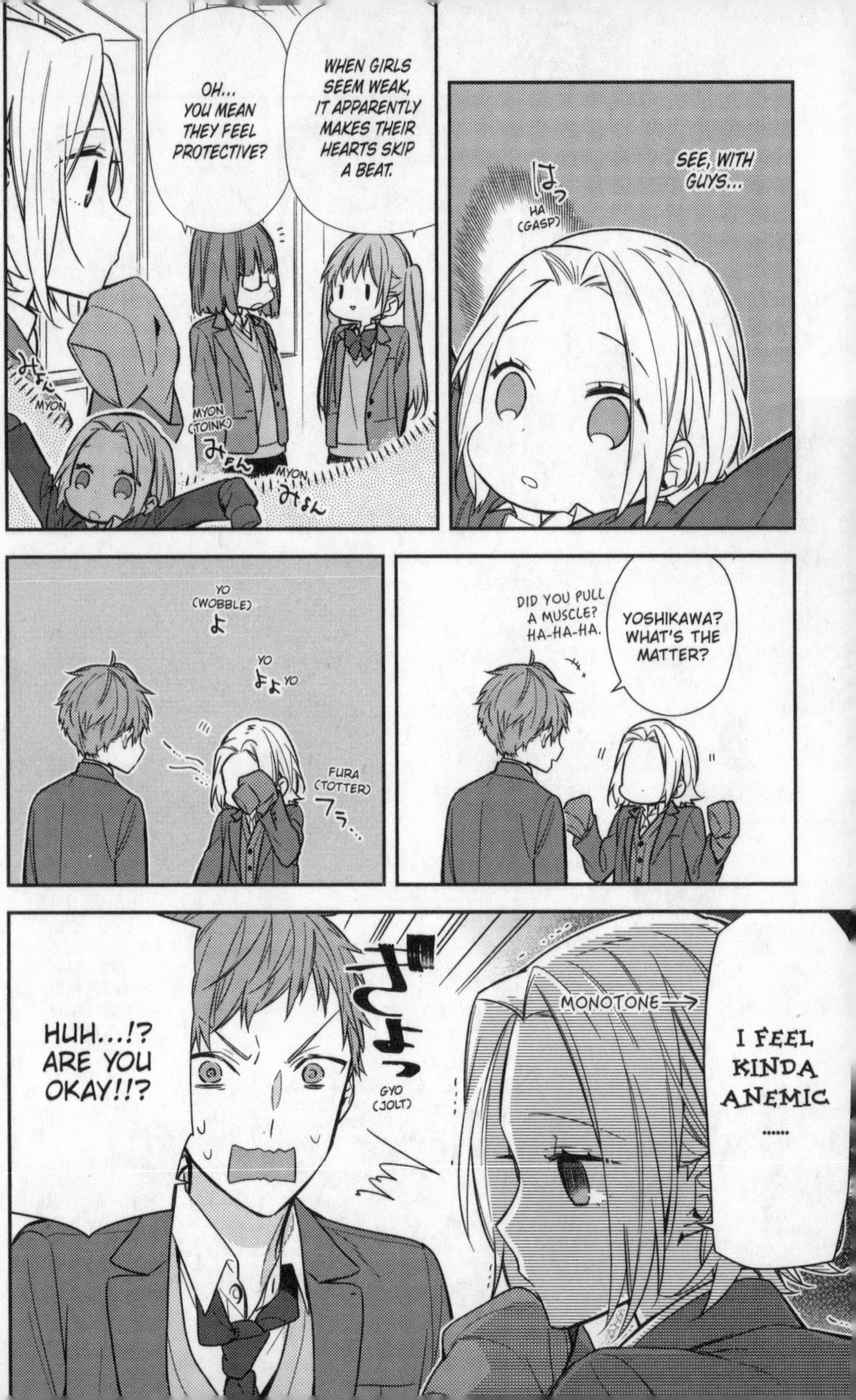
SEE, WITH GUYS...
はっ
HA (GASP)
WHEN GIRLS SEEM WEAK, IT APPARENTLY MAKES THEIR HEARTS SKIP A BEAT.
OH... YOU MEAN THEY FEEL PROTECTIVE?
みょん
MYON
MYON (TOINK)
みょん
MYON
みょん
YOSHIKAWA? WHAT'S THE MATTER?
DID YOU PULL A MUSCLE? HA-HA-HA.
YO (WOBBLE)
よ
YO
よよ
YO
FURA (TOTTER)
フラ...
I FEEL KINDA ANEMIC ......
MONOTONE→
ぎょっ
GYO (JOLT)
HUH...!? ARE YOU OKAY!!?

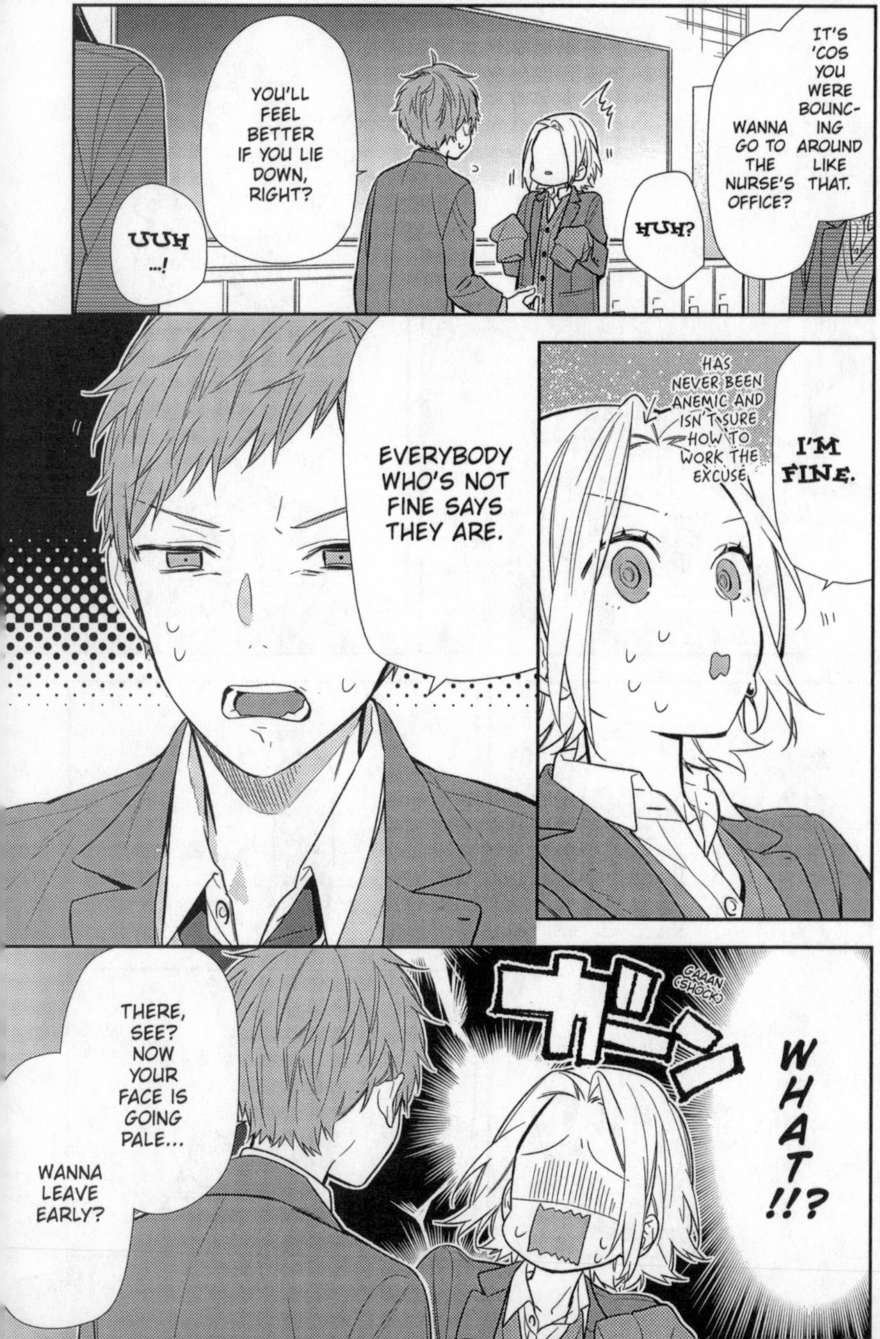
IT'S 'COS YOU WERE BOUNC-ING AROUND LIKE THAT.
WANNA GO TO THE NURSE'S OFFICE?
HUH?
YOU'LL FEEL BETTER IF YOU LIE DOWN, RIGHT?
UUH ...!
I'M FINE.
HAS NEVER BEEN ANEMIC AND ISN'T SURE HOW TO WORK THE EXCUSE
EVERYBODY WHO'S NOT FINE SAYS THEY ARE.
GAAAN (SHOCK)
WHAT!!?
THERE, SEE? NOW YOUR FACE IS GOING PALE...
WANNA LEAVE EARLY?

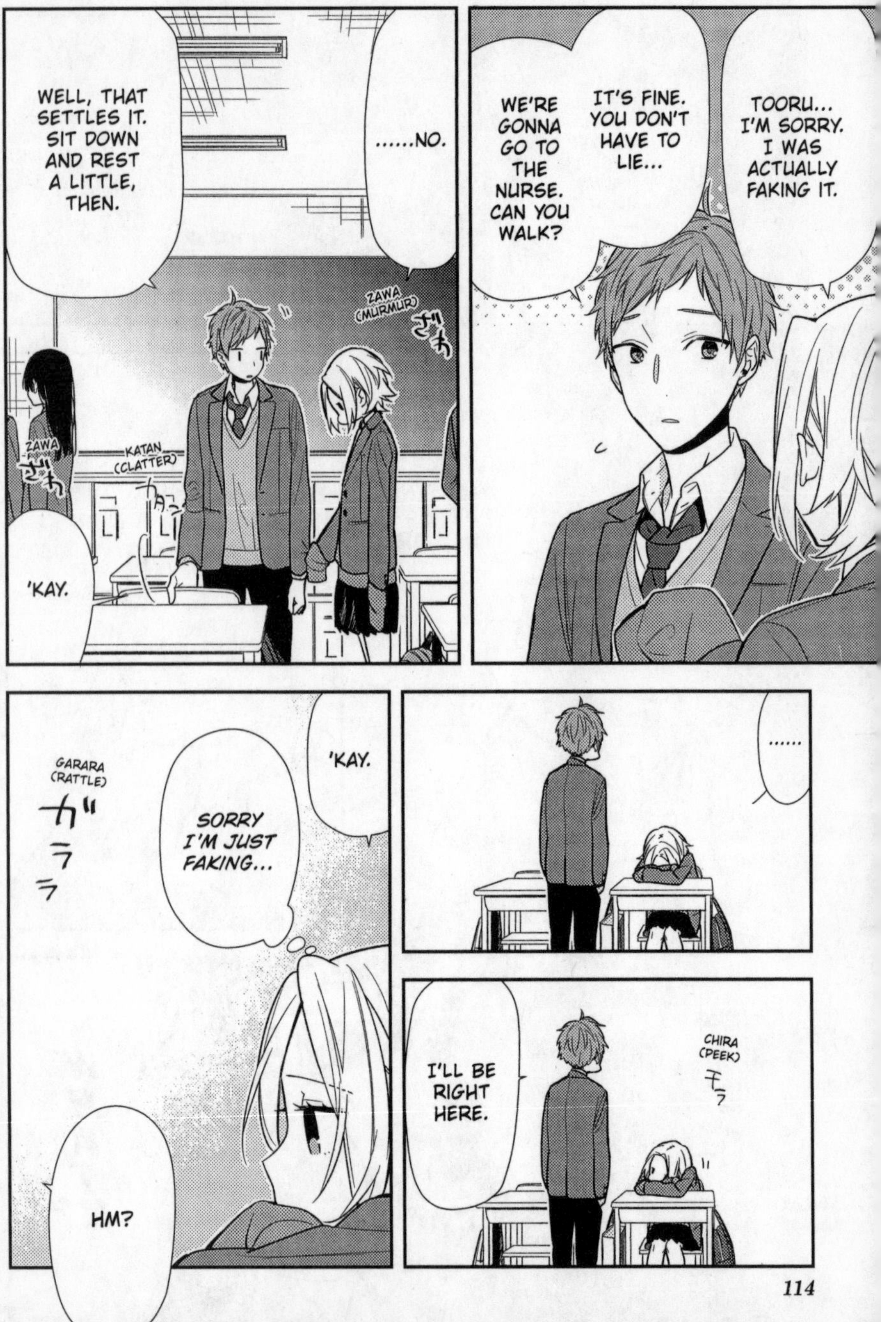
TOORU... I'M SORRY. I WAS ACTUALLY FAKING IT.
IT'S FINE. YOU DON'T HAVE TO LIE...
WE'RE GONNA GO TO THE NURSE. CAN YOU WALK?
......NO.
WELL, THAT SETTLES IT. SIT DOWN AND REST A LITTLE, THEN.
ZAWA (MURMUR)
KATAN (CLATTER)
ZAWA
'KAY.
......
CHIRA (PEEK)
I'LL BE RIGHT HERE.
'KAY.
SORRY I'M JUST FAKING...
GARARA (RATTLE)
HM?

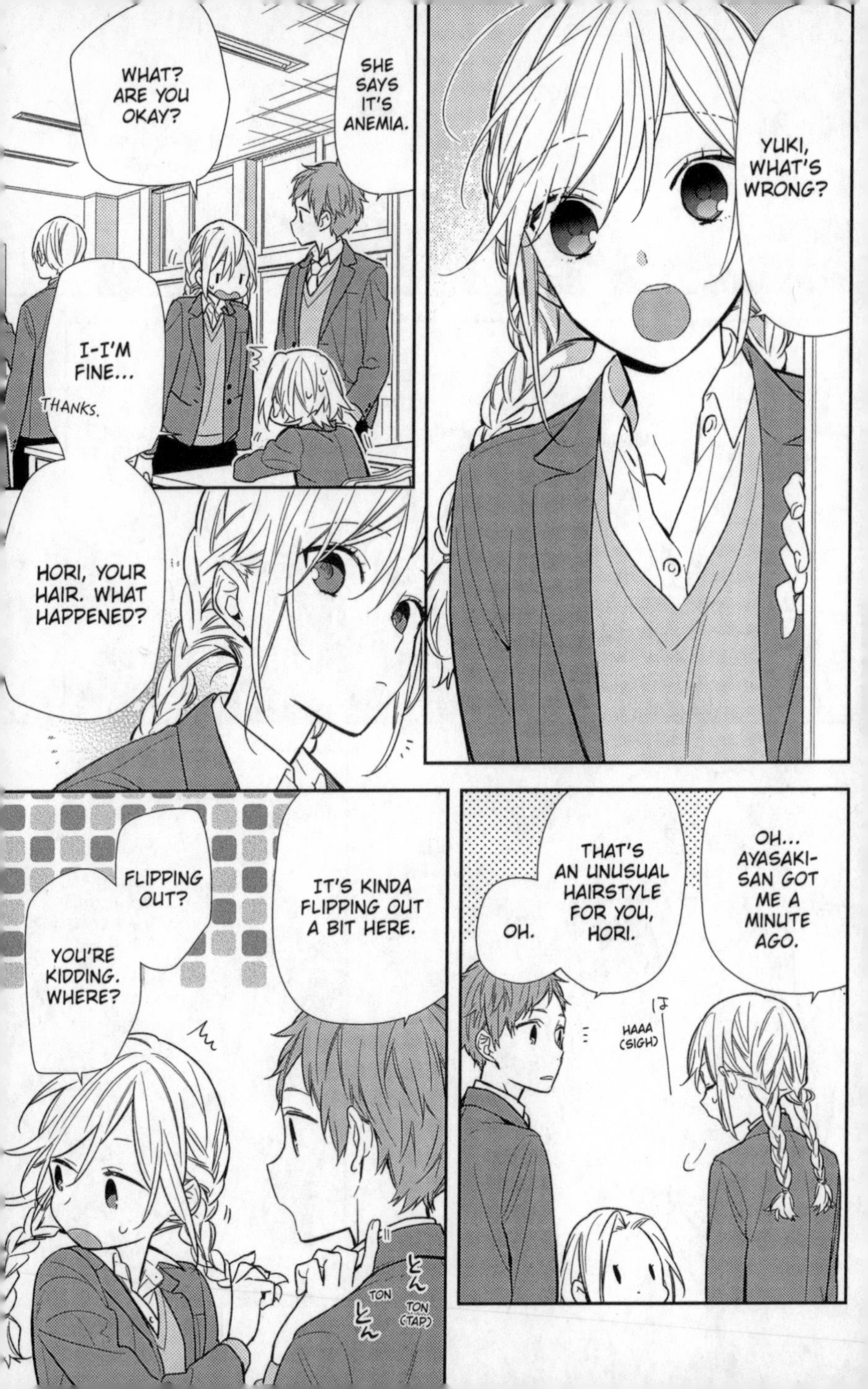
YUKI, WHAT'S WRONG?
SHE SAYS IT'S ANEMIA.
WHAT? ARE YOU OKAY?
I-I'M FINE...
THANKS.
HORI, YOUR HAIR. WHAT HAPPENED?
OH... AYASAKI-SAN GOT ME A MINUTE AGO.
THAT'S AN UNUSUAL HAIRSTYLE FOR YOU, HORI.
OH.
は
HAAA (SIGH)
IT'S KINDA FLIPPING OUT A BIT HERE.
FLIPPING OUT?
YOU'RE KIDDING. WHERE?
とん TON
とん TON (TAP)

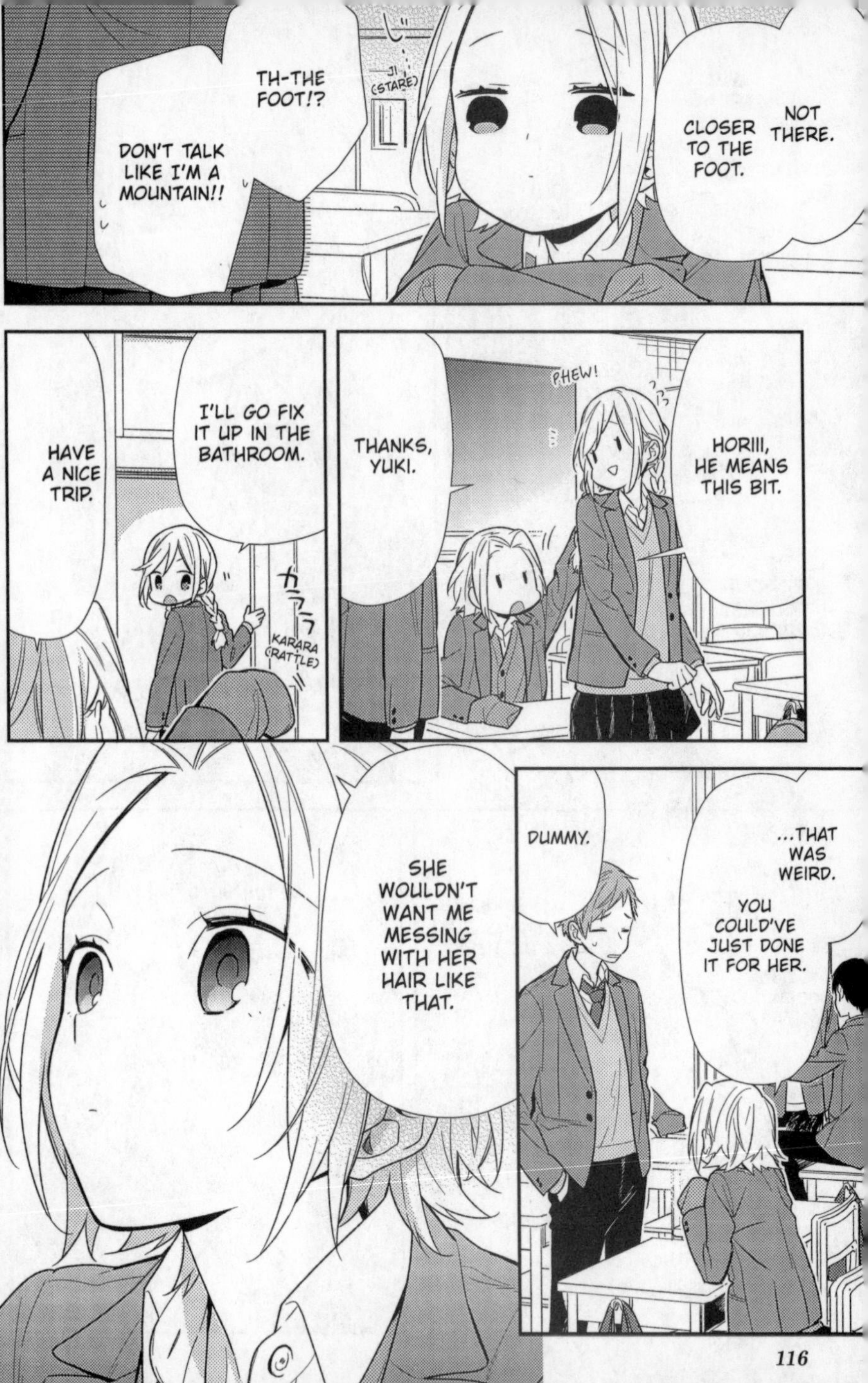

NOT THERE.
CLOSER TO THE FOOT.
JI (STARE)
TH-THE FOOT!?
DON'T TALK LIKE I'M A MOUNTAIN!!
HORIII, HE MEANS THIS BIT.
PHEW!
THANKS, YUKI.
I'LL GO FIX IT UP IN THE BATHROOM.
KARARA (RATTLE)
HAVE A NICE TRIP.
...THAT WAS WEIRD.
YOU COULD'VE JUST DONE IT FOR HER.
DUMMY.
SHE WOULDN'T WANT ME MESSING WITH HER HAIR LIKE THAT.

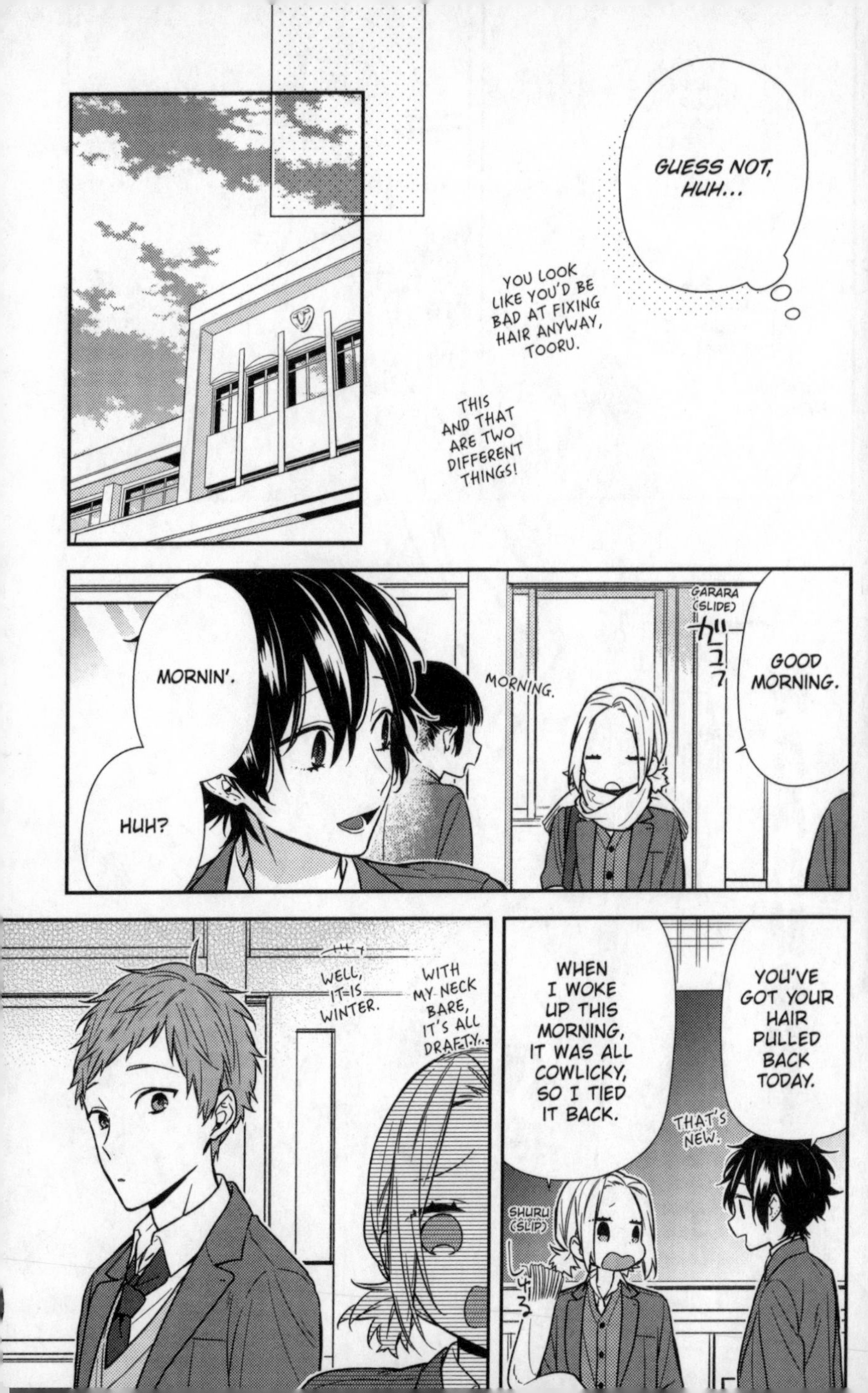
GUESS NOT, HUH...
YOU LOOK LIKE YOU'D BE BAD AT FIXING HAIR ANYWAY, TOORU.
THIS AND THAT ARE TWO DIFFERENT THINGS!
GARARA (SLIDE)
GOOD MORNING.
MORNING.
MORNIN'.
HUH?
YOU'VE GOT YOUR HAIR PULLED BACK TODAY.
THAT'S NEW.
WHEN I WOKE UP THIS MORNING, IT WAS ALL COWLICKY, SO I TIED IT BACK.
SHURU (SLIP)
WITH MY NECK BARE, IT'S ALL DRAFTY...
WELL, IT IS WINTER.

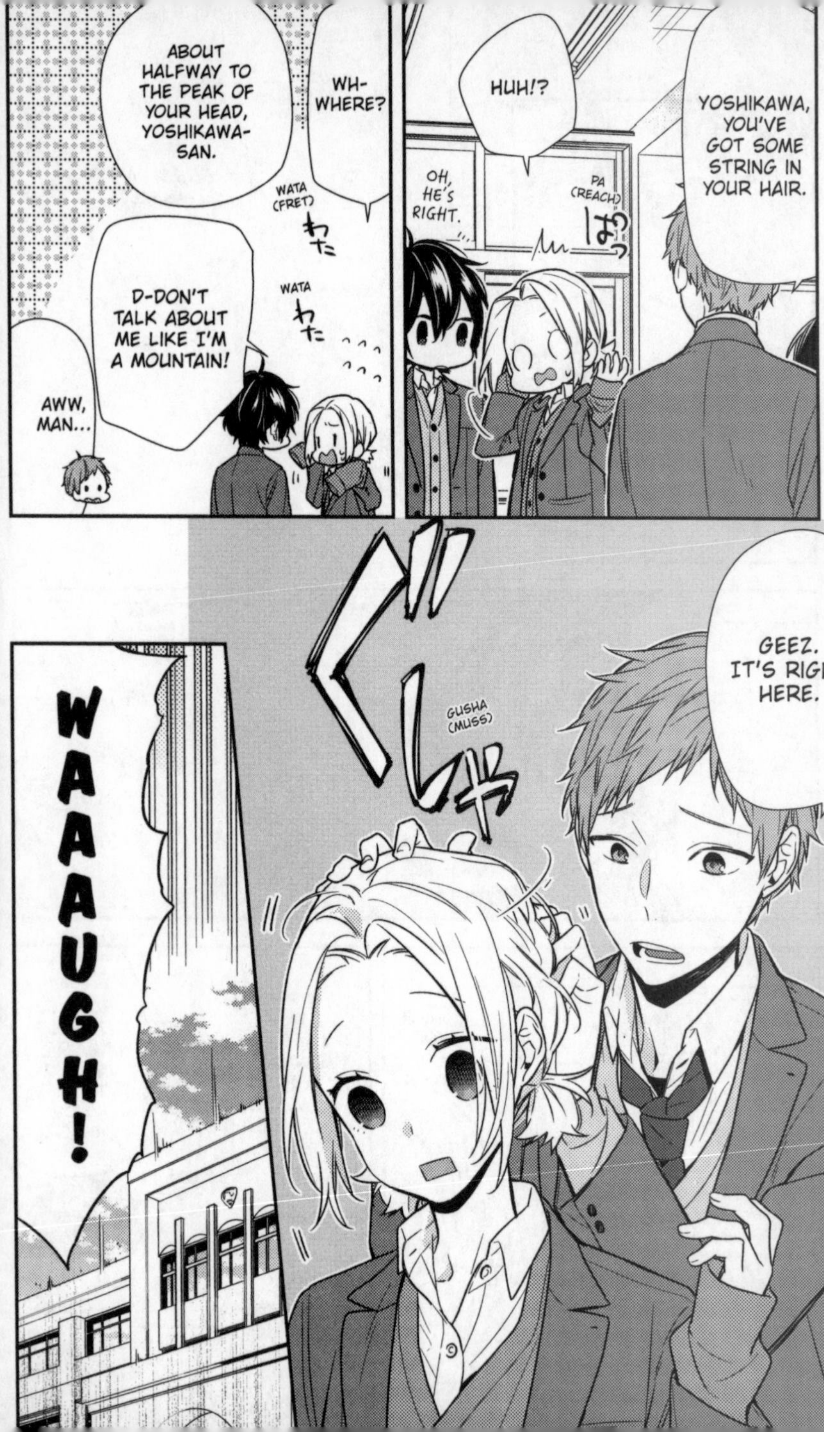
YOSHIKAWA, YOU'VE GOT SOME STRING IN YOUR HAIR.
HUH!?
PA (REACH)
ぱっ
OH, HE'S RIGHT.
WH-WHERE?
ABOUT HALFWAY TO THE PEAK OF YOUR HEAD, YOSHIKAWA-SAN.
WATA (FRET)
わた
WATA
わた
D-DON'T TALK ABOUT ME LIKE I'M A MOUNTAIN!
AWW, MAN...
GEEZ. IT'S RIGHT HERE.
GUSHA (MUSS)
ぐしゃ
WAAAAUGH!

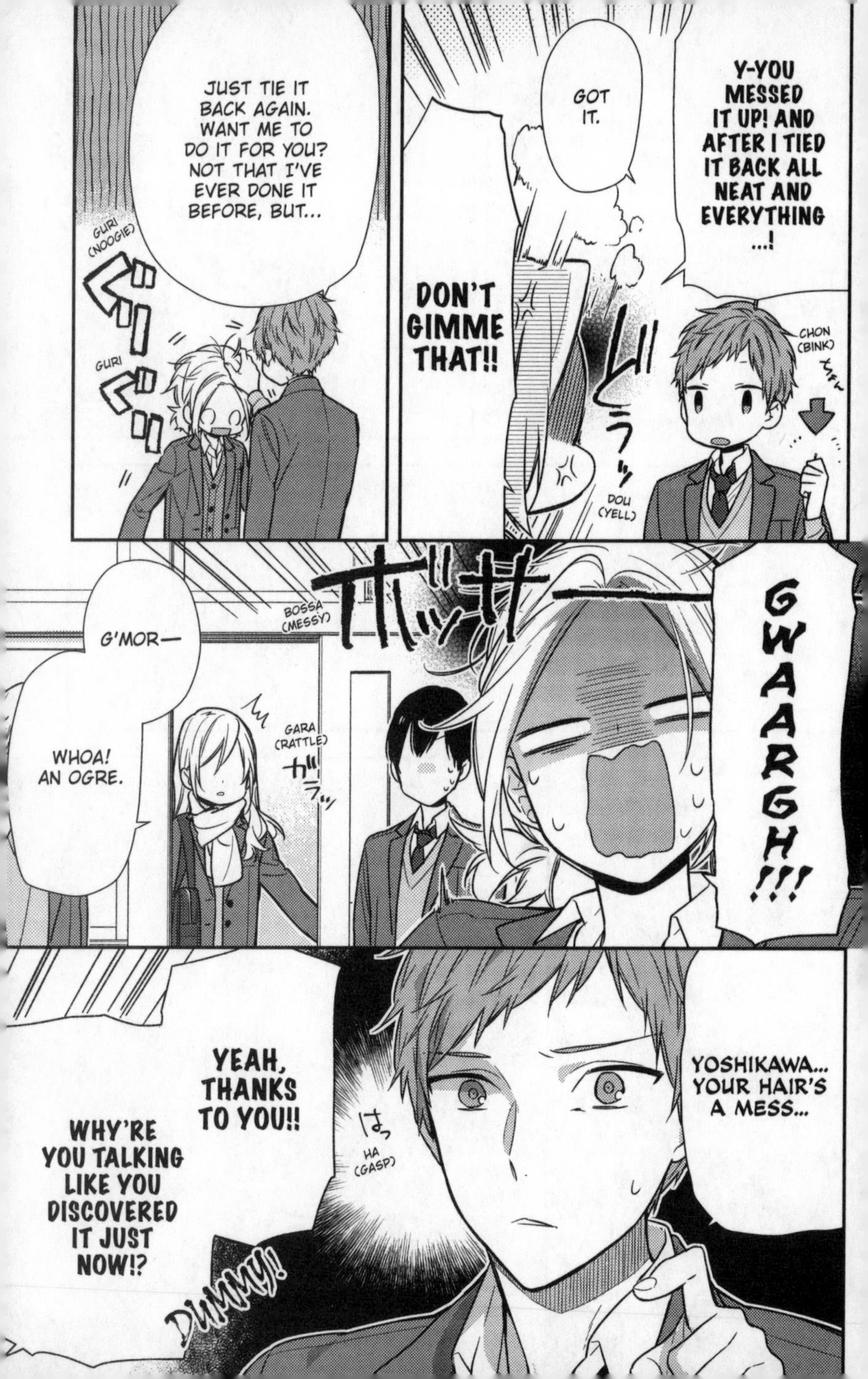
Y-YOU MESSED IT UP! AND AFTER I TIED IT BACK ALL NEAT AND EVERYTHING ...!
GOT IT.
CHON (BINK)
DON'T GIMME THAT!!
DOU (YELL)
JUST TIE IT BACK AGAIN. WANT ME TO DO IT FOR YOU? NOT THAT I'VE EVER DONE IT BEFORE, BUT...
GURI (NOOGIE)
GURI
GWAARGH!!!
BOSSA (MESSY)
GARA (RATTLE)
G'MOR—
WHOA! AN OGRE.
YOSHIKAWA... YOUR HAIR'S A MESS...
HA (GASP)
YEAH, THANKS TO YOU!!
WHY'RE YOU TALKING LIKE YOU DISCOVERED IT JUST NOW!?
DUMMY!

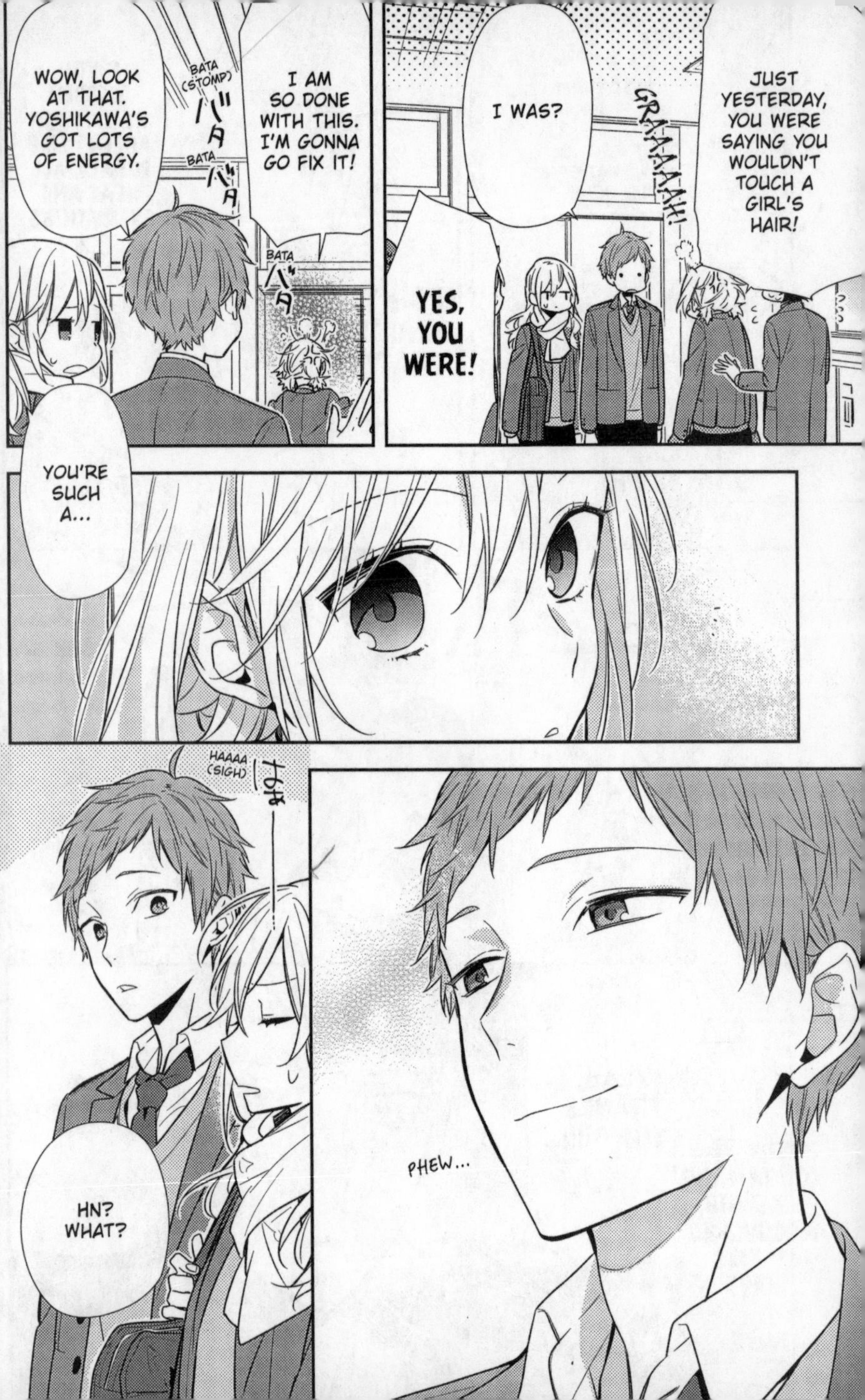
JUST YESTERDAY, YOU WERE SAYING YOU WOULDN'T TOUCH A GIRL'S HAIR!
I WAS?
GRAAAAAH!
YES, YOU WERE!
I AM SO DONE WITH THIS. I'M GONNA GO FIX IT!
BATA (STOMP)
バタ
BATA
バタ
BATA
バタ
WOW, LOOK AT THAT. YOSHIKAWA'S GOT LOTS OF ENERGY.
YOU'RE SUCH A...
PHEW...
HAAAA (SIGH)
はぁ—
HN? WHAT?

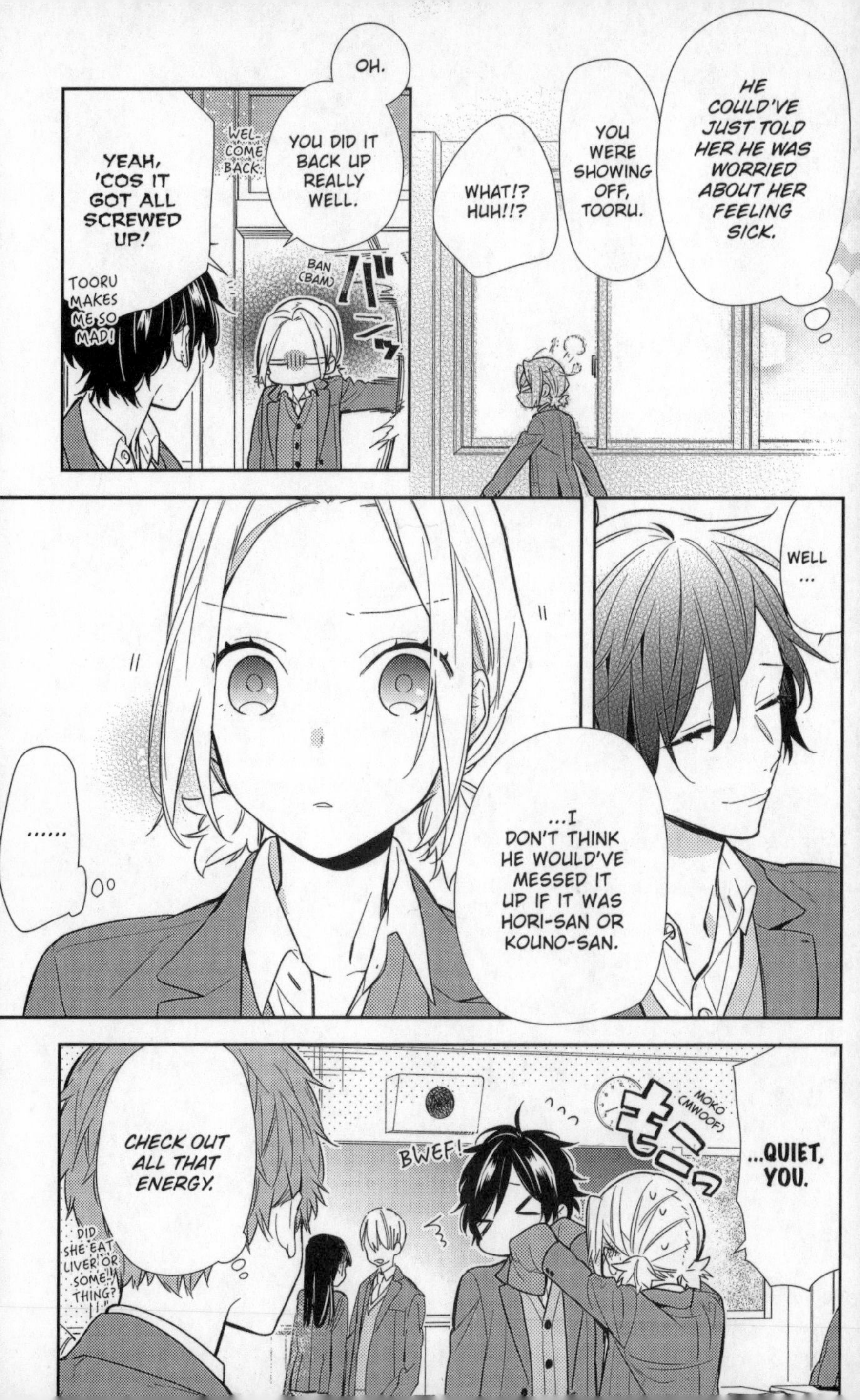
HE COULD'VE JUST TOLD HER HE WAS WORRIED ABOUT HER FEELING SICK.
YOU WERE SHOWING OFF, TOORU.
WHAT!? HUH!!?
OH.
YOU DID IT BACK UP REALLY WELL.
WEL-COME BACK.
YEAH, 'COS IT GOT ALL SCREWED UP!
BAN (BAM)
TOORU MAKES ME SO MAD!
WELL ...
...I DON'T THINK HE WOULD'VE MESSED IT UP IF IT WAS HORI-SAN OR KOUNO-SAN.
......
...QUIET, YOU.
MOKO (MWOOF)
BWEF!
CHECK OUT ALL THAT ENERGY.
DID SHE EAT LIVER OR SOME-THING?

HORIMIYA

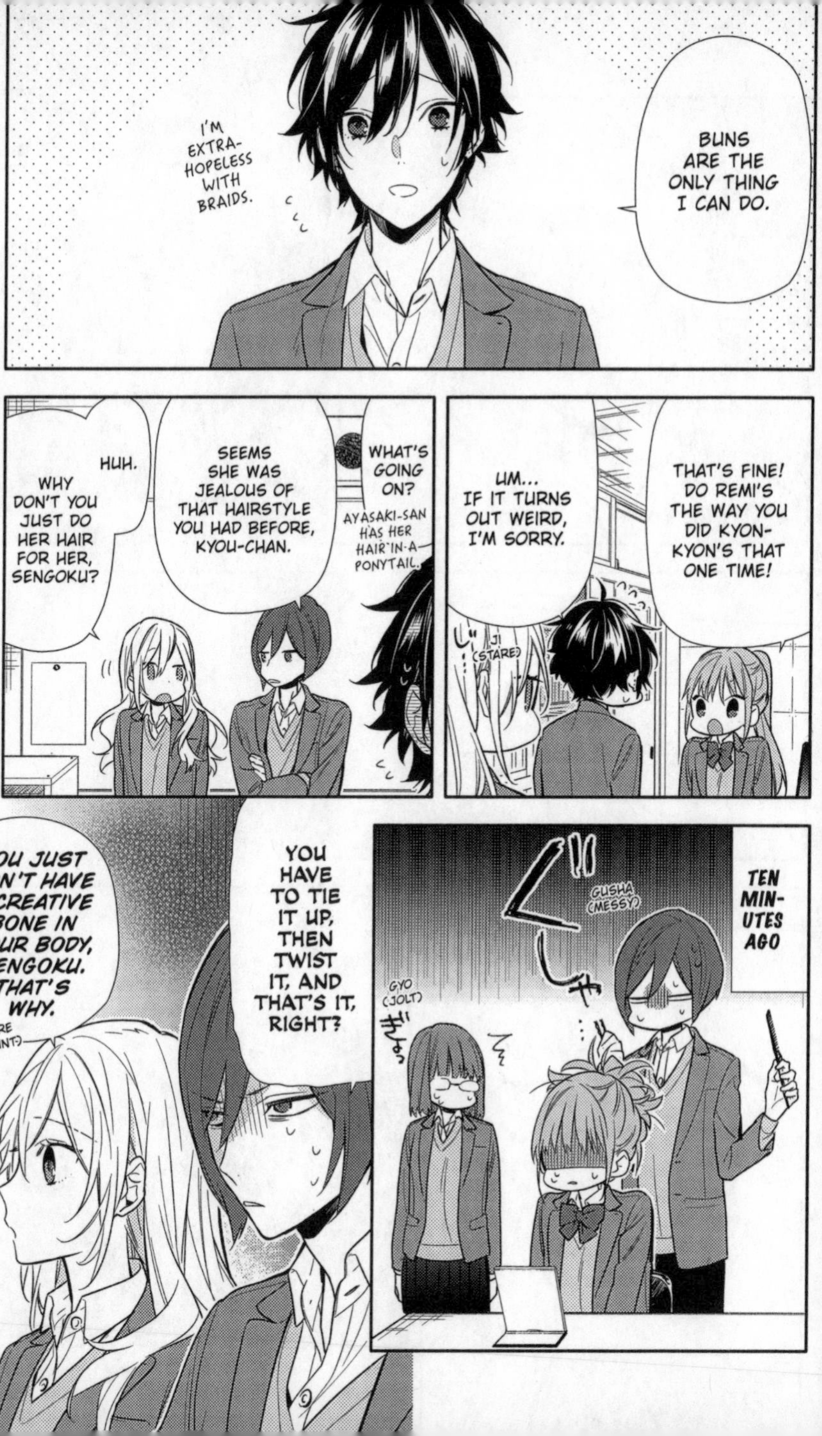
BUNS ARE THE ONLY THING I CAN DO.
I'M EXTRA-HOPELESS WITH BRAIDS.
THAT'S FINE! DO REMI'S THE WAY YOU DID KYON-KYON'S THAT ONE TIME!
UM... IF IT TURNS OUT WEIRD, I'M SORRY.
JI (STARE)
WHAT'S GOING ON?
AYASAKI-SAN HAS HER HAIR IN A PONYTAIL.
SEEMS SHE WAS JEALOUS OF THAT HAIRSTYLE YOU HAD BEFORE, KYOU-CHAN.
HUH.
WHY DON'T YOU JUST DO HER HAIR FOR HER, SENGOKU?
TEN MINUTES AGO
GUSHA (MESSY)
GYO (JOLT)
YOU HAVE TO TIE IT UP, THEN TWIST IT, AND THAT'S IT, RIGHT?
YOU JUST DON'T HAVE A CREATIVE BONE IN YOUR BODY, SENGOKU. THAT'S WHY.
SHIRE (BLUNT)

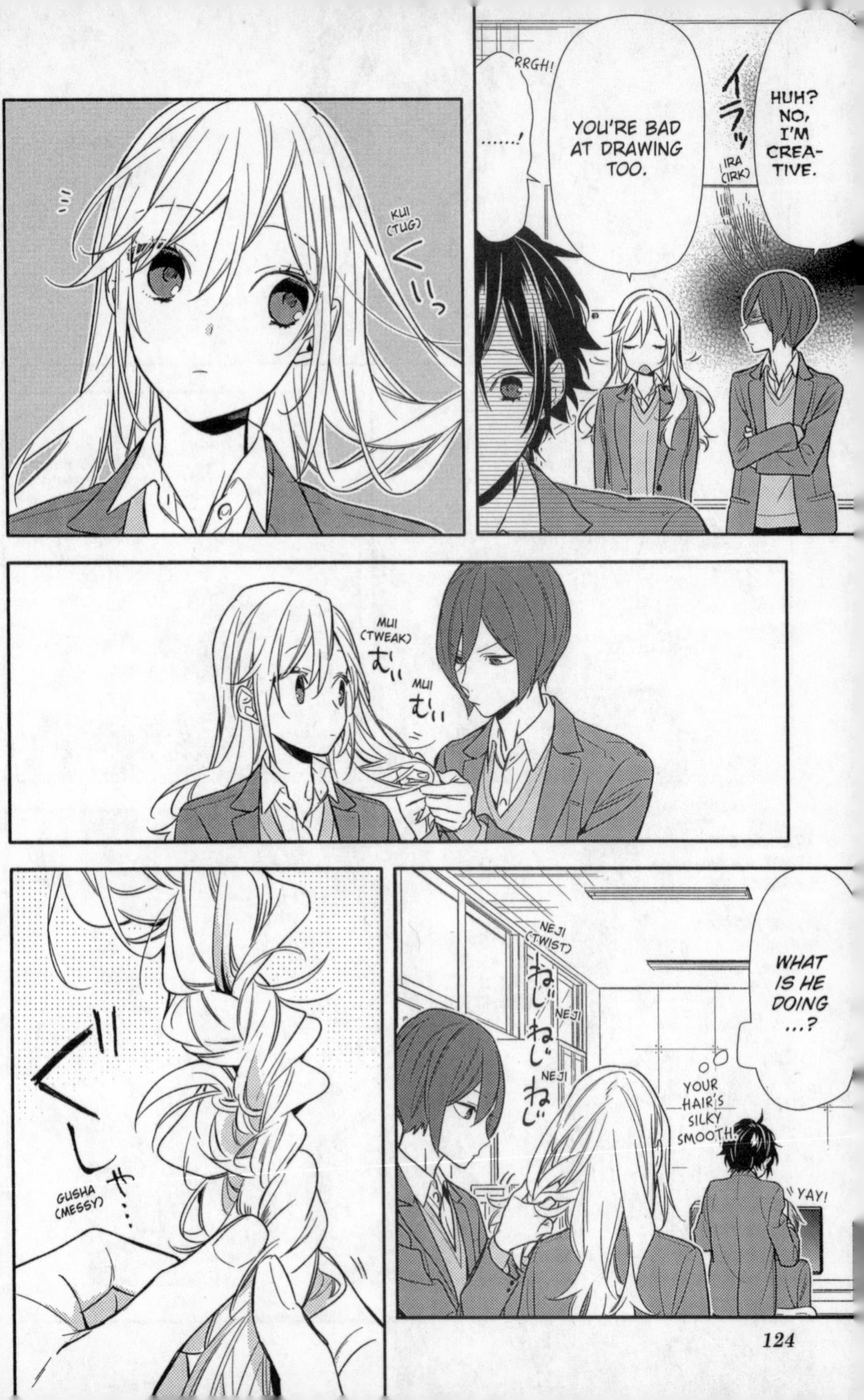
HUH? NO, I'M CREATIVE.
IRA (IRK)
YOU'RE BAD AT DRAWING TOO.
RRGH!
......!
KUI (TUG)
MUI (TWEAK)
MUI
WHAT IS HE DOING ...?
NEJI (TWIST)
NEJI
NEJI
YOUR HAIR'S SILKY SMOOTH.
YAY!
GUSHA (MESSY)

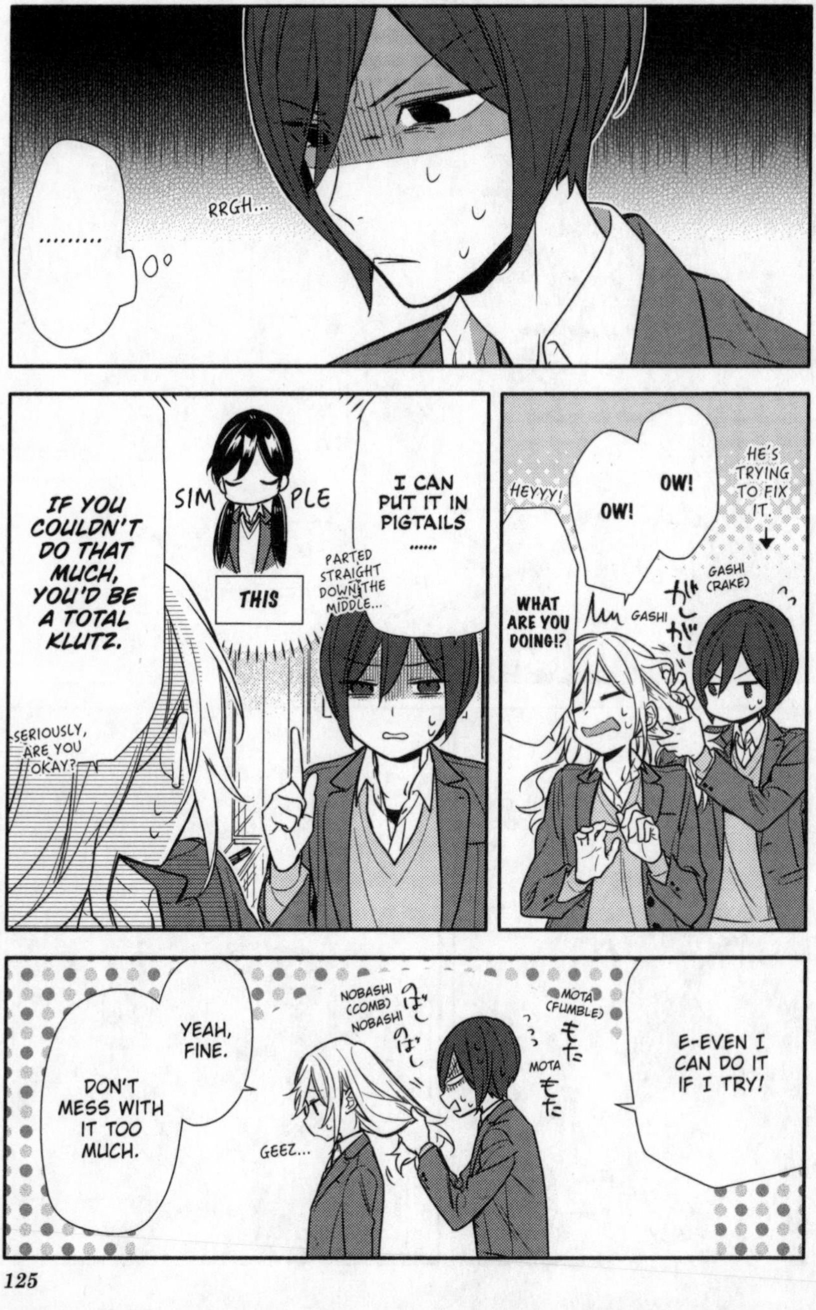

RRGH...
....
HE'S TRYING TO FIX IT.
OW!
OW!
HEYYY!
GASHI (RAKE)
がし
GASHI
がし
WHAT ARE YOU DOING!?
I CAN PUT IT IN PIGTAILS......
SIM PLE
THIS
PARTED STRAIGHT DOWN THE MIDDLE...
IF YOU COULDN'T DO THAT MUCH, YOU'D BE A TOTAL KLUTZ.
SERIOUSLY, ARE YOU OKAY?
E-EVEN I CAN DO IT IF I TRY!
MOTA (FUMBLE)
もた
MOTA
もた
NOBASHI (COMB)
のばし
NOBASHI
のばし
YEAH, FINE.
DON'T MESS WITH IT TOO MUCH.
GEEZ...

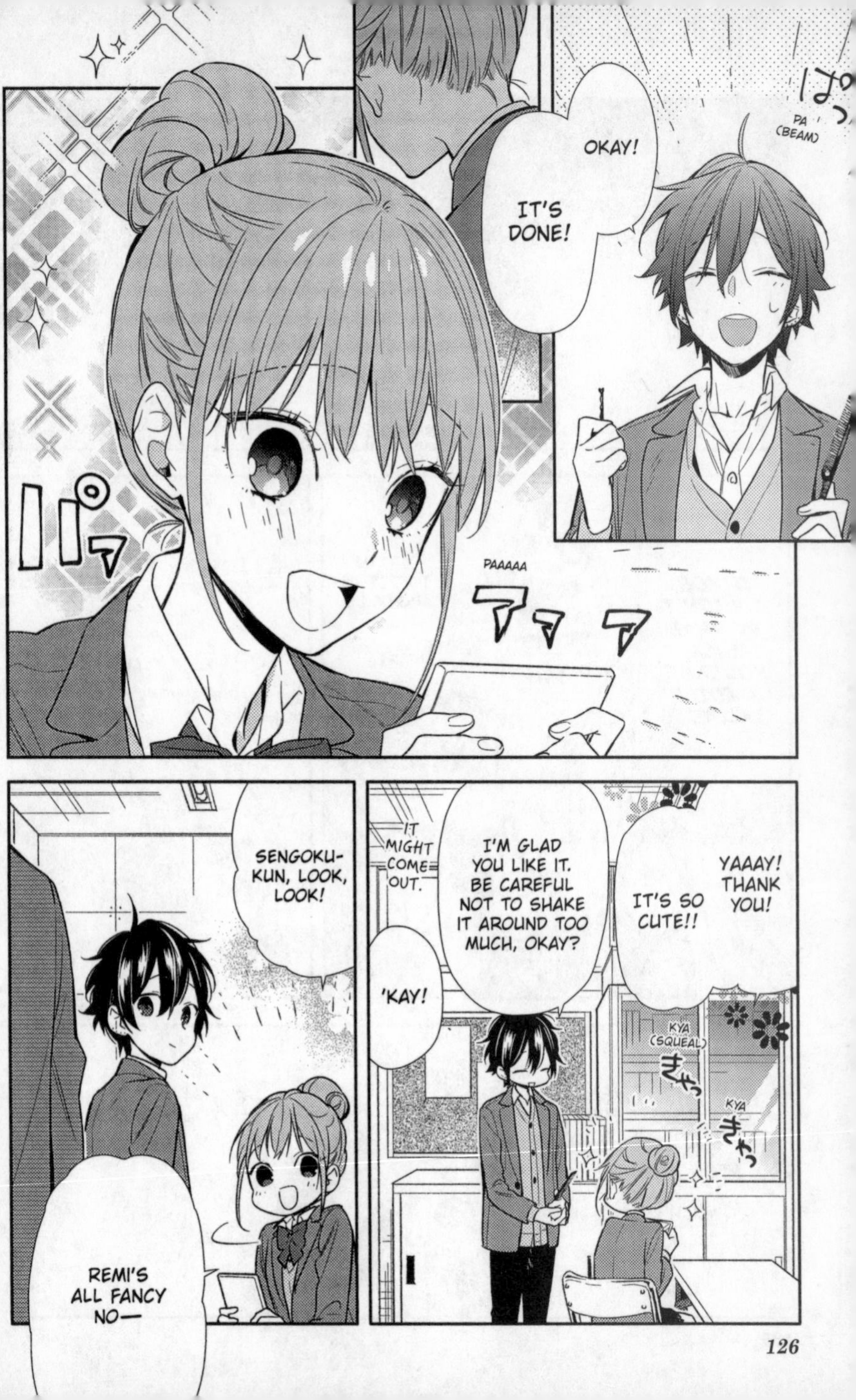
ぱっ
PA (BEAM)
OKAY!
IT'S DONE!
パァ
PAAAAA
アァァ
YAAAY! THANK YOU!
IT'S SO CUTE!!
I'M GLAD YOU LIKE IT. BE CAREFUL NOT TO SHAKE IT AROUND TOO MUCH, OKAY?
IT MIGHT COME OUT.
'KAY!
KYA (SQUEAL)
きゃっ
KYA
きゃっ
SENGOKU-KUN, LOOK, LOOK!
REMI'S ALL FANCY NO—

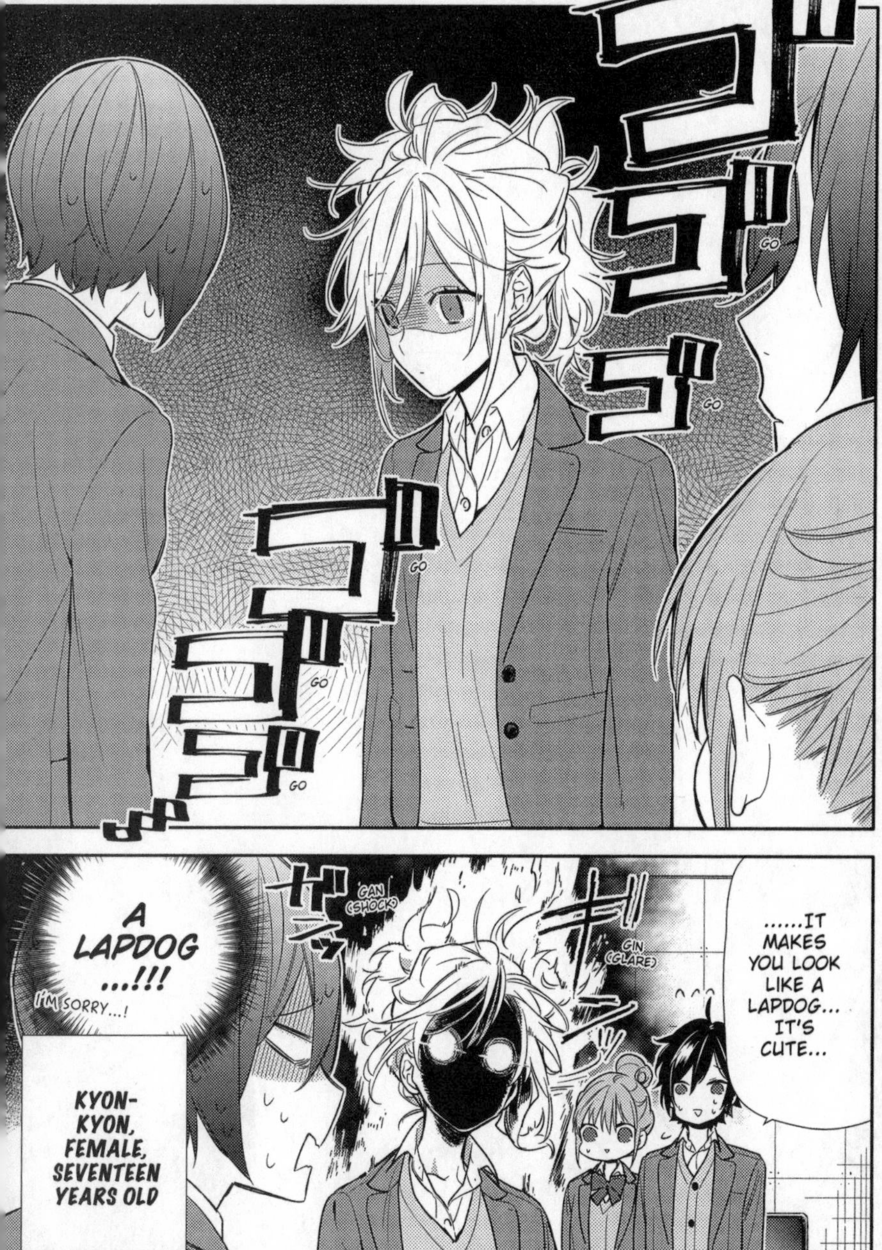
GO (RUMBLE)
GO
GO
GO
GO
GO
......IT MAKES YOU LOOK LIKE A LAPDOG... IT'S CUTE...
GIN (GLARE)
GAN (SHOCK)
A LAPDOG ...!!!
I'M SORRY...!
KYON-KYON, FEMALE, SEVENTEEN YEARS OLD

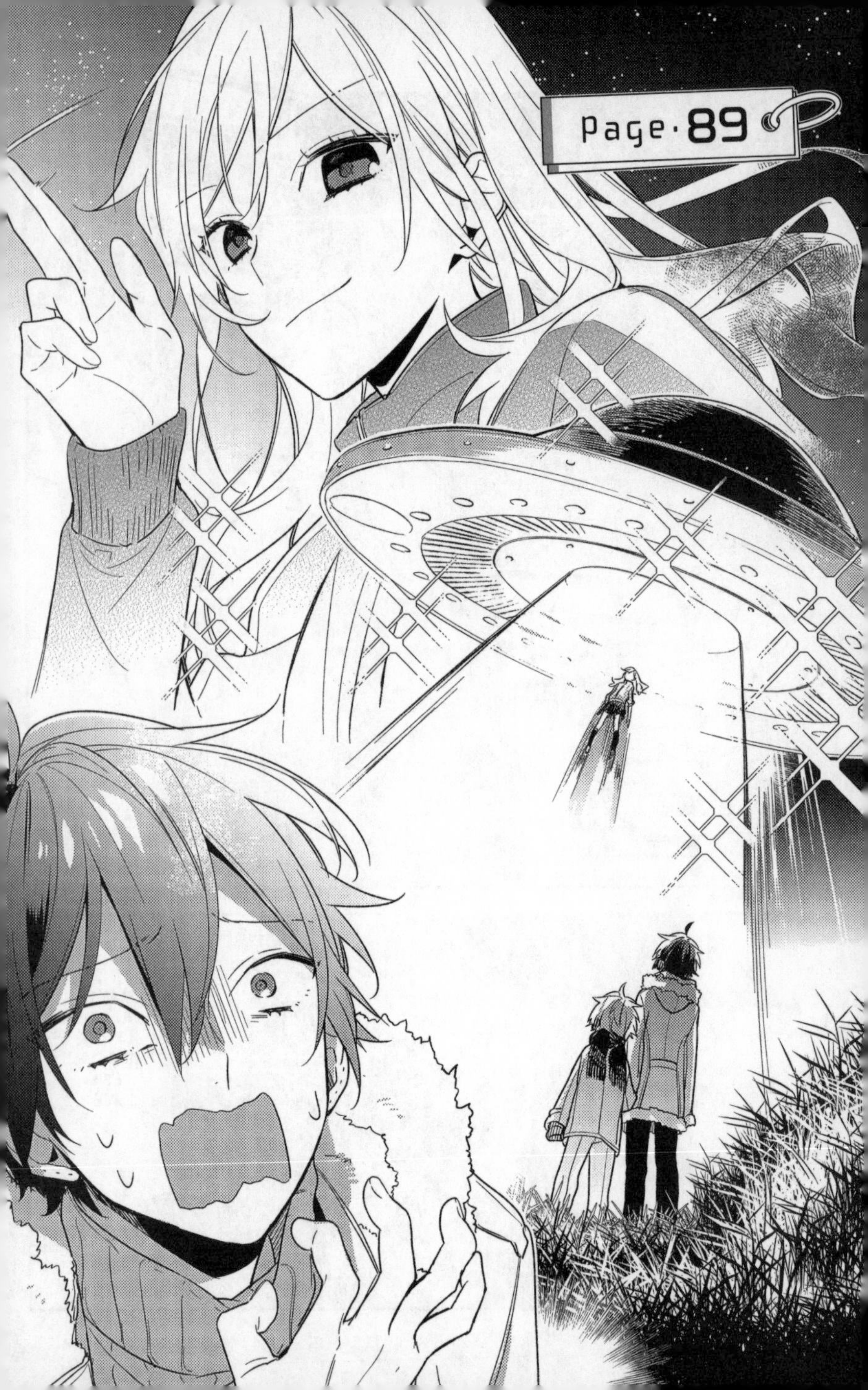
Page·89

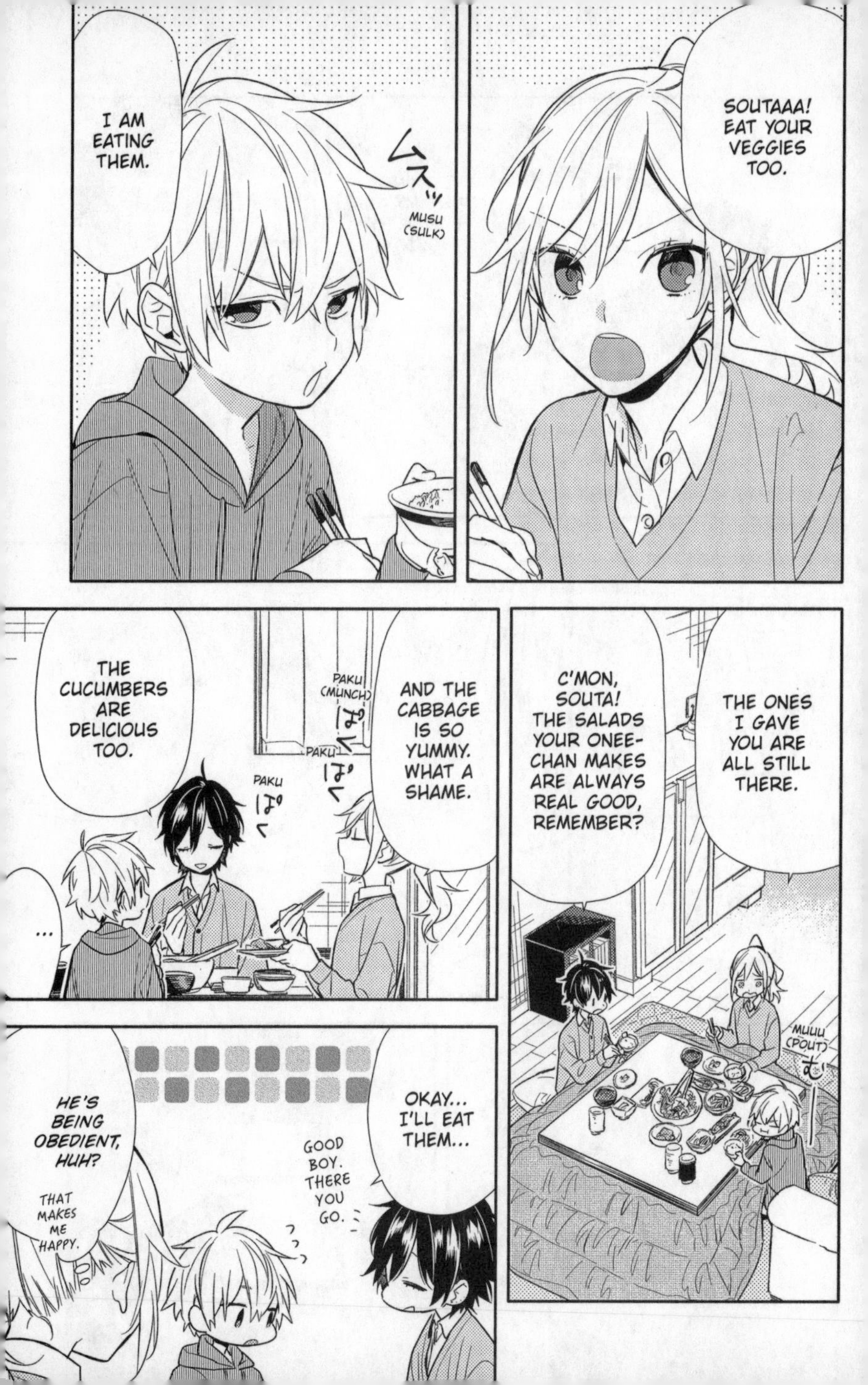

SOUTAAA! EAT YOUR VEGGIES TOO.
I AM EATING THEM.
ムスッ
MUSU (SULK)
THE ONES I GAVE YOU ARE ALL STILL THERE.
C'MON, SOUTA! THE SALADS YOUR ONEE-CHAN MAKES ARE ALWAYS REAL GOOD, REMEMBER?
MUUU (POUT)
む
AND THE CABBAGE IS SO YUMMY. WHAT A SHAME.
PAKU (MUNCH)
ぱく
PAKU
ぱく
PAKU
ぱく
THE CUCUMBERS ARE DELICIOUS TOO.
...
OKAY... I'LL EAT THEM...
GOOD BOY. THERE YOU GO.
HE'S BEING OBEDIENT, HUH?
THAT MAKES ME HAPPY.

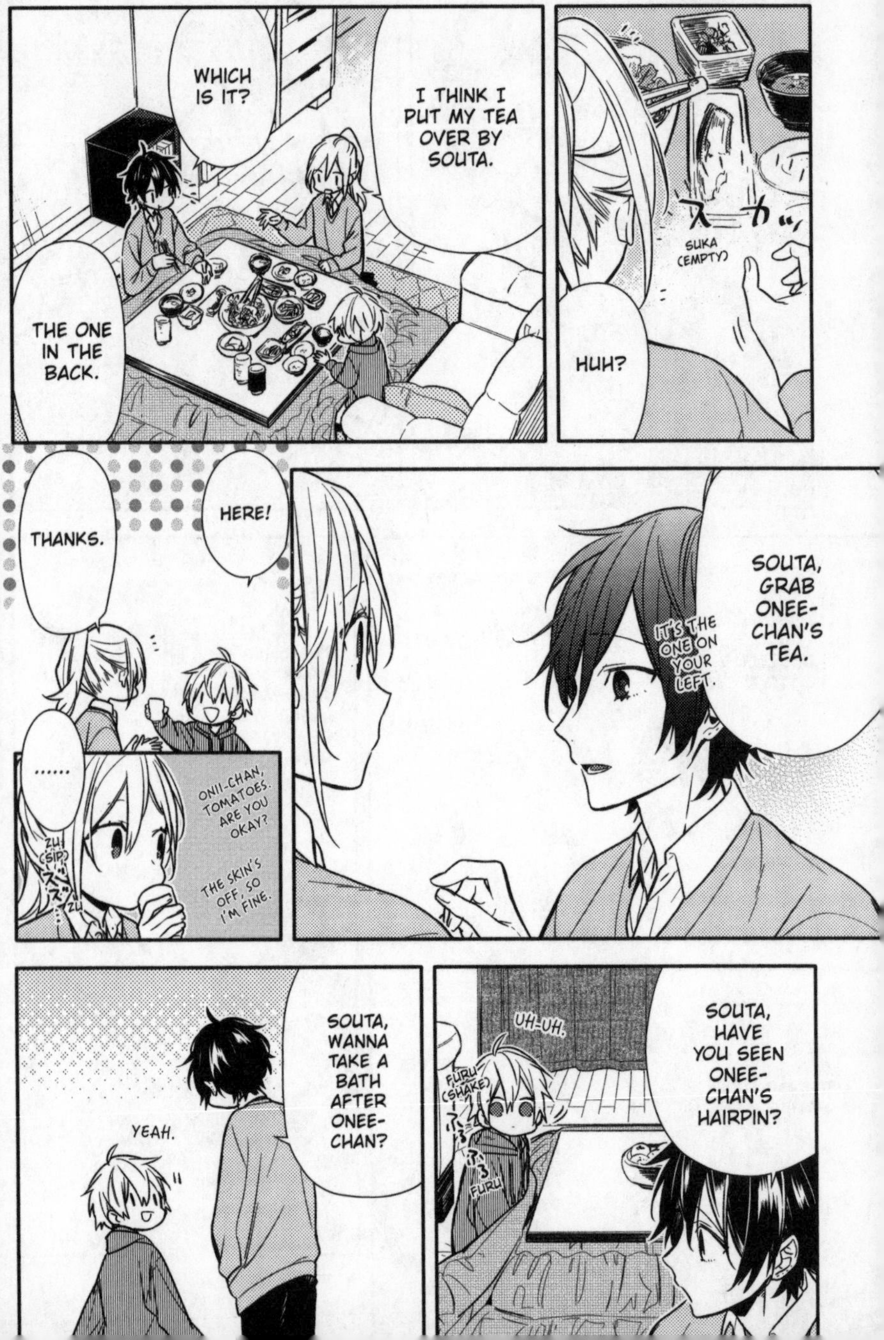
SUKA (EMPTY)
HUH?
I THINK I PUT MY TEA OVER BY SOUTA.
WHICH IS IT?
THE ONE IN THE BACK.
SOUTA, GRAB ONEE-CHAN'S TEA.
IT'S THE ONE ON YOUR LEFT.
HERE!
THANKS.
......
ONII-CHAN, TOMATOES. ARE YOU OKAY?
THE SKIN'S OFF, SO I'M FINE.
ZU (SIP) ZU
SOUTA, HAVE YOU SEEN ONEE-CHAN'S HAIRPIN?
UH-UH.
FURU (SHAKE) FURU
SOUTA, WANNA TAKE A BATH AFTER ONEE-CHAN?
YEAH.

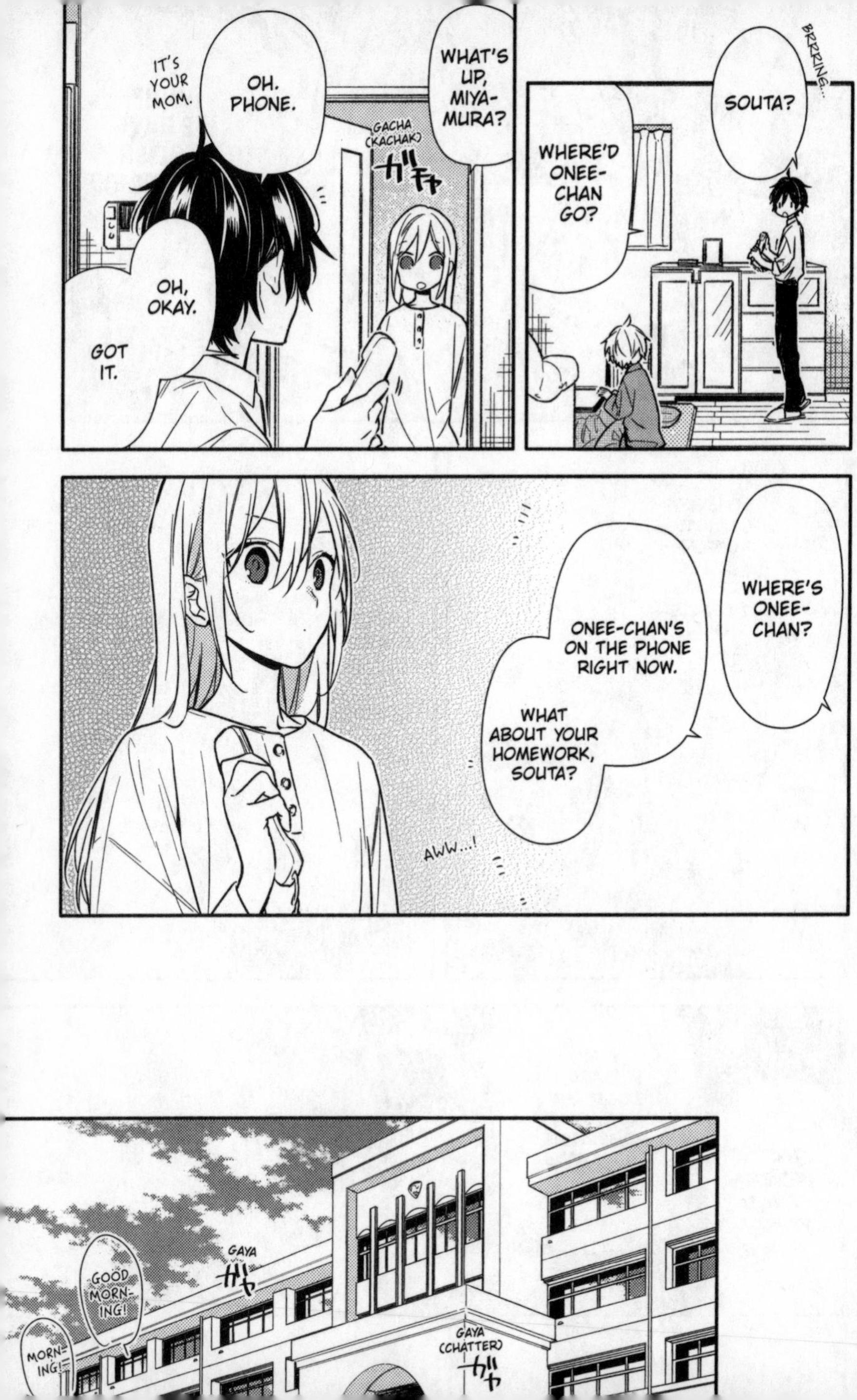
BRRRING...
SOUTA?
WHERE'D ONEE-CHAN GO?
WHAT'S UP, MIYAMURA?
GACHA (KACHAK)
OH. PHONE.
IT'S YOUR MOM.
OH, OKAY.
GOT IT.
WHERE'S ONEE-CHAN?
ONEE-CHAN'S ON THE PHONE RIGHT NOW.
WHAT ABOUT YOUR HOMEWORK, SOUTA?
AWW...!
GAYA (CHATTER)
GAYA
GOOD MORNING!
MORNING!

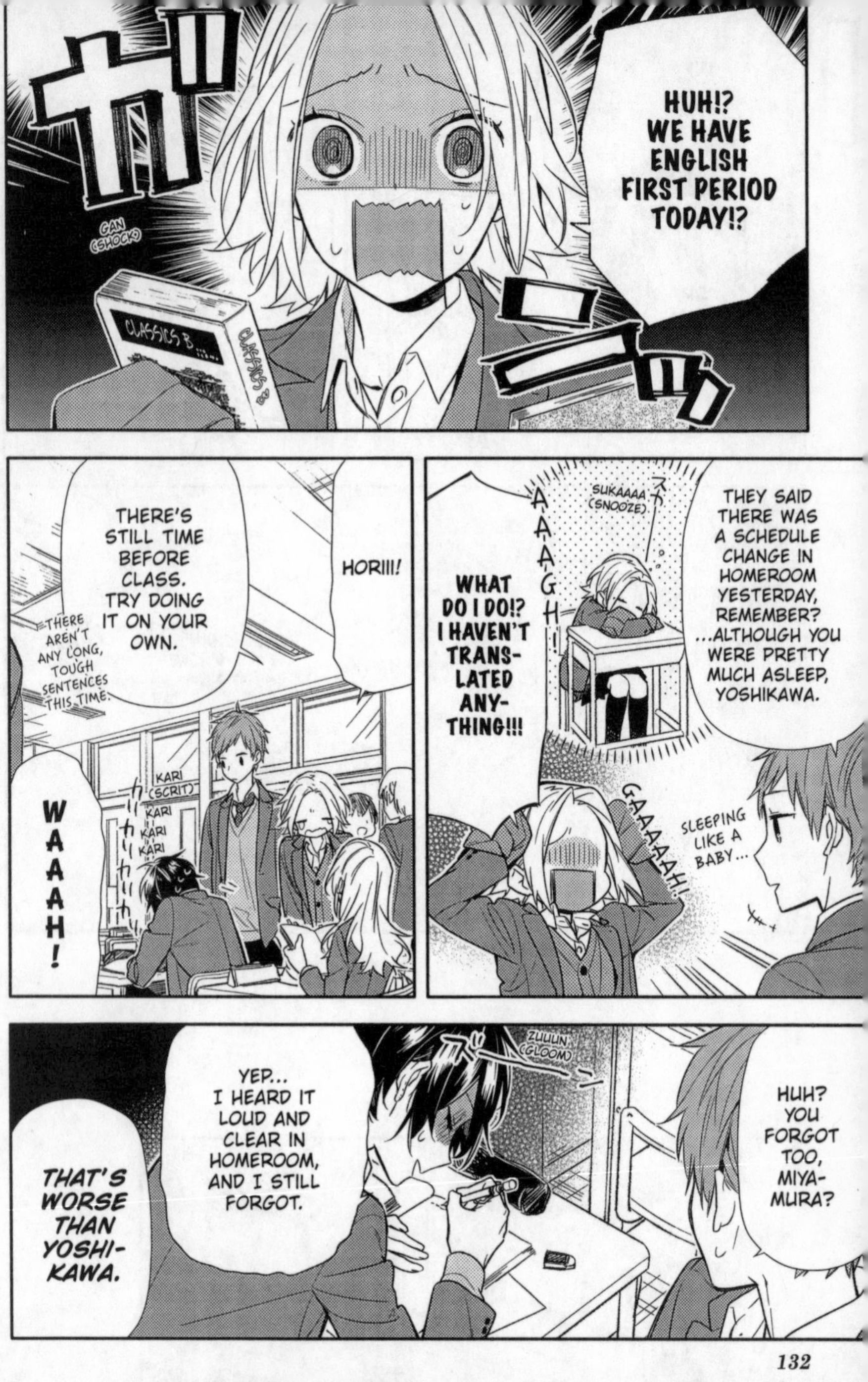

HUH!? WE HAVE ENGLISH FIRST PERIOD TODAY!?
GAN (SHOCK)
CLASSICS B
THEY SAID THERE WAS A SCHEDULE CHANGE IN HOMEROOM YESTERDAY, REMEMBER? ...ALTHOUGH YOU WERE PRETTY MUCH ASLEEP, YOSHIKAWA.
SUKAAAA (SNOOZE)
SLEEPING LIKE A BABY...
WHAT DO I DO!? I HAVEN'T TRANSLATED ANYTHING!!!
AAAAGH!
GAAAAAAH!
HORIII!
THERE'S STILL TIME BEFORE CLASS. TRY DOING IT ON YOUR OWN.
THERE AREN'T ANY LONG, TOUGH SENTENCES THIS TIME.
KARI (SCRIT)
KARI KARI KARI
WAAAAH!
HUH? YOU FORGOT TOO, MIYAMURA?
ZUUUN (GLOOM)
YEP... I HEARD IT LOUD AND CLEAR IN HOMEROOM, AND I STILL FORGOT.
THAT'S WORSE THAN YOSHIKAWA.

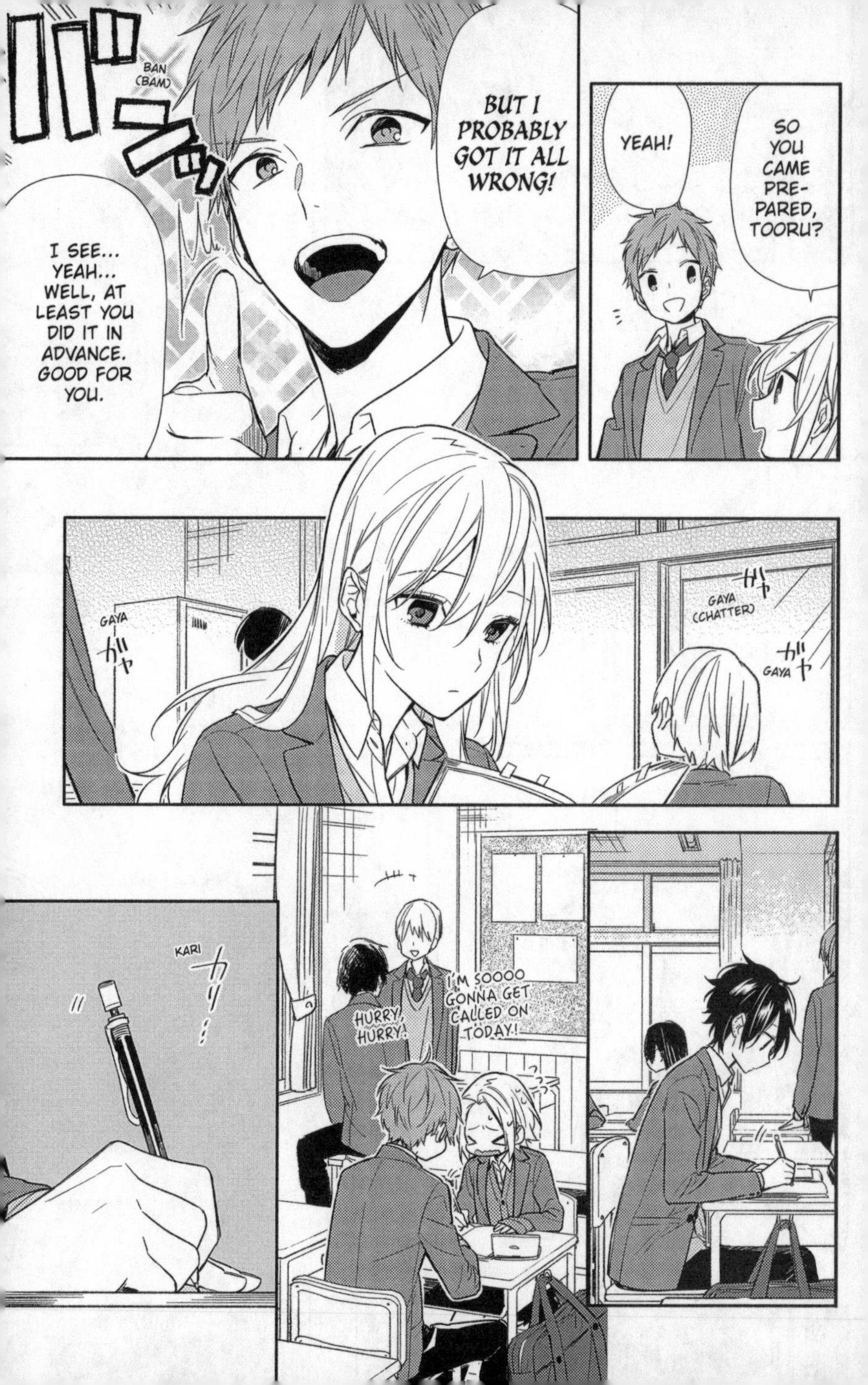
SO YOU CAME PRE-PARED, TOORU?
YEAH!
BUT I PROBABLY GOT IT ALL WRONG!
BAN (BAM)
I SEE... YEAH... WELL, AT LEAST YOU DID IT IN ADVANCE. GOOD FOR YOU.
GAYA (CHATTER)
GAYA
GAYA
I'M SOOOO GONNA GET CALLED ON TODAY!
HURRY, HURRY!
KARI

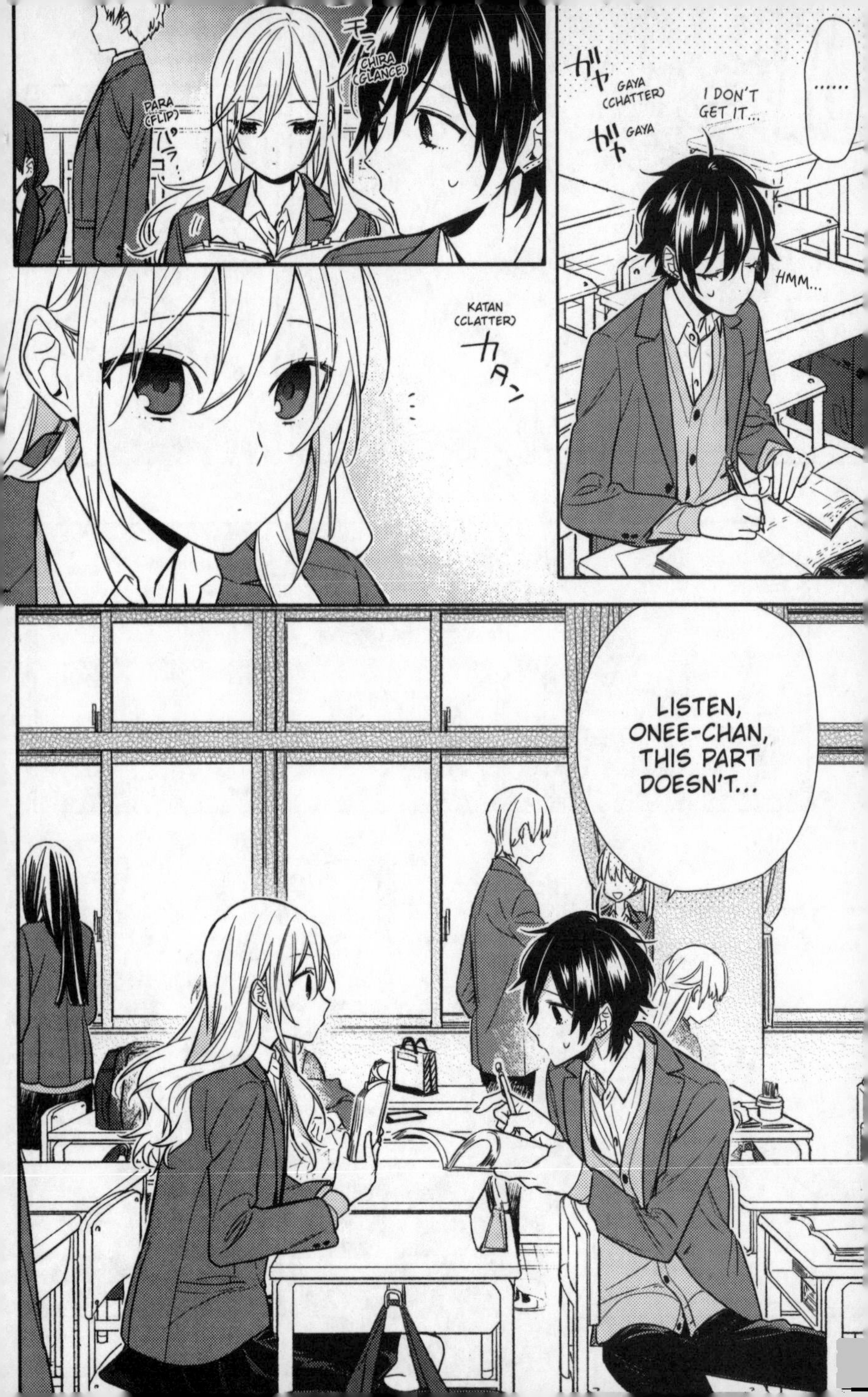
......
I DON'T GET IT...
GAYA (CHATTER)
GAYA
HMM...
CHIRA (GLANCE)
PARA (FLIP)
KATAN (CLATTER)
LISTEN, ONEE-CHAN, THIS PART DOESN'T...

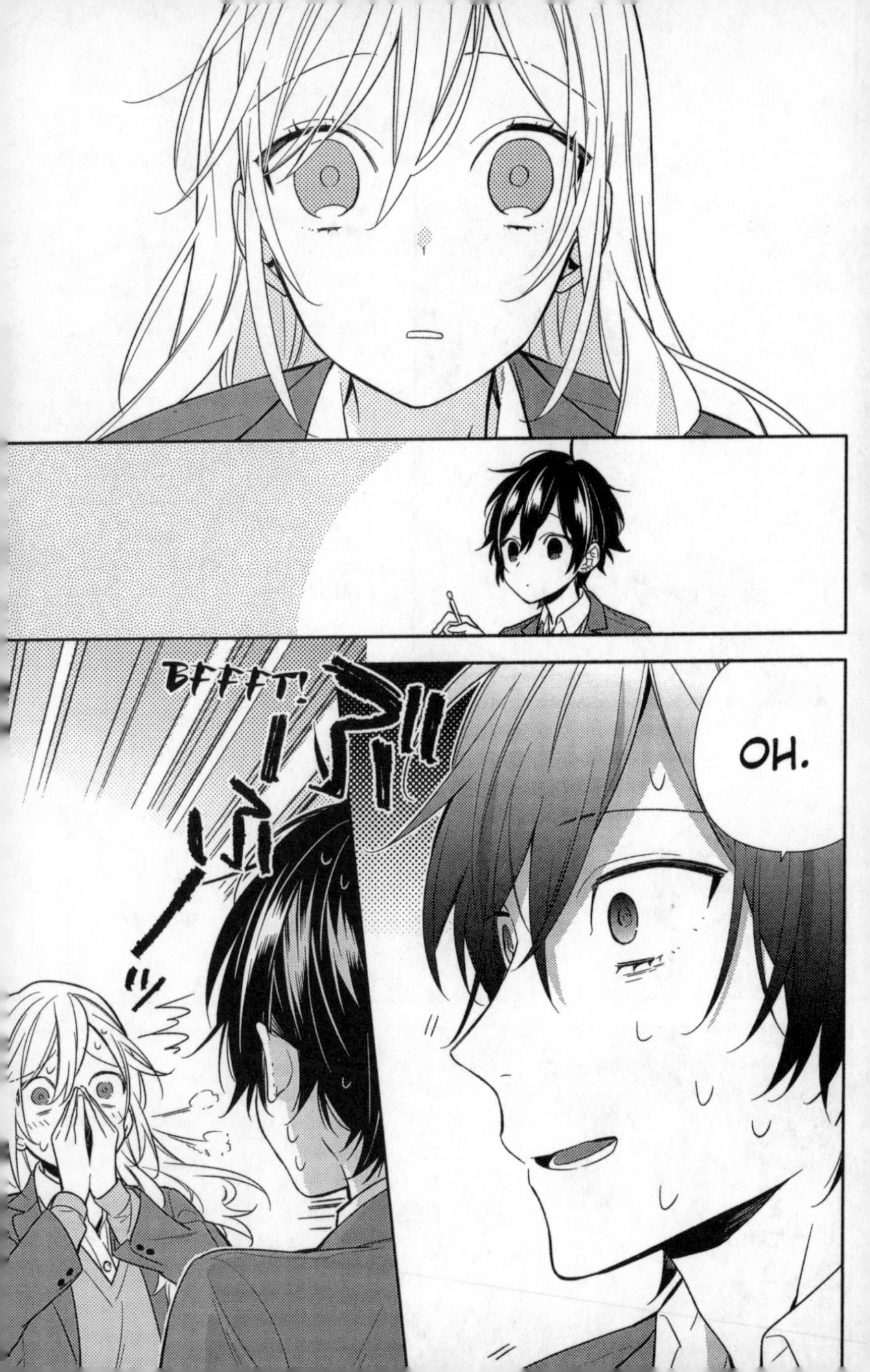
OH.
BFFFT!

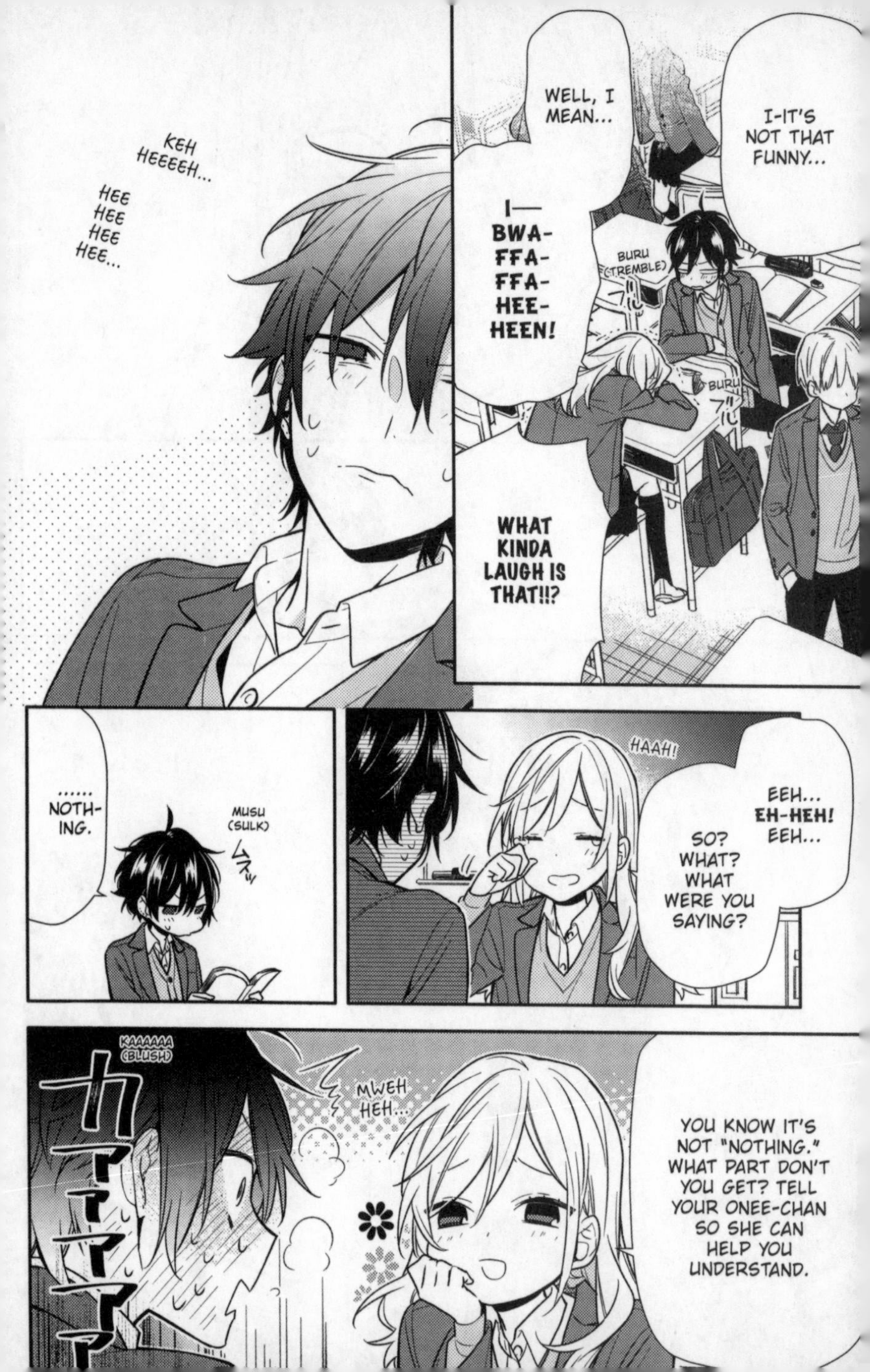
I-IT'S NOT THAT FUNNY...
WELL, I MEAN...
I— BWA-FFA-FFA-HEE-HEEN!
BURU (TREMBLE)
BURU
WHAT KINDA LAUGH IS THAT!!?
KEH HEEEEH...
HEE HEE HEE HEE...
HAAH!
EEH... EH-HEH! EEH...
SO? WHAT? WHAT WERE YOU SAYING?
...... NOTHING.
MUSU (SULK)
YOU KNOW IT'S NOT "NOTHING." WHAT PART DON'T YOU GET? TELL YOUR ONEE-CHAN SO SHE CAN HELP YOU UNDERSTAND.
MWEH HEH...
KAAAAAA (BLUSH)

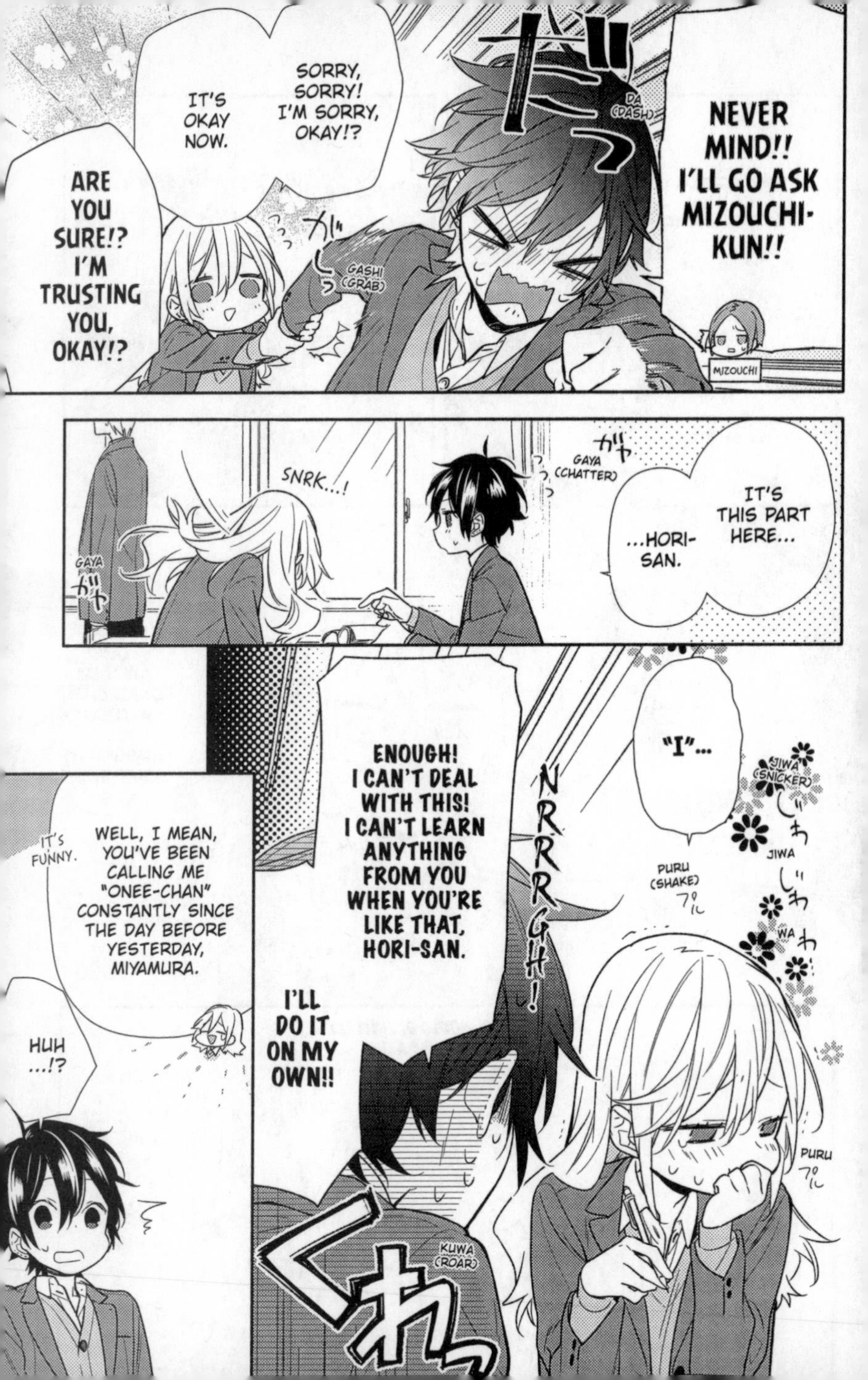
NEVER MIND!! I'LL GO ASK MIZOUCHI-KUN!!
DA (DASH)
SORRY, SORRY! I'M SORRY, OKAY!?
IT'S OKAY NOW.
GASHI (GRAB)
ARE YOU SURE!? I'M TRUSTING YOU, OKAY!?
MIZOUCHI
IT'S THIS PART HERE...
...HORI-SAN.
GAYA (CHATTER)
SNRK...!
GAYA
"I"...
JIWA (SNICKER)
JIWA
WA
PURU (SHAKE)
PURU
NRRRGH!
ENOUGH! I CAN'T DEAL WITH THIS! I CAN'T LEARN ANYTHING FROM YOU WHEN YOU'RE LIKE THAT, HORI-SAN.
I'LL DO IT ON MY OWN!!
KUWA (ROAR)
WELL, I MEAN, YOU'VE BEEN CALLING ME "ONEE-CHAN" CONSTANTLY SINCE THE DAY BEFORE YESTERDAY, MIYAMURA.
IT'S FUNNY.
HUH ...!?

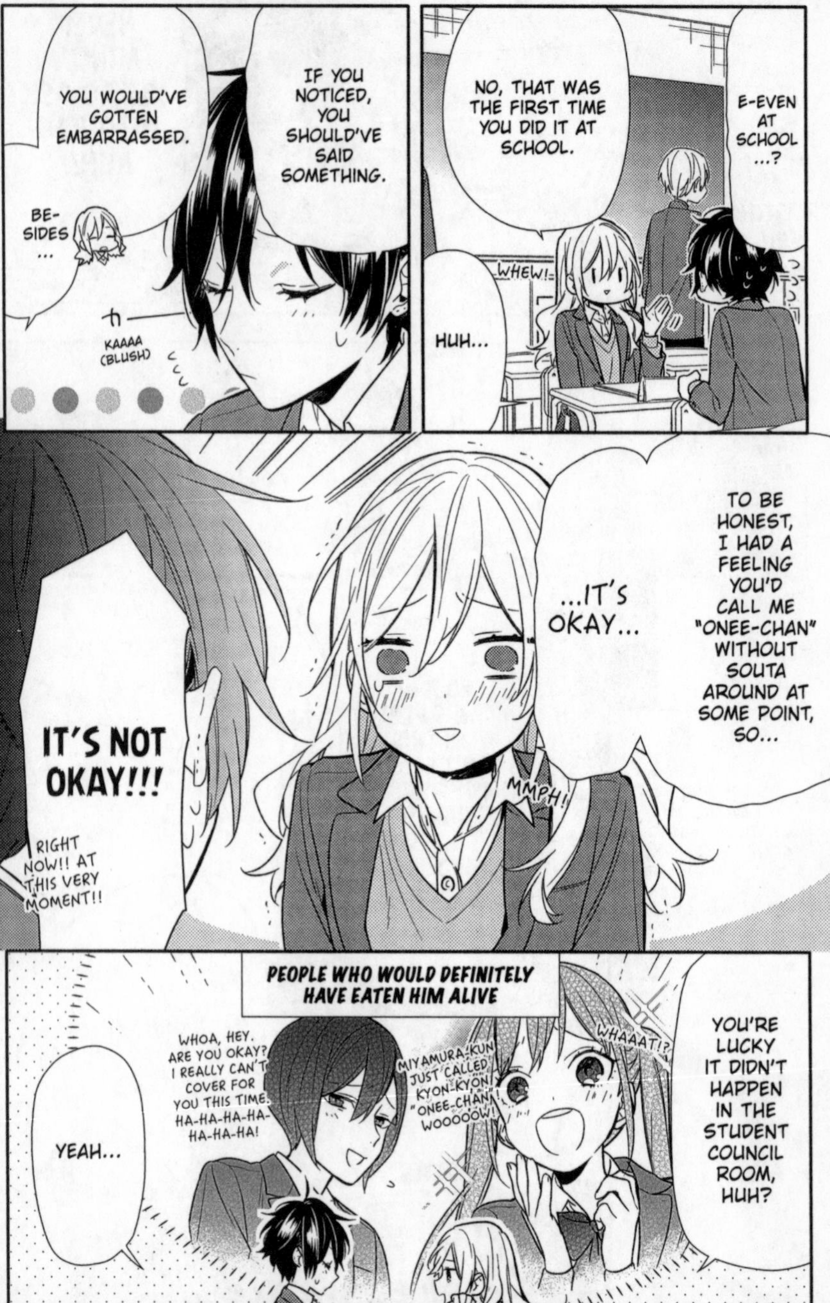
E-EVEN AT SCHOOL ...?
NO, THAT WAS THE FIRST TIME YOU DID IT AT SCHOOL.
WHEW!
HUH...
IF YOU NOTICED, YOU SHOULD'VE SAID SOMETHING.
YOU WOULD'VE GOTTEN EMBARRASSED.
BESIDES ...
カ
KAAAA (BLUSH)
TO BE HONEST, I HAD A FEELING YOU'D CALL ME "ONEE-CHAN" WITHOUT SOUTA AROUND AT SOME POINT, SO...
...IT'S OKAY...
MMPH!
IT'S NOT OKAY!!!
RIGHT NOW!! AT THIS VERY MOMENT!!
PEOPLE WHO WOULD DEFINITELY HAVE EATEN HIM ALIVE
YOU'RE LUCKY IT DIDN'T HAPPEN IN THE STUDENT COUNCIL ROOM, HUH?
WHAAAT!?
MIYAMURA-KUN JUST CALLED KYON-KYON "ONEE-CHAN"! WOOOOOW!
WHOA, HEY. ARE YOU OKAY? I REALLY CAN'T COVER FOR YOU THIS TIME. HA-HA-HA-HA-HA-HA-HA!
YEAH...

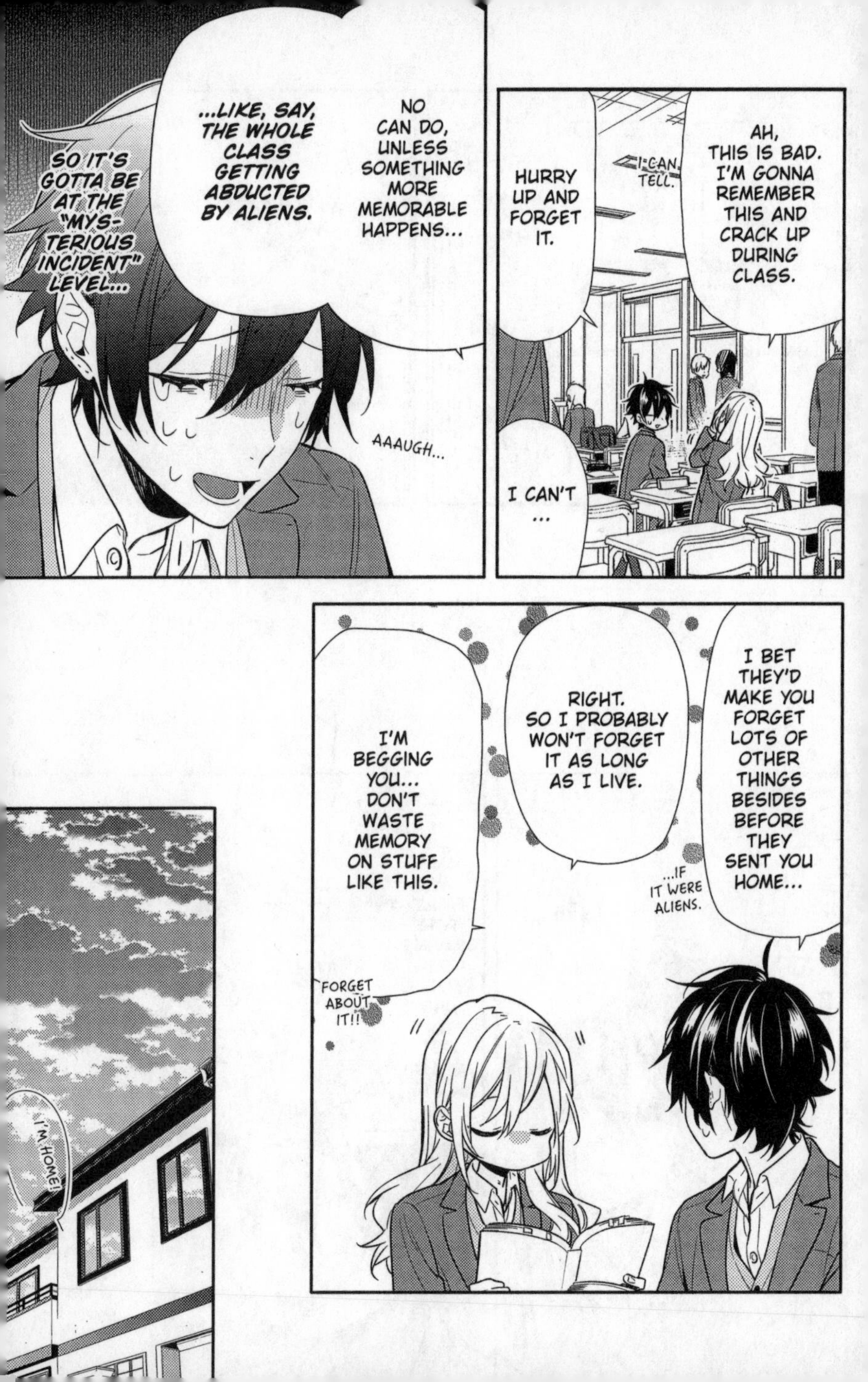
AH, THIS IS BAD. I'M GONNA REMEMBER THIS AND CRACK UP DURING CLASS.
I CAN. TELL.
HURRY UP AND FORGET IT.
I CAN'T ...
NO CAN DO, UNLESS SOMETHING MORE MEMORABLE HAPPENS...
...LIKE, SAY, THE WHOLE CLASS GETTING ABDUCTED BY ALIENS.
SO IT'S GOTTA BE AT THE "MYSTERIOUS INCIDENT" LEVEL...
AAAUGH...
I BET THEY'D MAKE YOU FORGET LOTS OF OTHER THINGS BESIDES BEFORE THEY SENT YOU HOME...
...IF IT WERE ALIENS.
RIGHT. SO I PROBABLY WON'T FORGET IT AS LONG AS I LIVE.
I'M BEGGING YOU... DON'T WASTE MEMORY ON STUFF LIKE THIS.
FORGET ABOUT IT!!
I'M HOME!

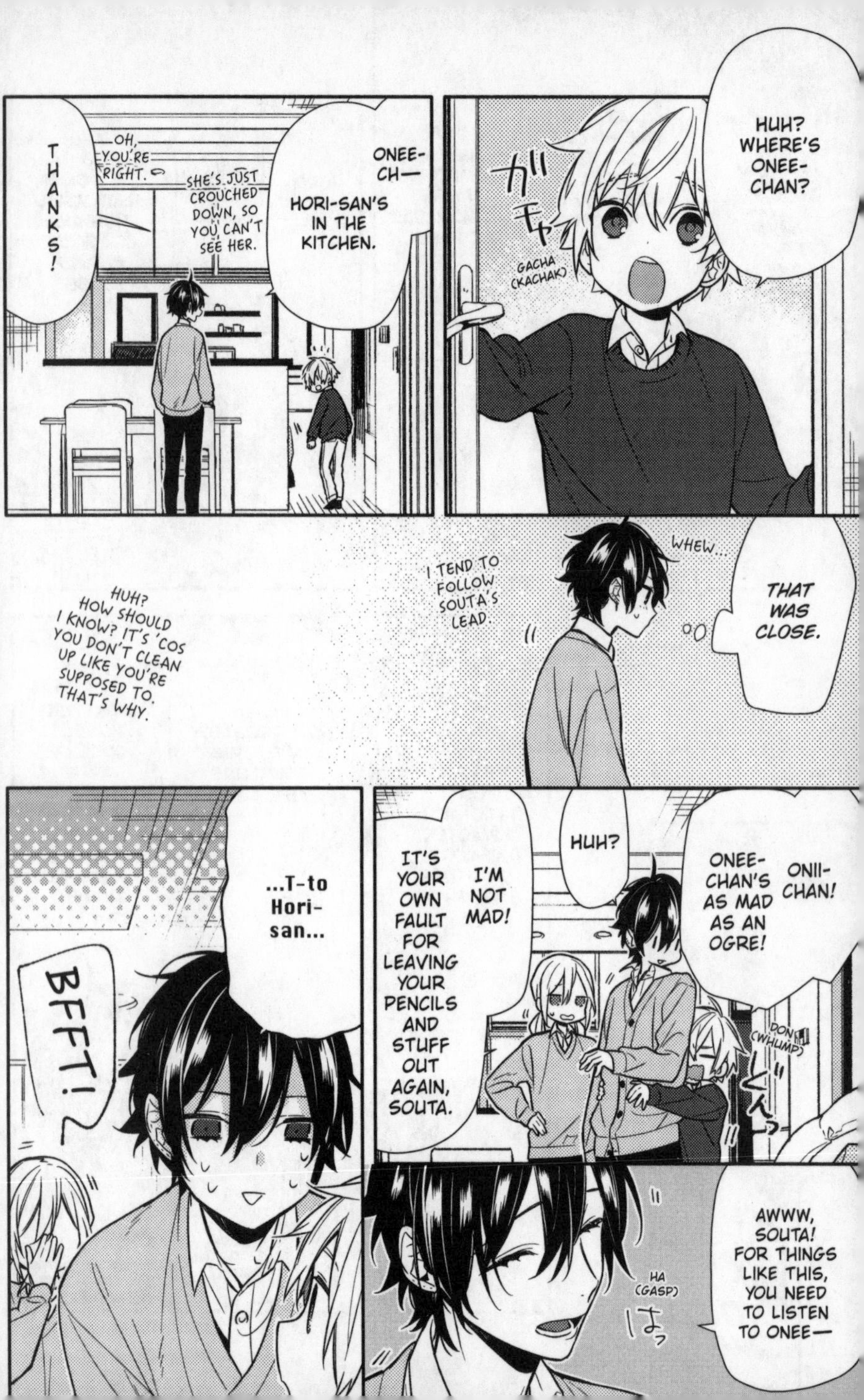
HUH? WHERE'S ONEE-CHAN?
GACHA (KACHAK)
ONEE-CH—
HORI-SAN'S IN THE KITCHEN.
SHE'S JUST CROUCHED DOWN, SO YOU CAN'T SEE HER.
—OH, YOU'RE RIGHT.
THANKS!
WHEW...
THAT WAS CLOSE.
I TEND TO FOLLOW SOUTA'S LEAD.
HUH? HOW SHOULD I KNOW? IT'S 'COS YOU DON'T CLEAN UP LIKE YOU'RE SUPPOSED TO. THAT'S WHY.
ONII-CHAN!
ONEE-CHAN'S AS MAD AS AN OGRE!
HUH?
I'M NOT MAD!
IT'S YOUR OWN FAULT FOR LEAVING YOUR PENCILS AND STUFF OUT AGAIN, SOUTA.
DON (WHUMP)
AWWW, SOUTA! FOR THINGS LIKE THIS, YOU NEED TO LISTEN TO ONEE—
HA (GASP)
...T-to Hori-san...
BFFT!

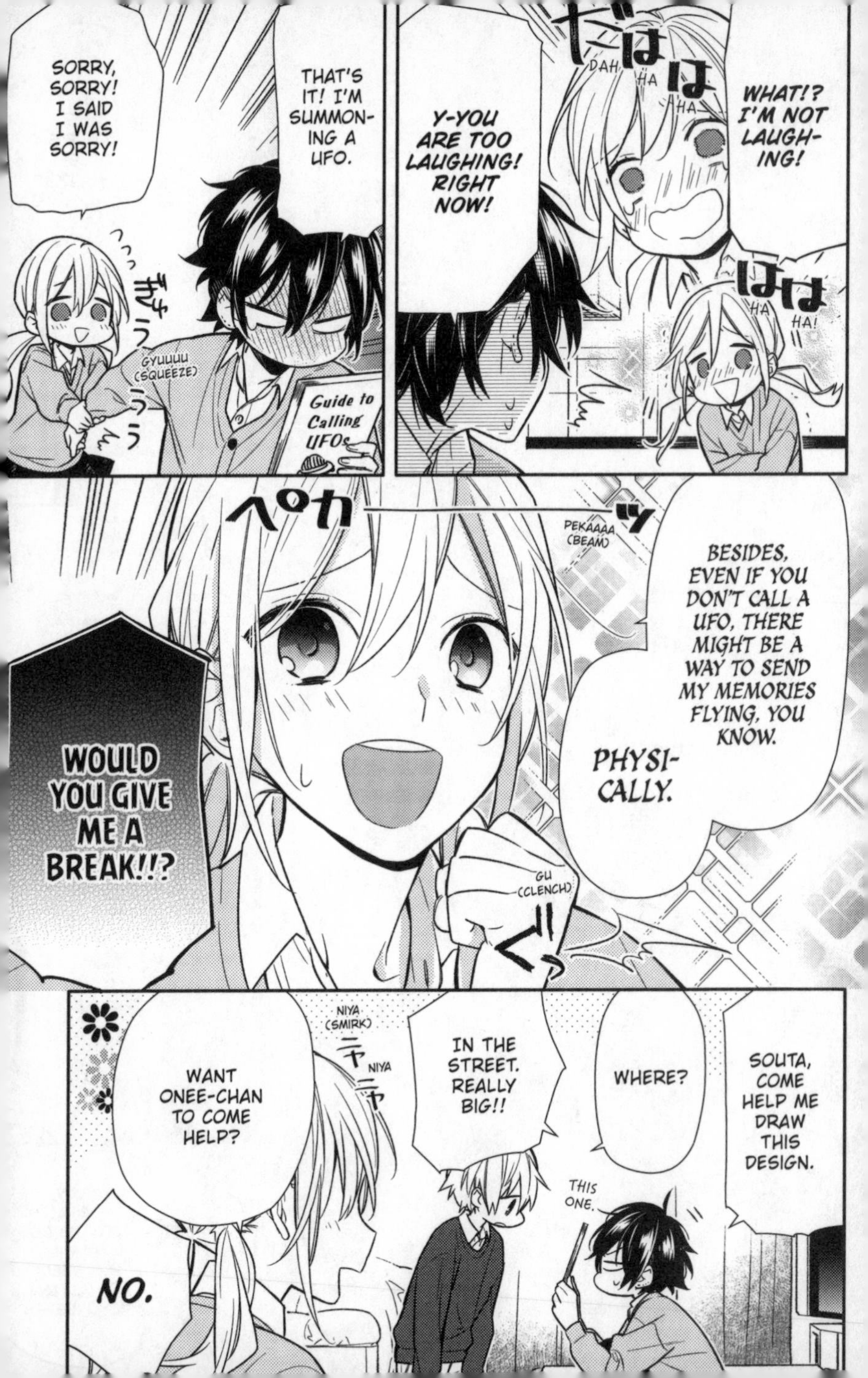
だはは
DAH HA HA
WHAT!? I'M NOT LAUGHING!
Y-YOU ARE TOO LAUGHING! RIGHT NOW!
はは
HA HA!
THAT'S IT! I'M SUMMONING A UFO.
SORRY, SORRY! I SAID I WAS SORRY!
GYUUUU (SQUEEZE)
Guide to Calling UFOs
PEKAAAA (BEAM)
BESIDES, EVEN IF YOU DON'T CALL A UFO, THERE MIGHT BE A WAY TO SEND MY MEMORIES FLYING, YOU KNOW.
PHYSICALLY.
GU (CLENCH)
WOULD YOU GIVE ME A BREAK!!?
SOUTA, COME HELP ME DRAW THIS DESIGN.
THIS ONE.
WHERE?
IN THE STREET. REALLY BIG!!
NIYA (SMIRK)
NIYA
WANT ONEE-CHAN TO COME HELP?
NO.

HORIMIYA

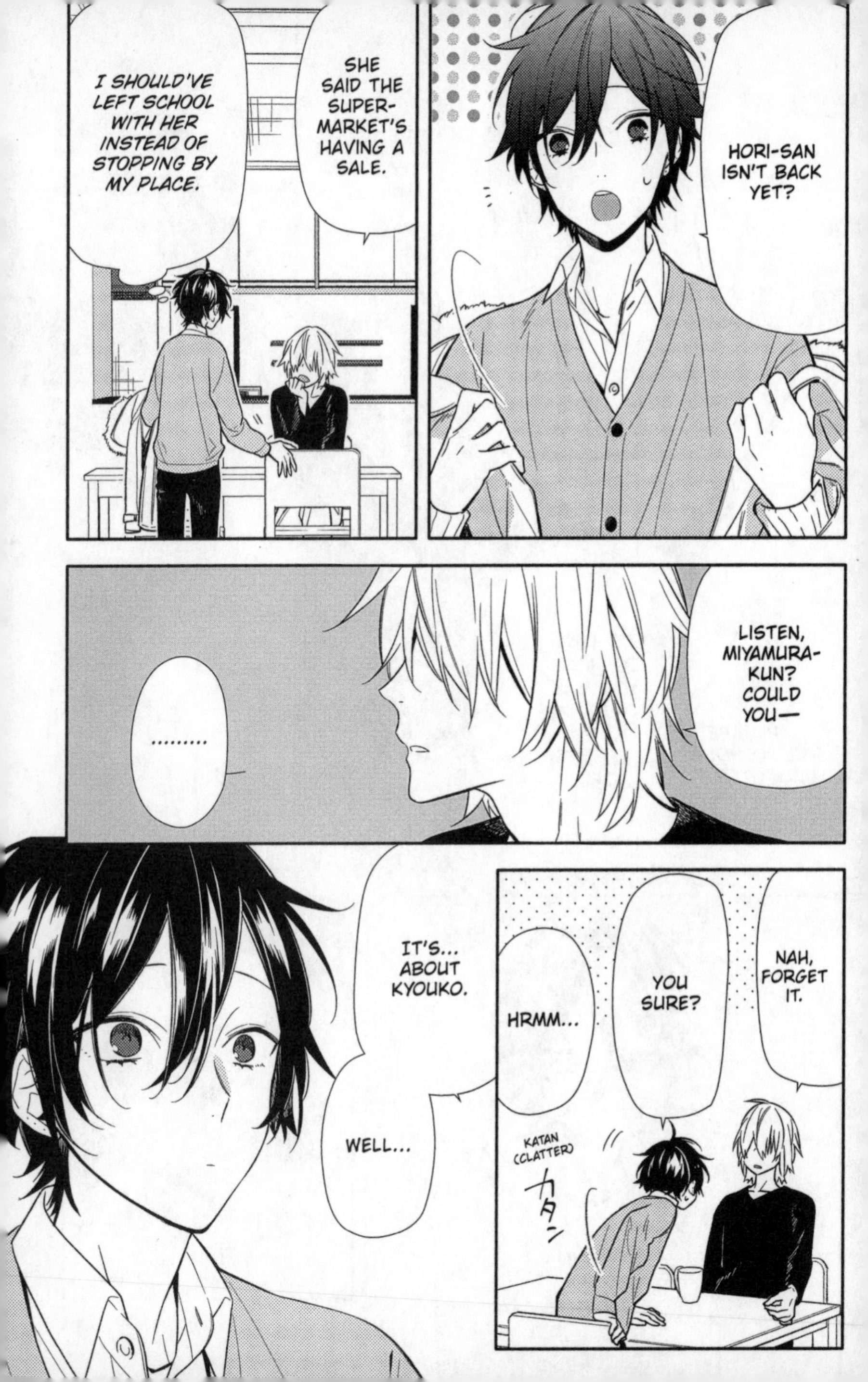
HORI-SAN ISN'T BACK YET?
SHE SAID THE SUPER-MARKET'S HAVING A SALE.
I SHOULD'VE LEFT SCHOOL WITH HER INSTEAD OF STOPPING BY MY PLACE.
LISTEN, MIYAMURA-KUN? COULD YOU—
....
NAH, FORGET IT.
YOU SURE?
HRMM...
KATAN (CLATTER)
カタン
IT'S... ABOUT KYOUKO.
WELL...

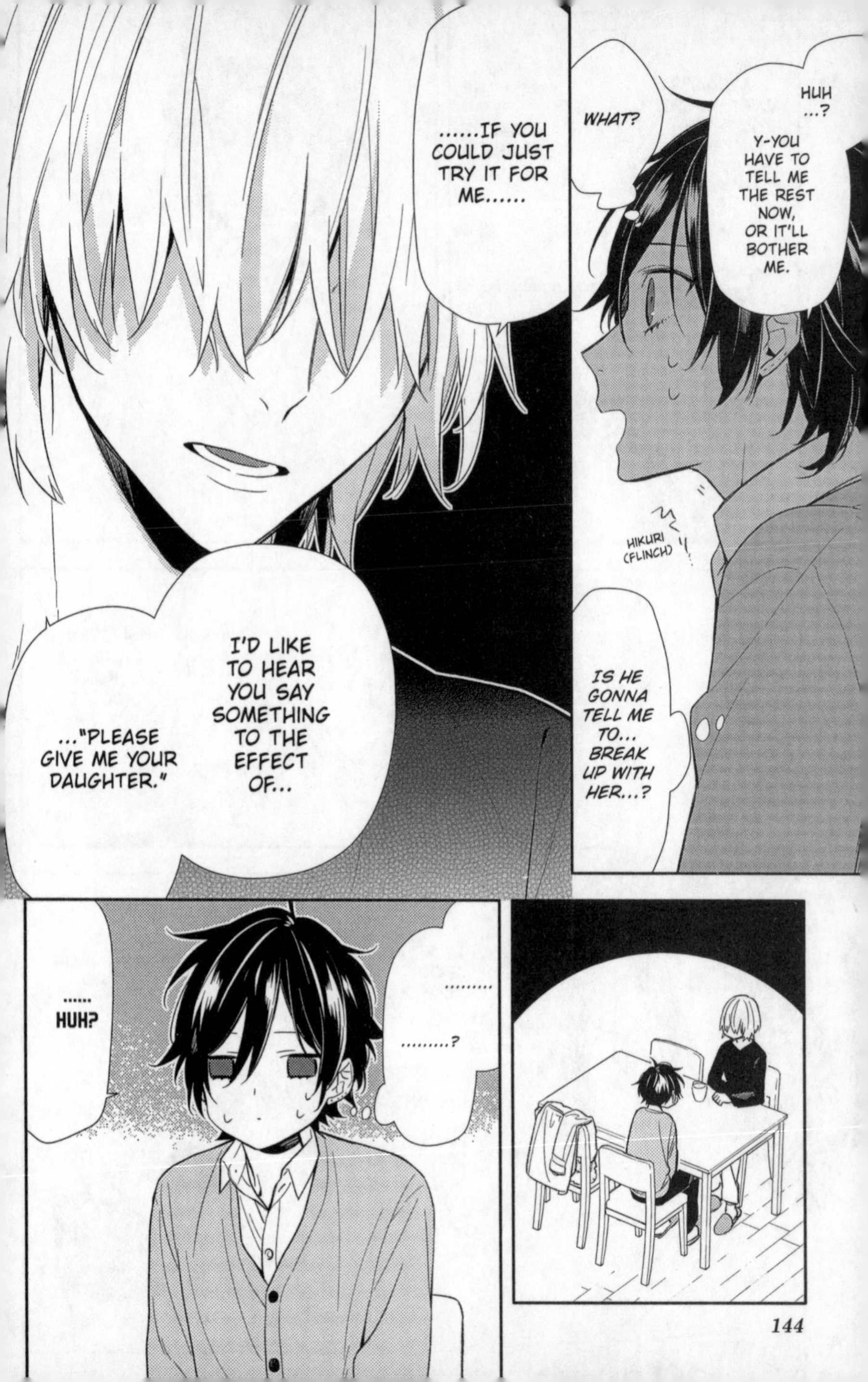
HUH ...?
Y-YOU HAVE TO TELL ME THE REST NOW, OR IT'LL BOTHER ME.
WHAT?
HIKURI (FLINCH)
IS HE GONNA TELL ME TO... BREAK UP WITH HER...?
......IF YOU COULD JUST TRY IT FOR ME......
I'D LIKE TO HEAR YOU SAY SOMETHING TO THE EFFECT OF...
..."PLEASE GIVE ME YOUR DAUGHTER."
....
.........?
...... HUH?

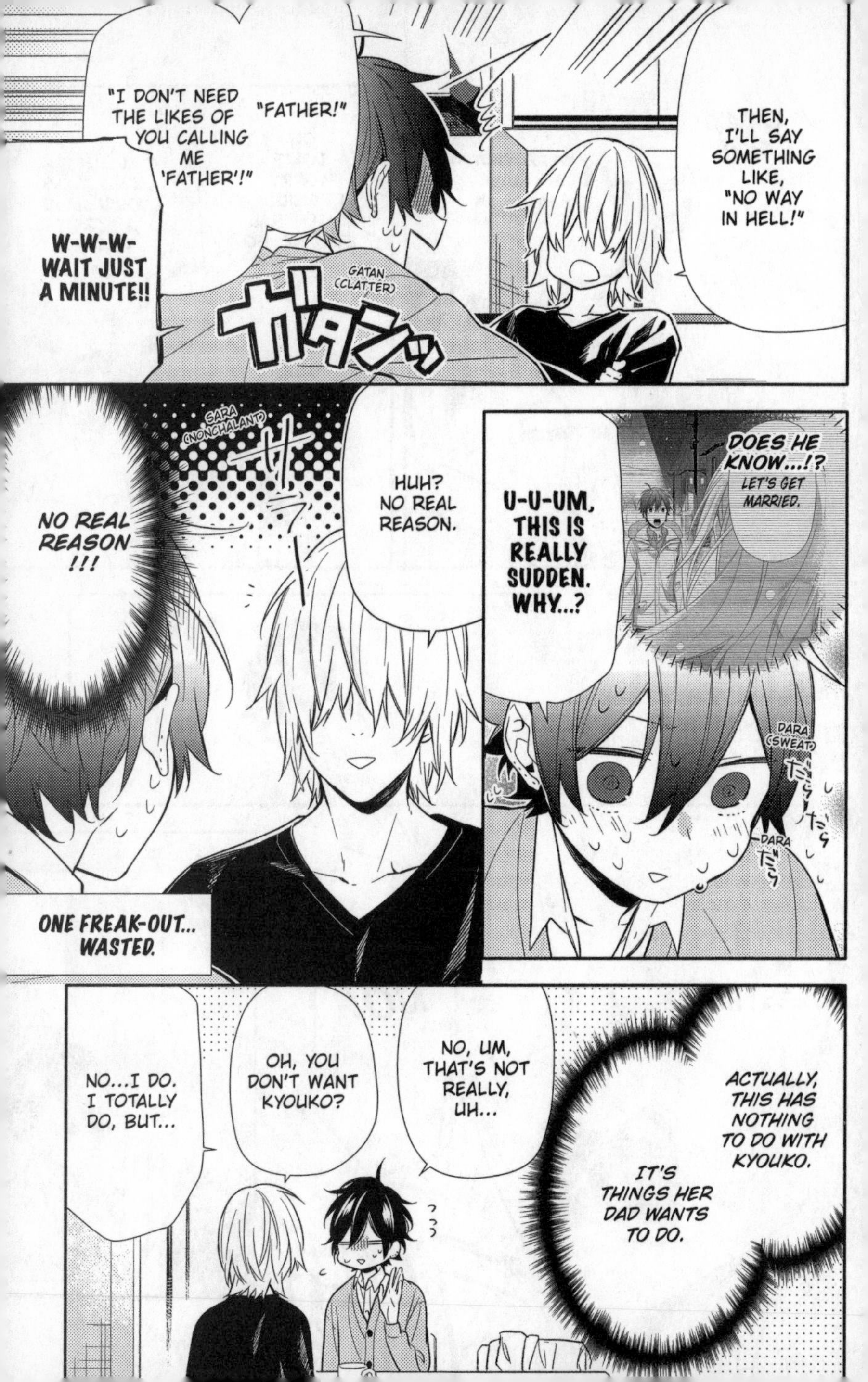
THEN, I'LL SAY SOMETHING LIKE, "NO WAY IN HELL!"
"FATHER!"
"I DON'T NEED THE LIKES OF YOU CALLING ME 'FATHER'!"
GATAN (CLATTER)
W-W-W-WAIT JUST A MINUTE!!
DOES HE KNOW...!?
LET'S GET MARRIED.
U-U-UM, THIS IS REALLY SUDDEN. WHY...?
DARA (SWEAT)
DARA
HUH? NO REAL REASON.
SARA (NONCHALANT)
NO REAL REASON !!!
ONE FREAK-OUT... WASTED.
ACTUALLY, THIS HAS NOTHING TO DO WITH KYOUKO.
IT'S THINGS HER DAD WANTS TO DO.
NO, UM, THAT'S NOT REALLY, UH...
OH, YOU DON'T WANT KYOUKO?
NO...I DO. I TOTALLY DO, BUT...

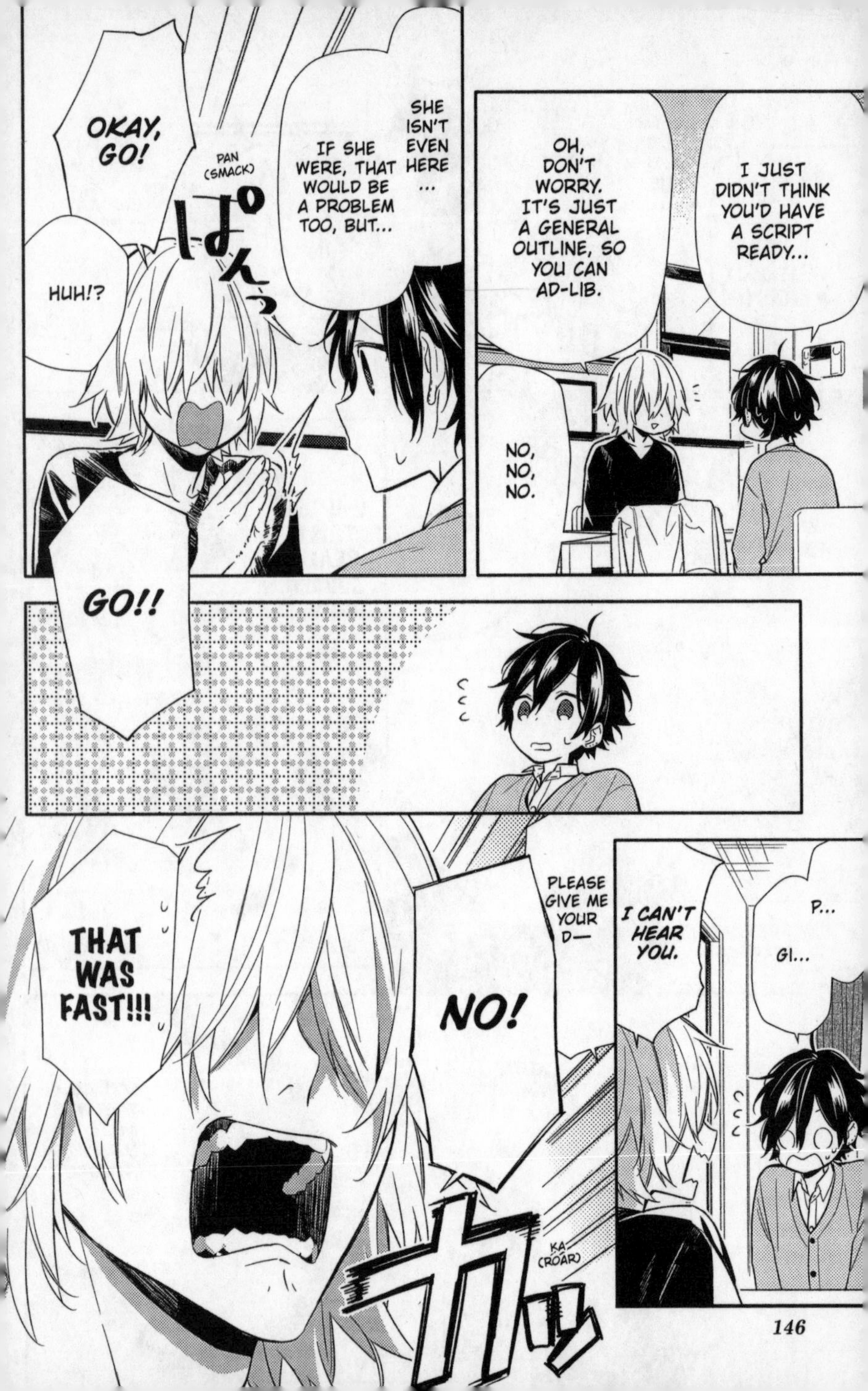
I JUST DIDN'T THINK YOU'D HAVE A SCRIPT READY...
OH, DON'T WORRY. IT'S JUST A GENERAL OUTLINE, SO YOU CAN AD-LIB.
NO, NO, NO.
SHE ISN'T EVEN HERE...
IF SHE WERE, THAT WOULD BE A PROBLEM TOO, BUT...
PAN (SMACK)
OKAY, GO!
HUH!?
GO!!
P...
GI...
I CAN'T HEAR YOU.
PLEASE GIVE ME YOUR D—
NO!
KA (ROAR)
THAT WAS FAST!!!

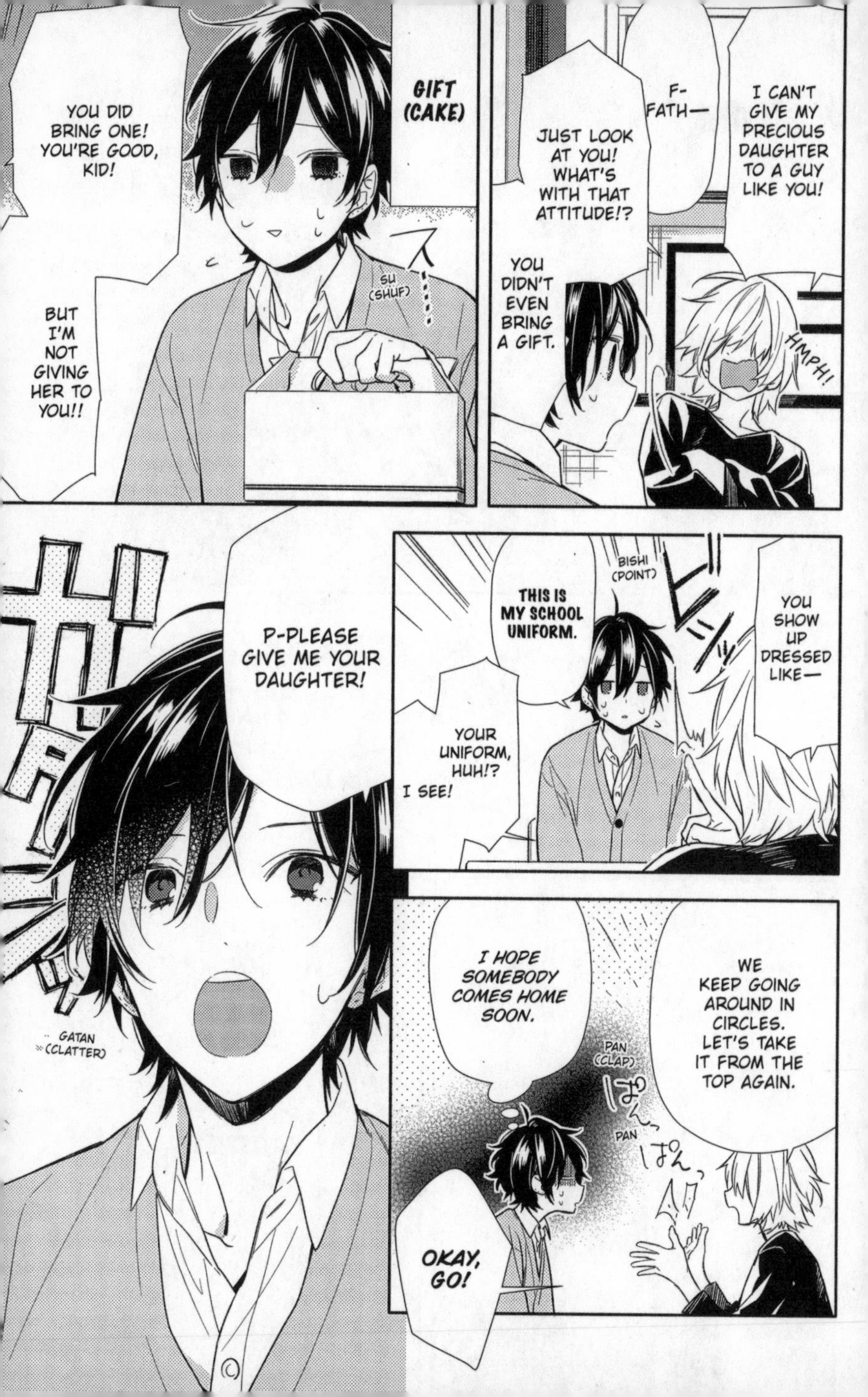
I CAN'T GIVE MY PRECIOUS DAUGHTER TO A GUY LIKE YOU!
F-FATH—
JUST LOOK AT YOU! WHAT'S WITH THAT ATTITUDE!?
YOU DIDN'T EVEN BRING A GIFT.
HMPH!
GIFT (CAKE)
SU (SHUF)
YOU DID BRING ONE! YOU'RE GOOD, KID!
BUT I'M NOT GIVING HER TO YOU!!
YOU SHOW UP DRESSED LIKE—
BISHI (POINT)
THIS IS MY SCHOOL UNIFORM.
YOUR UNIFORM, HUH!? I SEE!
WE KEEP GOING AROUND IN CIRCLES. LET'S TAKE IT FROM THE TOP AGAIN.
PAN (CLAP)
PAN
I HOPE SOMEBODY COMES HOME SOON.
OKAY, GO!
P-PLEASE GIVE ME YOUR DAUGHTER!
GATAN (CLATTER)

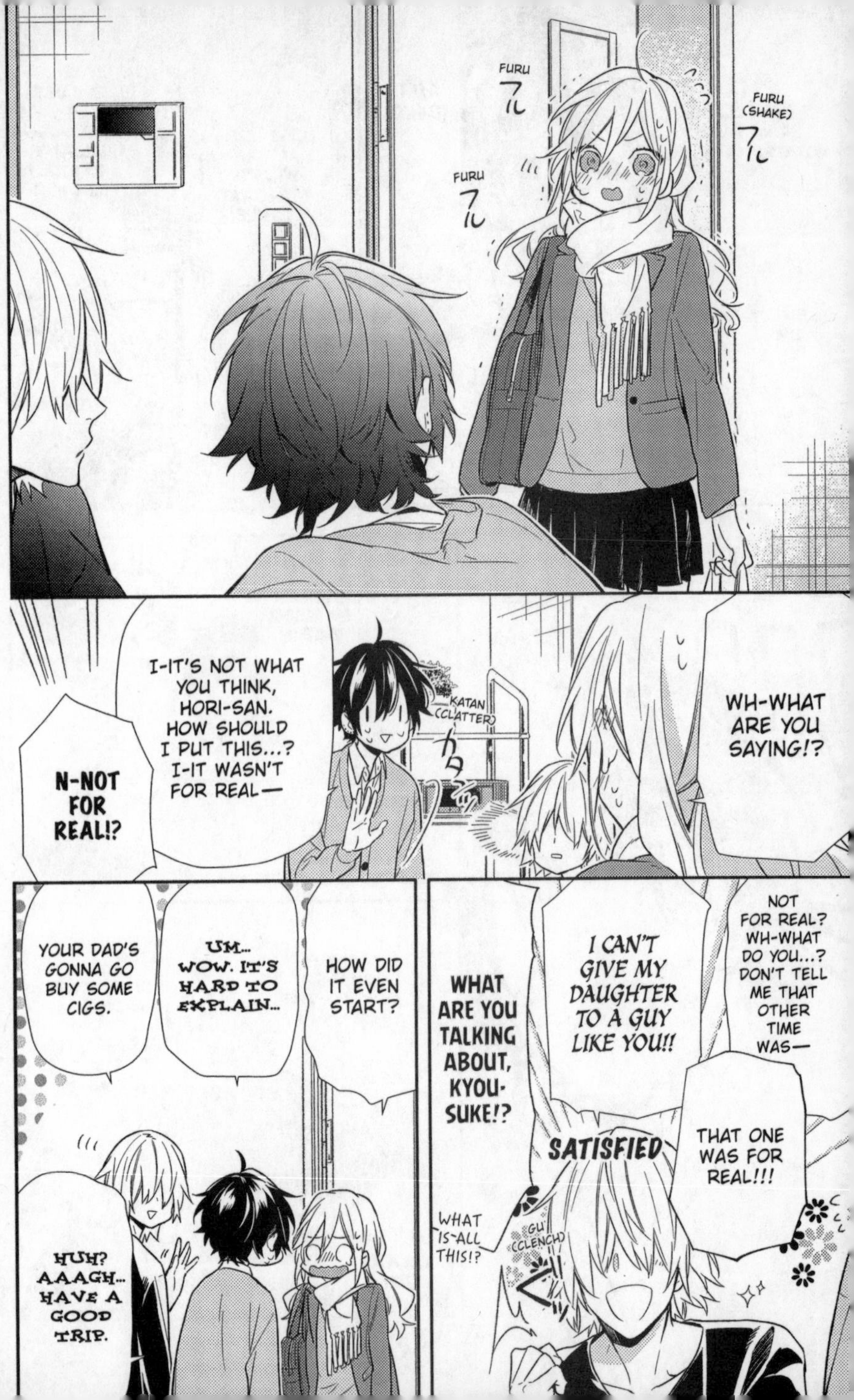
FURU (SHAKE)
フル
FURU
フル
FURU
フル
WH-WHAT ARE YOU SAYING!?
KATAN (CLATTER)
カタ
I-IT'S NOT WHAT YOU THINK, HORI-SAN. HOW SHOULD I PUT THIS...? I-IT WASN'T FOR REAL—
N-NOT FOR REAL!?
NOT FOR REAL? WH-WHAT DO YOU...? DON'T TELL ME THAT OTHER TIME WAS—
I CAN'T GIVE MY DAUGHTER TO A GUY LIKE YOU!!
WHAT ARE YOU TALKING ABOUT, KYOU-SUKE!?
THAT ONE WAS FOR REAL!!!
SATISFIED
GU (CLENCH)
WHAT IS ALL THIS!?
HOW DID IT EVEN START?
UM... WOW. IT'S HARD TO EXPLAIN...
YOUR DAD'S GONNA GO BUY SOME CIGS.
HUH? AAAGH... HAVE A GOOD TRIP.

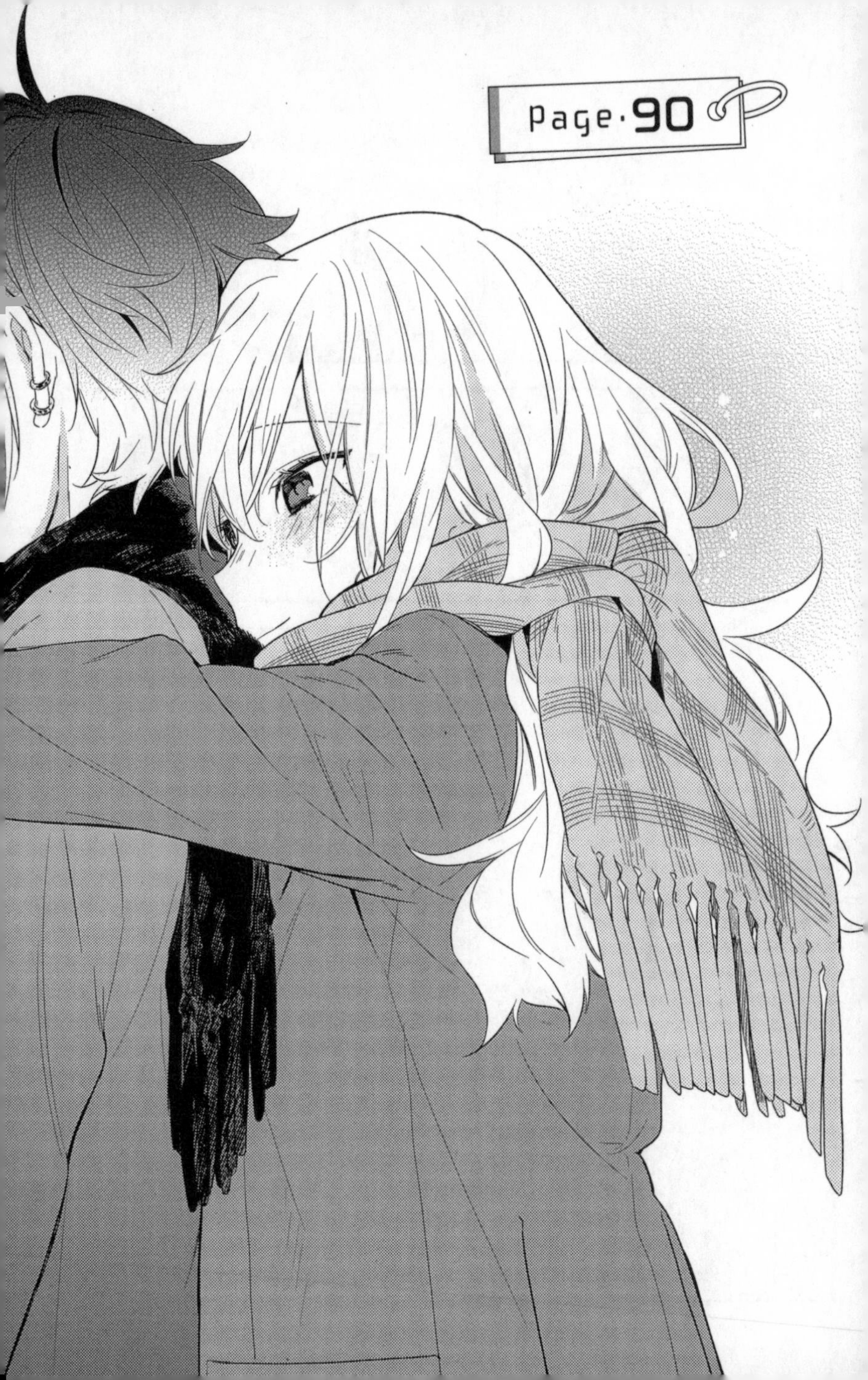
Page·90

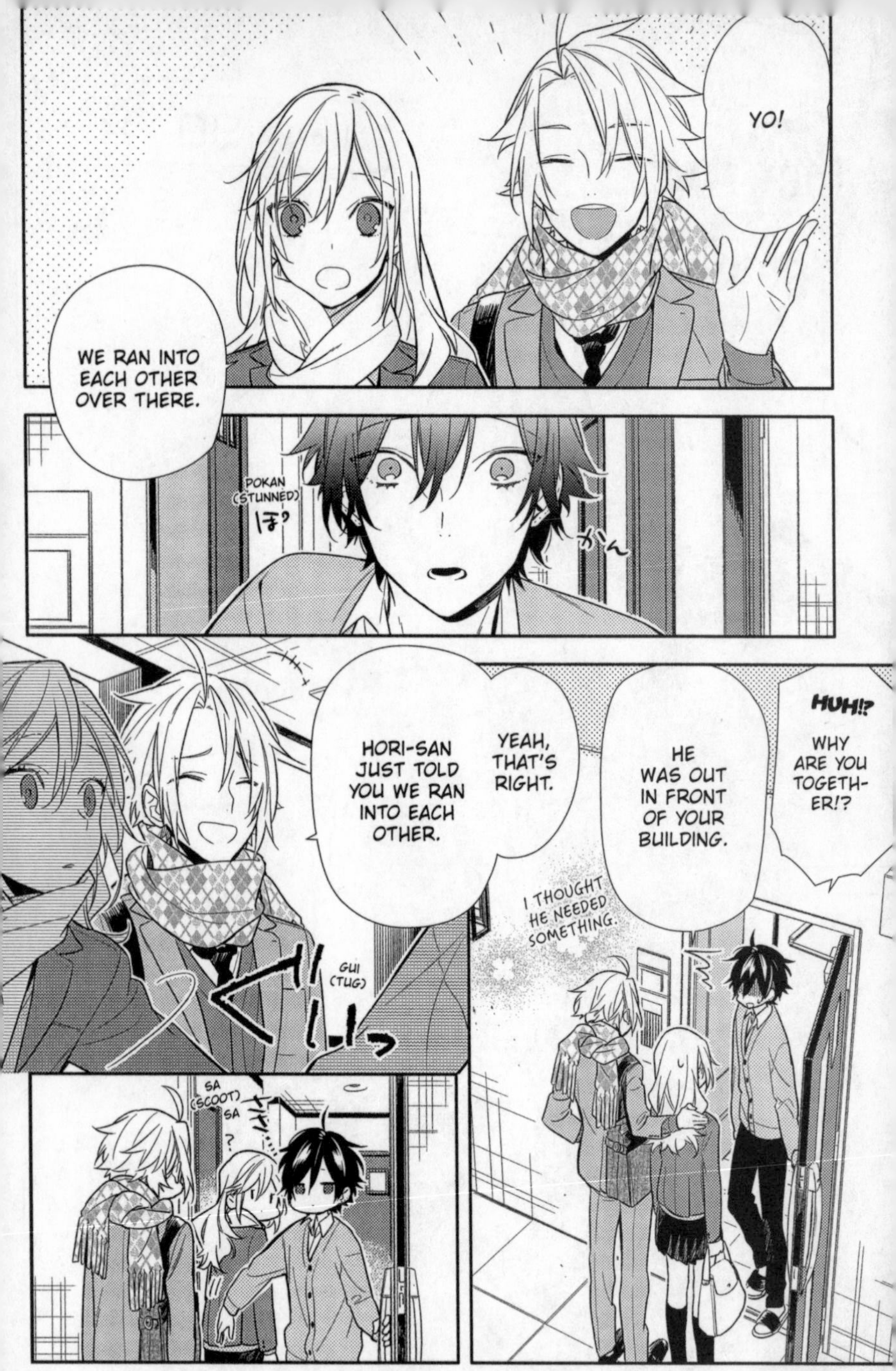
YO!
WE RAN INTO EACH OTHER OVER THERE.
POKAN (STUNNED)
HUH!? WHY ARE YOU TOGETH-ER!?
HE WAS OUT IN FRONT OF YOUR BUILDING.
I THOUGHT HE NEEDED SOMETHING.
YEAH, THAT'S RIGHT.
HORI-SAN JUST TOLD YOU WE RAN INTO EACH OTHER.
GUI (TUG)
SA (SCOOT) SA
?

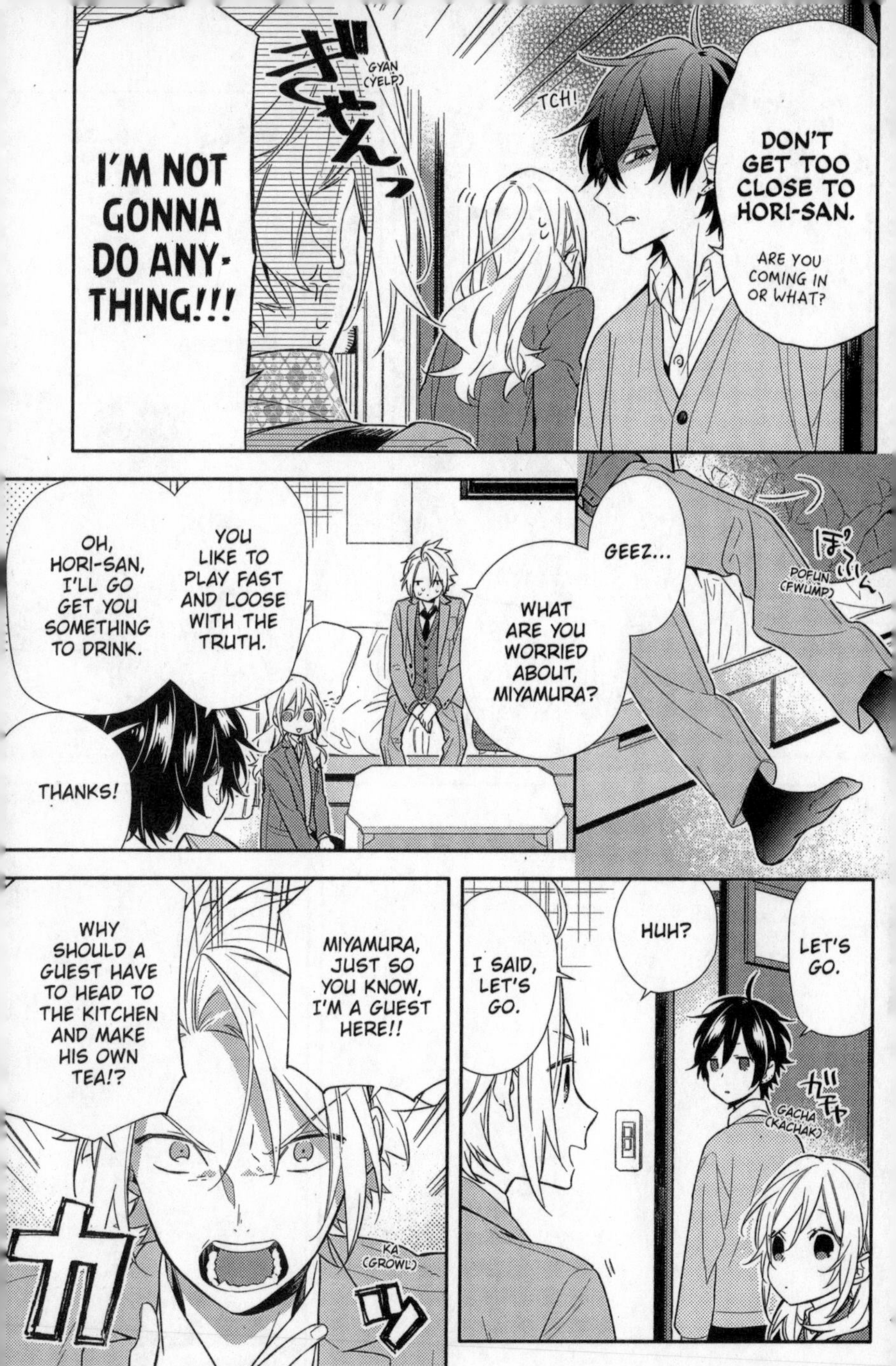
DON'T GET TOO CLOSE TO HORI-SAN.
ARE YOU COMING IN OR WHAT?
TCH!
GYAN (YELP)
I'M NOT GONNA DO ANY-THING!!!
POFUN (FWUMP)
GEEZ...
WHAT ARE YOU WORRIED ABOUT, MIYAMURA?
YOU LIKE TO PLAY FAST AND LOOSE WITH THE TRUTH.
OH, HORI-SAN, I'LL GO GET YOU SOMETHING TO DRINK.
THANKS!
LET'S GO.
HUH?
I SAID, LET'S GO.
GACHA (KACHAK)
MIYAMURA, JUST SO YOU KNOW, I'M A GUEST HERE!!
WHY SHOULD A GUEST HAVE TO HEAD TO THE KITCHEN AND MAKE HIS OWN TEA!?
KA (GROWL)

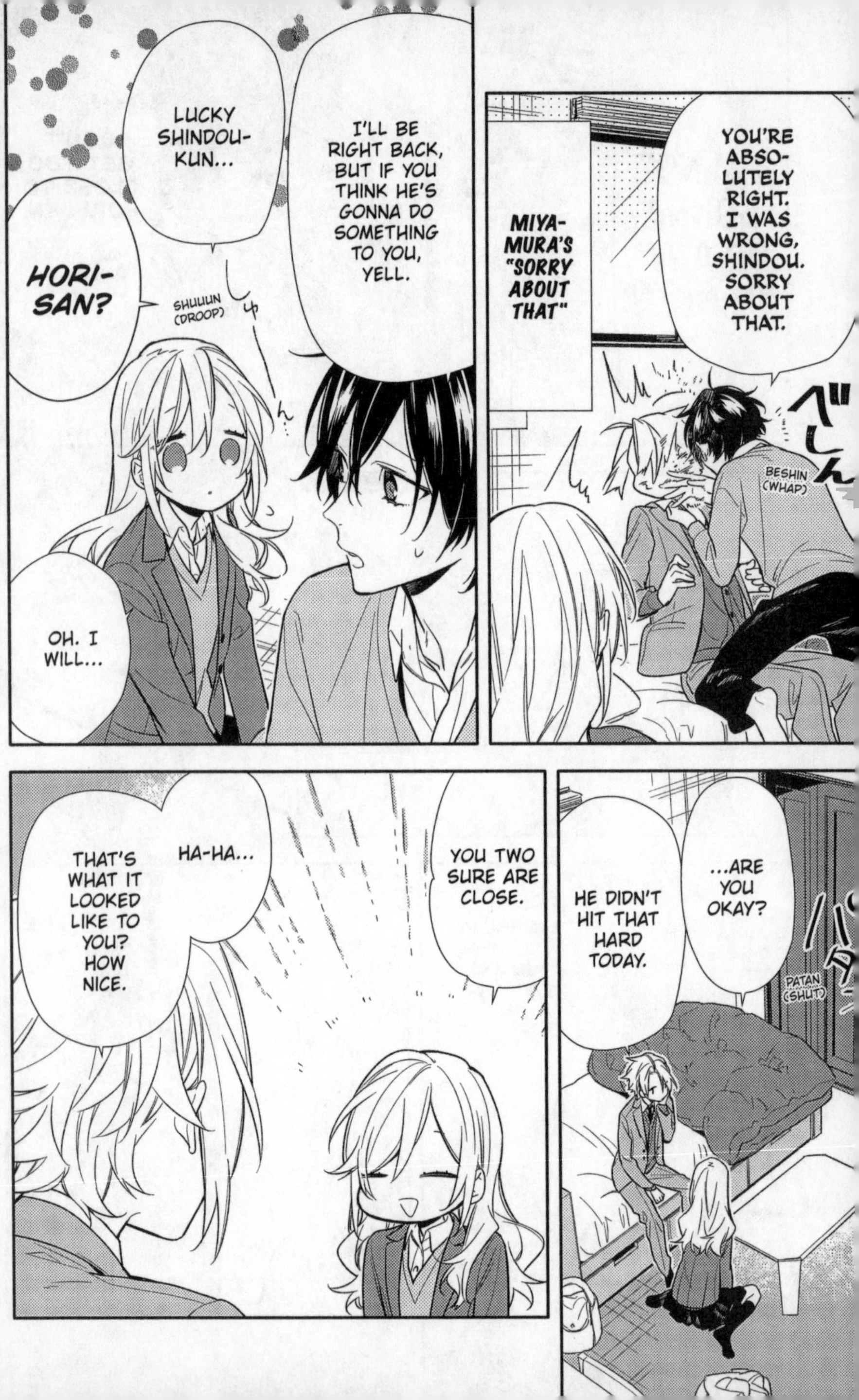
YOU'RE ABSOLUTELY RIGHT. I WAS WRONG, SHINDOU. SORRY ABOUT THAT.
MIYAMURA'S "SORRY ABOUT THAT"
べしん
BESHIN (WHAP)
I'LL BE RIGHT BACK, BUT IF YOU THINK HE'S GONNA DO SOMETHING TO YOU, YELL.
LUCKY SHINDOU-KUN...
HORI-SAN?
SHUUUN (DROOP)
OH. I WILL...
...ARE YOU OKAY?
HE DIDN'T HIT THAT HARD TODAY.
PATAN (SHUT)
YOU TWO SURE ARE CLOSE.
HA-HA...
THAT'S WHAT IT LOOKED LIKE TO YOU? HOW NICE.

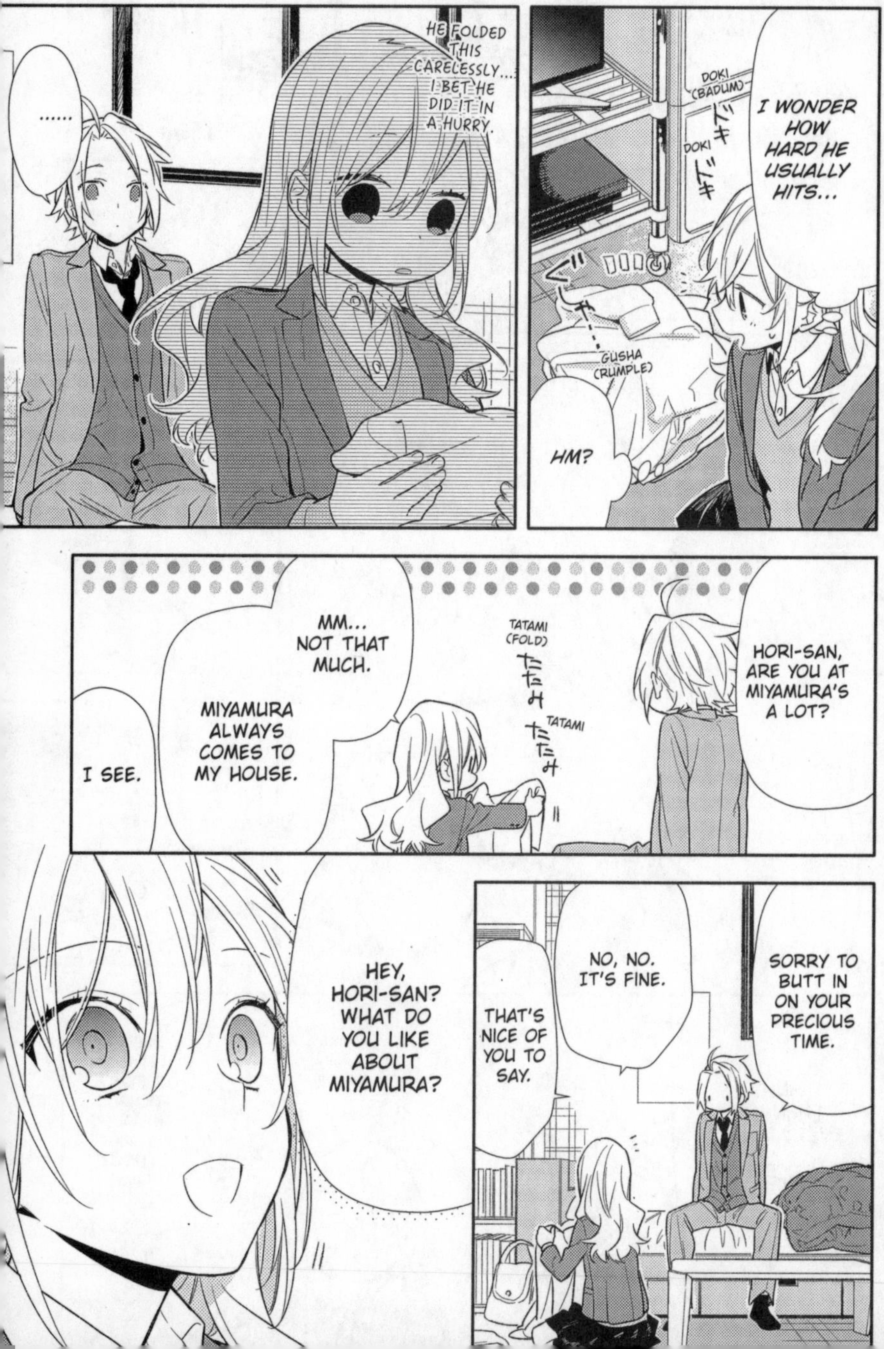
I WONDER HOW HARD HE USUALLY HITS...
DOKI (BADUM)
ドキ
DOKI
ドキ
GUSHA (RUMPLE)
HM?
HE FOLDED THIS CARELESSLY... I BET HE DID IT IN A HURRY.
......
HORI-SAN, ARE YOU AT MIYAMURA'S A LOT?
TATAMI (FOLD)
たたみ
TATAMI
たたみ
MM... NOT THAT MUCH.
MIYAMURA ALWAYS COMES TO MY HOUSE.
I SEE.
SORRY TO BUTT IN ON YOUR PRECIOUS TIME.
NO, NO. IT'S FINE.
THAT'S NICE OF YOU TO SAY.
HEY, HORI-SAN? WHAT DO YOU LIKE ABOUT MIYAMURA?

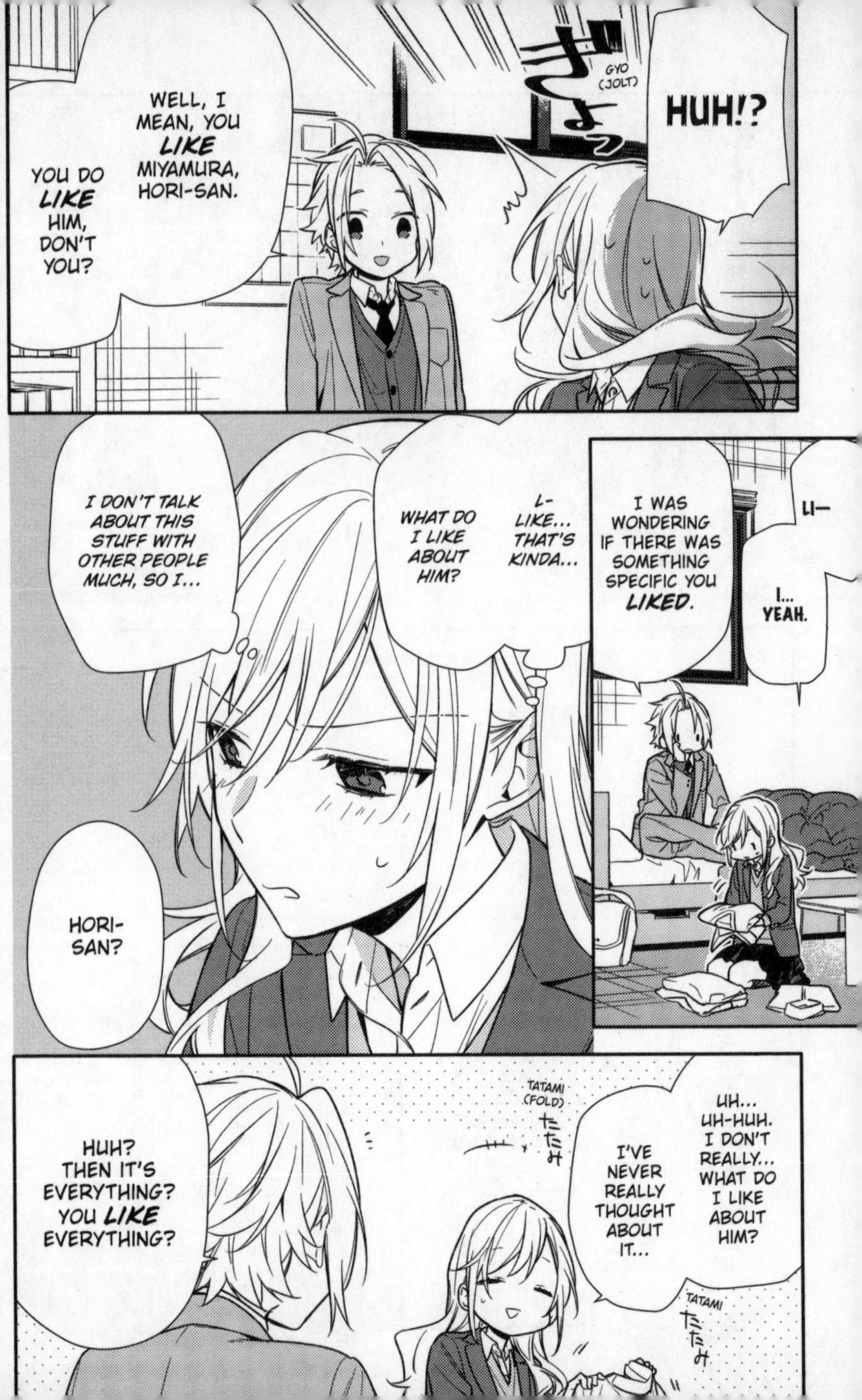
HUH!?
GYO (JOLT)
ぎょっ
WELL, I MEAN, YOU LIKE MIYAMURA, HORI-SAN.
YOU DO LIKE HIM, DON'T YOU?
LI—
I... YEAH.
I WAS WONDERING IF THERE WAS SOMETHING SPECIFIC YOU LIKED.
L- LIKE... THAT'S KINDA...
WHAT DO I LIKE ABOUT HIM?
I DON'T TALK ABOUT THIS STUFF WITH OTHER PEOPLE MUCH, SO I...
HORI-SAN?
UH... UH-HUH. I DON'T REALLY... WHAT DO I LIKE ABOUT HIM?
TATAMI
たたみ
I'VE NEVER REALLY THOUGHT ABOUT IT...
TATAMI (FOLD)
たたみ
HUH? THEN IT'S EVERYTHING? YOU LIKE EVERYTHING?

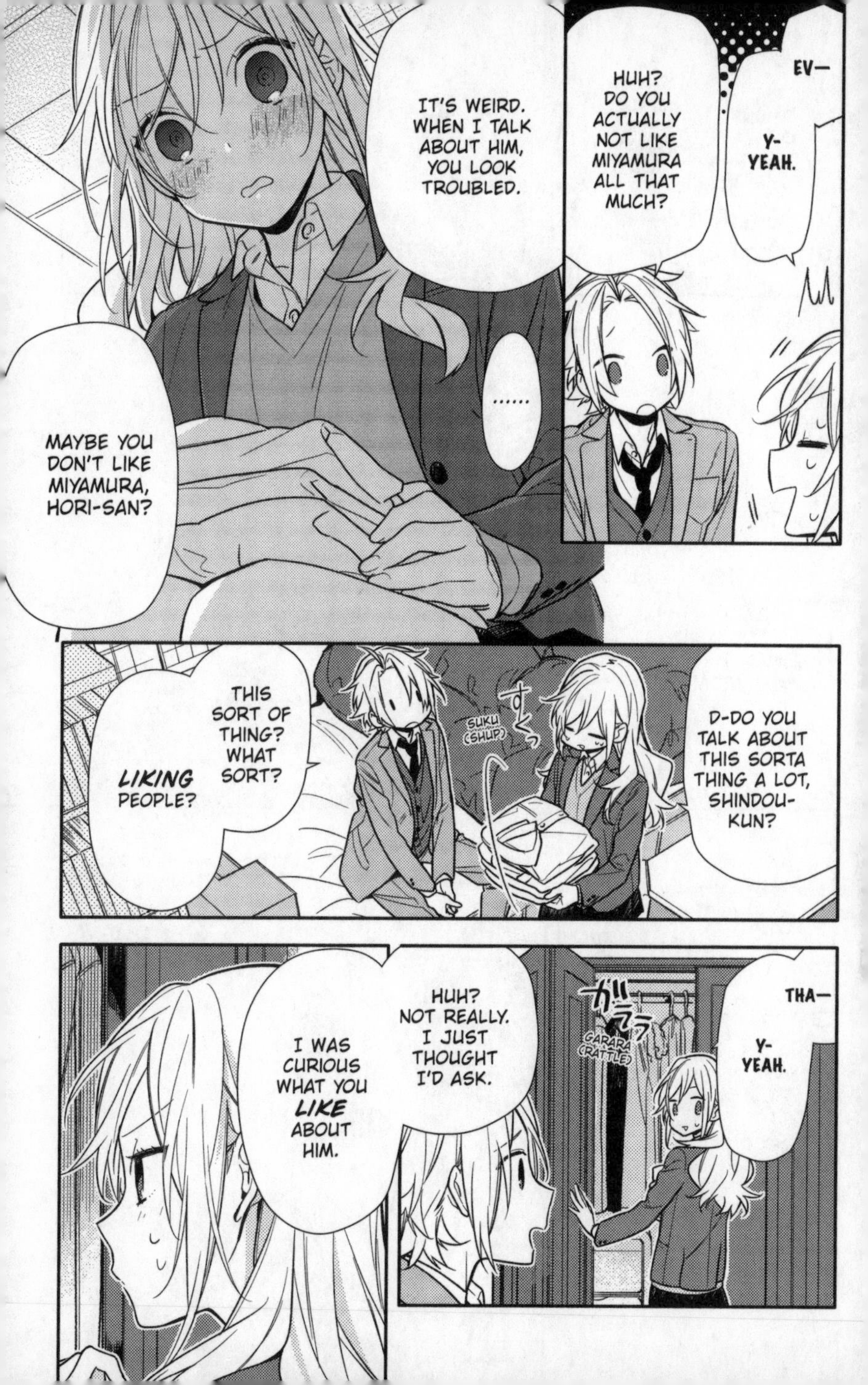
EV—
Y-YEAH.
HUH? DO YOU ACTUALLY NOT LIKE MIYAMURA ALL THAT MUCH?
IT'S WEIRD. WHEN I TALK ABOUT HIM, YOU LOOK TROUBLED.
......
MAYBE YOU DON'T LIKE MIYAMURA, HORI-SAN?
D-DO YOU TALK ABOUT THIS SORTA THING A LOT, SHINDOU-KUN?
すっ
SUKU (SHUP)
THIS SORT OF THING? WHAT SORT?
LIKING PEOPLE?
THA—
Y-YEAH.
ガラ
GARARA (RATTLE)
HUH? NOT REALLY. I JUST THOUGHT I'D ASK.
I WAS CURIOUS WHAT YOU LIKE ABOUT HIM.

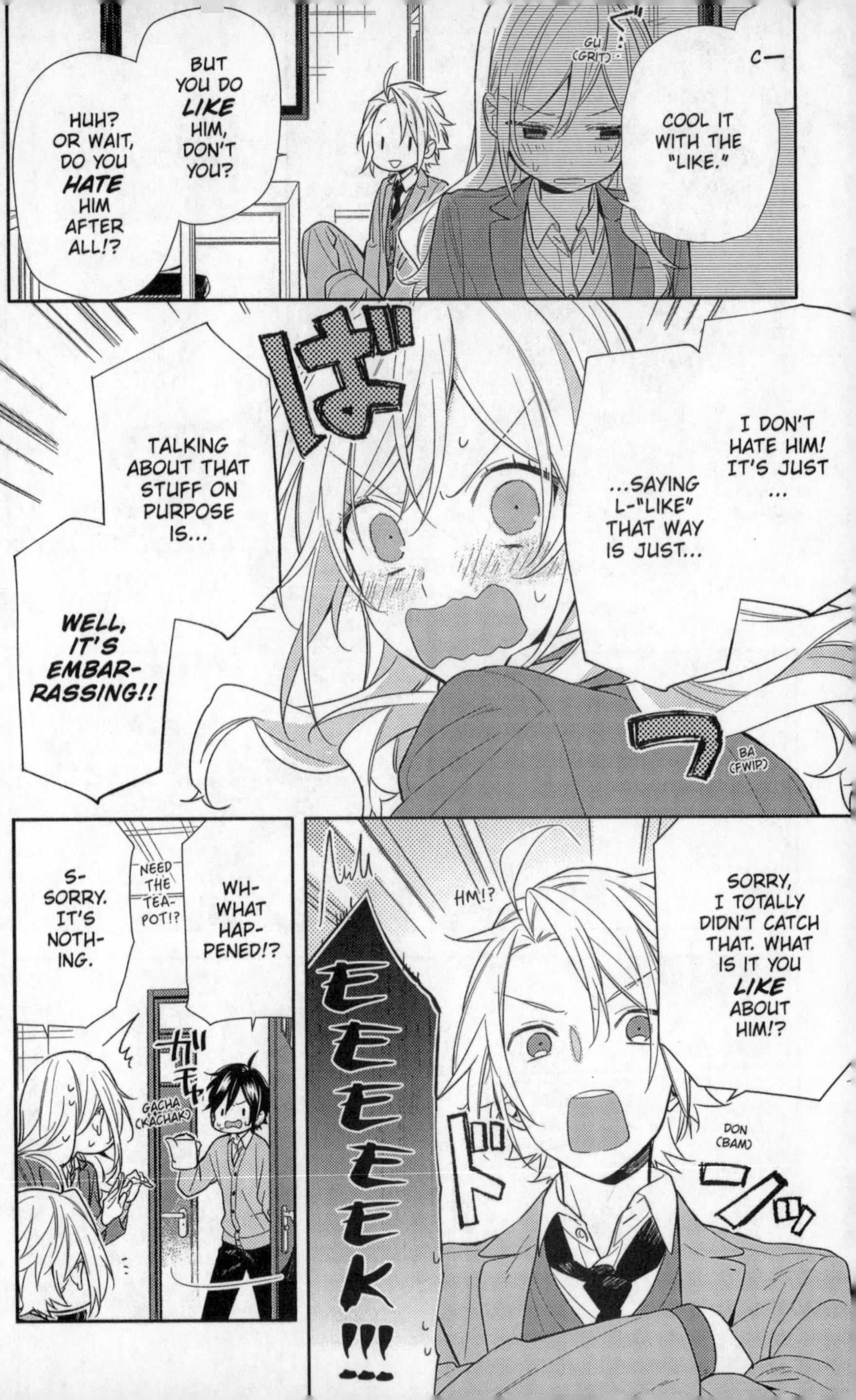
C—
COOL IT WITH THE "LIKE."
GU (GRIT)
BUT YOU DO LIKE HIM, DON'T YOU?
HUH? OR WAIT, DO YOU HATE HIM AFTER ALL!?
I DON'T HATE HIM! IT'S JUST ...
...SAYING L-"LIKE" THAT WAY IS JUST...
ばっ
TALKING ABOUT THAT STUFF ON PURPOSE IS...
WELL, IT'S EMBARRASSING!!
BA (FWIP)
SORRY, I TOTALLY DIDN'T CATCH THAT. WHAT IS IT YOU LIKE ABOUT HIM!?
HM!?
DON (BAM)
EEEEEK!!!
WH-WHAT HAP-PENED!?
NEED THE TEA-POT!?
S-SORRY. IT'S NOTH-ING.
GACHA (KACHAK)

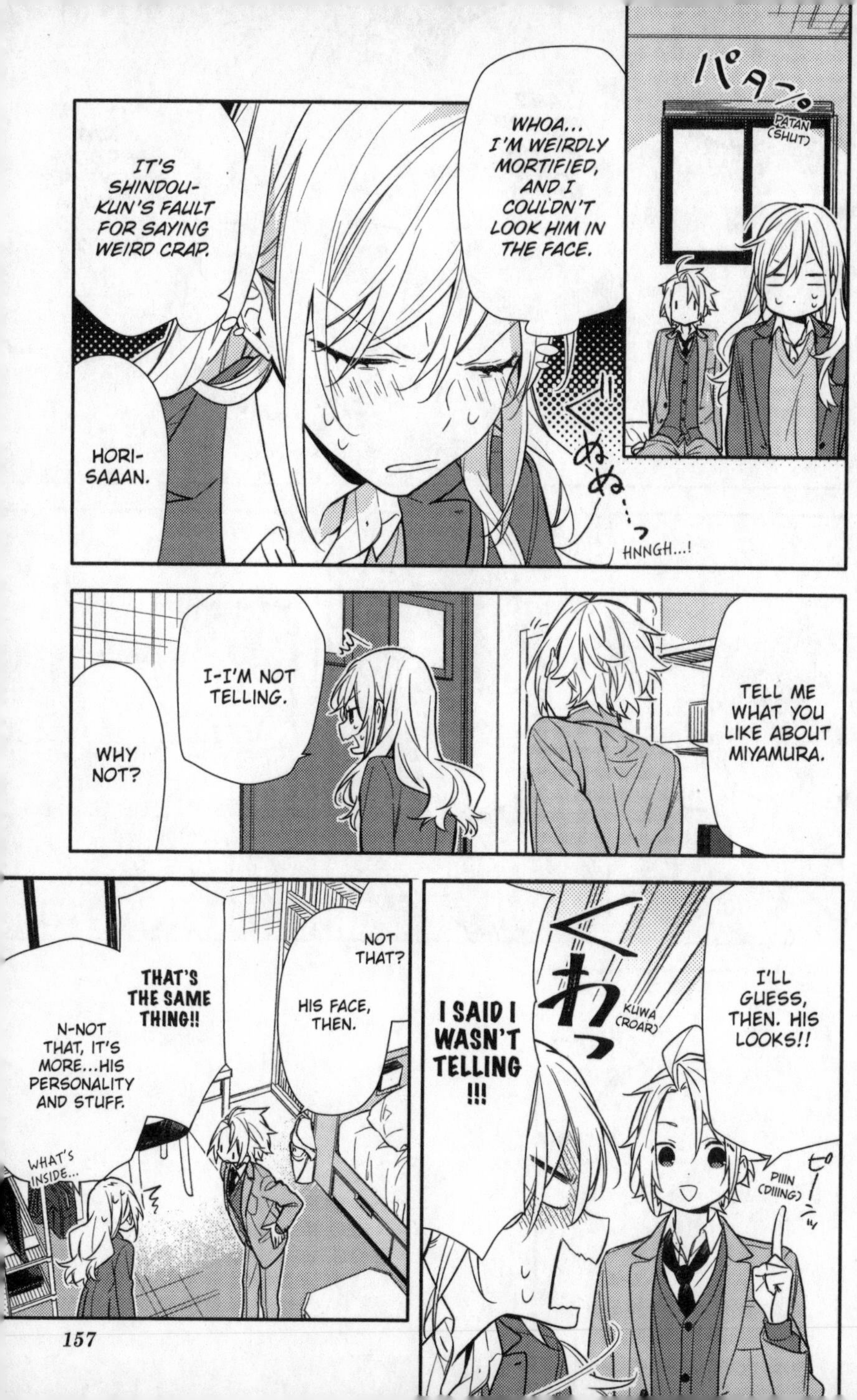
パタン。
PATAN (SHUT)
WHOA... I'M WEIRDLY MORTIFIED, AND I COULDN'T LOOK HIM IN THE FACE.
ぬぬ…っ
HNNGH...!
IT'S SHINDOU-KUN'S FAULT FOR SAYING WEIRD CRAP.
HORI-SAAAN.
TELL ME WHAT YOU LIKE ABOUT MIYAMURA.
I-I'M NOT TELLING.
WHY NOT?
I'LL GUESS, THEN. HIS LOOKS!!
ピーン
PIIIN (DIIING)
くわっ
KUWA (ROAR)
I SAID I WASN'T TELLING!!!
NOT THAT?
HIS FACE, THEN.
THAT'S THE SAME THING!!
N-NOT THAT, IT'S MORE...HIS PERSONALITY AND STUFF.
WHAT'S INSIDE...

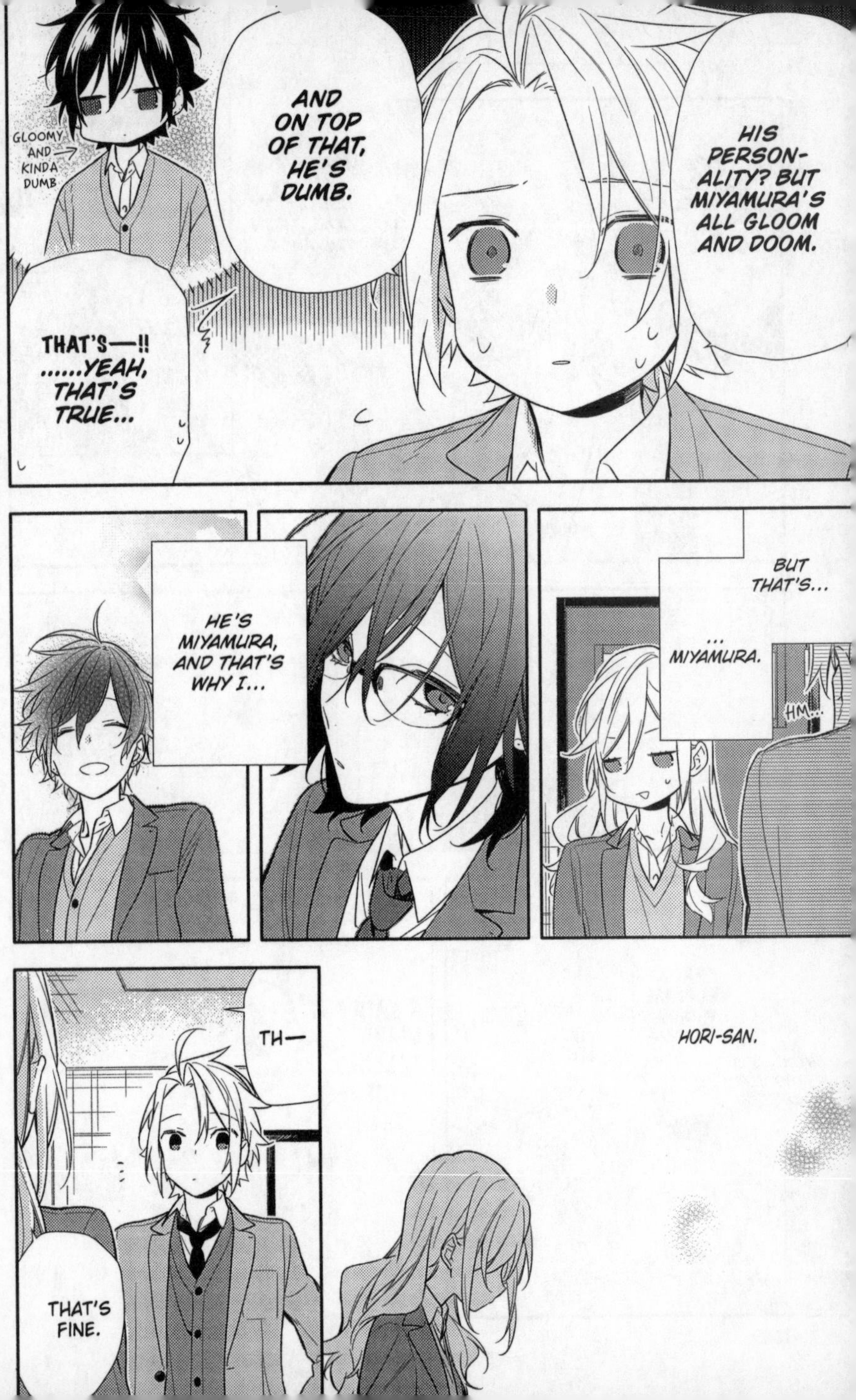
HIS PERSONALITY? BUT MIYAMURA'S ALL GLOOM AND DOOM.
AND ON TOP OF THAT, HE'S DUMB.
GLOOMY AND KINDA DUMB
THAT'S—!! ......YEAH, THAT'S TRUE...
BUT THAT'S...
... MIYAMURA.
HM...
HE'S MIYAMURA, AND THAT'S WHY I...
HORI-SAN.
TH—
THAT'S FINE.

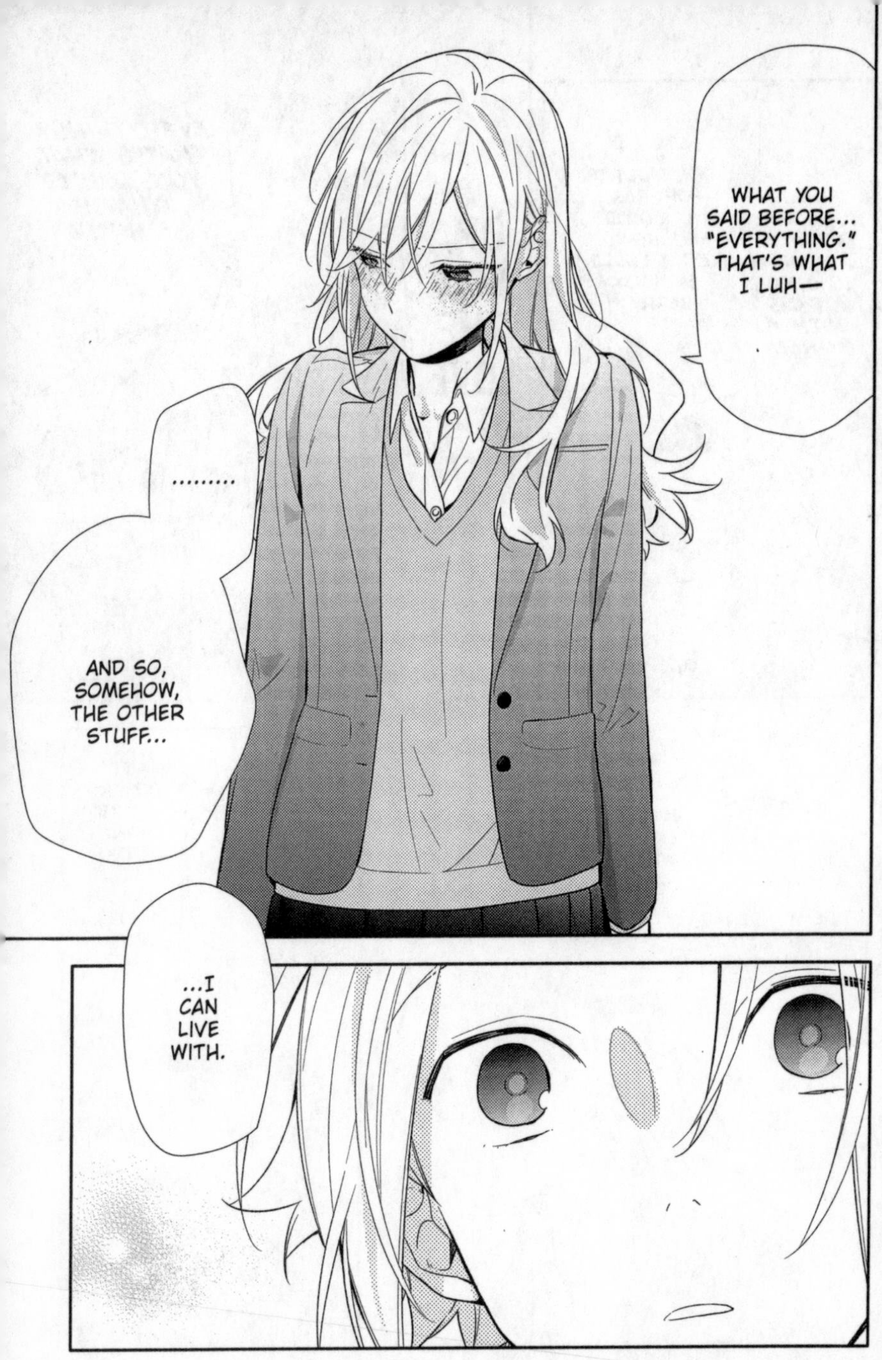
WHAT YOU SAID BEFORE... "EVERYTHING." THAT'S WHAT I LUH—
....
AND SO, SOMEHOW, THE OTHER STUFF...
...I CAN LIVE WITH.

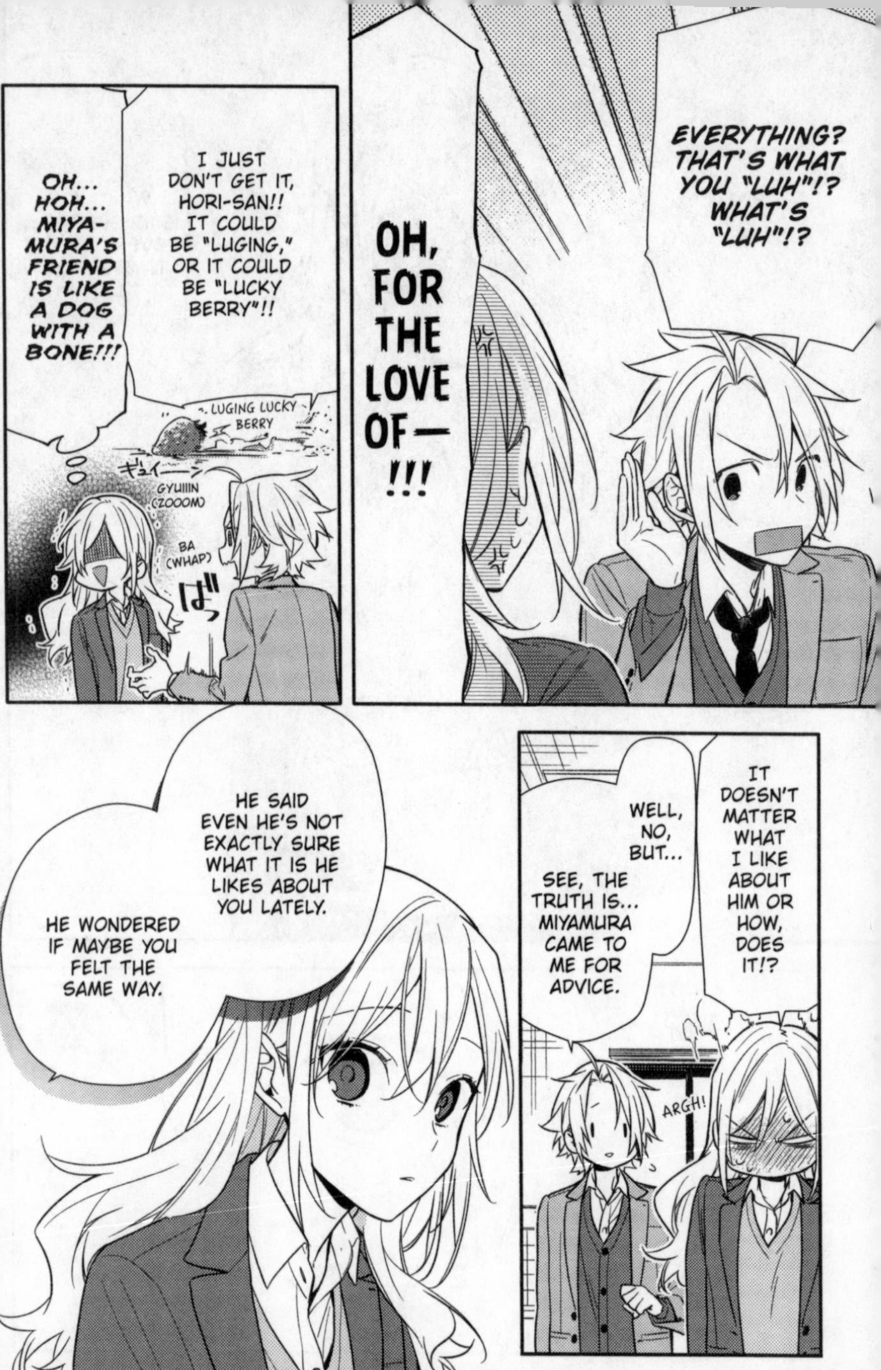
EVERYTHING? THAT'S WHAT YOU "LUH"!? WHAT'S "LUH"!?
OH, FOR THE LOVE OF—!!!
I JUST DON'T GET IT, HORI-SAN!! IT COULD BE "LUGING," OR IT COULD BE "LUCKY BERRY"!!
OH... HOH... MIYA-MURA'S FRIEND IS LIKE A DOG WITH A BONE!!!
LUGING LUCKY BERRY
ギュイーン
GYUIIIN (ZOOOM)
BA (WHAP)
ばっ
IT DOESN'T MATTER WHAT I LIKE ABOUT HIM OR HOW, DOES IT!?
WELL, NO, BUT...
SEE, THE TRUTH IS... MIYAMURA CAME TO ME FOR ADVICE.
ARGH!
HE SAID EVEN HE'S NOT EXACTLY SURE WHAT IT IS HE LIKES ABOUT YOU LATELY.
HE WONDERED IF MAYBE YOU FELT THE SAME WAY.

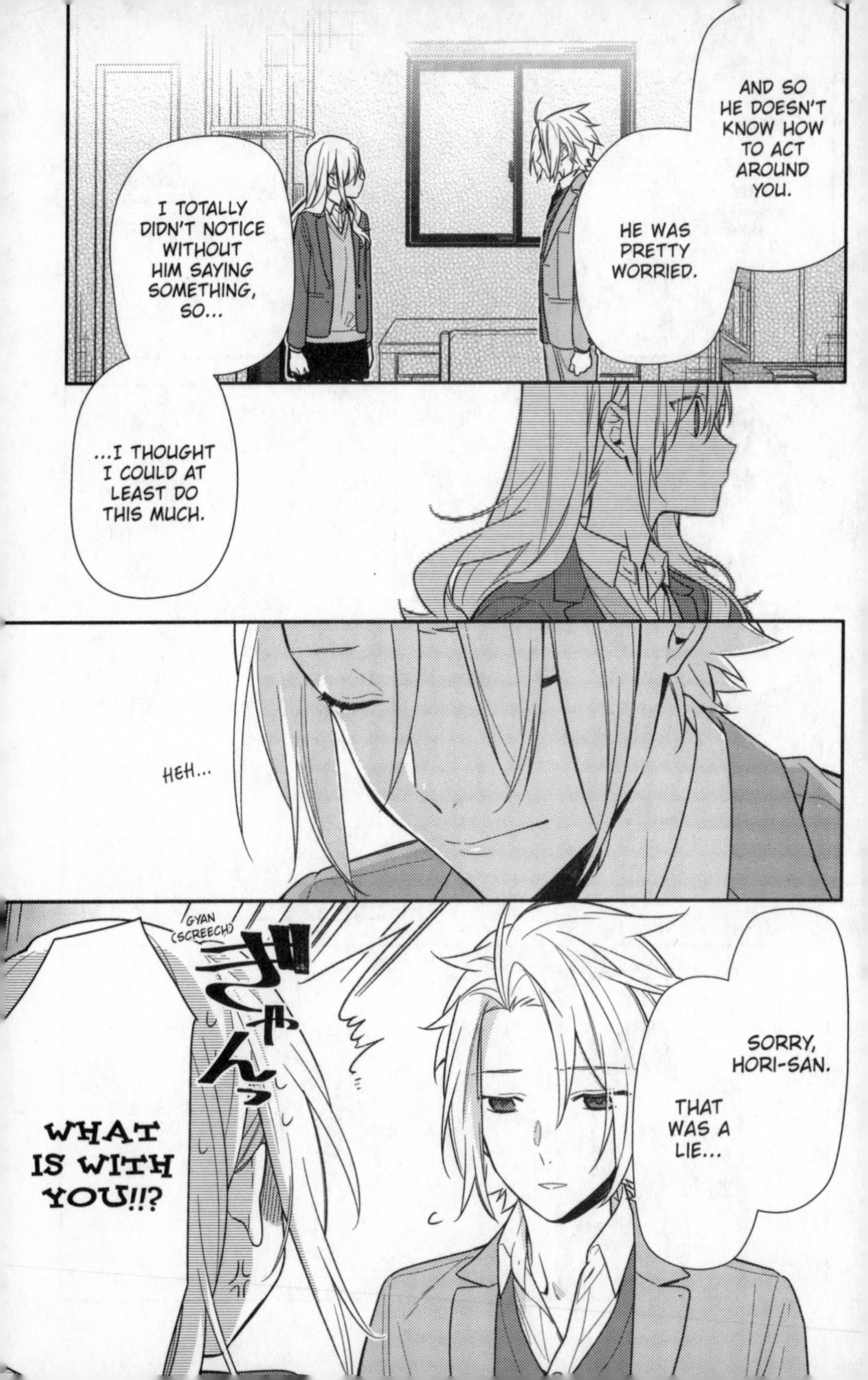
AND SO HE DOESN'T KNOW HOW TO ACT AROUND YOU.
HE WAS PRETTY WORRIED.
I TOTALLY DIDN'T NOTICE WITHOUT HIM SAYING SOMETHING, SO...
...I THOUGHT I COULD AT LEAST DO THIS MUCH.
HEH...
SORRY, HORI-SAN.
THAT WAS A LIE...
GYAN (SCREECH)
WHAT IS WITH YOU!!?

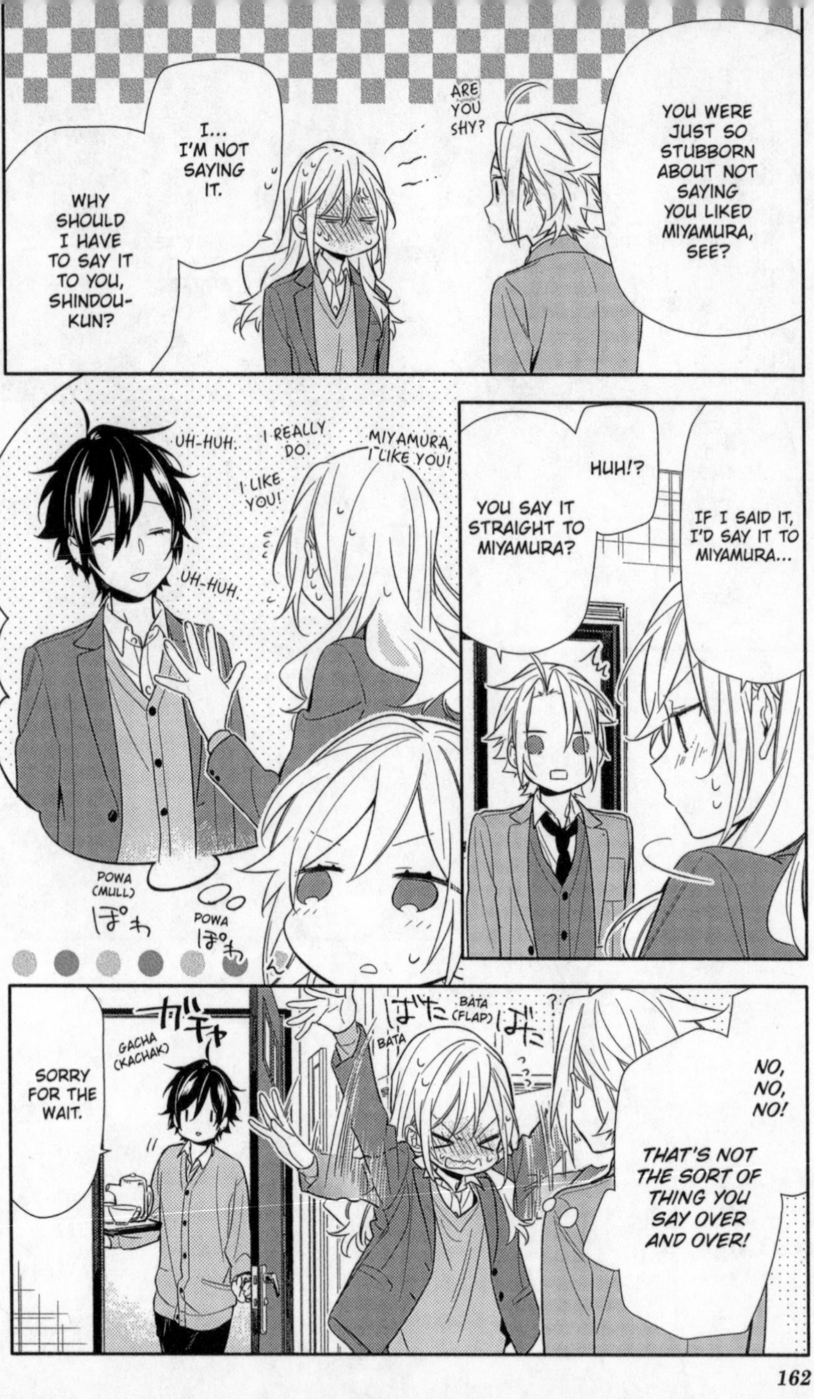
YOU WERE JUST SO STUBBORN ABOUT NOT SAYING YOU LIKED MIYAMURA, SEE?
ARE YOU SHY?
I... I'M NOT SAYING IT.
WHY SHOULD I HAVE TO SAY IT TO YOU, SHINDOU-KUN?
IF I SAID IT, I'D SAY IT TO MIYAMURA...
HUH!?
YOU SAY IT STRAIGHT TO MIYAMURA?
MIYAMURA, I LIKE YOU!
I REALLY DO.
UH-HUH.
I LIKE YOU!
UH-HUH.
POWA (MULL)
ぽわ
POWA
ぽわ
NO, NO, NO!
THAT'S NOT THE SORT OF THING YOU SAY OVER AND OVER!
BATA (FLAP)
ばた
ばた
BATA
GACHA (KACHAK)
ガチャ
SORRY FOR THE WAIT.

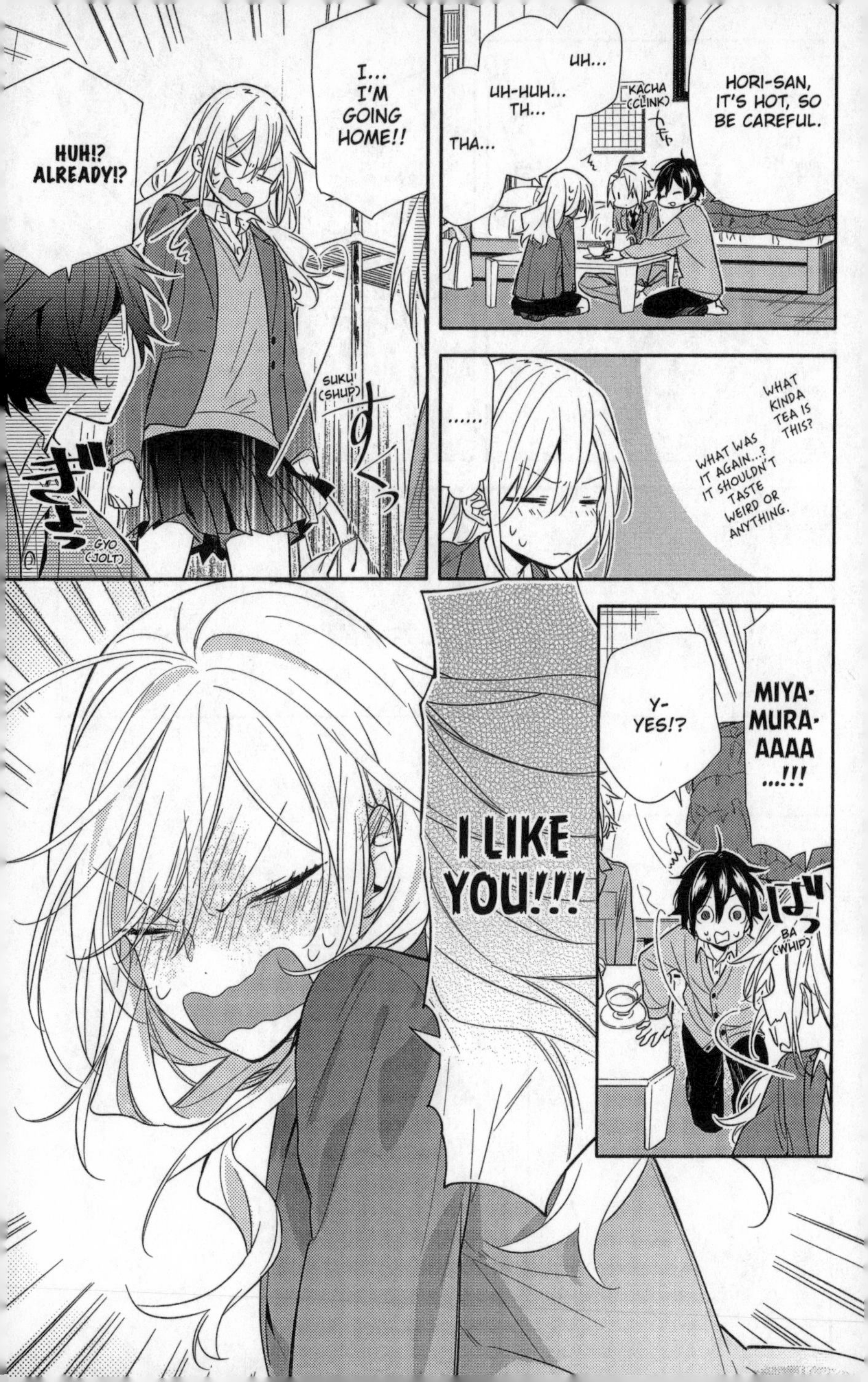
HORI-SAN, IT'S HOT, SO BE CAREFUL.
UH...
KACHA (CLINK)
UH-HUH... TH...
THA...
WHAT KINDA TEA IS THIS?
WHAT WAS IT AGAIN...? IT SHOULDN'T TASTE WEIRD OR ANYTHING.
......
I... I'M GOING HOME!!
SUKU' (SHUP)
HUH!? ALREADY!?
GYO (JOLT)
MIYA-MURA-AAAA ...!!!
Y-YES!?
BA (WHIP)
I LIKE YOU!!!

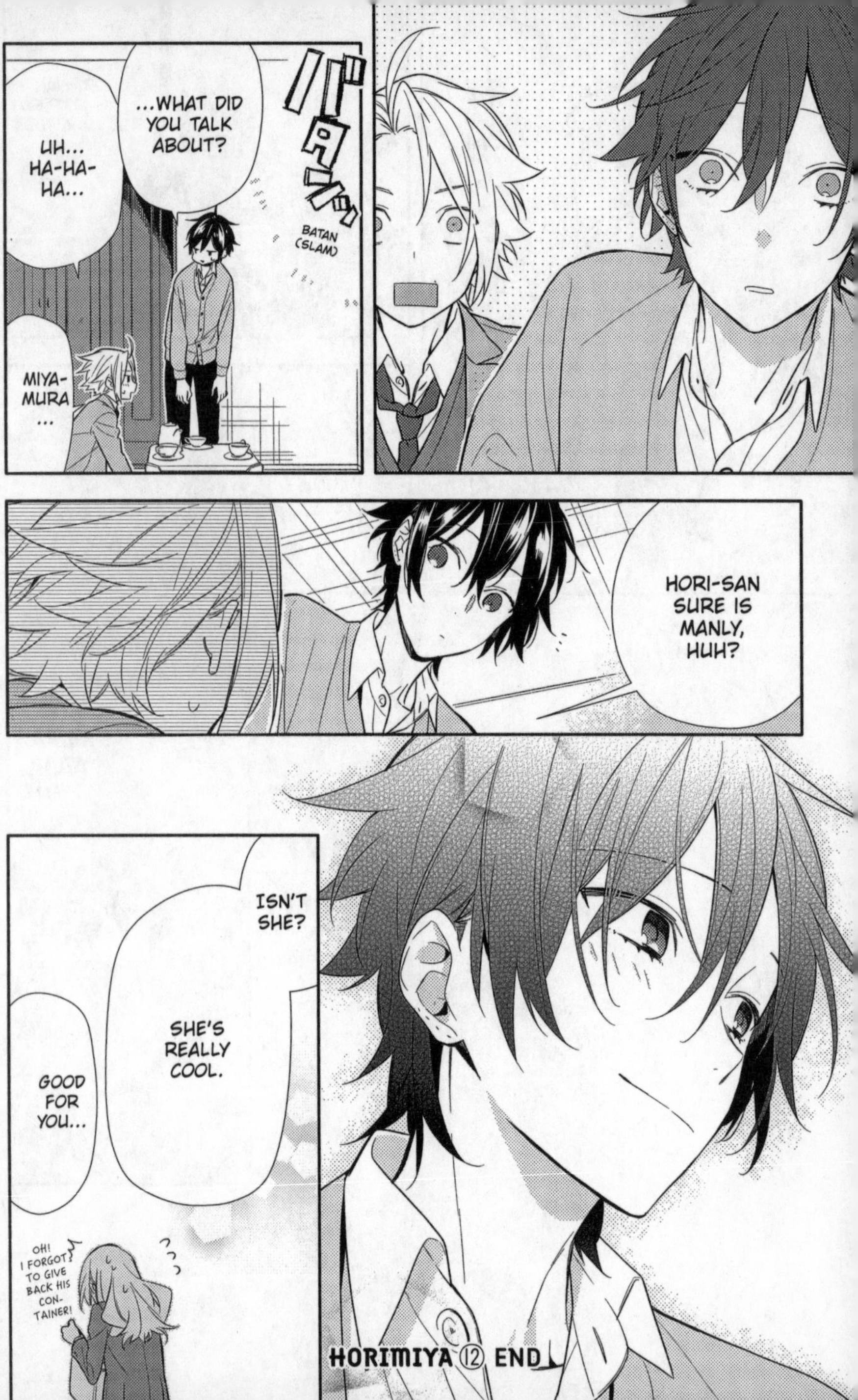
BATAN (SLAM)
...WHAT DID YOU TALK ABOUT?
UH... HA-HA-HA...
MIYAMURA ...
HORI-SAN SURE IS MANLY, HUH?
ISN'T SHE?
SHE'S REALLY COOL.
GOOD FOR YOU...
OH! I FORGOT TO GIVE BACK HIS CONTAINER!
HORIMIYA ⑫ END

To Be Continued...

HORIMIYA

BONUS MANGA: MYAMURA ⑩

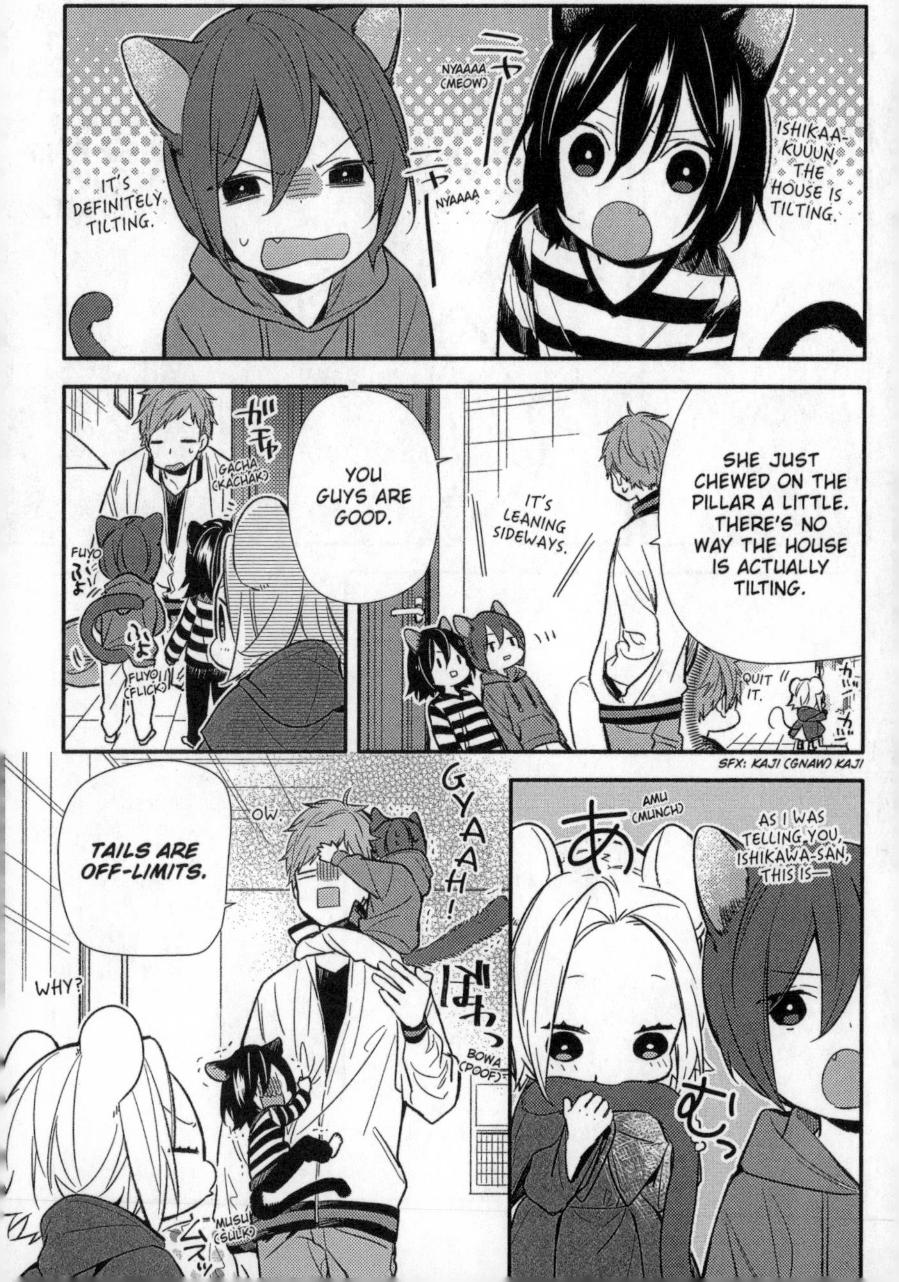
ISHIKAA-KUUUN, THE HOUSE IS TILTING.
NYAAAA (MEOW)
NYAAAA
IT'S DEFINITELY TILTING.
SHE JUST CHEWED ON THE PILLAR A LITTLE. THERE'S NO WAY THE HOUSE IS ACTUALLY TILTING.
IT'S LEANING SIDEWAYS.
QUIT IT.
SFX: KAJI (GNAW) KAJI
YOU GUYS ARE GOOD.
GACHA (KACHAK)
FUYO
FUYO (FLICK)
AS I WAS TELLING YOU, ISHIKAWA-SAN, THIS IS—
AMU (MUNCH)
GYAAH!
OW.
TAILS ARE OFF-LIMITS.
BOWA (POOF)
WHY?
MUSU (SULK)

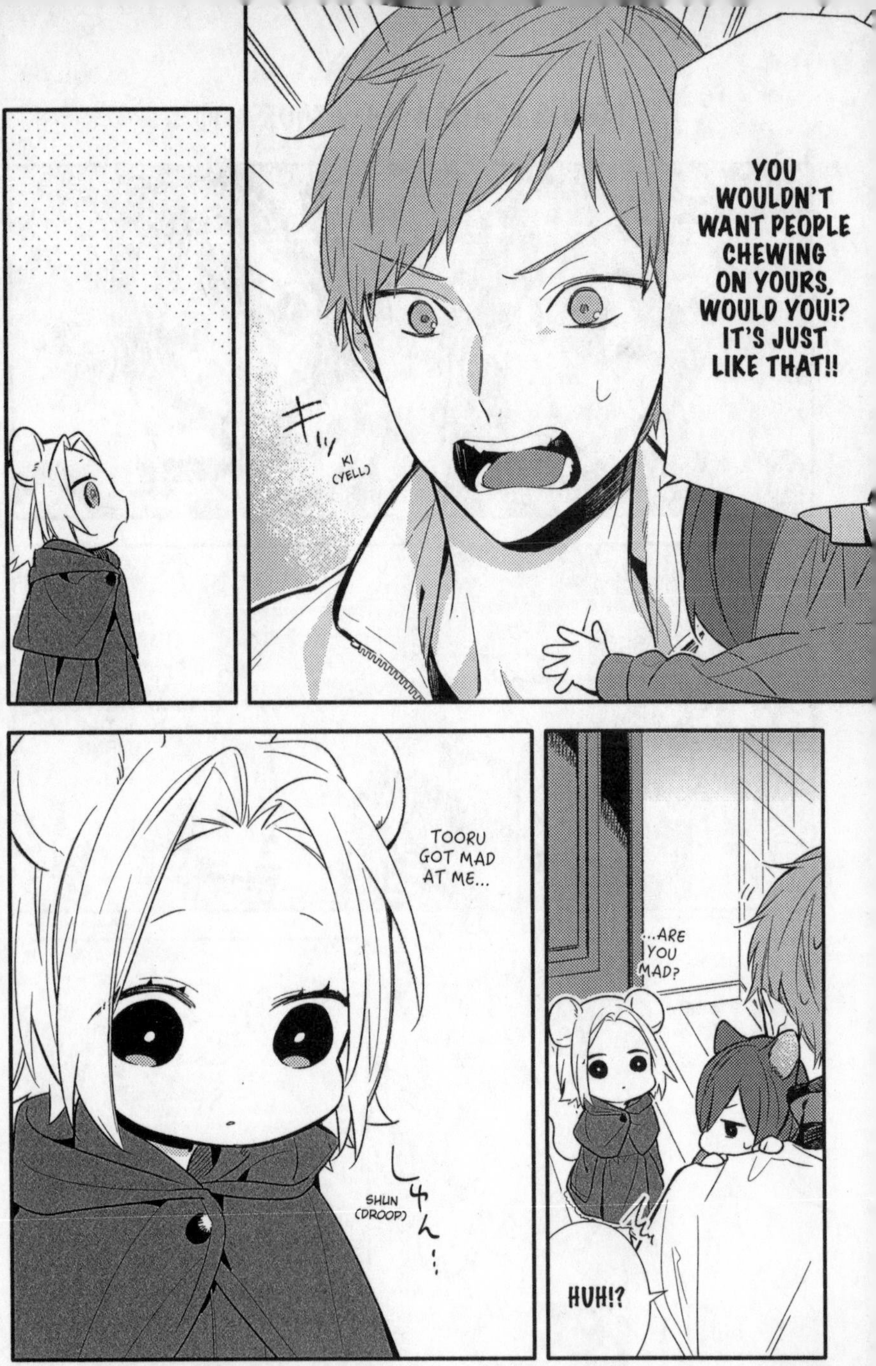

YOU WOULDN'T WANT PEOPLE CHEWING ON YOURS, WOULD YOU!? IT'S JUST LIKE THAT!!
KI (YELL)
...ARE YOU MAD?
HUH!?
TOORU GOT MAD AT ME...
SHUN (DROOP)

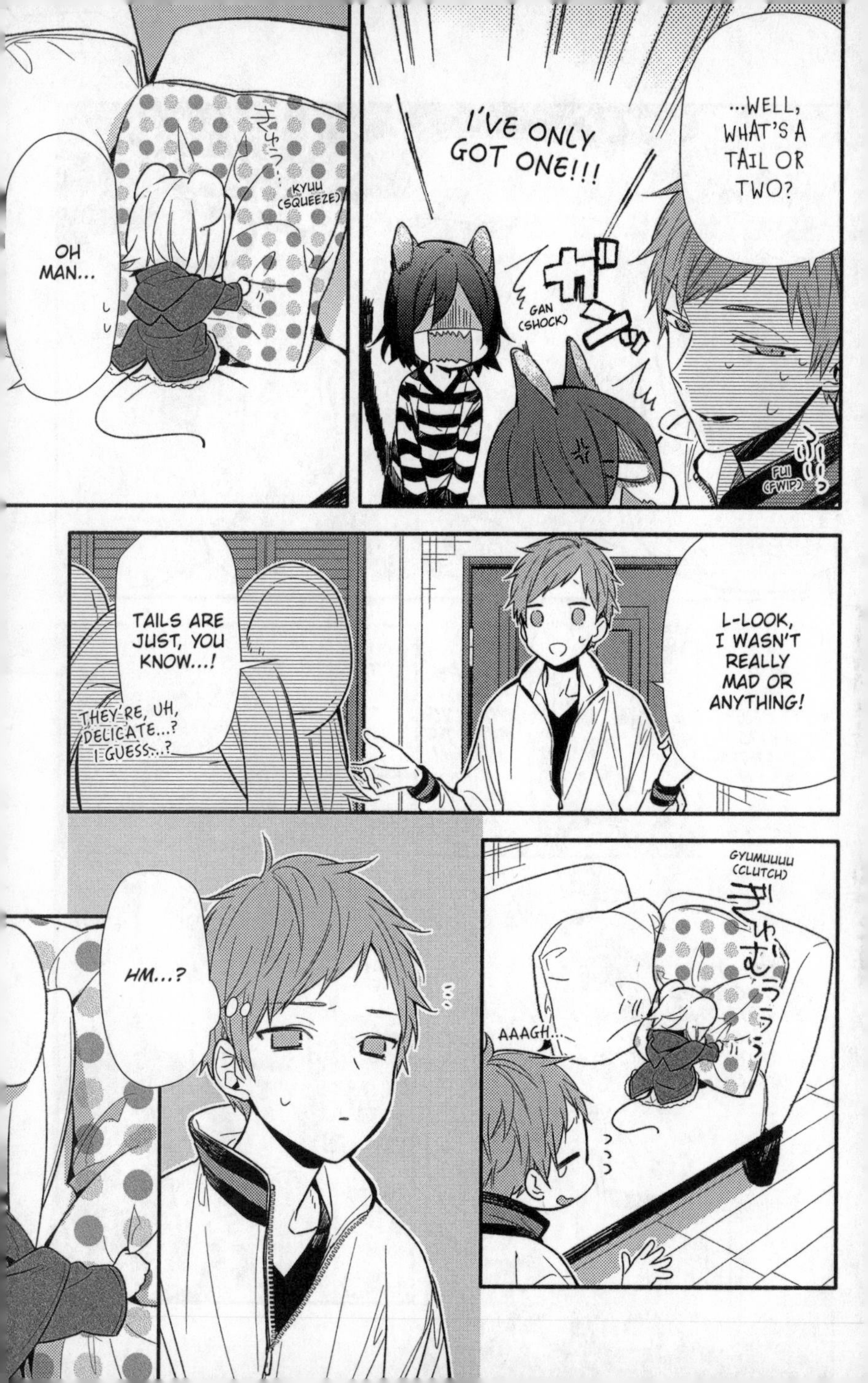
...WELL, WHAT'S A TAIL OR TWO?
FUI (FWIP)
I'VE ONLY GOT ONE!!!
GAN (SHOCK)
KYUU (SQUEEZE)
OH MAN...
L-LOOK, I WASN'T REALLY MAD OR ANYTHING!
TAILS ARE JUST, YOU KNOW...!
THEY'RE, UH, DELICATE...? I GUESS...?
GYUMUUUU (CLUTCH)
AAAGH...
HM...?

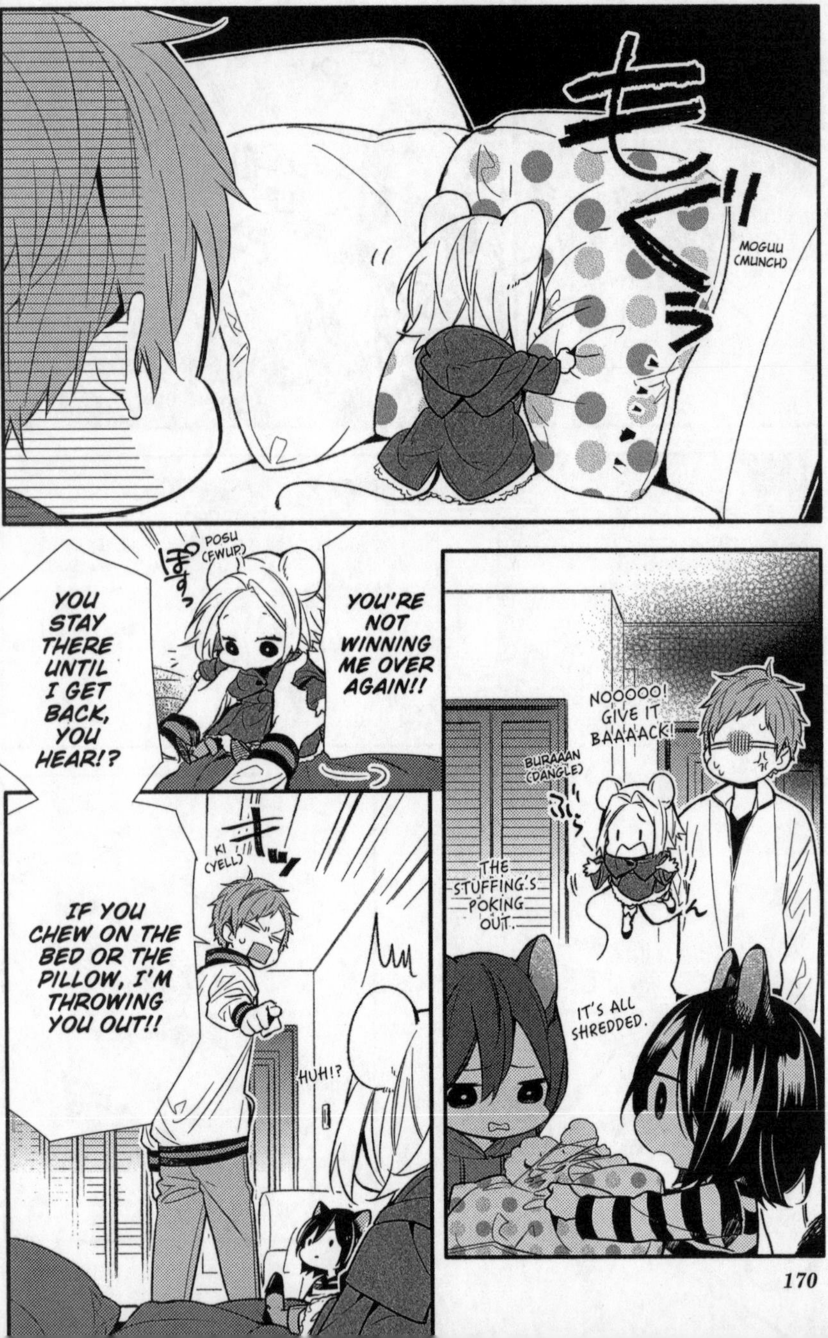
MOGUU (MUNCH)
NOOOOO! GIVE IT BAAAACK!
BURAAAN (DANGLE)
THE STUFFING'S POKING OUT.
IT'S ALL SHREDDED.
YOU'RE NOT WINNING ME OVER AGAIN!!
POSU (FWUP)
YOU STAY THERE UNTIL I GET BACK, YOU HEAR!?
KI (YELL)
IF YOU CHEW ON THE BED OR THE PILLOW, I'M THROWING YOU OUT!!
HUH!?

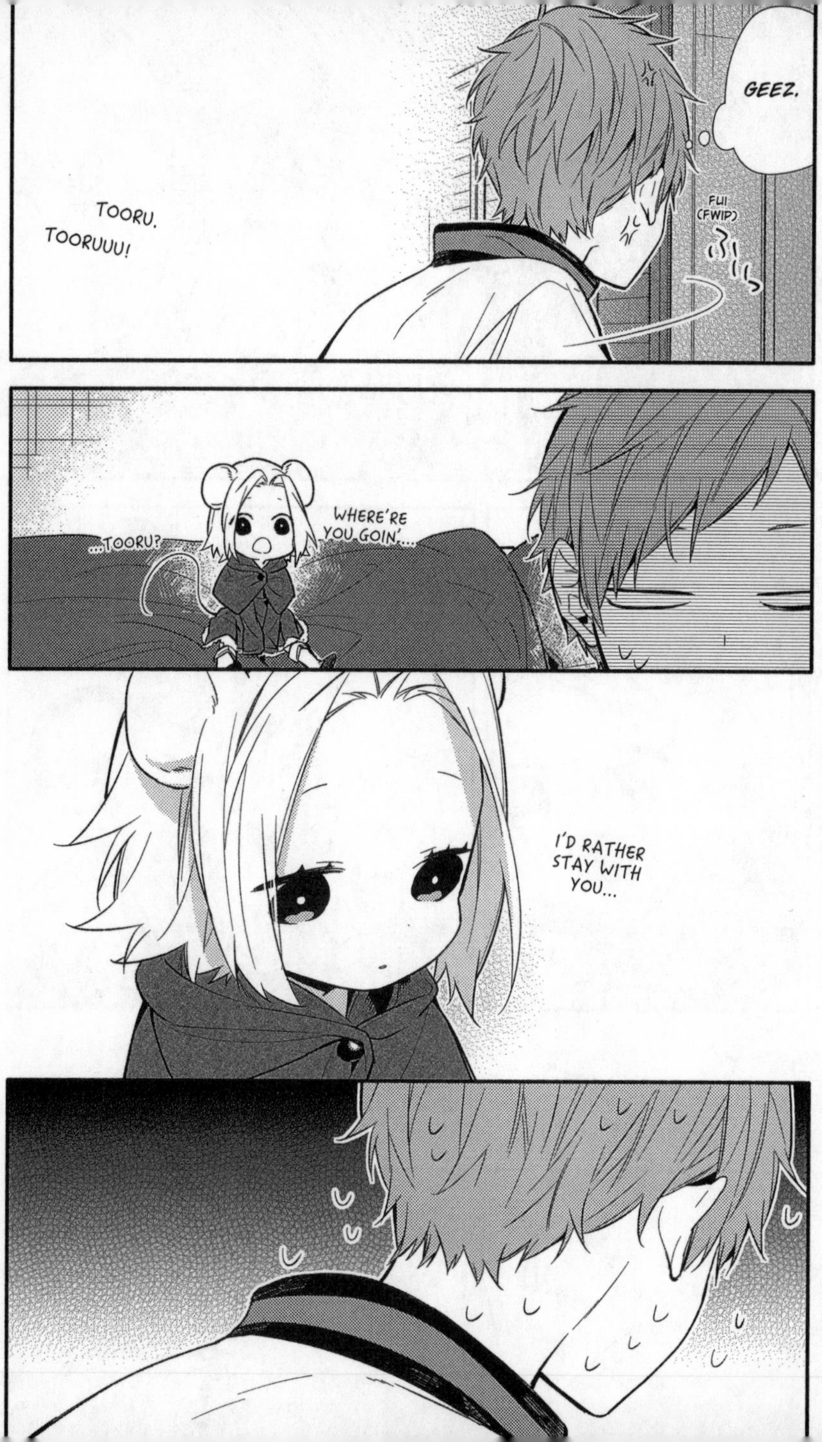
GEEZ.
FUI (FWIP)
ふいっ
TOORU. TOORUUU!
WHERE'RE YOU GOIN'...
...TOORU?
I'D RATHER STAY WITH YOU...

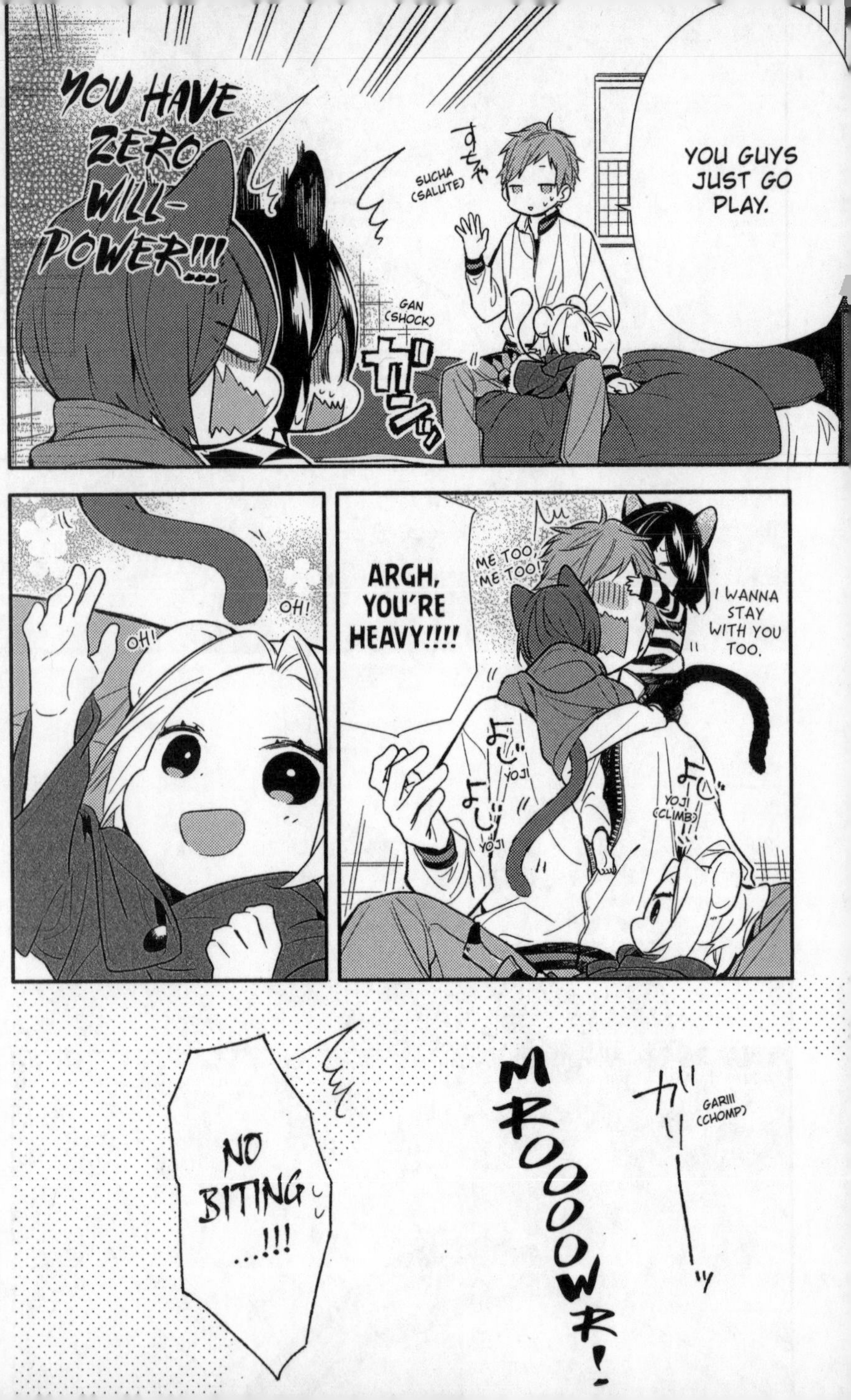
YOU GUYS JUST GO PLAY.
すちゃ
SUCHA (SALUTE)
GAN (SHOCK)
YOU HAVE ZERO WILL-POWER!!!...
I WANNA STAY WITH YOU TOO.
ME TOO, ME TOO!
ARGH, YOU'RE HEAVY!!!!
よじ
YOJI (CLIMB)
よじ
YOJI
よじ
YOJI
OH!
OH!
GARIII (CHOMP)
MROOOOWR!
NO BITING...!!!

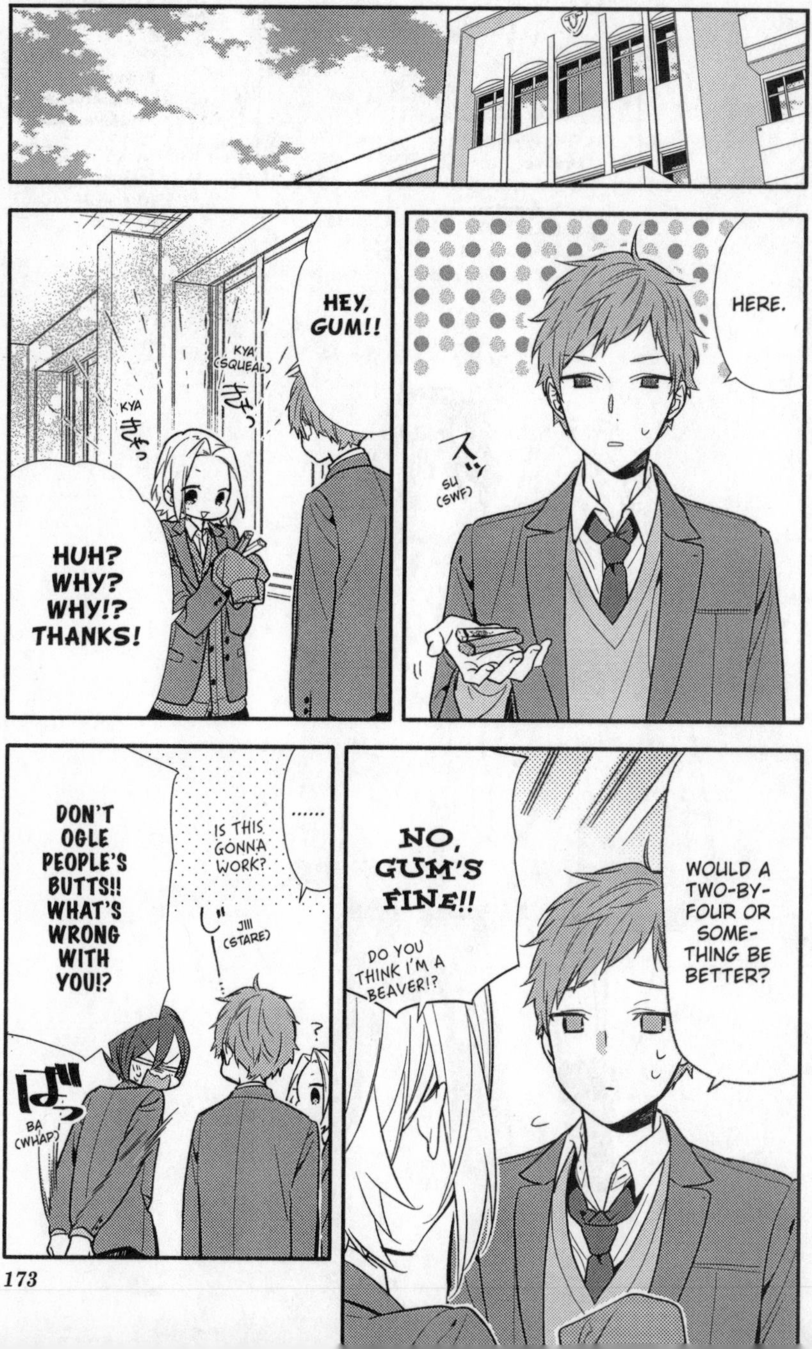
HERE.
SU (SWF)
HEY, GUM!!
KYA (SQUEAL)
KYA
HUH? WHY? WHY!? THANKS!
WOULD A TWO-BY-FOUR OR SOME-THING BE BETTER?
NO, GUM'S FINE!!
DO YOU THINK I'M A BEAVER!?
......
IS THIS GONNA WORK?
JIII (STARE)
?
DON'T OGLE PEOPLE'S BUTTS!! WHAT'S WRONG WITH YOU!?
BA (WHAP)

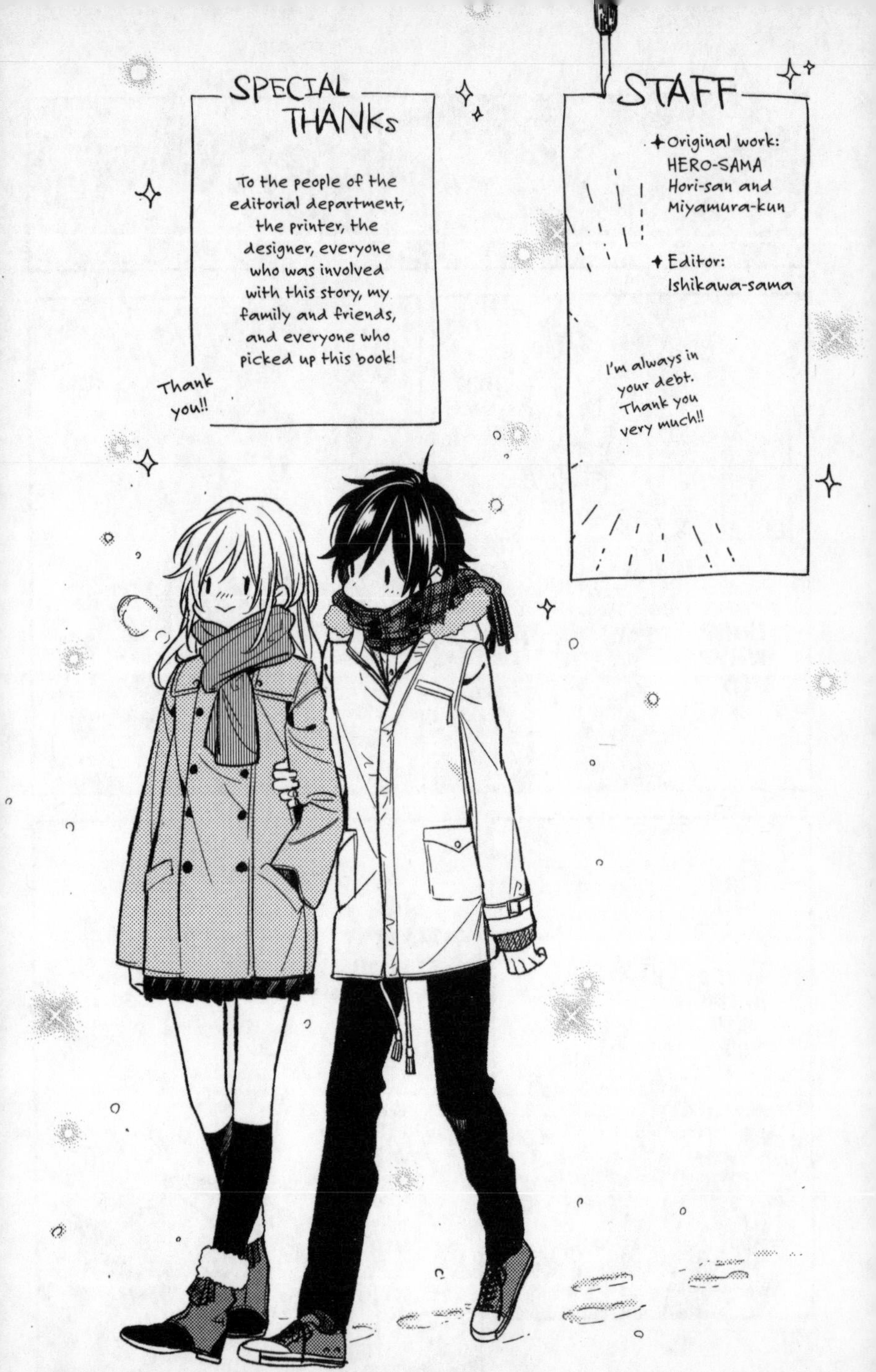
STAFF
Original work: HERO-SAMA
Hori-san and Miyamura-kun
Editor: Ishikawa-sama
I'm always in your debt. Thank you very much!!
SPECIAL THANKs
To the people of the editorial department, the printer, the designer, everyone who was involved with this story, my family and friends, and everyone who picked up this book!
Thank you!!

Translation Notes

Page 1 – Title page illustration
Both Sakura and Yanagi are using a mock ninja technique
seen in a lot of shounen manga to transform themselves into
two different types of *sakura-mochi*, or cherry-blossom
rice cake, a Japanese sweet that comes in a variety of
shapes. The common elements are mochi (usually pink, but
sometimes white) filled with red-bean jam, with a preserved,
green cherry-blossom leaf wrapped around the outside.
The leaves on their heads mark them as shape-shifters,
although that particular symbol is more commonly used with
shape-shifting animals (tanuki and foxes) than human ninja.

Page 26 – Salt
In Japan, the tradition of setting out salt to drive away evil,
purify an area, and attract good luck goes back to the Nara
(710–794) and Heian (794–1185) eras. You're supposed to use
salt which has been refined through natural processes and
is as unadulterated as possible (so ordinary table salt isn't
recommended). First, you clean the room in question thoroughly.
Then you create a mound of salt on a plate, one pinch at a time.
It's important that the mound be as peaked as you can make
it; salt that's spread in a dish isn't believed to be as effective.
There are even "mound" molds and dishes sold for this specific
purpose. The dish of salt should be changed once a week. "Used"
salt doesn't need to be disposed of in any particular way, but
since it's assumed to have absorbed things that aren't good
for you, you aren't supposed to eat it or use it for bathing.

Page 33 – *Chiiin* (ding)
This is the funeral bell ("this person is completely toast")
ding, and it means that the alarm clock is dead.

Page 50 – Yanagi, Sakura
Yanagi is the Japanese word for "willow tree," while *sakura*
means "cherry tree." Both trees are used to signify the season
of spring in haiku poetry. In the author note to this volume,
Hagiwara-sensei writes, "The pair with the coloring of
sakura-mochi are the cover stars for this volume, and that
makes it feel somehow spring-like. Though the volume itself
is set right smack in the middle of winter, its atmosphere is
soft and warm...If you enjoy it even a little bit, I'll be happy!"

Page 62 – "Why are you talking all melodramatically?"
Here, Sengoku uses *oneikei*, literally meaning "big sister type,"
but it refers specifically to men who speak in an exaggeratedly
feminine way, usually to project a female persona. In
entertainment, it's stereotypically used by gay men, drag queens,
and transgender women, but it's not all that common in real life.

Page 172 – "Me too, me too!"
In the original volume, both cat boys are copying mouse Yuki
and using her feminine pronoun (*atashi*) to refer to themselves.

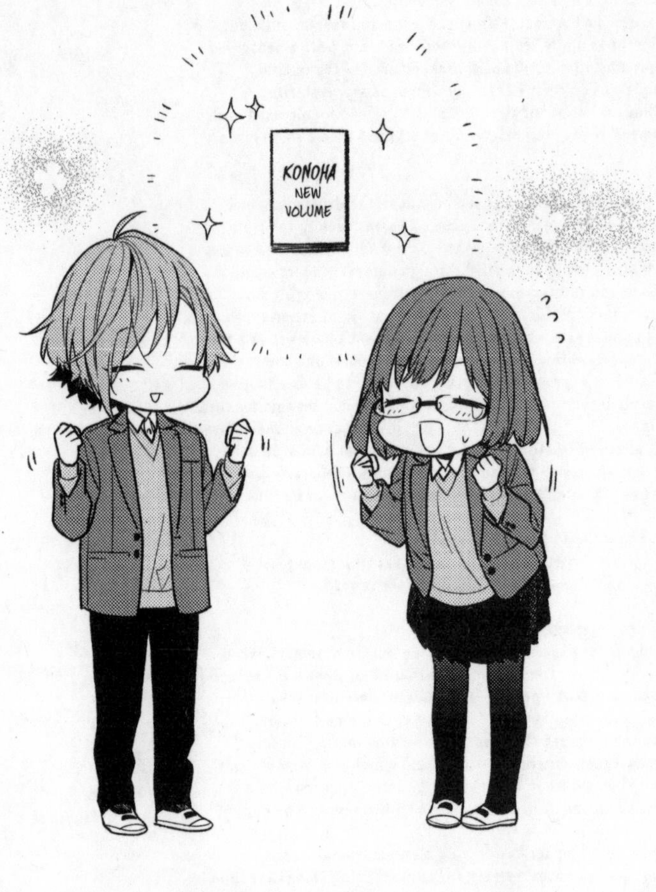
KONOHA
NEW
VOLUME

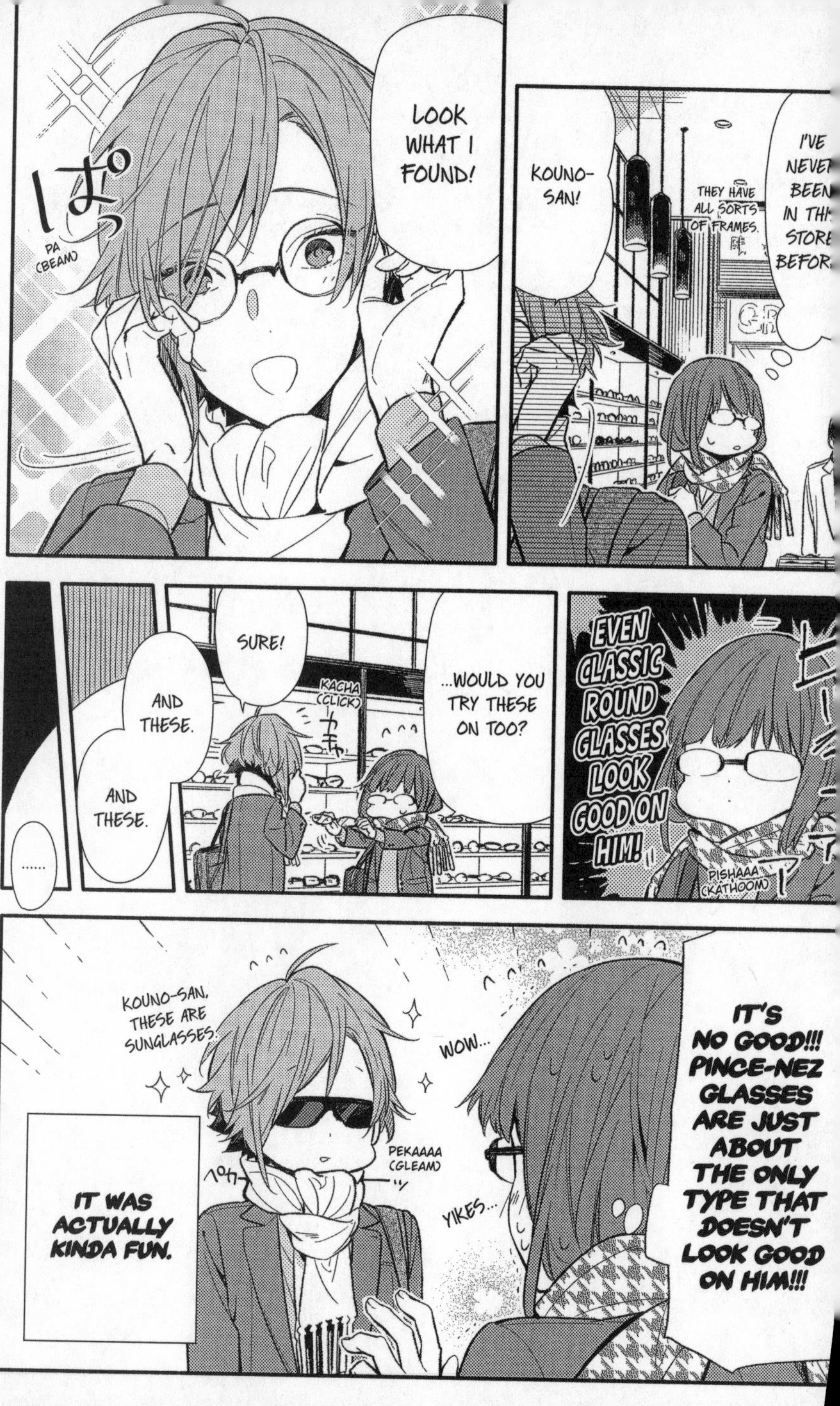
I'VE NEVE BEEN IN THI STORE BEFOR
THEY HAVE ALL SORTS OF FRAMES.
KOUNO-SAN!
LOOK WHAT I FOUND!
ぱっ
PA (BEAM)
EVEN CLASSIC ROUND GLASSES LOOK GOOD ON HIM!
PISHAAA (KATHOOM)
...WOULD YOU TRY THESE ON TOO?
KACHA (CLICK)
SURE!
AND THESE.
AND THESE.
......
IT'S NO GOOD!!! PINCE-NEZ GLASSES ARE JUST ABOUT THE ONLY TYPE THAT DOESN'T LOOK GOOD ON HIM!!!
WOW...
YIKES...
PEKAAAA (GLEAM)
KOUNO-SAN, THESE ARE SUNGLASSES.
IT WAS ACTUALLY KINDA FUN.

HERO × Daisuke Hagiwara

Translation: Taylor Engel
Lettering: Alexis Eckerman

HORIMIYA vol. 12
© HERO · OOZ
© 2018 Daisuke Hagiwara / SQUARE ENIX CO., LTD. First published in Japan in 2018 by SQUARE ENIX CO., LTD. English translation rights arranged with SQUARE ENIX CO., LTD. and Yen Press, LLC through Tuttle-Mori Agency, Inc.

English translation © 2018 by SQUARE ENIX CO., LTD.

Yen Press
150 West 30th Street, 19th Floor
New York, NY 10001

Visit us at yenpress.com • facebook.com/yenpress • twitter.com/yenpress • yenpress.tumblr.com • instagram.com/yenpress

First Yen Press Edition: December 2018

Yen Press is an imprint of Yen Press, LLC.
The Yen Press name and logo are trademarks of Yen Press, LLC.

The publisher is not responsible for websites (or their content) that are not owned by the publisher.

Library of Congress Control Number:
2015960115

ISBNs: 978-1-9753-2922-8 (paperback)
978-1-9753-2923-5 (ebook)

10 9 8 7 6 5 4

BVG

Printed in the United States of America